Rethinking Rhetorical Theory, Criticism, and Pedagogy

RHETORIC AND PUBLIC AFFAIRS SERIES

- *Eisenhower's War of Words: Rhetoric and Leadership*, Martin J. Medhurst, editor
- *The Nuclear Freeze Campaign: Rhetoric and Foreign Policy in the Telepolitical Age*, J. Michael Hogan
- *Mansfield and Vietnam: A Study in Rhetorical Adaptation*, Gregory A. Olson
- *Truman and the Hiroshima Cult*, Robert P. Newman
- *Post-Realism: The Rhetorical Turn in International Relations*, Francis A. Beer and Robert Hariman, editors
- *Rhetoric and Political Culture in Nineteenth-Century America*, Thomas W. Benson, editor
- *Frederick Douglass: Freedom's Voice, 1818–1845*, Gregory P. Lampe
- *Angelina Grimké: Rhetoric, Identity, and the Radical Imagination*, Stephen Howard Browne
- *Strategic Deception: Rhetoric, Science, and Politics in Missile Defense Advocacy*, Gordon R. Mitchell
- *Rostow, Kennedy, and the Rhetoric of Foreign Aid*, Kimber Charles Pearce
- *Visions of Poverty: Welfare Policy and Political Imagination*, Robert Asen
- *General Eisenhower: Ideology and Discourse*, Ira Chernus
- *The Reconstruction Desegregation Debate: The Politics of Equality and the Rhetoric of Place, 1870–1875*, Kirt H. Wilson
- *Shared Land/Conflicting Identity: Trajectories of Israeli and Palestinian Symbol Use*, Robert C. Rowland and David A. Frank
- *Darwinism, Design, and Public Education*, John Angus Campbell and Stephen C. Meyer, editors
- *Religious Expression and the American Constitution*, Franklyn S. Haiman
- *Christianity and the Mass Media in America: Toward a Democratic Accommodation*, Quentin J. Schultze
- *Bending Spines: The Propagandas of Nazi Germany and the German Democratic Republic*, Randall L. Bytwerk
- *Malcolm X: Inventing Radical Judgment*, Robert E. Terrill
- *Metaphorical World Politics*, Francis A. Beer and Christ'l De Landtsheer, editors
- *The Lyceum and Public Culture in the Nineteenth-Century United States*, Angela G. Ray
- *The Political Style of Conspiracy: Chase, Sumner, and Lincoln*, Michael William Pfau
- *The Character of Justice: Rhetoric, Law, and Politics in the Supreme Court Confirmation Process*, Trevor Parry-Giles
- *Rhetorical Vectors of Memory in National and International Holocaust Trials*, Marouf A. Hasian Jr.
- *Judging the Supreme Court: Constructions of Motives in* Bush *v.* Gore, Clarke Rountree
- *Everyday Subversion: From Joking to Revolting in the German Democratic Republic*, Kerry Kathleen Riley
- *In the Wake of Violence: Image and Social Reform*, Cheryl R. Jorgensen-Earp
- *Rhetoric and Democracy: Pedagogical and Political Practices*, Todd F. McDorman and David M. Timmerman, editors
- *Invoking the Invisible Hand: Social Security and the Privatization Debates*, Robert Asen
- *With Faith in the Works of Words: The Beginnings of Reconciliation in South Africa, 1985–1995*, Erik Doxtader
- *Public Address and Moral Judgment: Critical Studies in Ethical Tensions*, Shawn J. Parry-Giles and Trevor Parry-Giles, editors
- *Executing Democracy: Capital Punishment and the Making of America, 1683–1807*, Stephen John Hartnett
- *Enemyship: Democracy and Counter-revolution in the Early Republic*, Jeremy Engels
- *Spirits of the Cold War: Contesting Worldviews in the Classical Age of American Security Strategy*, Ned O'Gorman
- *Making the Case: Advocacy and Judgment in Public Argument*, Kathryn M. Olson, Michael William Pfau, Benjamin Ponder, and Kirt H. Wilson, editors
- *Executing Democracy: Capital Punishment and the Making of America, 1835–1843*, Stephen John Hartnett
- *William James and the Art of Popular Statement*, Paul Stob
- *On the Frontier of Science: An American Rhetoric of Exploration and Exploitation*, Leah Ceccarelli
- *The Good Neighbor: Franklin D. Roosevelt and the Rhetoric of American Power*, Mary E. Stuckey
- *Creating Conservatism: Postwar Words That Made an American Movement*, Michael J. Lee
- *Superchurch: The Rhetoric and Politics of American Fundamentalism*, Jonathan J. Edwards
- *Rethinking Rhetorical Theory, Criticism, and Pedagogy: The Living Art of Michael C. Leff*, Antonio de Velasco, John Angus Campbell, and David Henry, editors

Rethinking Rhetorical Theory, Criticism, and Pedagogy

The Living Art of Michael C. Leff

EDITED BY

Antonio de Velasco, John Angus Campbell, and David Henry

Michigan State University Press • *East Lansing*

♾ The paper used in this publication meets the minimum requirements
of ANSI/NISO Z39.48-1992 (R 1997) (Permanence of Paper).

Michigan State University Press
East Lansing, Michigan 48823-5245

Printed and bound in the United States of America.

22 21 20 19 18 17 16   1 2 3 4 5 6 7 8 9 10

LIBRARY OF CONGRESS CATALOGING-IN-PUBLICATION DATA
Library of Congress Cataloging-in-Publication Data
Names: Velasco, Antonio de, 1974– editor. | Campbell, John Angus, editor.
| Henry, David R., 1947– editor. | Leff, Michael C., honouree.
Title: Rethinking rhetorical theory, criticism, and pedagogy : the living art of Michael C. Leff
/ edited by Antonio de Velasco, John Angus Campbell and David Henry.
Description: East Lansing : Michigan State University Press, 2016.
| Series: Rhetoric and public affairs series | Includes bibliographical references.
Identifiers: LCCN 2015038945| ISBN 9781611862133 (pbk. : alk. paper) | ISBN 9781609175009 (pdf)
| ISBN 9781628952735 (epub) | ISBN 9781628962734 (kindle)
Subjects: LCSH: Rhetoric—Theory, etc. | Rhetoric—Study and teaching. | Criticism.
Classification: LCC P301 .R356 2016 | DDC 808—dc23 LC record available at http://lccn.loc.gov/2015038945

Book design by Charlie Sharp, Sharp Des!gns, Lansing, Michigan
Cover design by Erin Kirk New

green press INITIATIVE

Michigan State University Press is a member of the Green Press Initiative and is committed to developing and encouraging ecologically responsible publishing practices. For more information about the Green Press Initiative and the use of recycled paper in book publishing, please visit *www.greenpressinitiative.org*.

Visit Michigan State University Press at *www.msupress.org*

Contents

INTRODUCTION · ix

PART I. GREEK AND LATIN RHETORICAL THEORY · · · · · · · · · · · · · · · · · · **I**

Tradition and Agency in Humanistic Rhetoric · 7

The Uses of Aristotle's *Rhetoric* in Contemporary American Scholarship · 25

Genre and Paradigm in the Second Book of *De Oratore* · · · · · · · · · · · 47

The Topics of Argumentative Invention in Latin Rhetorical Theory from Cicero to Boethius · 65

PART 2. CONTEMPORARY EXTENSIONS OF CLASSICAL RHETORICAL THEORY · · · 87

Piety, Propriety, and Perspective: An Interpretation and Application of Key Terms in Kenneth Burke's *Permanence and Change* (with Thomas Rosteck) · · · 95

Topical Invention and Metaphoric Interaction · · · 115

Up from Theory: Or I Fought the Topoi and the Topoi Won · · · 133

The Habitation of Rhetoric · · · 143

Decorum and Rhetorical Interpretation: The Latin Humanistic Tradition and Contemporary Critical Theory · · · 163

In Search of Ariadne's Thread: A Review of the Recent Literature on Rhetorical Theory · · · 185

PART 3. THEORIES OF CRITICISM · · · 215

Interpretation and the Art of the Rhetorical Critic · · · 221

Textual Criticism: The Legacy of G. P. Mohrmann · · · 241

Words Most like Things: Iconicity and the Rhetorical Text (with Andrew Sachs) · · · 261

Things Made by Words: Reflections on Textual Criticism · · · 291

Hermeneutical Rhetoric · · · 307

PART 4. THE PRACTICE OF RHETORICAL CRITICISM · · · 331

Lincoln at Cooper Union: A Rhetorical Analysis of the Text (with G. P. Mohrmann) · · · 337

Lincoln at Cooper Union: A Rationale for Neo-Classical Criticism (with G. P. Mohrmann) · · · 359

Instrumental and Constitutive Rhetoric in Martin Luther King Jr.'s "Letter from Birmingham Jail" (with Ebony A. Utley) · · · · · 375

Lincoln among the Nineteenth-Century Orators · · · · · · · · · · · · · · · · 395

PART 5. RHETORICAL PEDAGOGY · 427

Teaching Public Speaking as Composition · 433

Kenneth Burke in the Classroom · 441

Theory and Practice in Undergraduate Education · · · · · · · · · · · · · · · 449

Cultivating the Useless: Rhetoric and Liberal Arts Education in an Age of Consumerism · 457

What Is Rhetoric? · 471

Introduction

> Rhetoric [is] a universal activity that finds its habitation only in the particular.
>
> —Michael C. Leff, "The Habitation of Rhetoric"

What distinguishes the study of rhetoric from other pursuits in the liberal arts? From what realms of human existence and expression, of human history, does such study draw its defining character? What, in the end, should be the purposes of rhetorical inquiry? And amid so many competing accounts of discourse, power, and judgment in the contemporary world, how might scholars achieve these purposes through the attitudes and strategies that animate their work? *Rethinking Rhetorical Theory, Criticism, and Pedagogy: The Living Art of Michael C. Leff* offers answers to these questions by collecting the key works and introducing the key insights of one of the twentieth century's most innovative and prolific rhetoricians, Michael C. Leff.[1]

In a career that spanned more than forty years, there seemed no meeting too small for Leff to attend, nor journal too obscure for him not to grace with a publication, nor regional, national, or international conference devoted to rhetoric in which he was not a principal figure. There was always the most recent Leff essay to discuss. A central player in the major disciplinary controversies of his time, Leff was nearly ubiquitous. The ambition of his reach and travel speaks to the passion he brought to scholarly discourse, to the value he found in the very act of argument, rebuttal, and revision, and to the love he had for the intellectual community he helped to build. When Leff died in 2010, he left a legacy forged not in isolation, but in the heat of intellectual debates in the humanities and social sciences that caught fire just as he emerged from graduate study in the late 1960s, and in the light of enduring tensions in the history of rhetoric that he first identified in his doctoral dissertation in 1972. With these immediate and long-term historical scenes in mind, and with an eye on the flexible and shifting manner in which Leff spoke to them over his career, *Living Art* discloses the story of an inimitable scholar's evolving, self-reflexive, and distinctly rhetorical intervention into the very meaning, and thus the future, of humanistic studies.

Leff's thought was singular in many ways but especially in its timing. At a moment when the field was rapidly changing, and almost anything associated with the ancien régime of what Edwin Black at once christened and buried as "neo-Aristotelianism" was held in suspicion, Leff attempted something counterintuitive and, at the time, countercultural. Given the winds of change that so many in what then was "speech" or "speech communication" found freeing and invigorating, Leff's proposal that rhetoricians focus on the individual speech and its immediate context and bring the full armamentarium of classical rhetoric to bear on its analysis was more than just outré. The very idea of tradition was discredited and boring. Why would anyone want to revisit a perspective that had so unambiguously failed to launch innovative analysis of its own favored object?

But it was worse. Leff's interests seemed outrageously rear-guard. Tradition, especially in the late 1960s and 1970s, carried the bad odor of every form of repressive elitism. In revisiting tradition, Leff risked not only sponsoring a program of reaction but also simultaneously placing himself (and anyone foolish enough to take his project seriously) on the wrong side of history. With so many great shifts in the academic landscape, hunks of theory were floating free of their disciplinary moorings and were there for the taking by rhetoricians eager to embrace change. The opportunities for fundamental innovation in a field that never did quite fit in to the research university's idea of a discipline were never clearer. For Leff's generation of scholars in rhetoric it was a boom time for rethinking fundamental issues. The suggestion that the boom might have certain elements of "bubble" about it, that revisiting the classical tradition might clear a path for fundamental insight and sustainable development, seemed wrongheaded.

Leff frequently observes that common to rhetorical practice is a certain sprawl of subject, genre, and forum. While Leff's essays are meticulously argued, the sprawl native to rhetorical inquiry emerges in the diversity of his thought and in the range of venues in which he published and presented his work. When his published and unpublished papers are combined, they include over 160 items on a sometimes dizzying variety of themes. This sprawl left its own legacy, one might observe, since, up until now, readers searching for a book that could capture Leff's thought in its variegated wholeness would have come up short. Leff himself left no single masterwork behind. Indeed, this is an irony both Leff and the late Michael Calvin McGee, his collegial nemesis, might have appreciated. Although Leff's best-known publications are essays in which he closely analyzed texts in their unity, his oeuvre has remained, until now, a series of fragments. No longer. *Living Art* integrates these fragments for the first time into a whole text. Realized as facets of an integrated rhetorical vision, Leff's texts reveal both an overall coherence and their own inter- and intratextual tensions. We therefore see the volume as a necessary encapsulation of the project Leff launched and developed through individual essays but never brought together in a single place.

A brief comment is needed to make clear the rationale for our title. Though the title is ours, we believe this volume is Leff's book and captures the depth, scope, originality, and variety of his work. Two words in our subtitle—*Living Art*—are consonant with Leff's Ciceronian emphasis on the priority of life and action in rhetoric and oratory. (Leff often used "metabolism" as a metaphor for the movement of a rhetorical text.) At the same time, *Living Art* acknowledges Leff's debt to Aristotle's emphasis on art or theory. The main title, *Rethinking Rhetorical Theory, Criticism, and Pedagogy*, reflects our understanding of the thrust of Leff's work as a development both with and against the grain of ancient, modern, and postmodern rhetoric. Indeed, amid his variety of topic and approach Leff's thought can be understood as a perspective on the history of rhetoric; a critique of the disciplinary assumptions of classical, Hellenistic, Renaissance, modern, and postmodern rhetoric, particularly of those assumptions that block growth in rhetorical theory or criticism; and, finally, a multipronged program for reinventing and revitalizing rhetorical study, criticism, and traditions based on an Isocratean and Ciceronian exemplar.

Throughout his career Leff always returned to history to ground interpretation. In such a spirit, we introduce the volume with a brief interpretive history of how Leff's understanding of rhetoric and the orator's art emerged from the context of his graduate study and early work.

Earliest Work

Leff's first scholarly study was his master's thesis, "The Status System in Fortunatus: A Translation of the First Book of the *Ars Rhetorica* of C. Chirius Fortunatus with Introduction and Commentary." Leff wrote his thesis at the University of California, Santa Barbara, in 1966. Six years later, he completed his PhD at University of California, Los Angeles, by writing "The Frozen Image: Sulpicius Victor and the Ancient Rhetorical Tradition."

Although it is well known that Leff began as a classical rhetorician with a special interest in late Latin treatises, less well known is Leff's early interpretation of the development of the rhetorical tradition. Leff's interpretation of the rhetorical tradition began in his master's thesis. He later incorporated the focus of his thesis on Fortunatus into the larger panorama of late Latin writers he examined in his dissertation. "The Frozen Image" encompasses more than a thousand years of history, and presages the general outline, at least in a topical sense, of many of the recurrent themes of his historical scholarship—though also, as we shall see, his attitude toward some themes would change.

Leff always saw the rhetorical tradition as both one and many. The tradition was one in that it was united by a common if diverse body of theory and by a common core of teaching and classroom exercises. The tradition was many in that its theoretical parts did not agree; in fact, they reflected very different perspectives on the nature of rhetoric and the role of the orator in society. Isocrates, for example, rejected what Plato and Aristotle called "philosophy," and focused not on the theoretical principles dear to them, but on cases. Aristotle developed the most rhetoric-friendly version of a philosophical approach to rhetoric, but he grounded his perspective in intellectual contemplation (*to theoresai* in Aristotle's famous definition) not in practice. Hermagoras in the second century BCE developed a decision machine for public questions independent equally of Isocrates and Aristotle. Cicero complicated and enriched matters further by embracing the Greek philosophy Isocrates rejected, while retaining his emphasis on developing the facility of the orator over knowledge of technical principles. In turn, as Leff points out in his dissertation, both Cicero's early, more technical, manual-centered work and his later more sophisticated view of invention and genre added distinct components even to this one influential branch of rhetorical thought.

Not only were rhetoric's theoretic components—originating in these separate traditions—less than coherent, but its teaching components were similarly fragmented. "The Frozen Image" opens with a beginning that is also an end. After centuries in which rhetorical treatises in Greek dominated Roman education, the fourth century CE saw a flourishing of rhetorical treatises in Latin. A dozen or so of these have come down to us, and the whole resurgence was unprecedented since the work of Cicero and Quintilian. These works—though reflecting the range of the tradition since its inception in fourth-century Greece and including figurist manuals, technical manuals (accounts of the whole techne or art), and writings or borrowings from Cicero and Quintilian—have none of the vitality of the originals; they are dry, formulaic, and unimaginative. Worse, many, indeed most, of them are inconsistent, confused, and lack clear understanding of their subject. Though known to specialist scholars, none of these works was available in English, nor likely to be made so. In the midst of an apparently unpromising, even useless, topic Leff found a series of questions worth asking.

Irrespective of their lack of significant content, why did these treatises exist? Why, two hundred years after the forums in which orators played a vital civic role had disappeared—and at a time when the only serious, if diminishing, outlet for oratory was the courts—would a series of texts emerge holding up the orator statesman as a cultural ideal? Why even as the empire declined would emperors, hard-strapped for cash, subsidize rhetorical schools and pay rhetoricians the highest salaries of any class of teacher? Rhetoric, it seems, was popular even among indigenous subjects in the provinces. The leading figures in Tacitus's *Dialogue on Orators*, for instance, are all Spaniards. And herein lay a paradox. An art that in its heyday had focused on flexibility and adaptation had become frozen in time. Cut off from the realities of communication in its own day, a system designed to train public orators to advise the state had become a system of classifications valued for its own sake and cherished as a badge of culture at a time when that culture was rapidly eroding. That the classroom was the principal forum for this backward-looking art underscored the triumph of form over content, of theory over practice.

Starting with a picture of the art in its most corrupt form at arguably its worst historical moment, Leff situates his project of philosophic and historical reflection. Leff's dissertation both illuminates earlier creative periods in which rhetoric was a viable cultural ideal and shows how, in response to various contingencies, it fell beneath self-parody and took on a form never imagined by the contending figures who originated it. Not least of the interest of Leff's study is his critique of contemporary scholarship for its misunderstanding of the classical tradition, for seeing it through too narrow (or too modern) a lens, and for lack of knowledge of or interest in the historically contingent interrelationships of its parts. Perhaps worst of all from Leff's perspective was the contemporary habit of using the classical tradition as a quarry for teaching criticism and composition without sufficiently attending to the political and cultural circumstances in which its various teachings developed. That the art in the period of its corruption was also a product of historical circumstance, and that its teachings, properly approached, could reveal something worth knowing about the contexts in which rhetorical thought has flourished or declined, added additional motivation to his project. In light of his early emphasis on the close relation of power and politics to the development of rhetorical practice and teaching, the complaint of his later professional antagonists, the critical rhetoricians, that Leff ignored power and ideology reveals a paradox that would bewitch scholarship for decades.

"The Frozen Image" ends with a poignant tribute to civic humanism even in its dotage. What long since had ceased to be an art that embodied the process by which citizens would learn to argue, deliberate, and judge public issues whether of policy or justice had become a memorial to a vanished way of life. The preservation of the cultural memory in which concern for the public good defined the citizen, and advancing it the task of the orator-statesman, recalled a time when rhetoric was substantive and its union of value, reason, and passion consequential.

Leff's immediate postdissertation publication indicates that his views of the late Latin tradition continued to develop. Leff's citations from the work of John Ward on the change in court practice in the late empire indicate he came to believe that the late Latin manuals' focus on preinvention and formal schematization may have represented, not so much the failure of the tradition to adapt, as he had argued in his dissertation, but an example of adaptation.[2] According to Ward, oral presentation played a lesser role in the late empire, and a greater emphasis on classification was evident in the courts. From this perspective late Latin rhetoric was not so much dead as changing with its times. Leff's account of St. Augustine and Martianus Capella underscores how the late Latin tradition seemed to be wholly unlike its civic republican ancestor, yet was derived from it.[3] In Augustine Leff analyzes how Cicero's very machinery of invention facilitated the salvation of the soul rather than illuminated more narrowly the civil questions of the courts or the forum! Similarly, in the pagan Martianus Capella's *Marriage of Philology and Mercury*, eloquence, in the form of Mercury, marries a mortal woman of great learning (Philology) who in response to courtship surrenders her life in this world to marry Mercury in the next.

At the expense of getting ahead of our story, it is pertinent to cite an observation about Augustine that Leff made seventeen years later in a conference keynote address aptly titled "Knowing What to Take Out of Egypt":

> Augustine, then, captures something of Cicero's spirit and turns it to productive use within the metabolism of his own Christian rhetoric. . . . Yet Augustine's purpose is not to understand Cicero; rather his understanding of Cicero serves his own rhetorical purposes. In other words, we have here a paradigm for hermeneutical rhetoric.[4]

The "frozen image" never appears in Leff's postdissertation scholarship, published or unpublished. Instead, in keeping with his revised interpretation of his object of study, Leff's view of rhetoric became increasingly innovative, fluid, multisided, cyclical, and adaptive.

The Development of Leff's Research Program

Given Leff's early knowledge of the contours and byways of the rhetorical traditions, one might assume that his subsequent critique of the presuppositions of his colleagues and even the germ of his own program of close reading were in some sense waiting to be launched. As two of his own retrospective essays make clear, however, his criticism of disciplinary assumptions and practices begins with a realization of how much he himself shared them.

In "Up from Theory: I Fought the Topoi and the Topoi Won," Leff recounts that in 1963, the year he began graduate study, Karl Wallace published "The Substance of Rhetoric: Good Reasons."[5] The aim of Wallace's essay, as Leff summarizes it, was to find "a distinctive, substantive, and coherent theory of rhetorical argumentation."[6] Having earlier that same year emerged from a study of the history of speech communication in the United States, Leff recognized how deeply Wallace's effort to find a substantive foundation for the discipline was rooted in its history. "Theory" and "substance" were buzzwords of the time, and the problem with speech was that it seemed to have neither. Speech lacked both a proper subject and a set of abstract principles positioned above and apart from its subject to give the phenomena it studied coherence. Other disciplines also studied popular discourse and argumentation, and so this relatively new research area needed to claim a distinctive approach. As Leff notes, it was common practice to mine the lore of the classical tradition to extract elements for a contemporary approach to invention. Leff began his lifelong study of the topics fully on board with Wallace's project. His own distinctive proposal was to approach "the substance of rhetoric" historically. Since the topics had always been central to rhetorical invention, yet were not well understood, perhaps the needed elements were already in the historical record awaiting their rediscovery.

In "Up from Theory," Leff describes this initial project as "a fool's errand." One has only to read his retrospective essay or any of the many essays on the topics that dot his career to see how different the perspective that emerged from his studies was from the presuppositions with which he began. Leff's historical perspective formed the part of this original project that would endure. As with so much else that he studied, Leff's discovery of the diversity of past practice and the teaching focus of that practice was revelatory. "As long as the rhetor knew how to get hold of a topic and use it," he concluded, "there was not much need to fuss about abstract considerations." One of Leff's favorite quotations from Quintilian on the topics was that rhetors who reduce them into a system and memorize it "will be the possessors of what I can only call a dumb science (*mutam quondam scientiam*)."

The early Leff, having seen through the modernist assumption that the topics were bits of information rather than teaching tools, was still far from seeing through modernist assumptions about theory in rhetorical criticism, however. A clear proof, for example, that for Leff rhetorical theory—including his own—develops through competition among differing versions of itself appears in his attempt in 1973 to account for Cicero's recurrent use of exaggeration in his Catilinarian orations. Having been drawn to Kenneth Burke's theory of "redemptive identification," Leff used Burke as his theoretical template in his first essay in rhetorical criticism, "Redemptive Identification in Cicero's Catilinarian Orations." Leff concludes the essay with a warning against the perspective that soon would become the signature of his program of studies:

> There is a temptation to concentrate on the text . . . in order to witness the practical conflict of one idea set against the other; we become so absorbed in the ideas themselves or in the process by which they are argued that it is easy to forget that these data may be applied to a wider

> field. . . . The critic, then, must face two realities, that of the document and that of the theory which explains it in humane terms. The theory of redemptive identification can assist the critic in bringing these two realities together.[7]

Twenty years later in his retrospective on this essay Leff reflects on how he shared the then-conventional view of theory "as a coherently organized body of principles distanced from and superior to any particular instance of practice." He goes on: "I did not pause to consider whether the resistance of the texts suggested a flawed conception of the nature of theory and its relationship to critical practice. Instead, I hastened to find another 'theory' as a replacement."[8]

Indeed, Leff's first essay of rhetorical criticism appears in a volume that explicitly aimed to multiply critical perspectives. Leff's effort fit right in, since his essay resolved to "apply" Burke to Cicero. What would seem obvious to him later was not at all apparent to him then:

> Had I studied Burke more attentively, I would have discovered an alternative conception of theory per se, rather than an alternative theory in the conventional sense. . . . I might have seen the theorist as a positioned subject engaged in a kind of rhetorical practice, and I might have recognized the possibility of grounding interpretive work in cases rather than in disembodied abstractions.[9]

Leff's essay and his later comment on it help frame what would become his close reading project as a task of reclamation developing from within, and in resistance to, a specific context of cultural and disciplinary history.

In the wake of Edwin Black's definitive critique of neo-Aristotelianism, the previous orthodoxy of the field, not only did critics face the challenge of engaging the oratorical/rhetorical text, but no longer did they even have a tradition—however inadequate or badly understood—to draw on to orient themselves to their task. Leff's collaboration with Mohrmann in the Cooper Union Address essays is important because in them he and Mohrmann open both a new approach to texts and a new understanding of tradition. The essays show that to move rhetorical criticism forward, one need not abandon past tradition but approach it more intelligently.

Mohrmann's insistence that critics engage the text rather than circle around it, and Leff's prior realization from his "fool's errand" of looking for packets of substantive information in an art designed to make students more limber thinkers, enabled them to suggest how aspects of prior tradition, properly understood, might creatively and appropriately be reinvented and redeployed. It is in this sense that what later became one of Leff's signature contributions to contemporary theory—"close reading"—can be seen most accurately as a development from classical Isocratean/Ciceronian pedagogy.

The Ciceronian spirit of celebrating the suppleness of even the formalistic categories of tradition, when selectively appropriated or reinvented, makes its debut in the Cooper Union essays. By making available for the critic a needed formalistic resource, the campaign oration—new to the tradition but not to the Aristotelian spirit of specifying rhetoric by genre, nor to the Ciceronian spirit of reenvisioning the resources of perceptive lore with an eye to their use—Leff and Mohrmann showed tradition as an inventional practice, not as an antique set of terms and distinctions frozen in time. So intimately tied is close reading to Leff's larger historical/historiographical project of diagnosis and case-specific prescription, that the two, while distinguishable in their parts, blend together in a single web of thought.

As Leff argues in "Genre and Paradigm in the Second Book of *De Oratore*," a central thesis of close reading is that knowledge embedded in the action of a text escapes the net of abstract theory. To be *seen*, then, and following the Isocratean practice of focusing instruction on texts and cases, the action implicit in the text must be *shown*. But this approach has intrinsic problems of its own. Gladstone, who ought to have known since he specialized in presenting budgets to Parliament, put the problem of the relativity of perception to audience well when he said, "The truth is not always loved when seen and is not always seen when shown."[10] The problem of enabling readers to see what has been shown, and to appreciate its value, already manifests itself in the Leff-Mohrmann collaboration.

The Leff-Mohrmann collaboration encompasses two separate, and very different, essays. The first could easily stand on its own as an historically well-motivated case study; the second explains the rationale of the first. On strictly Isocratean/Ciceronian standards the first essay should not require separate theoretical breakdown in a second essay.[11] In a well-structured Isocratean/Ciceronian world, imitation, or, as Leff called it, "concrete abstraction," should be sufficient to enable the reader to grasp the lesson of the model and reinvent its insights.[12] If the student cannot do this, then there is not much hope for the student to develop independent rhetorical skill—mere theorizing will not help. But Leff and Mohrmann lived not in an Isocratean world, and the important thing is they knew it. They attempted to revive several features of Isocratean/Ciceronian insight, specifically how civic humanism embedded theory in practice. A paradox of close reading from its very inception, then, is that for rhetorical theorists and critics to grasp the meaning of close reading, its precepts, theory, conditions, and explanatory ambitions have to be carefully spelled out. Not only that, but blockages occasioned by critical habits and expectations put in place by the scientific culture of modernity, or by the romantic reaction against rhetoric, and not challenged or unconsciously retained by postmodernity, have to be identified and addressed. The Isocratean/Ciceronian perspective of what it means to learn from a case rather than from a theory that explains it—the rationale of rhetoric having no true abode but in cases—has itself to be separately theorized and then exemplified in a case.

Thus if we reverse the order of the Leff-Mohrmann essays so that a detailed rationale making a theoretical point of rhetorical interest introduces the case, rather than the case coming first and being motivated by historical or political themes, we have the pattern of most of Leff's mature essays in rhetorical criticism. From his earliest work on, elaborate and detailed theorization precedes most of Leff's close reading. The heavily theory-laden nature of the opening motivational sections of Leff's essays sometimes occupy nearly half of the paper. That Leff's rhetorical criticism is typically so heavily front-loaded with theory as opposed to being primarily motivated by the contexts or circumstances of the speeches examined in no way detracts from its demonstration that rhetorical theory, to be grounded, can only be understood in relation to specific cases. The extensive rationales preceding most of Leff's close readings provide the appropriate degree of abstraction necessary for the particulars of the case analysis to be brought into view. They also point us to the truth that, to be properly understood, each of Leff's essays needs to be seen in relation to what we take to be the explanatory ambitions of his larger body of work—in particular in relation to the grounding of rhetoric in its teaching traditions.

If there is one takeaway from our study of Leff's oeuvre in its entirety, it is this: Leffian criticism consistently finds itself implicated in purposes that reach beyond any single case, and that instead find their true home in a pedagogical vision of rhetoric as a living, transformative art aimed at cultivating the productive capacities of its students. A short piece from late in his career is instructive on this point. Leff argues for the significance of his style of criticism not in light of its analytic precision in relation to other approaches, but rather in light of its place in a wider network of purposes and values he aligns with rhetoric as a teaching art. Leff defined his approach "as a mode of isolating and appreciating important resources for rhetorical art as embodied in use and as a propaedeutic for disciplining and developing the sensibilities of rhetorical critics."[13]

Skeptics of Leff's work, most of whom embrace the broader sociological, philosophical, and ideological approaches to discourse so dominant in the contemporary humanities, have typically ignored the "propaedeutic" ethos of Leff's scholarship. They have treated Leff's imperative to examine particular texts and speakers, instead, as evidence of naïveté about language and power, of devotion to an elitist hermeneutic detached from the reality of hegemonic struggles that, by definition, transcend the ambit of any single rhetorical performance and that therefore outstrip the capacities of rhetorical inquiry. For such skeptics, the big-picture vista ostensibly enabled by the mastery of ideological criticism or philosophical reflection trumped the kind of knowledge yielded by studying what Leff once called "public address at the rough ground of its practice."[14] And yet Leff was never opposed to big-picture pronouncements or even to theorizing rhetoric at the global level. Rather, as this volume shows, he simply had his sights set on a different big picture, and this "big picture" was itself always at play in the norms and forms that guided Leff's writing. To look at a text closely was not merely to uncover its formal artistry at the cellular level but to go in search of "the fundamental operations of rhetorical language" as they uniquely inhabited particular loci of controversy and performance. Leff, in fact, resisted the notion of a "direct encounter with rhetorical texts" unmediated by history or ideology, and spoke of his aims in a much different key. As he recalls in "Things Made by Words," he had built much to his own surprise "something very like a 'theory' of rhetorical reading" in which certain features of rhetorical art are stressed over others, certain judgments are made about the primary materials of this art, and certain goals are kept in sight all the while.

Organization of the Volume

Living Art strives to clarify these goals and to bring focus to their implications for current scholars. As we wrote at the outset, Leff's thought can be understood as a perspective on the history of rhetoric; a critique of the disciplinary assumptions of classical, Hellenistic, Renaissance, modern, and postmodern rhetoric, particularly of those assumptions that block growth in rhetorical theory or criticism; and, finally, a multipronged program for reinventing and revitalizing rhetorical study, criticism, and tradition(s) based on an Isocratean/Ciceronian exemplar. While these themes weave through all of Leff's work, their development is not always linear. We thus present Leff's essays in the order that we believe makes it easiest for readers to discern the sweep of his thought, even if this means presenting the essays—and previewing them in an introduction to each of the book's five sections—in a sequence that does not always follow the chronology in which they first appeared. Finally, the limits of space and the need to represent the range of Leff's interests have required difficult choices on which essays to include in each section. Fortunately, *Living Art*'s accompanying website makes it possible for readers to locate Leff essays not included in our text, to encounter work that is barely known, and to bring their own judgment to bear on the full legacy of a scholar, colleague, and friend who left his mark on us all.

NOTES

1. For an account of Leff's stature and contributions to rhetorical scholarship see David Zarefsky, "Introduction: Michael Leff et la tradition des études rhétoriques

aux Etats-Unis," *Argumentation et Analyse du Discours* 6 (2011): http://aad.revues.org/1082; Stephen Howard Browne, "Introduction," *Philosophy and Rhetoric* 45 (2012): 99–106. For a tribute to Leff's influence on the study of argument beyond rhetorical studies proper, see J. Anthony Blair, "Rhetoric, Dialectic and Logic as Related to Argument," *Philosophy and Rhetoric* 45 (2012): 148, 156, 163. See, too, the special section "Celebrating the Life of Michael Leff, 1941–2010," *Rhetoric and Public Affairs* 13 (2010): 653–716.

2. Michael C. Leff, "The *Institutiones Oratoriae* of Sulpitius Victor," *Quarterly Journal of Speech* 63 (1977): 442–43; "The Topics of Argumentative Invention in Latin Rhetorical Theory from Cicero to Boethius," *Rhetorica* 1 (1983): 41.
3. Michael C. Leff, "St. Augustine and Martianus Capella: Continuity and Change in Fifth Century Latin Rhetorical Theory," *Communication Quarterly* 24 (1976): 2–9.
4. Michael C. Leff, "Knowing What to Take Out of Egypt: Notes toward Hermeneutical Rhetoric," keynote address, Pennsylvania State University Conference on Rhetoric and Composition, State College, PA, 1993.
5. Karl R. Wallace, "The Substance of Rhetoric: Good Reasons," *Quarterly Journal of Speech* 40 (1963): 239–49.
6. Michael C. Leff, "Up from Theory: Or I Fought the Topoi and the Topoi Won," Abstract, *Rhetoric Society Quarterly* 36 (2006): 203–11.
7. Michael C. Leff, "Redemptive Identification: Cicero's Catilinarian Orations," in *Explorations in Rhetorical Criticism*, ed. G. P. Mohrmann, Charles J. Stewart, and Donovan J. Ochs (University Park: Pennsylvania State University Press, 1973), 157–77.
8. Michael C. Leff, "Cicero's Redemptive Identification: Commentary," in *Critical Questions: Invention, Creativity, and the Criticism of Discourse and Media*, ed. William L. Nothstine, Carole Blair, and Gary A. Copeland (New York: St. Martin's Press, 1994), 325.
9. Leff, "Cicero's Redemptive Identification," 325.
10. William Ewart Gladstone, "Public Speaking," cited in Loren Reid, "Gladstone's Essay on Public Speaking," *Quarterly Journal of Speech* 39 (October 1953): 267.
11. Leff himself notes this point in his essay on Mohrmann. "Paradoxically then, the attempt to displace theory with action leads from action back to theory." See "Textual Criticism: The Legacy of G. P. Mohrmann" in this volume.
12. Michael C. Leff, "Concrete Abstractions: A Response to Anderson and Skopec," *Pennsylvania Speech Communication Annual* 38 (1982): 21–24.

13. Michael C. Leff, "Close Textual Analysis," Leff Conference Papers and Lectures, 2006 Department of Communication, University of Memphis.
14. Michael C. Leff, "From Madison to Nashville: How Far South Public Address Has Gone," lecture, Tenth Biennial Public Address Conference, Vanderbilt University, Nashville, TN, 2006.

PART ONE

Greek and Latin Rhetorical Theory

Readers in search of an entry point into Michael C. Leff's signature talent for weaving histories of rhetoric together with theoretical innovations attuned to the present will want to start with "Tradition and Agency in Humanistic Rhetoric." For Leff, the standard opposition of individual agency to collective tradition had to be reconfigured and rethought for rhetoric's intelligibility to break through the grid of modernist and postmodernist attitudes towards language, culture, and power. Leff notes how in both ancient and modern times rhetoricians have been taxed with not being independent agents but merely mouthpieces for popular and received opinion. And yet, by calling attention to the tension between agent- and audience-centered views of an orator's agency, Leff strives to make a more mixed understanding of agency viable. He uses Ralph Ellison's account of jazz improvisation as an example of how an individual rhetor, like a jazz artist, innovates within tradition while at the same time finds ways to preserve the ability of tradition to provide a common focus for community identity as tradition changes.

Seeing tradition in terms of change and action involves, for Leff, seeing traditions of rhetorical theory, too, in terms of the internal diversities that invite multiple and sometimes contradictory interpretations of the same text or author. In "The Uses of Aristotle's *Rhetoric* in Contemporary American Scholarship," Leff shows how disputes over Aristotle's rhetorical thought are as instructive regarding the nature of rhetorical theory as anything in the text itself. As though taking a cue from Hans-Georg Gadamer that the meaning of a text must include the history of its interpretation, Leff's review of the different receptions of Aristotle in the twentieth century suggests one way that rhetorical theorizing itself should be conducted. In the final portion of the essay, Leff notes that Aristotle divided the arts into productive, practical, and theoretic, and that Richard

McKeon's account of Aristotle's *Rhetoric* as "an architectonic, productive art" placed the *Rhetoric* in two of Aristotle's categories. In response, Leff suggests almost off-handedly that foundationalists and antifoundationalists share the same unexamined assumption that Aristotle's *Rhetoric* must be understood in just one way. An unfortunate consequence of such a monological hermeneutic has been to assume that rhetoric *itself* was also always one thing. The reductionism shared by various parties to the dispute over Aristotle's *Rhetoric* has tended, Leff suggests, to occlude from historical consciousness the actual variety of practices and understandings of rhetoric, even those variously derived from Aristotle, that have actually operated at different times and places.

Thinking carefully through the productive often underappreciated nature of such multiplicities came naturally to Leff, and in "Genre and Paradigm in the Second Book of *De oratore*" one finds such subtlety on vivid display. The essay spotlights the central role of irony in both the subject of rhetoric and Leff's approach to theorizing. An instructive exposition of *De oratore*, it also reveals Cicero's deft use of irony in appropriating Aristotle's categories for organizing his own, logically incompatible view of rhetoric. Again, tensions in rhetoric's varieties of tradition, agency, and change become visible in Leff's historically-grounded interpretive practice. One gets a glimpse into the reach and scope of the knowledge behind such practice in Leff's synoptic treatment of one of the most often talked about (but most difficult to understand) features of classical rhetoric—the topics. In "The Topics of Argumentative Invention in Latin Rhetorical Theory from Cicero to Boethius"—published first in the inaugural issue of the journal *Rhetorica*, which Leff helped to found—readers will find, at the very least, a starting place for sorting through "a bewildering diversity of meanings" associated with the topics. In particular, readers will gain insight into how a constant, if variegated, return to the distinctions between Aristotelian and Ciceronian approaches to the topics informed much of Leff's thought on the history and future of rhetoric study.

FURTHER READING

"Boethius and the History of Medieval Rhetoric." *Central States Speech Journal* 25 (1974): 135–41.

"Cicero's 'Pro Murena' and the Strong Case for Rhetoric." *Rhetoric and Public Affairs* 1 (1998): 61–88.

"Commonplaces and Argumentation in Cicero and Quintilian." *Argumentation* 10 (1996): 445–52.

"Forms of Reality in Plato's *Phaedrus*." *Rhetoric Society Quarterly* 11 (1981): 21–23.

"The Latin Stylistic Rhetorics of Antiquity." *Speech Monographs* 40 (1973): 273–79.

"The Material of the Art in the Latin Handbooks of the Fourth Century A.D." In *Rhetoric Revalued*, ed. Brian Vickers (Binghamton, NY: Medieval and Renaissance Texts and Studies, 1982), 71–78

"Recovering Aristotle: Rhetoric, Politics, and the Limits of Rationality." *Quarterly Journal of Speech* 71 (1985): 262–72.

"Reinterpreting Plato's *Phaedrus*." *Quarterly Journal of Speech* 57 (1971): 344–47.

Tradition and Agency in Humanistic Rhetoric

I intend to approach the issue of tradition indirectly by first considering some problems connected with rhetorical agency. This strategy might seem awkward, if not actually dangerous, since it entangles two equally complex and disputed concepts. Nevertheless, I hope to show that, within the humanistic strand of rhetoric, these concepts are linked in a way that is not now recognized but has an important bearing on our understanding of both. Specifically, I argue that the humanistic approach entails a productively ambiguous notion of agency that positions the orator both as an individual who leads an audience and as a member of a community who is shaped and constrained by the demands of the audience. This tension, I maintain, becomes intelligible when we understand how tradition can function as a mediating force between individual and collective identities, and once

From *Philosophy and Rhetoric* 36 (2003): 135–47.

viewed from this angle, tradition emerges as the primary resource for rhetorical invention.

Before proceeding to this argument, I need to explain the sense in which I am using the term "humanistic," since humanism, like tradition and agency, is also a concept that carries with it a variety of different and largely unrelated meanings. Consequently, I want to be clear that I am not referring to a kind of secular religion, as in a "religion of humanity," or to the version of pragmatic philosophy developed by William James and F. S. C. Schiller, or to the ideological formation often called "liberal humanism." Instead, I have in mind a rather specific development in the history of rhetoric that begins in classical Greece with Protagoras and Isocrates, appears in Rome under the sponsorship of Cicero and Quintilian, rises to prominence again in the Renaissance "humanists," and still commands attention and respect from some contemporary rhetoricians.[1] Throughout most of the history of this development, Cicero has been the dominating presence, and so it is often characterized as "Ciceronian rhetoric," and while this history is complex and includes much local variation, at least some features of the approach are consistent. These include a suspicious attitude toward abstract theory not only in respect to rhetoric but also to ethics and politics,[2] a conviction that discourse, especially discourse that allows for argument on both sides of an issue, has a constitutive role to play in civic life,[3] a valorization and idealization of eloquence that entails a strong connection between eloquence and virtue,[4] and a conception of virtue that is decisively linked to political activity.[5] In what follows, I hope to demonstrate that certain views about agency and tradition also fall within this cluster of common attitudes.

Agency in Humanistic Rhetoric

Among contemporary rhetorical scholars, one of the most widely accepted judgments about traditional humanistic rhetoric is that it contains a strong, almost totalizing, emphasis on the agency of the rhetor. Robert Scott sums up this position in a sentence: "To take the speaker as active and the audience as passive is quite traditional,"[6] and Wayne Brockriede elaborates on the point when he asserts that the perspective placing "the speaker at the center of the transaction" is "a pervasive one historically. From the practice of the sophists and the writings of Isocrates and Cicero to the thrust of many twentieth-century textbooks in public speaking, the rhetorical transaction has been seen as one in which a speaker seeks to have his way with an audience—both to achieve an immediate end and to achieve power or glory as a respected member of society."[7]

Brockriede's remarks have a political and ethical subtext that Lois McNamara Byham makes explicit: "Old rhetoric was unidirectional thereby vesting those with authority the power to impart information to inferiors," and its goal, she adds, was to manipulate and exploit.[8] More recently, Dilip Gaonkar translates these observations into postmodern argot when he identifies classical rhetoric with "an ideology of human agency," which, among other things, regards the speaker as a "seat of origin rather than a point of articulation."[9]

The classical treatises on rhetoric contain much that supports the claims I have just reviewed. The technical apparatus always is informed and organized from the speaker's perspective, and the humanistic rhetoricians construct the orator as a cultural hero and celebrate the magnitude and apparent autonomy of oratorical power. One of the earliest and most noteworthy examples of this homage to the rhetor appears in Plato's *Gorgias*. In that dialogue, Gorgias immodestly claims that rhetoricians hold absolute sway in public debate. They can speak more persuasively than the expert on any given topic and overwhelm "all opposition of any kind," since the force of their art is so great and splendid that no one can address "a crowd, on any subject in the world, more persuasively than the rhetorician."[10]

Plato, of course, is no friend of rhetoric, and he presents this view only to refute it. But the testimony of the rhetoricians themselves proves that Plato was not constructing a straw man. Isocrates, in his *Antidosis*, offers an elegant hymn to the power of speech that associates rhetorical eloquence with sound thought and concludes by asserting that the power of discourse is so important "that nothing done prudently occurs without speech, that speech is the leader of all thoughts and actions, and the most intelligent people use it most often" (257).[11] This power is the possession of the speaker, and elsewhere, Isocrates explains that mastery of eloquence requires much study and is "the work of a brave and imaginative soul" (*Against the Sophists*, 17). Cicero addresses the same themes. In his *De inventione*, the orator emerges as the heroic agent who, by combining wisdom and eloquence, persuaded humanity to abandon its naturally savage condition and adopt a civilized and just way of life.[12] In the *De oratore*, he refashions this topos so as to embody the eloquence that is being praised: "There is . . . no more excellent thing than the power, by means of oratory, to get a hold on assemblies of men, win their good will, direct their inclinations wherever the speaker wishes. . . . For what is so marvelous as that, out of the innumerable company of mankind, a single being should arise . . . who can make effective a faculty bestowed by nature on every man? . . . Or what achievement is so mighty and glorious as that the impulses of the crowd, the consciences of the judges, the austerity of the Senate, should suffer transformation through the eloquence of one man? What function again is so kingly, so worthy of the free, so generous as to bring help to the suppliant, to raise up those that are cast down, to bestow security, to set free from peril, to maintain men in their civil rights?" (1.30–32).[13]

These Ciceronian sentiments reverberate through the history of humanism. During the twelfth-century revival of classical learning, for example, John of Salisbury defines the eloquent speaker as the one "who fittingly and efficaciously expresses himself as he intends," and John find himself at a loss "to see how anything could be more generally useful; more helpful in acquiring wealth, more reliable for winning favor, more suited for gaining fame, than is eloquence."[14] Two centuries later, the Florentine humanist Coluccio Saltutati offers another variation on this theme when he asserts that nothing is "more important than to control the motions of the mind, to turn your hearer where you will and to lead him back again to the place from which you moved him, pleasantly and with love. These, unless I am mistaken, are the powers of eloquence; this is its work. All the force and power of rhetoricians strains to attain it. To be sure, it is a great thing to adorn writing with words and maxims, but the greatest—however embellished and dignified by the language—is to move the minds of the listeners. Only eloquence achieves these things."[15]

This list of witnesses could be extended at some length, but even the short version justifies the conclusion that humanistic rhetoric valorizes and centers itself on the individual agent. Nevertheless, there is another side to this story, a complication embedded within this apparently simple conception of agency. John Witherspoon hints at this underside of rhetorical agency when he observes that the highest achievement in the art of speaking must coincide with "the greatest reserve and self-denial in the use of it, otherwise it will defeat its own purpose."[16] That is, the power of the orator ironically implies humility before the audience, because the power to move and persuade an audience requires accommodation and adaptation to its sentiments. The audience necessarily constrains the orator's intellectual horizons, modes of expression, and even representation of self, and so, if orators are to exert influence, they must yield to the people they seek to influence.

Isocrates and Cicero mark and emphasize this dependency on audience and social context. Hence, while Isocrates sometimes underscores the bold imagination needed for success in political discourse, he also warns his reader not to expect novelty, since his is a type of discourse that allows "no room for paradox, or for what is incredible or unconventional. Instead we should consider most accomplished the man who is able to draw together the most ideas held by others and articulate them most elegantly" (*To Nicocles*, 44). Likewise Cicero explains that "the whole art of oratory lies open to the view, and is concerned in some measure with the common practice, custom, and speech of mankind, so that, whereas in all other arts that is most excellent which is farthest removed from the understanding and mental capacity of the untrained, in oratory the very cardinal sin is to depart from the language of everyday life, and the usage approved by the sense of the community" (*De oratore* 1.12). Orators must adapt their thinking to "the understanding of the crowd" (1.108) and regulate their eloquence to conform with "the good sense of the audience, since all who desire to win approval have regard to the goodwill of their auditors, and shape and adapt themselves completely according to this and their opinion and approval" (*Orator* 24).[17]

In the first book of *De oratore*, Cicero offers a dramatic representation of this point. When Crassus, one of the two main interlocutors in the dialogue, considers the special burdens placed upon the orator, he stresses the anxiety caused by the demands of the audience. Based on his own experience, he has learned that the best orators are most "frightened by the difficulty of speaking," the doubtful outcome of the effort, and the

"the anticipations of the audience." He confesses that he "turns pale" and "quakes in every limb and in all my soul" when he begins to speak, and he recalls one incident where he was so overcome by fear that the presiding magistrate had to adjourn the court. Crassus, we should remember, is portrayed as an imposing figure. The other characters in the dialogue display attitudes toward him that range from deep respect to reverence, and he is a distinguished political leader and a preeminent orator, whose special talent is the arousing of emotion. Paradoxically, then, this man who strikes awe into the heart of his listeners is himself awed by his audience (*De oratore* 1.123–24).

As Jerrold Seigel has demonstrated, the Renaissance humanists, owing largely to their commitment to Christian notions of virtue, were forced to acknowledge the discrepancy implicit in this dual perspective on the orator and made elaborate efforts to resolve it.[18] Among the classical writers, however, no such tension surfaced, and the two perspectives coexisted within a symmetrically balanced pattern: The orator led the people, bent their will, and won applause but was also lead by the people, bent by their will, and dependent on their applause. The orator was simultaneously active and passive.

The critics of *ars oratoria* (and the humanism associated with it) do not recognize this complexity and regard the conception of agency as all one thing or the other. As Gaonkar's comments indicate, the postmodern inclination is to associate humanistic rhetoric with a view of the orator as an autonomous agent. On the other hand, Enlightenment thinkers condemned *ars oratoria* for precisely the opposite reason: Since it demanded accommodation to concrete circumstances, motives, and audience interests, it rendered the orator heteronomous and therefore incapable of exercising either imaginative freedom or clear, unfettered reason. Thus, Locke, in a now much quoted passage, maintained that the devices of rhetoric worked to no other purpose than "to insinuate wrong *Ideas*, move the Passions, and thereby mislead the Judgment; and so indeed are perfect cheat."[19] Kant regarded the rhetorical art of persuasion suspect because it deceived through a beautiful show and catered to human weakness so as to promote "one's own designs." It did not matter, in Kant's view, whether such designs were "well meant or even actually true," since an art based upon this compunction to accommodate was, in principle, "worthy of no respect."[20]

The Enlightenment antipathy toward humanistic rhetoric arises from many causes, but one of the most basic—and one that has a special bearing on the question of agency—is the systematic discrediting of tradition. As Alasdair MacIntyre has argued, tradition collapses under the weight of Enlightenment rationality because it never begins with "unassailable self-evident truths" and because it can never aim toward achievement of a final and universal rationality. Traditions are always embedded in the contingencies of history, are always subject to internal alteration, and are "always and ineradicably local."[21] As applied to agency, this means that whoever thinks or acts in terms of tradition cannot pass the test for autonomous judgment required by Enlightenment epistemology.

Tradition entails a different conception of agency and self. In place of the isolated self of modernity (or the alienated self of some versions of postmodernity), tradition constitutes the self through social interaction and as part of an ongoing historical development. Both the individual agent and the tradition achieve and change identity through a reciprocal circulation of influence. Inclusion within a tradition shapes the individual self, but also, and as a direct result of submitting to the mores and practices of the community, the individual gains the power to shape tradition. Moreover, the agents who succeed in effecting change in tradition also change their self-conception since individual and affiliative identities never lose connection with one another. Ralph Ellison explains how this process works in the performative tradition of jazz: "Each true jazz moment springs from a contest in which each artist challenges all the rest; each solo flight, or improvisation, represents (like successive canvases of a painter) a definition of his identity: as individual, as member of the collectivity, and as link in the chain of traditions."[22] This fluid relationship between individual and community also seems to describe the conception of agency implicit within humanistic rhetoric. Like the jazz artist, the orator leads the community by merging with it, and identifies the self not as a still, isolated essence but as something realized in and through public performance. The individual and the collective, as Greg Clark has said, "interact in relationships of collaboration."[23]

Tradition and Rhetorical Performance: The Case of Isocrates

To this point, I have attempted to show that the humanistic conception of rhetorical agency entails a complex interaction between speaker and audience and that this conception makes senses once we appreciate how tradition mediates between the individual and the community. This argument presupposes that a special and intimate relationship exists between humanistic rhetoric and tradition, and I now want to explain and justify this point. My claim is that, for the rhetorical humanists, tradition serves as the source and ground for civic discourse, since such discourse draws from and works to sustain the identity of the community, while it also functions as an instrument to effect change. From the humanistic perspective, rhetoric has constitutive force because it comes at the intersection of past memory and current interests and balances and adjusts both considerations. This is, of course, a very general and ambitious claim, and I can hardly pretend to deal with it adequately in this short essay. But I hope to make it plausible by referring to Isocrates, who provides us with an intriguing case study located at the origin of rhetorical humanism.

Although long dismissed as a mundane and unoriginal thinker, Isocrates is now the subject of a notable revival. The recent scholarship, impressive both in its quantity and quality, opens new perspectives on Isocrates's educational program, its place in fourth-century Athens, and its importance as a contribution to humanistic thought.[24] For our purposes, three aspects of this revisionist development merit special attention: (1) Despite a long-established tradition to the contrary, Isocrates and Plato ought not to be set in a polar opposition to one another, with one standing for practical realism and the other for idealism. While Isocrates vigorously rejects Plato's commitment to abstract, objective truth, he is equally opposed to the extreme relativism associated with Gorgias and other Sophists. Isocrates tries to situate himself between Plato and Gorgias by constructing a practical standard of knowledge that responds to ordinary experience, that develops within the medium of political discourse, and that generally allows for appropriate judgments in particular cases. (2) Isocrates is as much concerned about educating to virtue as Plato, and his version of *paideia*, though more practical than

Plato's, contains a good bit of idealism. For Isocrates, the goal of rhetorical education is deliberative excellence, and this goal cannot be reduced to mere success in pleasing or persuading an audience. Rather, its realization demands self-restraint, breadth of knowledge, and a cultivated sense of the common good, and as a result, it must reflect and manifest virtues intimately connected with moral character. Moreover, since neither technical skill nor persuasive efficacy determines deliberative excellence, the concept represents an idealization. That is, it must refer to standards that transcend the immediate partisan context and rest upon reasonably stable and durable principles of virtue. (3) Given Isocrates's pragmatic theory of knowledge and his thoroughly social and political conception of virtue, these principles could not arise from a purely abstract source. They had to come from within the experience of the community, and hence Isocrates's ideals had to be derived from history, or more specifically, from the Athenian political tradition. In short, Isocratean rhetoric is inherently embedded in tradition.[25]

Consistent with the humanistic aversion to theory, Isocrates never produces a systematic, conceptual account of his program. Instead, he teaches by example and writes political discourses that engage particular situations even as they illustrate how a rhetor can and should engage tradition. One of the most straightforward and interesting of these examples is his *Areopagiticus*, a speech that has been studied carefully by Josiah Ober and David Konstan, two leading proponents of the revisionist approach to Isocrates.[26] In what follows, I will borrow heavily from them to explain how the *Areopagiticus* simultaneously grounds itself in tradition and uses tradition for rhetorical purposes.

The speech is part of Isocrates's general effort to reform Athenian politics in a conservative direction. His goal is to persuade his fellow citizens to revise the existing populist form of democracy and replace it with a more restrained constitution—a variant of democratic government in which the masses would voluntarily defer to elite leaders who, in Isocrates's opinion, were properly equipped to make sound political judgments. The speech is highly critical of Athenian democracy as practiced in the mid-fourth century, but it carefully and skillfully avoids criticism of democratic government per se. Thus, the rhetoric of the text involves a dissociation between the current populist regime and another, better type of Athenian democracy, which is identified as the old regime founded by Solon and reestablished by Cleisthenes. Isocrates praises the Solonic constitution both because of the virtues it embodied and promoted and for the material advantages it brought to Athens. By contrast, he represents the existing populist democracy as immoderate, inclined to mistake license for freedom, and the cause of material ruin at home and abroad.

As Konstan has demonstrated, the speech pivots on the authority of Solon, since Isocrates promotes the Solonic constitution as the authentic source of the Athenian democratic tradition and as the model for a reformed and restrained version of democratic government appropriate for his own time. Solon's authority, of course, is hardly an inert historical given. It is not inscribed in an "objective" history of Athens, nor is it already fixed in the collective memory of fourth-century Athenian citizens. It is a rhetorical possibility that Isocrates can exploit to suit his own purposes. Isocrates chooses Solon as the touchstone for the Athenian tradition, and not Theseus or some other equally plausible character, because that choice corresponds with his immediate political interests, and he explains the nature and consequences of the Solonic regime in terms that tilt history decisively in the direction of his attitudes about the present. Tradition is not infinitely malleable, and so there are many things Isocrates cannot do; he cannot tell tales that have no basis in Athenian cultural memory, and he cannot construe persons and events in a way that offends his audience's sensibilities. Yet these limits are broad enough to allow Isocrates to do his rhetorical work and ground his objections to the existing regime in a plausible historical context.

When read from this perspective, the *Areopagiticus* becomes an exercise in the rhetorical and hermeneutic uses of history. The Athenian tradition frames and justifies the argument, but the tradition is fabricated (or at least tailored) as it is invoked, and the text works to fashion a reciprocal interaction between the past and the present. To the extent that it is persuasive, Isocrates's representation of the Solonic constitution at one and the same time alters understanding of its historical referent and of the immediate political context. Tradition surrounds and constrains the rhetorical field, but it also remains open to new rhetorical constructions, so that it is able to "develop while still maintaining its identity and continuity."[27]

Before concluding, we should also consider Josiah Ober's somewhat different but complementary reading of the *Areopagiticus*. Invoking Michael Walzer's conception of immanent criticism, Ober underscores the political differences between Plato and Isocrates in a way that highlights some of the distinctive features of Isocratean *paideia*. Ober notes that, like Plato, Isocrates regarded populist democracy with disdain, but, unlike Plato, he would not step outside the political process altogether and adopt a perspective alien to existing attitudes and practices. Thus, Isocrates did not reject democracy in favor of a more abstractly coherent type of government, but instead he differentiated forms of democracy and located (or invented) alternatives within the history of the polity: "Rather than working back to and then forward from fundamental knowledge of reality, rather than attempting to ground politics in a secure apprehension of the world as it is really, Isocrates remained rooted in his society. Isocrates again portrays himself . . . very much an internal critic, one who sees his role as calling his fellow citizens to abide by the best and highest ideals within their own political tradition."[28] Moreover, I would add that this immanent stance seems an almost unavoidable concomitant of Isocrates's rhetorical humanism. Since his version of *paideia* treats virtue as a social achievement and as something disseminated and regulated through political discourse, Isocrates cannot step outside the polity. Consequently, existing social and political forces constrain his individuality and the range of his thought, but they also enable rhetorical virtuosity since they provide resources for innovative modes of expression and forms of argument that work within tradition as they work to alter it.

The notion that tradition facilitates inventiveness may seem strange to those of us who, living in the wake of Enlightenment rationality, have been coached to believe that "tradition is like the handing over of a pound of tea, which enables us to brew exactly the same drink as our fathers,"[29] or as Lyotard and Thebaud put the point more abstractly, that tradition is "is a relation to time that would be a relation of preservation in which the important thing would be to keep things from being used up by time."[30] As the case of Isocrates demonstrates, however, rhetorical humanists present and deploy a much livelier sense of tradition. Tradition, in this sense, is a living force that requires constant change and adaptation if it is to serve a stabilizing function. Without it, rhetorical art could not exist, since lacking the conceptual support provided by tradition, the orator would not have a platform sufficiently stable to allow for performance. But the platform is only temporarily and locally stable, since it is constantly altered by the rhetorical performances it makes possible. Tradition, then, constrains and enables rhetorical art, limits the range of performance, but makes rhetorical performance count as a meaningful part of the history of the community and affords the community opportunities to perform new versions of itself without losing a sense of identity.

Finally, to return to my opening theme, this conception of tradition seems intimately connected with an ambiguous and interactive conception of rhetorical agency. Since tradition is not something that can be preserved in a pristine, original form, it must come to life through interventions that interpret the relationship between past and present. For the rhetorical humanists, orators are the agents who undertake this kind of intervention. If they are to succeed, they must persuade the community to alter its attitudes toward history, and this task involves a collaborative effort in which communal memory must expand, refocus, and change as circumstances demand. The orator, therefore, must display individual virtuosity in presenting and representing the tradition while also affirming solidarity with his audience. Orators work within a bounded but fluid medium, and they must exercise great inventive powers to shift the medium without appearing to subvert it, and this requires a special, delicate, and contextually sensitive relationship between self and community—a relationship that allows individual agents to stand apart as leaders because they stand with and serve the people they lead.

NOTES

1. Among the contemporary scholars who reflect this perspective, we might include Richard Lanham, *The Motives of Eloquence: Literary Rhetoric in the Renaissance* (New Haven: Yale University Press, 1976); and *The Electronic Word: Democracy, Technology and the Arts* (Chicago: University of Chicago Press, 1993); Thomas Sloane, *On the Contrary: The Protocol of Traditional Rhetoric* (Washington, DC: Catholic University of America Press, 1997); Walter Jost, "Teaching the Topics: Character, Rhetoric, and Liberal Education," *Rhetoric Society Quarterly* 21 (1991): 1–16; Michael Mendelson, "Everything Must Be Argued: Rhetorical Theory and

Pedagogical Practice in Cicero's *De oratore*," *Journal of Education* 179 (1997): 15–47; and *Many Sides: A Protagorean Approach to the Theory, Practice and Pedagogy of Argument* (Dordrecht: Kluwer, 2002); and David Fleming, "Rhetoric as a Course of Study," *College English* 61 (1998): 169–91. It may not be a coincidence that every author listed above is (1) a Renaissance specialist, or (2) seriously interested in the connection between the history of rhetoric and pedagogy, or (3) both of the above.

2. See Victoria Kahn, "Humanism and the Resistance to Theory," in *Rhetoric and Hermeneutics in Our Time: A Reader*, ed. Walter Jost and Michael Hyde (New Haven: Yale University Press, 1997), 149–70; and Kathy Eden, *Hermeneutics and the Rhetorical Tradition: Chapters in the Ancient Legacy and Its Humanist Reception* (New Haven: Yale University Press, 1997).
3. See Sloane, *On the Contrary*; and Mendelson, "Everything Must Be Argued."
4. See Lanham, *The Electronic Word*, 186–92.
5. For a more detailed account of "humanistic rhetoric," see Thomas Conley, *Rhetoric in the European Tradition* (New York: Longman, 1990), esp. 17–20, 34–42, and 109–50; and Nancy Stuerver, *The Language of History in the Renaissance: Rhetoric and Historical Consciousness in Florentine Humanism* (Princeton, NJ: Princeton University Press, 1970), 5–39.
6. Robert Scott, "A Synoptic View of Systems of Western Rhetoric," *Quarterly Journal of Speech* 61 (1975): 440.
7. Wayne Brockriede, "Trends in Rhetoric: Blending Criticism and Science," in *The Prospect of Rhetoric: Report of the National Developmental Project*, ed. Lloyd Bitzer and Edwin Black (Englewood Cliffs, NJ: Prentice-Hall, 1971), 124–25. Notably Brockriede regards Aristotle as a possible or partial exception to this myopic concentration on the rhetorical agent. This is, I think, an unreflective but very clear indication of the extent to which the humanistic tradition (Isocrates and Cicero rather than Aristotle) comes to be associated with the manipulative interests of the orator and of the failure to distinguish between a theoretically oriented rhetoric and one oriented to practice and teaching.
8. Lois McNamara Byham, "Rhetoric-as-Epistemic: A Reexamination," in *Rhetoric 78*, ed. Robert Brown and Martin Steinman (Minneapolis: University of Minnesota Center for Advanced Studies in Language, Style, and Literary Theory, 1979), 22.
9. Dilip Gaonkar, "The Idea of Rhetoric in the Rhetoric of Science," in *Rhetorical Hermeneutics: Invention and Interpretation in the Age of Science*, ed. Alan Gross

and William Keith (Albany: SUNY Press, 1997), 32. The shifting line of orthodoxy from Brockriede's high modernism to Gaonkar's postmodernism does meet with some resistance. Lanham, for example, presents a much more fluid conception of agency in the tradition (see especially, *The Electronic Word*, 186–91), though agency is not his most direct or primary concern. Janet Atwill, "Instituting the Art of Rhetoric: Theory, Practice, and Productive Knowledge in Interpretation," in *Rethinking the History of Rhetoric: Multidisciplinary Essays on the Rhetorical Tradition*, ed. Takis Poulakos (Boulder, CO: Westview Press, 1993), 91–118, offers a view of "productive knowledge" embedded in the tradition that suggests a different and more ambiguous notion of agency than the standard version acknowledges, but again she does not focus directly on the question of agency. John Angus Campbell, in a vigorous response to Gaonkar, does deal with agency explicitly and in some detail, but his argument does not refer directly to the tradition or to the interpretation placed upon it either by Gaonkar or by earlier proponents of an agent-dominated view; see John Angus Campbell, "Strategic Reading: Rhetoric, Intention, and Interpretation," in *Rhetorical Hermeneutics: Invention and Interpretation in the Age of Science*, ed. Alan Gross and William Keith (Albany: SUNY Press, 1997), 113–37, esp. 118–23.

10. Plato, *Gorgias*, trans. W. C. Helmbold (Indianapolis: Bobbs-Merrill, 1952), 456.
11. All translations of Isocrates are quoted from *Isocrates I*, trans. David Mirhady and Yun Lee Too (Austin: University of Texas Press, 2000).
12. *De inventione* 1.2–3.
13. All quotations from *De oratore* are taken from the Loeb edition, trans. E. W. Sutton and H. Rackham (Cambridge, MA: Harvard University Press, 1942).
14. *The Metalogicon of John of Salisbury: A Twelfth-Century Defense of the Verbal and Logical Arts of the Trivium*, trans. David D. McGarry (Berkeley: University of California Press, 1962), 26.
15. Coluccio Saltutati, *Rhetoric and Philosophy in Renaissance Humanism*, trans. Jerrold Seigel (Princeton, NJ: Princeton University Press, 1968), 76–77.
16. *Selected Writings of John Witherspoon*, ed. Thomas Miller (Carbondale: Southern Illinois Press, 1990), 232.
17. The quotation is from the Loeb edition, trans. H. M. Hubbell (Cambridge, MA: Harvard University Press, 1939).
18. Seigel, *Rhetoric and Philosophy*.
19. John Locke, *An Essay on Human Understanding* (Oxford: Oxford University Press, 1979), 508.

20. Immanuel Kant, *Critique of Judgment*, trans. J. H. Bernard (New York: Hafner, 1966), 172 n. 50.
21. Alasdair MacIntyre, *Whose Justice? Which Rationality?* (Notre Dame, IN: University of Notre Dame Press, 1988), 361.
22. Quoted by Robert Bone, "Ralph Ellison and the Uses of Imagination," in *Modern Critical Interpretations: "Invisible Man"*, ed. Harold Bloom (Philadelphia: Chelsea House, 1999), 6.
23. Gregory Clark, "Virtuosos and Ensembles: Rhetorical Lessons from Jazz," in *The Private, the Public, and the Published: Reconciling Private Lives and Public Rhetoric*, ed. Thomas Kent and Barbara Couture (Logan: Utah State University Press, 2004), 33. Another similar relationship between individual and collectivity has been observed among storytellers in traditional societies. Jean-François Lyotard and Jean Loup Thebaud note that "the subject of the enunciation makes no claims of autonomy with respect to his discourse. On the contrary, both through his name and through the story he tells, he claims to belong to the traditions. . . . The relevant feature [of good stories] is not faithfulness. . . . On the contrary, it is because one 'hams' it up, because one invents novel episodes that stand out as motifs against the narrative plot line, which for its part remains stable, that one is successful." Jean-François Lyotard and Jean Loup Thebaud, *Just Gaming*, trans. Wlad Godzich (Minneapolis: University of Minnesota Press, 1979), 33. Maurice Charland, whose article in *Philosophy and Rhetoric* develops the theme in greater detail, brought this passage to my attention.
24. Among the more important entries in this literature are Yun Lee Too, *The Rhetoric of Identity in Isocrates: Text, Power, Pedagogy* (Cambridge: Cambridge University Press, 1995); Takis Poulakis, *Speaking for the Polis: Isocrates' Rhetorical Education* (Columbia: University of South Carolina Press, 1997); Josiah Ober, "Eloquence, Leadership, Memory: Isocrates *Antidosis* and *Areopagiticus*," in *Political Dissent in Democratic Athens: Intellectual Critics of Popular Rule* (Princeton, NJ: Princeton University Press, 1999), 248–89; and Takis Poulakos and David Depew, eds., *Isocrates and Civic Education* (Austin: University of Texas Press, 2003).
25. A more detailed account of these developments appears in my paper "Isocrates, Tradition, and the Rhetorical Version of Civic Education," in Poulakos and Depew, *Isocrates and Civic Education*, 235–54.
26. Ober, *Political Dissent in Democratic Athens*, 277–89; and David Konstan, "Isocrates' Republic," in Poulakos and Depew, *Isocrates and Civic Education*, 107–24.

27. Jaroslav Pelikan, *The Vindication of Tradition* (New Haven: Yale University Press, 1984), 58.
28. Ober, *Political Dissent in Democratic Athens*, 282.
29. Davis McCaughey, *Tradition and Dissent* (Melbourne: Melbourne University Press, 1997), 56.
30. Lyotard and Thebaud, *Just Gaming*, 33.

WORKS CITED

Atwill, Janet. 1993. "Instituting the Art of Rhetoric: Theory, Practice, and Productive Knowledge in Interpretation." In *Rethinking the History of Rhetoric: Multidisciplinary Essays on Interpretation*, ed. Takis Poulakos. Boulder, CO: Westview Press.

Bone, Robert. 1999. "Ralph Ellison and the Uses of Imagination." In *Modern Critical Interpretations: "Invisible Man"*, ed. Harold Bloom. Philadelphia: Chelsea House.

Brockriede, Wayne. 1971. "Trends in Rhetoric: Blending Criticism and Science." In *The Prospect of Rhetoric: Report of the National Developmental Project*, ed. Lloyd Bitzer and Edwin Black. Englewood Cliff, NJ: Prentice Hall.

Bynham, Lois McNamara. 1979. "Rhetoric-as-Epistemic: A Reexamination." In *Rhetoric 78*, ed. Robert Brown and Martin Steinman. Minneapolis: University of Minnesota Center for Advanced Studies in Language, Style, and Literary Theory.

Campbell, John Angus. 1997. "Strategic Reading: Rhetoric, Intention, and Interpretation." In *Rhetorical Hermeneutics: Invention and Interpretation in the Age of Science*, ed. Alan Gross and William Keith, 113–37. Albany: SUNY Press.

Cicero. 1942. *De oratore*. Trans. E. W. Sutton and H. Rackham. Cambridge, MA: Harvard University Press.

———. 1939. *Orator and Brutus*. Trans. H. M. Hubbell. Cambridge, MA: Harvard University Press.

Clark, Gregory. 2004. "Virtuosos and Ensembles: Rhetorical Lessons From Jazz." In *The Private, The Public, and the Published: Reconciling Private Lives and Public Rhetoric*, ed. Thomas Kent and Barbara Couture. Logan: Utah State University Press.

Conley, Thomas. 1990. *Rhetoric in the European Tradition*. New York: Longman.

Eden, Kathy. 1997. *Hermeneutics and the Rhetorical Tradition: Chapters in the Ancient Legacy and Its Humanist Reception*. New Haven: Yale University.

Fleming, David. 1998. "Rhetoric as a Course of Study." *College English* 61:169–91.

Gaonkar, Dilip. 1997. "The Idea of Rhetoric in the Rhetoric of Science." In *Rhetorical Hermeneutics: Invention and Interpretation in the Age of Science*, ed. Alan Gross and William Keith. Albany: SUNY Press.

Isocrates. 2000. *Isocrates I*. Trans. David Mirhady and Yun Lee Too. Austin: University of Texas.

John of Salisbury. 1962. *The Metalogicon of John of Salisbury: A Twelfth-Century Defense of the Verbal and Logical Arts of the Trivium*. Trans. David D. McGarry. Berkeley: University of California Press.

Jost, Walter. 1991. "Teaching the Topics: Character, Rhetoric, and Liberal Education." *Rhetoric Society Quarterly* 21:1–16.

Kahn, Victoria. 1997. "Humanism and the Resistance to Theory." In *Rhetoric and Hermeneutics in Our Time: A Reader*, ed. Walter Jost and Michael Hyde. New Haven: Yale University Press.

Kant, Immanuel. 1966. *Critique of Judgment*. Trans., J. H. Bernard. New York: Haffner.

Lanham, Richard. 1976. *The Motives of Eloquence: Literary Rhetoric in the Renaissance*. New Haven: Yale University Press.

———. 1993. *The Electronic Word: Democracy, Technology, and the Arts*. Chicago: University of Chicago Press.

Locke, John. 1979. *An Essay on Human Understanding*. Ed. Peter Nidditch. Oxford: Oxford University Press.

Lyotard, Jean-Francois, and Jean Loup Thebaud. 1979. *Just Gaming*. Trans. Wlad Godzich. Minneapolis: University of Minnesota Press.

McCaughey, Davis. 1997. *Tradition and Dissent*. Melbourne: Melbourne University Press.

McIntrye, Aladair. 1988. *Whose Justice? Which Rationality?* Notre Dame, IN: University of Notre Dame Press.

Mendelson, Michael. 1997. "Everything Must Be Argued: Rhetorical Theory and Pedagogical Practice in Cicero's *De oratore*." *Journal of Education* 179:15–47.

Mendelson, Michael. 2002. *Many Sides: A Protagorean Approach to the Theory, Practice, and Pedagogy of Argument*. Dordrecht: Kluwer.

Ober, Josiah. 1999. *Political Dissent in Democratic Athens: Intellectual Critics of Popular Rule*. Princeton, NJ: Princeton University Press.

Pelikan, Jaroslav. 1984. *The Vindication of Tradition*. New Haven: Yale University Press.

Plato. 1952. *Gorgias*. Trans. W. C. Helmbold. Indianapolis: Bobbs-Merrill.

Poulakos, Takis. 1997. *Speaking for the Polis: Isocrates' Rhetorical Education*. Columbia: University of South Carolina Press.

Poulakos, Takis, and David Depew, eds. 2003. *Isocrates and Civic Education*. Austin: University of Texas Press.

Scott, Robert. 1975. "A Synoptic View of Systems of Western Rhetoric." *Quarterly Journal of Speech* 61:448–53.

Seigel, Jerrold. 1968. *Rhetoric and Philosophy in Renaissance Humanism*. Princeton, NJ: Princeton University Press.

Sloane, Thomas. 1997. *On the Contrary: The Protocol of Traditional Rhetoric*. Washington, DC: Catholic University of America Press.

Too, Yun Lee. 1995. *The Rhetoric of Identity in Isocrates: Text, Power, Pedagogy*. Cambridge: Cambridge University Press.

Witherspoon, John. 1990. *Selected Writings of John Witherspoon*. Ed. Thomas Miller. Carbondale: Southern Illinois University Press.

The Uses of Aristotle's *Rhetoric* in Contemporary American Scholarship

The reception of Aristotle's *Rhetoric* in the twentieth century presents us with a complicated and somewhat ironic tale. Through much of the century, while rhetoric remained an unfashionable subject, the treatise was largely ignored or dismissed by philologists and philosophers, but it was studied avidly by scholars in the language arts, especially by those in the emerging discipline of speech communication and by literary critics concerned about close, formalistic readings of poetic texts. More recently, as interest in rhetoric has revived, the *Rhetoric* has attracted broader attention: Classicists, after a long hiatus, have produced new commentaries and translations; philosophers have reclaimed the work, arguing that it has real significance for ethics and philosophical psychology; political scientists have used it to support a revisionist approach to political theory, and it has attracted notice even

From *Argumentation* 7 (1993): 313–27.

in such apparently remote disciplines as economics and social psychology. At the same time, however, in the area where its authority was once secure, the status of the *Rhetoric* has declined precipitously. Rhetoricians in American departments of English and speech communication now commonly associate Aristotle with the "old rhetoric," which, in their view, was at best moribund and at worst actually opposed to the formation of a genuine rhetorical consciousness. Hence the repeated calls for a new rhetoric conventionally include an attack on Aristotle as the *fons et origo* of the sins committed by the older generation. Yet, while this attitude is widespread, it is not universal, since some scholars hold that the liabilities of "neo-Aristotelianism" resulted from the "neo" rather than the "Aristotelian"; that is, the problem was not the *Rhetoric*, but the inaccurate or misguided interpretations placed upon it by modern readers. And from this perspective, the *Rhetoric*, when properly interpreted, has a perennial value; it continues to speak to current interests and should remain a central, if not the central, text in rhetorical scholarship.

This whole development is extremely complex, but the actions and reactions of the professional rhetoricians seem to follow a familiar pattern. As Richard McKeon has noted, the general history of Aristotle's influence often takes form "as revolts against his outworn authority or as discovery of his forgotten methods."[1] On a much reduced scale, twentieth-century rhetoricians appear to have reenacted this tension, and the disciplinary history of rhetoric (which is only a small part of its entire history in our century) turns on the attitude toward Aristotle. Traditionalists accept Aristotle's authority; radical revisionists deny it altogether; and moderate revisionists seek to rediscover its meaning and significance. In this context, interpretation of Aristotle hardly becomes a disinterested exegetical task, but instead functions as a vehicle for articulating different visions of what rhetoric is or should be.

This is not to say that the *Rhetoric* simply has become a Rorschach test, dividing contemporary rhetoricians into different philosophical camps. In fact, the literature contains lively debates about the interpretation and application of specific Aristotelian principles. In this context, we encounter issues such as these: Is the enthymeme a truncated formal syllogism, or does its identity depend upon more subtle features?[2] Does the rhetorical induction (*paradeigma*) require some kind of mediating generalization between particulars, or does it move directly from particular to particular?[3] Do the topoi in the *Rhetoric* provide formal, material, or both formal and material resources for invention?[4] Is the theory of metaphor in book 3 substantially connected with the theory of invention in the first two books, or does it address a different aspect of the rhetorical process?[5] Rhetoricians who raise these issues are concerned about their application to current problems, but they also seek to understand the text. Thus, if they do not always adhere to the most scrupulous standards of philological inquiry, they at least recognize these standards as relevant to their arguments. As a result, controversies about these matters, while often sharp and theoretically significant, retain a degree of stability, since the criteria for settling them seem reasonably clear and consistent.

More typically, however,—and this is especially true since the coming of the postmodern revolution—contemporary rhetoricians assess the *Rhetoric* in global, metatheoretical terms. At this level, the issues define and impart attitudes toward the *Rhetoric* as a whole. Differing views rarely make much argumentative contact with one another, since opposition is either unrecognized or used to distinguish the infidels from the true believers. The grounds for settling controversy are obscure, and necessarily so, because, as Rosalin Gabin has noted, the disagreements are "not logical but ontological." And so to choose a position is to choose "a total view of language and its human use, and a total view of Aristotle's *Rhetoric* and what it offers us as a text."[6]

In order to illustrate and clarify this larger arena of controversy, I have isolated three issues that seem especially prominent, and in what follows, I will summarize the opposing positions concerning each of them. These issues are the placement of Aristotelian *Rhetoric* in reference to Plato; Aristotle's conception of the epistemological and ethical status of rhetoric; and the location of rhetoric within the Aristotelian system of the arts and sciences. Within the discussion of these issues, I will also comment here and there about two other matters that deserve separate consideration, but which I do not have the time to address in detail—the scope of Aristotelian rhetoric and the relationship between rhetoric and extra-verbal reality in Aristotelian thought.

Plato and Aristotle

Contemporary rhetoricians display great concern about the origins of the art and routinely set out the possibilities for rhetorical theory within the parameters of its development in classical Greek thought. In charting this development, the conventional method is to follow a sequence that first compares the Sophists with Plato and then Plato with Aristotle. Since this progression places Aristotle at the conclusion of the process and Plato as the middle term, the relationship between the two emerges as a conceptual pivot. As we might expect, there is no consensus about this matter.

In an influential essay that does much to establish the method I have just described, Everett Lee Hunt disputes interpretations that stress the affinity between the *Rhetoric* and the Platonic dialogues. Reading the *Rhetoric* as a practical and popular treatise, Hunt concludes that Aristotle's theory "bears more resemblance to that of Protagoras and Gorgias than to that of Plato."[7] James Kinneavy reaches a somewhat more restricted but basically similar conclusion. Since Aristotle accepts contingency and probability as the legitimate domain of rhetoric, Kinneavy holds that Aristotle "sides with Isocrates in the epistemological debate with Plato."[8] John Gage agrees that the attitude toward probability marks a crucial distinction between Plato and Aristotle, but Gage also insists that Aristotle's position departs sharply from that of the Sophists. Like Plato, Aristotle objects to the technical and eristic emphasis in the sophistic manuals, and he views rhetoric as connected with knowledge. But, Gage adds, unlike Plato, Aristotle conceives knowledge in the rhetorical sphere as a product of contingency and social interaction—not as something discovered outside the process of deliberation, but as an activity which develops in and through discursive exchange. On this view, Aristotle occupies a well-demarcated middle ground between Platonic idealism and sophistical relativism.[9]

While Hunt and Kinneavy draw heavily from Cope's commentaries, Gage is much more influenced by William Grimaldi. Grimaldi, however, presses well beyond Gage in aligning Aristotle with Plato. Agreeing with During that the *Rhetoric* is composed against the background of the *Phaedrus*, Grimaldi contends that Aristotle "clearly sides with Plato . . . on the relation between rhetoric and truth: one must know the subject and present its truth."[10] Consequently, Aristotle fully justifies "rhetoric for the most Platonic Platonist."[11] This strong association between Aristotle and Plato allows Grimaldi to make a sharp contrast between Aristotle and the sophistic rhetoricians, and in his view, the contrast serves to vindicate Aristotelian rhetoric.

In other quarters, however, this same alignment works to vindicate the Sophists, since Plato and Aristotle come to represent a closed, metaphysically tainted conception of the art. Thus, Eric Charles White argues that Aristotle's rhetoric of probability presupposes a stable and ordered reality as its referent, and so it is decisively opposed to "Gorgias' skepticism concerning the possibility of final truth.[12] The *Rhetoric*, on White's account, circumscribes "the merely probable" within the ambit "of certain knowledge," and while it assumes a more practical guise than Platonic rhetoric, Aristotelian rhetoric remains committed to the metaphysical premise that the function of language is to reproduce knowledge of the real.[13] In this respect, Aristotelian and Platonic rhetoric are essentially the same, and both suppress the open-ended, constantly mutable, and tropological forms of invention that characterize Gorgianic rhetoric. Other contemporary scholars who support this postmodern rehabilitation of the Sophists also stress the metaphysical—and therefore Platonic—basis of the *Rhetoric*.[14]

Rhetoric, Ethics, and Epistemology

Aristotle never clearly and systematically explains his conception of the relationships among rhetoric, truth, and ethics, but contemporary scholars often make strong, unqualified claims in interpreting his position. On one side, there are those who insist that the connections are intimate and fundamental. Thus, Charles S. Baldwin maintains that Aristotle establishes for all time "the true theory of rhetoric as the energizing of knowledge."[15] Lester Thonnsen and A. Craig Baird assert that "Aristotle's basic philosophy did not tolerate compromise with the moral integrity and design of the speaker," and that "a fair reading of the *Rhetoric* reveals no significant departures from the high moral principles enunciated in the *Nicomachean Ethics*."[16] Larry Arnhart, who has pursued the issue in much greater detail, reaches a similar conclusion: "Although Aristotle recognizes the differences between rhetoric and moral philosophy, and although these differences are reflected in his treatment of nobility and virtue in the *Rhetoric*, what he says in the *Rhetoric* does not fundamentally contradict what he says in the *Ethics*."[17] As I have already noted, the strong link Grimaldi forges between Aristotle and Plato rests on the conviction that the *Rhetoric* is committed to truth. For Grimaldi, Aristotle's attitude is "simply that rhetoric qua rhetoric stretches out to truth." As a linguistic art, then, rhetoric is mimetic and "is supposed to re-present the real (i.e., truth and justice) in any situation for an auditor."[18] And this formulation, strange though it may seem, corresponds quite closely to the orthodox postmodern view of the *Rhetoric*'s method and purpose. The difference here is not descriptive but evaluative; Aristotle emerges as hero or villain depending on the attitude toward this sort of representational theory of language and its ethical implications.

On the other side, we find an equally long list of those who regard the *Rhetoric* as a purely practical and instrumental treatise. In part, this interpretation arises from Aristotle's shrewd and pragmatic treatment of specific rhetorical tactics, and in truth, it is difficult to read parts of the *Rhetoric* without noting the agonistic and even eristic tone. Troubled by the apparent inconsistency between these sections and the more philosophical stance Aristotle adopts elsewhere in the text, Whitney Oates concludes that the *Rhetoric* is ambivalent in its attitude toward ethical values. At times, Aristotle behaves as a proper philosopher, attending to questions of value as he tries to link rhetoric with logic, ethics, and politics. But once he launches into the barnyard of tactics, he becomes transformed into a sophistical Mr. Hyde, approving of conventional response as a standard for values, reducing the craft of persuasion to a mere matter of words, and adopting the view that "anything goes if only persuasion emerges."[19] More impressed by the strategic than the philosophical moments in the *Rhetoric*, B. A. G. Fuller argues that Aristotle assumes a medical and not a moral posture concerning rhetoric. Thus, rhetoric becomes a clinical power, since whether it is used "in the interests of truth or falsehood, or right or wrong makes no difference. Rhetoric is good or bad according as it wins the case."[20] Likewise, W. D. Ross believes that the *Rhetoric* has "a purely practical purpose." It is not a theoretical work, but "a manual for speakers."[21]

The views I have just summarized come from an older generation of philologists and philosophers, who are skeptical about rhetoric in general and who seem almost embarrassed by the fact that Aristotle had written about the subject. Nevertheless, the instrumental interpretation of the *Rhetoric* has also commanded the attention of professional rhetoricians, and it emerges most clearly among those who emphasize the distance between Aristotelian and Platonic rhetoric. Hunt, for example, repeatedly stresses the moral neutrality of the *Rhetoric*. In an often cited passage, he asserts that "Aristotle's *Rhetoric* is largely detached from both morality and pedagogy. It is neither a manual of rules nor a collection of injunctions. It is an unmoral and scientific analysis of the means of persuasion."[22] In assessing Aristotle's treatment of forensic oratory, Hunt observes that "once engaged in the classification of arguments, [Aristotle] is concerned with rhetorical effectiveness and not with moral justifiability."[23] Finally, Aristotle's treatment of delivery reveals that he regarded the art as an "instrument of persuasion detached from the moral nature of the rhetorician."[24]

This disjunction between persuasive effect and the moral quality of the act yields a reasonably clear and technical basis for defining the position of rhetoric within a disciplinary matrix. J. Robert Olian explains that the key issue here is the distinction between "rhetoric as productive art and ethics or politics as practical arts."[25] Productive arts concern themselves only with making, while practical arts "suggest modes of conduct." Consequently, rhetoric, in the Aristotelian scheme, is purely instrumental and cannot entail intrinsic ethical or political standards. The social uses of rhetoric are regulated externally by ethics and politics. Accepting this view, Forbes Hill maintains that Aristotelian rhetoric "is a neutral instrument that sees impartially the arguments on both sides of a question. It is subservient, politics is the architectonic art."[26] Moreover, Hill extends and refines this position to formulate a theory of rhetorical criticism in which the critic assumes a neutral, politically disinterested stance with respect to persuasive discourse.[27]

Recently, a third approach to this issue has emerged, one that stands between the idealism suggested by Grimaldi and the pure functionalism advocated by Hunt and Hill. Scholars such as Lois Self,[28] Christopher Johnstone,[29] Ronald Beiner,[30] and Eugene Garver[31] attempt to discover the connection between rhetoric and ethics in Aristotle neither by considering the representational solidity of rhetoric nor by comparing specific doctrines in the *Nicomachean Ethics* or the *Politics* with sections of the *Rhetoric*. Instead, they concentrate on apparent similarities between Aristotle's account of the rhetorical process and the operation of practical wisdom, as it is explained in the *Nicomachean Ethics*. Their studies indicate three important points of convergence between rhetoric and *phronesis*. First, both must balance reason and passion, intellect and desire, and deal with a unified activity of the whole being. Second, the object of both rhetorical and ethical deliberation concerns particulars that are not yet determined and cannot be determined through universals. And third, rhetoric, like *phronesis*, does not find its end in judgment or understanding but in action.[32] Taken together, these points suggest a conceptual affinity between rhetoric and ethics in Aristotelian thought, and rhetoric begins to emerge as a deliberative faculty rather than as a technical instrument. Conceived in this way, rhetoric assumes a civic rather than a professional identity, and within the economy of Aristotelian thought, it must incorporate intrinsic standards for success. This requirement involves a serious complication, since in order to satisfy it, rhetoric must be defined as a practical art, and as I hope to show in the next section of this paper, the placement of rhetoric within the Aristotelian system of the arts poses a vexing problem.

Rhetoric in the System of the Arts

Everyone agrees that Aristotle regards rhetoric as an art, but no agreement exists about how he classifies it as an art. There are four possibilities: a productive art, a practical art, a theoretical art, or some combination of the above. Each of these possibilities is instanced in the literature, and, ironically, the Aristotelian classifications, often cited as an example of his effort to order and clarify matters, prove a source of contention and confusion.

Traditional scholarship places rhetoric among the productive arts, and this placement tacitly informs the perspective adopted by Hunt,

Thonssen, and Baird, and other rhetoricians of the past generation. As we have noted, Olian makes this assumption explicit, arguing that its status as a productive art is the key to understanding Aristotelian rhetoric. Olian, however, merely asserts and does not justify this categorization.

In her essay "Judgment, Probability, and Aristotle's *Rhetoric*," Barbara Warnick presents a rationale for this position.[33] Warnick's motive is to counter interpretations, such as those sponsored by Grimaldi and Johnstone, which expand the scope of Aristotelian rhetoric beyond the arenas of traditional civic discourse. While she does not make this point fully explicit, these extensions of the scope of the *Rhetoric* follow from a classification of it as something other than a productive art. Grimaldi, although he recognizes practical and productive considerations found within the text, heavily stresses the theoretical aspect of the *Rhetoric*. Consequently, he claims that Aristotle offers us a rhetoric that functions as a universal faculty and operates throughout the spectrum of discursive practices, finding application in the physical sciences as well as in politics. Johnstone, who flatly asserts that Aristotle's *Rhetoric* is a practical art, maintains that it functions as a general faculty of deliberation concerning contingent particulars. Consequently, its domain includes all situations that engage ethical or political issues, even ethical self-deliberation.

Both these views, Warnick argues, violate Aristotle's intentions. Referring to *Posterior Analytics* 89b7–9 and *Nicomachean Ethics* 1139b15, Warnick notes the schematic divisions among the domains of inquiry and emphasizes the fact that techne is distinguished from theoretical, scientific, or practical knowledge because it finds its end in production. Since Aristotle labels rhetoric as a techne, Warnick contends that its identity and its relationship to other disciplines are fully apparent. Like dialectic and unlike all other arts or rational activities, rhetoric produces arguments, and the distinction between rhetoric and dialectic corresponds to differences in the institutional contexts, the modes of discourse (i.e., monologue as opposed to dialogue), and the specificity or generality of the premises that characterize the two arts. On this analysis, rhetoric emerges not as a general faculty of deliberation but as a method for making arguments, whose range of operation is restricted to specific social and political environments.

Warnick's argument works to yield a relatively bounded and determinate conception of Aristotelian rhetoric, and in this respect, her position corresponds to the traditional attitude associated with the theory that rhetoric is a productive art. Janet Atwill, however, departs from this tradition and argues that the productive status of Aristotelian rhetoric indicates that its functions are indeterminate, and thus it is fundamentally and not just schematically different from other disciplines in the Aristotelian system. Theoretical and practical knowledge, Atwill explains, ultimately refer to the self-contained activity of the individual subject: theoretical knowledge manifests itself in disinterested contemplation, and practical wisdom eventuates in action undertaken for its own sake. In both cases, Aristotle stresses aims, dispositions, and habits possessed by the human subject and thus capable of being regulated without reference to extrinsic standards. A productive art, on Atwill's account, presents a very different situation since it works within a medium of exchange. In this exchange between the maker and the user of the art, neither party can control its operations or outcomes, and thus productive knowledge is itself contingent and indeterminate: "Subjects of productive knowledge are defined by social exchange rather than private possession; and just as a techne could never be a form of private property, neither could the makers and users with which it is identified be private, stable entities. The subject defined by techne is mutable and social, and rather than embodying the culture's highest value, that subject functions as the very nexus of competing standards of value. . . . Rather than securing boundaries, it would seem that productive knowledge is inevitably implicated in their transgression and renegotiation. . . . Thus productive knowledge becomes a significant stumbling block for those who attempt to invoke Aristotle to authorize either a philosophical or deliberative rhetoric."[34] As Susan Jarrett notes, this interest in the indeterminacy of the subject has a distinctively postmodern ring.[35]

Thus, in comparing Warnick and Atwill, we arrive at another interesting paradox. The classification of the *Rhetoric* as a productive art may justify the "modernist" bias in favor of a rhetoric that fits neatly into the corporation of disciplines; or it may justify the "postmodern" bias in favor of a rhetoric that destabilizes the entire system. Further complications arise when we consider the objections that exist, in principle, to any definition of Aristotelian rhetoric as a productive art.

George Kennedy, who considers Aristotelian rhetoric a theoretical art, raises one of these objections succinctly and clearly. Given that rhetoric involves "creativity," it might be regarded, like poetry, as a productive art. Aristotle, however, "fails to make the identification. Rhetoric in his view does not produce oratory in the same sense that poetics produces poetry, for it stands at a different stage in the productive process."[36] Significantly, neither Warnick nor Atwill compares rhetoric to poetic, even though poetic, as its very names suggests, seems to offer the prototype of a productive art. Had they attempted the comparison, the problem Kennedy raises would have emerged immediately. What is it that a productive art produces? In the case of poetic, the answer is clear—a poem. In the case of rhetoric, the answer is not at all clear. Warnick asserts that it is argument, but the status of argument as a product is hardly the same as the status of a poem. To claim that argument is the product of rhetorical art seems equivalent to the claim that *muthos* is the product of poetic; it is to single out a part without regard to the whole. Atwill, since she emphasizes the process of exchange, probably would hold that persuasion is the product of rhetoric. But again this response does not seem adequate, since persuasion clearly is not a product in the same sense that shoes or poems are products.

The anomaly is highlighted if we consider an important observation made by Richard McKeon. McKeon notes that the ancestor to the *Rhetoric* was Aristotle's *Collection of the Arts*, a work which "summarized the characteristics of rhetorical systems." On the other hand, the ancestor to the *Poetics* was *On Poets*, which devoted itself to the history of poetry per se. Thus, "Aristotle's interests in poetry seem to have followed the analogy of his interests in politics and to have been concerned rather more with the history of the subject of inquiry than with previous theories."[37] In other words, Aristotle has an interest in the products of the poetic: art which is not matched, as it is in Cicero, by an interest in the products of the rhetorical art. This difference becomes obvious when we compare the place of the poets in the *Poetics* to the place of the orators in the *Rhetoric*. In the former, the great works of Greek tragedy, especially the plays of Sophocles, form the basis of inquiry. In the latter, as Hunt remarks, Aristotle refers to "any existing examples of eloquence only most casually for the sake of illustration."[38] Consistent with this inattention to actual rhetorical production, Aristotle omits two things which, whether we judge by the standard of the *Poetics* or by the standard established in other classical rhetorics, would seem necessary components of a productive art—a doctrine of organic form[39] and reference to paradigmatic works that embody the principles of the art.

Now, the evidence being what it is, and intentions—even of the simpleminded, let alone Aristotle—being as elusive as they are, I think it possible that Aristotle's conception of productive art was sufficiently elastic to include the *Rhetoric*. Nevertheless, the contrast between the *Rhetoric* and the *Poetics* surely indicates that the issue is not simple and cannot be resolved by a direct deduction from the schemata of the arts and sciences that Aristotle presents in other works.

As I indicated at the end of the preceding section of this paper, the view that Aristotelian rhetoric is "civic" or "deliberative" leads to its classification as a practical art. This alignment is not obvious, and those attempting to justify it face serious obstacles. Perhaps the most serious arises from a point Janet Atwill has made and which I summarized above. Practical arts are self-regulative because they find their end in action undertaken for its own sake. Persuasion, however, occurs through exchange, accommodation, and social interaction. How, then, can an art of persuasion assume a self-regulative function? How can Aristotle assign an autonomous end to an activity that seems to require heteronomous judgment?

A relatively simple answer is to argue that, for Aristotle, the end of rhetoric is not to persuade but to discover the available means of persuasion as they apply to particular cases. The need to deal with particulars counters Kennedy's claim that this definition indicates that the art is theoretical. That is, the rhetorician not only needs to discover the means of persuasion but to apply them to contingent particulars. Since this process is clearly deliberative, rhetoric itself must be a deliberative or practical art, and if its standards refer to the quality of the act rather than its effects, then the art can sustain an autonomous end—namely, to deliberate well. But this argument, as Warnick suggests, is not sufficient, because, even if accepted, it would only justify placing rhetoric within the genus of deliberation; it does not distinguish rhetoric from other practical arts and hence simply collapses it into ethics and politics. Thus, to sustain the classification of rhetoric as practical art, it is necessary to locate a specific deliberative function performed by the art that is distinct from other types of deliberative practice.

In a recent series of articles, Eugene Garver makes a direct and sustained effort to solve this problem.[40] His starting premise is that rhetoric entails two possible standards of success—an external standard based upon actual results and an internal standard which depends upon the way the agent acts so as to produce the result. The first criterion, which Garver associates with sophistic, "pre-philosophical" rhetoric, refers to what is done by words and resists artistic treatment. The second criterion refers to what is done in words, and since it specifies something in the power of the agent, it offers the basis for an art of rhetoric. Aristotle, Garver argues, accepts the second criterion, and the consequences of this choice become evident in terms of a familiar comparison: "Neither the art of rhetoric nor the analogous art of medicine in fact aims at producing that product, persuasion or health. Each aims at producing everything in its power to achieve that end."[41] Viewed from this angle, the practical aspect of rhetoric takes priority over its productive aspect: "Doing everything in one's power is precisely a doing as opposed to a making, even if it is doing everything in one's power to make something."[42] Furthermore, since the function of the art is not realized in a product, it must depend upon the agent's action.

What, then, is the function of artistic rhetoric? On this point, Garver notes that Aristotle has a fairly clear position. The function of rhetoric is to deliberate about matters where there is no specific art or method to guide us. As Garver interprets it, this view indicates that rhetoric deals with indeterminate issues, which cannot be resolved by determinate methods of science or logic. Rhetoric may enter into the discourse of a determinate subject, such as physics, but in such a case it fulfills a secondary or supplementary purpose. Rhetoric fulfills its own function only in contexts where the deliberative process is self-regulative, where there is no appeal to fixed principles that stand outside the process. Persuasion, Garver explains, is entirely general, but for Aristotle, artistic rhetoric can occur only in situations where the deliberative function is autonomous and thus can be said to operate for its sake.[43]

This conception of function, however, applies generally to practical knowledge, and Garver still must account for the distinctive status of the rhetorical art. For this purpose, he returns to his point about the dual standards for success that can apply to rhetoric. Unlike ethics, which directly engages *praxis*, rhetoric arises from and occurs within social institutions where productive results (i.e., persuasion) inform the agent's actions. Yet it is also possible to conceive rhetoric as an artistic power in which the agent's actions have an intrinsic value. (Garver cautions that this value cannot be fully equivalent to the autonomy of right conduct in ethics, but it must be sufficient to allow for standards that are not determined by sheer results.) To establish rhetoric as a practical art, therefore, it is necessary to make an inference from *poesis* to *praxis*—an inference that allows for recognition of inherent value embedded in the productive process. Persuasion in general cannot offer a basis for this inference, since its function is to produce an effect, a matter that is entirely extrinsic. Nevertheless, there are institutional settings in which the rhetorical function becomes the only available standard for deliberative proceedings, and by limiting artistic rhetoric to these contexts, Aristotle can locate intrinsic value in the exercise of that function. Thus, on Garver's account, the Aristotelian genres of rhetoric do not represent an exhaustive classification of types of persuasive discourse, but rather they designate the contexts in which persuasion can manifest itself as a practical art, since in these three settings, the proper exercise of the art can have a value in and of itself. In the political, forensic, and epideictic species of rhetoric, it is possible to establish a role for both speaker and auditor that corresponds to the internal demands of the rhetorical function; and hence, in delimiting artistic rhetoric to these types, Aristotle establishes rhetoric as a practical art, generically similar to ethics but specifically different from it.[44]

This summary does not adequately represent the complexity of Garver's argument. And, in fact, this very complexity is one of its notable features, since it indicates the difficulty involved in presenting an adequate case for rhetoric as practical art. Garver's long and involved chain of reasoning is sustained only by filtering the opening chapters of the *Rhetoric* through Aristotle's ethical doctrine. It is plausible, of course, that this method places us in contact with Aristotle's own thought process, but the connection remains a matter of conjecture. Moreover, I wonder how well Garver's theory can account for the more technical sections of the *Rhetoric* (the middle and later chapter of book 1, for example), or how it can dismiss or accommodate the whole of book 3. Nevertheless, Garver certainly opens a number of interesting issues, and whatever the gaps or problems in his position, I think he has succeeded, where others have failed, in making a prima facie case to justify Aristotelian rhetoric as a practical art. In summary, this survey demonstrates that existing scholarly opinion covers the spectrum of possibilities concerning the classification of Aristotelian rhetoric as an art: It is variously conceived as a productive, a theoretical, or a practical art. Moreover, efforts to establish one of these categories as absolute and to dismiss the others do not seem convincing. And even the more reasonable effort to elevate one of the three to a coordinating position entails great difficulty, perhaps revealing more about the interests of the interpreter than the disposition of the issue. These disagreements and problems, therefore, lend support to Richard McKeon's thesis that the Aristotelian classifications are "reduced to confusion and contradiction" if one limits the process of classification to a single basis.[45] Mindful of his own admonition, McKeon considers Aristotelian rhetoric to be an architectonic, productive art, and since an architectonic art involves "a doing," this means that rhetoric is at once an art of making and of doing.[46] Furthermore, it seems consistent with the spirit of McKeon's thought to regard this combination as only one of the possible and plausible alternatives. Apparently, then, rhetoric has productive, practical, and theoretical aspects that all play significant roles in the Aristotelian conception of the art, and efforts to file the *Rhetoric* in only one folder are bound to prove frustrating. Nevertheless, many rhetoricians—a clear majority, I suspect—still firmly believe that on this matter Aristotelian rhetoric is all one thing.

Conclusion

What is true of the classification of Aristotelian rhetoric among the arts also holds good through the whole range of the metatheoretical arguments. The rhetorical literature is filled with articles, monographs, and books that offer equally global but incompatible interpretations of the *Rhetoric*. A short list of the entries might include the following: Aristotle's *Rhetoric* accepts the key premises of sophistic epistemology; Aristotle's *Rhetoric* presents the definitive and final refutation of sophistic epistemology; Aristotle's *Rhetoric* is relevant only to civic issues; Aristotle's *Rhetoric* is relevant to all types of discourse; Aristotle's *Rhetoric* reflects its author's metaphysical bias and thus circumscribes the function of the art within a fixed, determinate conception of reality; Aristotle's *Rhetoric* presents the art as a generative force that works within the indeterminate world of human relations; Aristotle's *Rhetoric* is a neutral, scientific treatise; Aristotle's *Rhetoric* describes instruments designed to repress political dissent; Aristotle's *Rhetoric* embodies lofty principles of ethical conduct; Aristotle's *Rhetoric* is a bag of tricks. Anyone who works through this literature and its conflicting pronouncements might well conclude—if I may use a yuppie variant on an ancient analogy—that the *Rhetoric* is like tofu; it is something whose color and flavor depends on the other ingredients and thus turns out to be completely different in each recipe.

The tendency to oversimplify Aristotelian rhetoric is often accompanied by a strong tendency to oversimplify his role in the history of rhetoric. Thus, the *Rhetoric* is often taken to represent the whole of classical rhetoric, or the whole of "traditional rhetoric" (that is, everything between Aristotle and, for example, Derrida). Although the revival of interest in Isocrates and the Latin rhetoricians has begun to erode this assumption, it is difficult to exaggerate how deeply it has affected the collective unconscious of twentieth-century rhetoricians. Thus, in Thonssen and Baird's enormously influential textbook, *Speech Criticism*, the whole of Roman rhetoric is covered in a chapter entitled "Elaborations of Aristotelian Principles."[47] A more recent composition text offers this thumbnail sketch: Classical rhetoric became "fixed as a definite body of doctrine by Aristotle's book, *Rhetoric*. The working out of what was inherent in Aristotle's *Rhetoric* continued throughout the life of the Roman Empire."[48] And much more recently, Richard Lanham, a scholar with formidable credentials, has asserted that the "Aristotelian pattern . . . has characterized the Western rhetorical tradition ever since Aristotle."[49]

Put these two tendencies together, and we get a double distortion of the *Rhetoric*. First, it is contracted to the point that it represents a single, uncomplicated perspective, and then it is expanded to the point that it blocks perception of anything else in the history of rhetoric. The result is to promote some very simple stories about Aristotle and the rhetorical tradition. And I close by presenting two versions of the story that reduce things to the greatest simplicity—the older "modernist" version and the new, unexpurgated "postmodernist" version.

The older variant reads, more or less, as follows:

> Once upon a time, there existed a group of miscreants who called themselves Sophists. Since they hated truth, justice, and healthful daily exercise, they invented something called false rhetoric and peddled it throughout Hellas. Just in the nick of time, however, Plato rose up and smote them with dialectical logic, shattering their evil plans. Some time later Plato's faithful Macedonian companion picked up the pieces and fashioned a proper rhetoric; he domesticated rhetoric by giving priority to content over form, reason over emotion, and argument over style. This philosophical rhetoric put the art in its proper place, and all later development ought to be gauged against this Aristotelian standard.

This story (and I hardly exaggerate its general tendency) offers a perfect target for the weapons of deconstruction; it is filled with subtexts and hidden ideological premises, and it is blindly logocentric, homological, and patriarchal. Thus, even without bothering to check the historical sources, it is an easy task to "detonate" this story, to reveal its misplaced seriousness, and through the magic of binary opposition to replace it with a mirror image. The new version reads something like this:

> In the beginning were the Sophists, and they were liberated, creative users of the word—free spirits innocent of any lust for logical order. Unhappily, however, an evil metaphysician, named Plato, noticed the way they frolicked with words. Since he hated unrepressed, free use of language—or for that matter, the possibility that anyone might be having a good lime—he thundered mightily and with much effect against them. Worst of all, he incited a gullible student, a logic-besotted wretch

known as Aristotle, to trap their precious rhetoric within the labyrinth of philosophical categories. There, in the prison called the *Rhetoric*, true rhetoric atrophied and eventually died a horrible death, much to the delight or the whole brigade of philosophical prigs. In the face of this systematic repression, our only course, as rhetoricians or as humans beings, is to tear down this Aristotelian prison-house and to return to our sophistic origins.

NOTES

1. Richard McKeon, "Rhetoric and Poetic in Aristotle," in *Aristotle's Poetics and English Literature: A Collection of Critical Essays*, ed. Elder Olson (Chicago: University of Chicago Press, 1965), 233.
2. See, for example, Lloyd Bitzer, "Aristotle's Enthymeme Revisited," *Quarterly Journal of Speech* 45 (1959): 399–408; and Charles Mudd, "The Enthymeme and Logical Validity," *Quarterly Journal of Speech* 45 (1959): 409–14. Concerning more recent developments, see Thomas Conley, "The Enthymeme in Perspective," *Quarterly Journal of Speech* 70 (1984): 168–87; and Michael Hood, "The Enthymeme: A Brief Bibliography of Modern Sources," *Rhetoric Society Quarterly* 14 (1984): 159–62.
3. Gerard Hauser, "The Example in Aristotle's *Rhetoric*: Bifurcation or Contradiction?," *Philosophy and Rhetoric* 1 (1968): 78–90; "Aristotle's Example Revisited," *Philosophy and Rhetoric* 18 (1985): 171–80; and "Reply to Benoit," *Philosophy and Rhetoric* 20 (1987): 268–73; Scott Consigny, "The Rhetorical Example," *Southern Speech Communication Journal* 41 (1976): 121–34; William Benoit, "Aristotle's Example: The Rhetorical Induction," *Quarterly Journal of Speech* 66 (1980): 182–92; and "On Aristotle's Example," *Philosophy and Rhetoric* 20 (1987): 261–67; Michael McGuire, "Some Problems with Rhetorical Example," *Pre/Text* 3 (1982): 121–36; James Raymond, "Enthymemes, Examples, and Rhetorical Method," in *Essays on Classical and Modern Discourse*, ed. Robert Connors, Lisa Ede, and Andrea Lunsford (Carbondale: Southern Illinois University Press, 1984), 144–48.
4. William Grimaldi, "A Note on the *Pisteis* in Aristotle's *Rhetoric*, 1354–1356," *American Journal of Philology* 78 (1957): 188–92; George Brake, "A Reconsideration of Aristotle's Concept of Topics," *Central States Speech Journal* 16 (1965): 106–12; Richard Huseman, "Aristotle's System of Topics," *Southern Speech*

Communication Journal 30 (1964): 243–52; Donovan Ochs, "Aristotle's Concept of Formal Topics," *Speech Monographs* 36 (1969): 419–25; Thomas Conley, "'Logical Hylomorphism' and Aristotle's *Koinoi Topoi*," *Central State Speech Journal* 29 (1978): 92–97.

5. Paul Ricoeur, *The Rule of Metaphor*, trans. Robert Czerny (London: Routledge and Kegan Paul, 1978), 9–43; Samuel R. Levin, "Aristotle's Theory of Metaphor," *Philosophy and Rhetoric* 15 (1982): 24–46; Eugene E. Ryan, *Aristotle's Theory of Rhetorical Argumentation* (Montreal: Bellarmin, 1984), 157–72.
6. Rosalin Gabin, "Aristotle and the New Rhetoric: Grimaldi and Valesio," *Philosophy and Rhetoric* 20 (1987): 180.
7. Everett Lee Hunt, "Plato and Aristotle on Rhetoric and Rhetoricians," in *Historical Studies of Rhetoric and Rhetoricians*, ed. Raymond F. Howes (Ithaca, NY: Cornell University Press, 1961), 70.
8. James Kinneavy, "Translating Theory into Practice in Teaching Composition," in Connors, Ede, and Lunsford, *Essays on Classical Rhetoric*, 1, 76.
9. John Gage, "An Adequate Epistemology for Composition: Classical and Modern Perspectives," in Connors, Ede, and Lunsford, *Essays on Classical Rhetoric*, 152–69.
10. William Grimaldi, "Rhetoric and Truth: A Note on Aristotle, *Rhetoric* 1355a 21–24," *Philosophy and Rhetoric* 11 (1978): 173.
11. William Grimaldi, *Studies in the Philosophy of Aristotle's Rhetoric* (Wiesbaden: F. Steiner, 1972), 151.
12. Eric Charles White, *Kaironomia: On the Will to Invent* (Ithaca, NY: Cornell University Press, 1987), 22.
13. White, *Kaironomia*, 22, and see 23–31 for White's elaboration of this assertion.
14. John Poulakos, "Rhetoric, the Sophists, and the Possible," *Communication Monographs* 51 (1984): 215–26; Victor Vitanza, "Critical Sub/Versions of the History of Philosophical Rhetoric," *Rhetoric Review* 6 (1987): 41–66; Jane Sutton, "The Death of Rhetoric and Its Rebirth in Philosophy," *Rhetorica* 4 (1986): 203–27; and "Rereading Sophistical Arguments: A Political Intervention," *Argumentation* 5 (1991): 141–58.
15. Charles S. Baldwin, *Medieval Rhetoric and Poetic* (New York: Macmillan, 1928), 3.
16. Lester Thonnsen and A. Craig Baird, *Speech Criticism* (New York: Ronald Press, 1948), 74–75.
17. Larry Arnhart, *Aristotle on Political Reasoning: A Commentary on the "Rhetoric"* (De Kalb: Northern Illinois University Press, 1981), 78.

18. Grimaldi, "Rhetoric and Truth," 176.
19. Whitney Oates, "Aristotle and the Problem of Value," in *Aristotle: The Classical Heritage of Rhetoric*, ed. Keith Erickson Metuchen (Metuchen, NJ: Scarecrow Press, 1974), 105–6.
20. B. A. G. Fuller, *A History of Greek Philosophy: Aristotle* (New York: Macmillan, 1931), 294.
21. W. D. Ross, *Aristotle*, 5th ed. (London: Methuen, 1949), 276.
22. Hunt, "Plato and Aristotle," 56.
23. Hunt, "Plato and Aristotle," 61.
24. Hunt, "Plato and Aristotle," 63–64.
25. J. Robert Olian, "The Intended Uses of Aristotle's *Rhetoric*," *Speech Monographs* 35 (1968): 140.
26. Forbes Hill, "The *Rhetoric* of Aristotle," in *A Synoptic History of Classical Rhetoric*, ed. James J. Murphy (New York: Random House, 1972), 25.
27. Forbes Hill, "Conventional Wisdom—Traditional Form: The President's Message of November 3, 1969," *Quarterly Journal of Speech* 58 (1972): 373–86.
28. Lois Self, "Rhetoric and Phronesis: The Aristotelian Ideal," *Philosophy and Rhetoric* 12 (1979): 130–45.
29. Christopher Johnstone, "An Aristotelian Trilogy: Ethics, Rhetoric, Politics, and the Search for Moral Truth," *Philosophy and Rhetoric* 13 (1980): 1–24.
30. Ronald Beiner, *Political Judgment* (Chicago: University of Chicago Press, 1983), 83–97.
31. Eugene Garver, "Aristotle's *Rhetoric* as a Work of Philosophy," *Philosophy and Rhetoric* 19 (1986): 1–22; "Aristotle's *Rhetoric* on Unintentionally Hitting the Principles of the Sciences," *Rhetorica* 6 (1988): 381–94; "The Human Function and Aristotle's Art of *Rhetoric*," *History of Philosophy Quarterly* 6 (1989): 133–46; "Making Discourse Ethical: The Lessons of Aristotle's *Rhetoric*," *Proceedings of the Boston Area Colloquium in Ancient Philosophy* 5 (1990): 73–96.
32. The first point is stressed by Self and Johnstone (see "Conventional Wisdom" and "Rhetoric and Phronesis"), and also relevant here is Arthur B. Miller and John D. Bee, "Enthymemes: Body and Soul," *Philosophy and Rhetoric* 5 (1972): 201–14. The second point is stressed by both Beiner (*Political Judgment*) and Garver ("Making Discourse Ethical"). The last point is most clearly formulated by Beiner.
33. Barbara Warnick, "Judgment, Probability, and Aristotle's *Rhetoric*," *Quarterly Journal of Speech* 75 (1989): 299–311.
34. I am quoting from pages 221, 222, and 223 of Janet Atwill's dissertation,

"Refiguring Rhetoric as Art: Aristotle's Concept of *Techne* and the Humanist Paradigm," Department of English, Purdue University, 1990. I am indebted to Professor Atwill for giving me access to sections of her dissertation that bear on the themes of this paper.

35. Susan Jarrett, *Rereading the Sophists: Classical Rhetoric Refigured* (Carbondale: Southern Illinois University Press, 1991), 122 n. 7.
36. George Kennedy, *Classical Rhetoric and Its Christian and Secular Tradition from Ancient Times to Modern* (Chapel Hill: University of North Carolina Press, 1980), 63.
37. Baldwin, "Rhetoric and Poetic," 206.
38. Hunt, "Plato and Aristotle," 56.
39. Hill's comments on this matter (*Synoptic History*, 69), are very much to the point.
40. See above, note 31. In the first essay in this series, "Aristotle's *Rhetoric* as a work of Philosophy," some of Garver's remarks indicate that he views Aristotelian rhetoric as a productive art (8). By the last essay in the series, "Making Discourse Ethical," he maintains that "the *Rhetoric* constructs a new kind of art, which is practical rather than productive, an art which is a doing rather than a making" (74).
41. Garver, "The Human Function," 136. Garver makes the distinction between the intrinsic and extrinsic aspects of rhetoric in several of his essays, but perhaps it is most fully explained in "Aristotle's *Rhetoric* as a Work of Philosophy," 2–7, 10–15.
42. Garver, "The Human Function," 136.
43. This argument is most clearly developed in Garver, "The Human Function."
44. In this paragraph, I am referring mainly to Garver, "The Human Function," 138–41.
45. Baldwin, "Rhetoric and Poetic," 244ff.
46. Richard McKeon, "The Uses of Rhetoric in a Technological Age: Architectonic Productive Arts," *The Prospect of Rhetoric*, ed. Edwin Black and Lloyd Bitzer (Englewood Cliffs, NJ: Prentice Hall, 1971), 44–63.
47. I refer to Thonssen and Baird, *Speech Criticism*, chap. 3.
48. John H. Mackin, *Classical Rhetoric for Modern Discourse* (New York: Free Press, 1969), 34–45.
49. Richard Lanham, *Literacy and the Survival of the Humanities* (New Haven: Yale University Press, 1983), 15.

Genre and Paradigm in the Second Book of *De Oratore*

In Cicero's rhetorical works, the concept of genre appears in two rather different and largely independent contexts. One of these involves the division of style into three general types (*tria genera dicendi*), while the other has to do with the conventional tripartite division of types of speeches (*tria genera causarum*). Among recent scholars, attention has centered on the first of these divisions, and for good reason. Although Cicero did not originate these stylistic categories, his formulation of them proved to have an abiding influence,[1] and he applied them in ways that suggest a striking and probably original contribution to rhetorical theory.[2] On the other hand, his thought concerning the genres of oratory has attracted only passing and technical interest, also apparently for good reason. Cicero's contribution on this matter seems nugatory, nothing more than a confused restatement of Aristotle. True enough, in the second book

From *Southern Journal of Speech Communication* 51 (1986): 308–25.

of *De oratore*, Cicero attempts a critique of Aristotle by denying epideictic a generic status equivalent to forensic and deliberative discourse. But the critics, both ancient and modern, have found little to commend in his analysis. Quintilian, avid Ciceronian though he is, calls the argument "a feeble attempt."[3] And modern commentators find it unconvincing,[4] a product of misunderstanding[5] or worse, evidence of why *De oratore* is "an exasperating work," for immediately after claiming that epideictic needs no rules, Cicero "proceeds to give some."[6]

When read as an isolated and technical statement, Cicero's remarks about oratorical genres invite such dismissive criticism. Yet I believe that his analysis of genre in book 2 of *De oratore* is open to interpretation from another perspective, one that stresses the larger issues animating that work and that places his use of Aristotelian theory in the context of his own synthetic purposes. From this perspective, passages that seem confused or inconsistent in isolation become intelligible as part of a subtle effort to balance conflicting theoretical positions within a single ironic structure.[7] Before attempting this reinterpretation, however, I must say something about what Cicero is attempting to synthesize and how genre theory bears on his project.

Shortly after completing *De oratore*, Cicero wrote a letter to a friend announcing that his new work rejected the "common precepts" and embraced "the oratorical theory of all the ancients, both Aristotelian and Isocratean."[8] Many contemporary scholars accept this statement as an accurate indication of Cicero's major sources, and they have produced important studies detailing Aristotelian and Isocratean influences on *De oratore*.[9] What is surprising, however, is the failure to recognize that in embracing these two sources, Cicero faced a problem of considerable magnitude. Isocratean and Aristotelian theory are not fully compatible, and the differences between them refer to matters of general theoretical significance as well as specific technical detail. This tension emerges rather clearly when we contrast Aristotle's theory of genre with some basic tenets of Isocratean thought.

Aristotle's theory of genre is teleological and deductive. It begins with the definition of the end of a type of discourse and proceeds through systematic divisions based upon the consideration of ends. Thus, poetic and rhetoric are distinct because imitation is the *telos* of the one, persuasion the *telos* of the other. Within the domain of rhetoric, the general end of the art informs the typology of the basic forms of discourse. And so, the dominant criterion is the speaker's goal relative to the various functions of the audience.[10] This yields the familiar three-part division into deliberative, epideictic, and forensic; in turn, the topics specific to each genre depend upon the aims that control it. Deliberative rhetoric, for example, seeks to influence the making of choices, and people make choices in reference to the ends of happiness, goodness, and utility.[11] Finally, these three ends become the source for identifying the particular premises (usually called "special topics") which function as the elementary units of artistic proof in deliberative oratory.[12]

As he constructs this system, Aristotle proceeds in a way that recalls the diaeretic method described in the *Phaedrus*.[13] Solmsen, in fact, argues that the Aristotelian genres emerge through "a deductive reasoning which is Platonic in form and content."[14] This method results in a fundamentally analytic approach to the art. The rhetor must first grasp the defining characteristic of the art as a whole, then divide and subdivide it into logical classes, and only at the end of the process does one arrive at elements which apply to the composition of a particular discourse. Furthermore, while this analytic procedure helps to secure the integrity of the art per se, in practical terms, it stresses the production of discrete argumentative units rather than a discourse as a unified whole.[15]

Isocrates approaches the subject from an entirely different angle. Whereas Aristotle emphasizes the art as a coherent body of precepts, Isocrates emphasizes the art as creative performance. For Isocrates, rhetoric is first and foremost a kind of action, action that must encompass an infinite variety of changing circumstances. No set of abstractly derived precepts is sufficient to produce eloquence, and it is eloquence that Isocrates seeks to teach. This is, of course, not to say that precepts are useless or that the orator should ignore formal principles that appear in different oratorical types. But, in the Isocratean scheme, these matters are ancillary to the real task—the production of harmonious and unified discourses that respond to actual situations. Thus, a command of the elements of rhetoric is a simple and insignificant task compared to the problem of choosing from among these elements "those which should be employed for each subject, to join them together, to arrange them properly, and also not to miss what the occasion demands but appropriately to adorn the whole speech with striking thoughts, and to clothe it in flowing and melodious phrase."[16]

Such concentration on synthetic performance obviously demands methods of instruction that differ from Aristotle's analytic principles. The orator must not simply learn precepts, but must understand how they are materialized in particular contexts, and knowledge of the art as an abstract entity must be subordinated to knowledge of how particular discourses operate as integrated fields of action. Consequently, the axis of Isocratean pedagogy shifts from theory per se to practice and imitation. The student learns the art primarily by experience and by reference to concrete example.[17] The role of imitation is crucial, since it forces the student to grapple with instantiated principles of eloquence even as it establishes material artifacts as the standard of rhetorical excellence. A command of paradigm cases allows the orator to move from concrete usage in the past to concrete problems in a case at hand without recourse to disembodied precepts.

Imitation and practice can and often do operate comfortably within a generic framework. Composition exercises normally refer to a particular kind of rhetorical activity, and models for imitation usually fall under the divisions of a conventional typology. Nevertheless, Isocratean pedagogy greatly reduces the centrality of genre. In the first place, attention is directed toward concrete models within a genre and not toward the abstract features of the genre itself. This orientation encourages an empirical focus, and the concept of genre becomes less instructive than the particular characteristics of paradigm cases. Second, when the art proceeds from genre to cases, as it does in Aristotle, the generic categories function to limit and define the art; the logic of generic analysis constructs the orator's field of operation. On the other hand, when the emphasis falls on performance and imitation, boundaries become blurred and a more extensive territory opens for the orator. The art is constituted by its performance, and its application can expand in unlimited and unpredictable ways as oratorical principles are transferred into new domains of practice. In short, as contrasted with a perspective grounded in genre, the Isocratean bias in favor of paradigm cases and imitative methods not only provides a more concrete referent for rhetorical composition, but also renders the conception of the art less coherent and less manageable at a general level.

If the two major sources for *De oratore* were Isocratean and Aristotelian, then it also would appear that the Isocratean influence exercised the stronger grip on Cicero's thought. Like Isocrates and unlike Aristotle, Cicero was more concerned about the orator than the art of rhetoric, more interested in concrete practice than abstract precept, and more inclined to view oratory as the central force in civilized life than as one among a number of practical activities open to theoretical investigation. In idealizing the orator's vocation, Cicero seemed to invoke the spirit of Isocrates, and H. L. Hubbell scarcely exaggerated when he asserted that Cicero's "whole attitude toward oratory as an art" was "drawn from Isocrates."[18] Yet, when Cicero considered the art of rhetoric, he was clearly and decisively drawn toward Aristotelian doctrine. He relied upon the peripatetic divisions of the art to organize *De oratore*, and he revived a number of peripatetic concepts as key elements in his theory of eloquence.[19]

As a consequence of this uneven, dual loyalty, *De oratore* superimposed an Isocratean conception of oratory on an Aristotelian conception of rhetoric. Since the fit was not precise, a peculiar tension inhabited the entire work. This tension, however, need not be dismissed as the product of mindless conflation, but can be interpreted as a consistent application of Cicero's philosophical skepticism. As an adherent of the New Academy, Cicero believed that no single system or doctrine could articulate truth. The wise man, therefore, avoided dogmatic commitment to any single perspective and continually sought to engage opposing positions.[20] And if this principle held good in general, it had special force in respect to the study of oratory, a subject located within the unstable realm of opinion. Consequently, in *De oratore*, Cicero balanced his own neo-Isocratean perspective against a plausible and useful alternative. The analytic Aristotelian theory allowed for a coherent and well-ordered survey of the art, and its technical divisions governed the external frame of the dialogue. At the same time, the more expansive Isocratean ideal compensated for this Aristotelian ballast, as it worked to discount, supplement, and subvert the technical scheme. In some instances, the two perspectives blended together to yield better results than either could achieve in isolation. Elsewhere, however, their opposition proved intractable, and

Cicero elected to tolerate this friction rather than jettison either one of these approaches.

As I have indicated above, the problem of defining the scope of the art represents one of the clearest and strongest points of conflict between Isocratean and Aristotelian theory. Cicero addresses this problem at *De oratore* 2.41–73, where he deals specifically with the Aristotelian genres. The significance of this particular passage, however, is unclear without reference to its immediate context. Consequently, in what follows, I must deal with the entire section of the text (2.30–98) which functions as an introduction to Cicero's technical analysis of invention.

The plan of the dialogue calls for Antonius to explain the principles of oratorical invention. Before undertaking this task, however, he presents a lengthy disquisition concerning the nature of the art in general. This discourse seems divided into three parts: first, there is a praise of oratory (30–40), then an analysis of the "business" (*negotium*) proper to the orator (41–73), and finally a discussion of the prerequisites for oratorical success (74–98). These topics are all conventional elements of the *accessus* to a rhetorical treatise, but Antonius is made to treat them in a somewhat unconventional and nontechnical fashion. As a result, important themes recur throughout the discourse, and they accumulate to provide a rationale for the split focus of the text as a whole.

Antonius begins by declaring that oratorical excellence rests more on ability (*facultate*) than on art. Art, he contends, deals with objects of knowledge, whereas oratory traffics in opinion and relies upon judgments that inconstantly shift from one occasion to the next. Nevertheless, he concedes that it is possible to lay down some shrewd principles for influencing the minds of an audience. And if someone should claim that "knowledge of such devices is an art of real significance," Antonius will "not quarrel with him."[21] There follows a brief justification for the view that rhetoric is an art—a justification that closely follows Aristotle's argument in the opening paragraph of the *Rhetoric*. Antonius then concludes that investigation into the subject as a whole (*toto in genere*) can produce "that which, though not absolutely an art, yet wears the likeness of an art (*quasi artem*)" (2.32). The focus shifts quickly back to the orator, as Antonius argues that even if oratory is not one of the arts, nothing is "more splendid than the complete orator" (2.33). This reflection offers the occasion for an enthusiastic and unrestrained encomium on eloquence, which Antonius commends as magnificent in itself and as a great force in directing civic affairs. The power of eloquence, he adds, is distinct and belongs solely to the orator, but since it applies to any subject that calls for embellished and impressive treatment, its range is vast.

This brief introductory segment establishes the terms for coordinating the Isocratean and Aristotelian perspectives. Cicero clearly indicates his primary commitment to the expansive Isocratean conception of the art; his attention centers on the power of the orator, not the precepts of a system, and this power expresses itself concretely throughout the domain of human action. Still, he acknowledges that an abstract, systematic approach to the subject has a legitimate function. It can generalize what occurs in practice and thus identify principles potentially valuable to the orator engaged in real controversies. Owing to the nature of the subject studied, this preceptive lore can never amount to anything genuine in itself. The precepts can form only the semblance of an art, a sort of fiction at least once removed from the actuality of eloquence in use. But it is a useful fiction that should not be ignored. In the second major section of his discourse, where Antonius considers the scope and subject matter of oratory, the tone changes considerably. There is a more interactive and dialectical orientation, since several key points arise from objections raised by another character in the dialogue, Catulus. Moreover, some rather technical issues now enter into the discussion. Nevertheless, although Antonius begins on a narrow and technical note, his argument leads back to the general themes articulated in his opening statement. The sweep of this argument indicates a conscious recognition of the opposition between the Isocratean view that eloquence is a distinctive, unified force ranging through all human affairs and the more restricted Aristotelian theory of generic divisions. Before the section concludes, Antonius develops a subtle means for resolving this tension.

Antonius begins by arguing that only forensic and deliberative discourse merit recognition as separate genres. The third Aristotelian genre, panegyric (*laudationes*),[22] is less essential, and it should not be granted an independent status, since it is unwise to try to reduce everything to rule or precept. In any event, the precepts for panegyric flow from the same sources that apply to all other forms of oratory, and the topics commonly associated with it lie open to common sense and do not require formulation as "scholastic rudiments" (2.45).

Catulus objects to this position. He maintains that rational analysis of the subject justifies the generic status of panegyric, and, in his view, the fact that it is easy to master is no reason to eliminate it. This brief argument precipitates a lengthy response from Antonius.

At the outset, Antonius reiterates his earlier point. The attempt to enclose all species of oratory within a system is misguided, since it encourages the scholastic bias that nothing can be achieved without rules. Experience clearly reveals that specific precepts are unnecessary for all the types of oratorical activity that rational analysis can uncover. For example, the presentation of evidence and the composition of official dispatches are tasks that often require considerable rhetorical skill. Yet, since a competent orator can accomplish them by relying on his past experience and his general fund of knowledge, it would be absurd to regard such tasks as belonging to separate departments of the art. Likewise, Antonius argues, panegyric does not deserve a separate generic identity simply because it falls within the province of the orator and entails problems somewhat different from those encountered in other contexts.

This argument is logically complete as it stands, but in typically Ciceronian fashion, Antonius proceeds to amplify and extend his point by means of an apparent digression. The subject of this digression (2.51–61) is historical writing, and, among other things, Antonius asserts that history is part of oratory, or, at any rate, that it is an art whose proper exercise involves oratorical powers. The historian must possess an almost unmatched command over the resources of language and argument. Yet the rhetoricians do not supply any independent directives for writing history. And there is no need for such precepts, since all that is required is common sense and the creative ability to adapt the methods used in forensic eloquence.

On the surface, Antonius has done nothing more than offer another example supporting his contention that oratorical practice need not depend upon generically specific rules. But this particular example suggests a more important point. An open-ended conception of eloquence permits an association between oratory and history. Strict adherence to theoretical categories, however, would block perception of this relationship. That is, a thoroughgoing generic system would blind us to the oratorical qualities of history because it would wall the oratorical faculty within a territory prescribed by static academic categories.

The implications of this example are easily generalized; thus the "digression" on history discloses the full significance of Antonius's position. In effect, the elimination of panegyric becomes the vehicle for subverting a generically motivated definition of the scope of the art. The practical objections to panegyric as independent genre open the way to a general argument from consequence: A rational generic analysis of the art must not be driven to perfection, for to do so would yield results at once too expansive and too confining—too expansive because it would entail an almost endless proliferation of generic categories and too confining because it would constrict the range of eloquence within the limits of conventional, rule-governed domains. A preoccupation with generic rationality, therefore, stultifies creative adaptation, the hallmark of the orator's vocation, and diminishes the power of oratory by dividing it into arbitrary and isolated compartments.

This recognition of the limits of analysis recalls Antonius to the theme developed in his encomium on oratory. Once again, he asserts that oratory encompasses an unbounded field. The orator, he now adds, must not only engage the infinite variety of special subjects presented for debate, but must also deal with the abstract, general issues that lie at the base of these subjects (2.67). In short, all matters that bear on the human condition fall within the orator's ken. But just as this Isocratean vision is about to be perfected, Antonius acknowledges that his position raises certain difficulties and that it requires qualification. An entirely global conception of the scope of oratory may render the subject amorphous and apparently impossible to learn or manage. In confronting this problem, Antonius locates a modified but important place for genre in the education of the orator.

Antonius's argument follows from the premise that whoever has mastered the most difficult part of an art can master all its other aspects without specific instruction. Thus, an artist who can paint the human figure can easily and naturally paint any other type of figure. And, on the same principle, an orator who can sway an audience on topics of public concern is capable of speaking eloquently on all other topics without having to consider each one as a special type. In other words, oratorical eloquence has no delimited boundaries, but its power is most completely expressed in the paradigm of civic discourse, that is, in the territory delimited by the Aristotelian *ars rhetorica*.

Catulus endorses this argument and applauds Antonius for his admirable account of what the orator ought to learn and what he ought to absorb without independent study. Antonius, he explains, restricts formal instruction to "just two kinds of subjects";[23] everything else is left to practice and analogy. Nevertheless, Catulus is not completely satisfied that the right paradigm has been chosen. Antonius merely assumes that legal controversies constitute the hardest part of the art, but Catulus contends that debates about abstract issues involve the most formidable problems.

Antonius vigorously denies this contention. Discourse in other contexts, he asserts, requires some ability, but the law court presents the most arduous arena for eloquence. It is here that the orator must confront a skillful and well-prepared adversary, must allay prejudice and arouse emotion, and must deploy all the resources of speech and thought to meet the situation. Thus, "In such labors, if any man shall have so firmly grasped this art as to be able to produce a statue of Minerva in the manner of Phidias, assuredly he will have no trouble in learning how to carry out the lesser details, as that same Master did, upon the shield" (2.73).

This exchange between Catulus and Antonius represents a crucial though not entirely justified shift in Cicero's argument. At the outset of this section, Antonius accepts two of the Aristotelian genres and argues only for the omission of panegyric. As the section closes, however, he simply ignores the deliberative genre and concentrates solely on forensic oratory. No reason is presented to warrant this narrowing of focus, and, in fact, the privileged status given to the forensic genre is not consistent with either of Cicero's major sources. Both Isocrates and Aristotle assign the highest priority to deliberative discourse.

Nevertheless, whatever its logical flaws, this maneuver is necessary for Cicero to round out his position. The whole of the rhetorical art is now funneled into a single field of action, and the genre of forensic oratory becomes the paradigm for all eloquence. Among other things, this arrangement justifies the prevailing Hellenistic and Roman conventions, which emphasize the theory of forensic oratory to the virtual exclusion of all else. More important for present purposes, however, it gives Cicero a conceptual pivot on which he can balance the influence of his two pre-Hellenistic sources. He has identified a point of coalescence between the Aristotelian generic apparatus and the Isocratean emphasis on exemplary cases, and hence he can reconcile the boundary conditions needed for analytic pedagogy with the expansiveness needed to account for concrete practice. The precepts of forensic discourse provide an orderly and rational frame for teaching the art, but these precepts refer specifically only to a representative type of eloquence; hence a confusion between the theory of rhetoric and the art of oratory is unlikely to occur. Every oratorical type that falls outside the forensic realm must be encountered either through practical experience or through analogies drawn from the paradigm genre. Theory cannot become reified as an autonomous and autotelic enterprise, since it remains an incomplete structure unable to incorporate all of the phenomena to which it refers. At the same time, the integrity of eloquence is not compromised. Mastery of one oratorical form implies mastery of the whole field. Forensic oratory, as the paradigm of eloquence, is complete within its own sphere of action and embraces all the principles of eloquence.[24]

The genuine principles of eloquence, however, should not be confused with the preceptive lore of the handbooks. This distinction emerges as one of the themes of the third and final section of Antonius's introductory discourse. Following the conventional pattern, Antonius identifies art, natural talent, and practice as the components that enter into the making of the orator. Like Isocrates, he maintains that natural talent is the most important of these elements and that practice, especially when coupled with imitation, is the best resource for refining innate ability. Art is the least significant member of this triad. Given these priorities, it follows that genuine principles of eloquence are embedded in concrete performance and that they are products of keen and practiced intellects. Precepts are abstractions drawn from practice; they are conditional and equivocal, incapable of capturing the essence of the art, and reveal nothing that common sense and experience cannot teach. Consequently, formal art should function only as an ancilla, a general guide for the novice or as a promptuary for the mature orator.

The existing theoretical texts are, in Antonius's judgment, "utterly ludicrous" (2.77). Their fault, however, is not that they teach false or useless doctrine. Instead, the problem is one of arrogance. The authors of these texts, men bereft of any real oratorical experience, invest the precepts with a dignity of their own and treat them as immutable axioms. This fault, Antonius explains, devolves from the mistaken view that the art of oratory is a science that can be organized through precise definition and logically exhaustive division into species. In truth, oratory is not so orderly a business; its rules are never more than rough generalizations that must be tempered by experience and conditioned by recognition of the changing requirements of real circumstances.

Antonius, of course, is no academic. He is (not coincidentally, like Cicero himself) a man of action, an experienced advocate and orator. Ironically, it is this characteristic that makes him an ideal candidate to teach the academic precepts of the art. He fully understands their limitations and is capable of measuring them against the standard of actual proceedings in legal cases. Moreover, consistent with the Ciceronian emphasis on paradigms, Antonius can display the principles of the art in what he says about its precepts. Since he is an orator, he can provide a model of eloquence for students even as he sets forth the scholastic rudiments. These virtues are stressed by Catulus, who offers choral comments throughout the text. At one point, for example, he interrupts Antonius in order to praise not only what he is saying but also the skill he demonstrates in saying it (2.39). Later, Catulus explains that he is eager to hear Antonius discuss the methods and precepts of the eloquence because he is not some Greek professor chanting "a series of hackneyed axioms, when he himself never had a glimpse of a law-court or judicial proceeding" (2.75). In short, since Antonius has lived his life in the forum and the courtroom and not in the halls of academe, what he says about oratory displays the texture of experience within it.

The benefits of this experience surface throughout the later sections of book 2, where Antonius turns to the technical content of rhetorical theory. His analysis of the precepts is studded with references to actual cases, many of them drawn from his own practice. These references often function in a way that goes beyond mere illustration. They usually supplement and sometimes displace the standard preceptive dicta. Thus, in the course of his analysis of the emotions, Antonius pauses to recount the strategy he used in an important trial. After explaining the difficult rhetorical problems he faced, he comments: "In these circumstances how can I say I used any particular technique? What I did I will relate, if you think fit, you will give my line of defense some place or other in your system" (2.198). But when he has finished, the recourse to precepts seems unnecessary, for, as Sulpicius explains, the "actual reproduction" of Antonius's methods, in his own words, constitutes "the most instructive of teaching" (2.204).

Throughout the second book of *De oratore*, Antonius sustains an ironic role. His first words call attention to the irony involved in his assignment. He is to speak as though he were a "man of the schools" and to teach the theory of oratory, a subject he professes not to know (2.28–29). As the dialogue proceeds, however, this disclaimer itself proves ironic. Antonius's speeches disclose undeniable signs of the very learning and erudition that he claims not to possess; his discourse, as Crassus puts the point, unmasks and strips his veil "of pretended ignorance" (2.350). Moreover, we can add to this list the ironies we have already noted above: Antonius proves to be an ideal teacher of academic rhetoric precisely because he is not an academic, and he presents a detailed analysis of the standard precepts of the art, even though he often treats these precepts in a way that discounts or trivializes their importance.

The paradoxes that attach themselves to Antonius, the dominant speaker in this book, obviously apply to the book as a whole. Thus, the structure of the work is fundamentally ironic; it is, in an important sense, as much an exercise in tropological thinking as it is a rhetorical treatise. Consequently, since the tropes are themselves rhetorical devices, it appears that Cicero applies a rhetorical method to the theory of rhetoric; he relies upon ironic eloquence to explain the nature of eloquence, and, through this merger of theory and practice, the rival conceptions of oratory as systematic art and oratory as synthetic practice coalesce within the text, the two perspectives interacting to produce a development that incorporates both.[25]

This pattern of irony, as I have tried to demonstrate, explains Cicero's critique of the conventional theory of oratorical genres and indicates the significance of what seems, in other terms, a technical and rather peculiar argument. In addressing the problem of genre, Cicero locates an issue that reaches beneath the level of convention and defines an essential tension between the Isocratean and Aristotelian approaches to the art. The attempt to develop systematic and exhaustive generic categories yields a theory of oratory grounded in an abstract typology and committed to the abstract coherence of the preceptive lore. This orientation, even when adopted through the blind force of convention, strains against the Isocratean view that oratory is a performing art whose substance is found in concrete action. Primarily committed to the Isocratean perspective, Cicero argues that the generic system cannot achieve its own technical goal, since, as the anomalous case of panegyric reveals, it cannot generate an exhaustive and coherent typology. But Cicero does not simply discard the generic method. Instead, he exploits its imperfection in order to redefine and redeem it. Once seen as incomplete at the theoretical level, genre can be conceived in less systematic and more empirical terms—it can be used to demarcate and describe a particular sphere of action without any pretensions that the particular category reflects a grand theoretical structure. Restrained in this fashion, the generic apparatus can now do its analytical work, since the divisions it generates refer only to a paradigm type and cannot claim authority over the whole field. Moreover, systematic analysis of a genre performs an important function, since it offers a general frame of reference which can organize the otherwise scattered insights gleaned from particular cases. This analysis, of course, cannot adequately represent the data of the art, for the actual practice of eloquence does not produce results that fall neatly into rational categories. The generic frame, therefore, is only a convenient fiction, and its fictive status must not be forgotten. For this reason, the preceptive system must be discounted even as it is presented; its static divisions must be set in opposition to the ambiguous particularity that governs the practice of the art. Thus, Cicero converts the simple dialectical opposition between genre and paradigm into a complex rhetorical interaction. Both perspectives retain their identity, and, in effect, are allowed to argue against one another. The pull of generic abstraction and the push of material exemplars coexist in cooperative competition. This interaction serves to define the limits of both perspectives and to compensate for the deficiencies found in each of them.

Finally, I want to suggest that Cicero's ironic method recommends itself as a paradigm for the study of rhetorical theory. Through his effort to understand competing theoretical systems, Cicero identifies an issue of abiding concern—the opposition between a perspective grounded in the concrete experience of the rhetorical act and a perspective directed toward the abstract principles that define rhetoric as a coherent realm of experience. Our own recent literature testifies to the persistence of this conceptual dichotomy. Some contemporary scholars define rhetoric as a material phenomenon whose study must remain consistent with our experience of its particular embodiments. Others, however, argue for a more scientific approach that locates the substance of the art in the abstract regularities that characterize various types of rhetorical action.[26] This opposition is, I believe, irreconcilable from a logical point of view, since the two perspectives originate from equally cogent but incompatible conceptions of the subject of inquiry. Yet the differences involved seem so fundamental and urgent that they cannot be ignored. Ultimately, the theorist must choose sides. Nevertheless, as Cicero shows us, the choice need not entail simple exclusion, since we can exercise a rhetorical choice and accept rather than resist the oppositions that follow from dialogue about the ambiguities of substance.

NOTES

1. See, for example, Franz Quadlbauer, *Die antike Theorie der genera dicendi im lateinischen Millelalter* (Vienna: Akademie der Wissenschaft, 1962).
2. A. E. Douglas, "A Ciceronian Contribution to Rhetorical Theory," *Eranos* 55 (1957): 18–26; and Elaine Fantham, "Orator 69–74," *Central States Speech Journal* 35 (1981); 123–25.
3. *Institutio oratoriae* 3.4.2.
4. Charles Sears Baldwin, *Ancient Rhetoric and Poetic: Interpreted from Representative Sources* (New York: Macmillan, 1924), 47.
5. D. A. G. Hinks, "Tria Genera Causarum," *Classical Quarterly* 30 (1936): 176.
6. L. P. Wilkinson, "Cicero and the Relationship of Oratory to Literature," in *The Cambridge History of Classical Literature*, vol. 2, ed. E. J. Kenney, advisory editor W. V. Clausen (Cambridge: Cambridge University Press, 1982), 85.
7. I am using the term "irony" as Kenneth Burke defines it in his essay "Four

Master Tropes": "Irony arises when one tries, by the interaction of terms upon one another, to produce a *development* which uses all the terms." *A Grammar of Motives* (Berkeley: University of California Press, 1969), 512. Irony, in other words, is a strategy whereby the action in a text absorbs rather than discards rival perspectives.

8. *Ad familiares* 19.23. The adjectival form of the proper names is probably significant. While Aristotelian and Isocratean influences certainly play an important role in *De oratore*, it is not entirely clear how much direct knowledge Cicero had of either author. See George Kennedy, *The Art of Rhetoric in the Roman World* (Princeton, NJ: Princeton University Press, 1972), 220–24.
9. Friedrich Solmsen, "The Aristotelian Tradition, in Ancient Rhetoric," *American Journal of Philology* 62 (1941): 35–50, 169–90; "Aristotle and Cicero on the Orator's Playing upon the Feelings," *Classical Philology* 33 (1938): 390–404; H. L. Hubbell, *The Influence of Isocrates on Cicero, Dionysius, and Aristides* (New Haven: Yale University Press, 1914); and S. E. Smethurst, "Cicero and Isocrates," *Transactions and Proceedings of the American Philological Association* 84 (1953): 262–320.
10. *Rhetoric* 1.3.
11. *Rhetoric* 1.5–6.
12. See Hinks, "Tria Genera Causarum," 172–73. As Hinks notes, Aristotle reserves his strict method for classification of special topics, and the method is not used for other elements of the art. There is some inconsistency in the text on this matter, and Aristotle is not always so single-mindedly analytic as he is in respect to the division of genres. Hinks (171–72) also presents an interesting discussion, based on the evidence found in the *Rhetorica ad Alexandrum*, concerning the relationship between Aristotle's genres and the more empirical forms of generic classification current at the time he wrote the *Rhetoric*.
13. *Rhetoric* 1.265–66.
14. Solmsen, "The Aristotelian Tradition," 42.
15. Cicero seems aware of the way this system concentrates attention on the art itself rather than on the integrity of its particular manifestations. See *De oratore* 2.33.
16. Isocrates, "Against the Sophists," in *Isocrates*, vol. 1, trans. by George Norlin (Cambridge, MA: Harvard University Press, 1929), 16–17.
17. The Greek term, which is the root for the English "paradigm," literally means a showing beside or alongside of. Its primary meaning as "pattern," "model," or "example" comes from the manner in which we can learn about one thing by reference to another thing that falls within the same class. Concerning the use of

paradigm in Greek ethics, see Werner Jaeger, *Paideia: The Ideals of Greek Culture*, trans. Gilbert Highet, vol. 1 (New York: Oxford University Press, 1945), 42–43, 428 n. 18. Also see Jaeger, *Paideia: The Ideals of Greek Culture*, trans. Gilbert Highet, vol. 3 (New York: Oxford University Press, 1944), 61–64, concerning the opposition between "schemata" and "paradigm" in Isocrates's theory of oratory. Aristotle, incidentally, uses the word παραδειγμα to designate the "example" or rhetorical induction, a form of proof which concerns the relation of part to part or like to like (*Rhetoric*, 1357b).

18. Hubbell, *The Influence of Isocrates*, 17.
19. See Solmsen, "The Aristotelian Tradition," 190.
20. Concerning the influence of the New Academy and its skepticism on *De oratore*, see Alain Michel, *Rhetorique et philosophie chez Ciceron: Essai sur les fondements de l'art de parler* (Paris: Presses Universitaires de France, 1960), 81–149, esp. 136ff.
21. *De oratore* 2.32, trans. by H. W. Sutton and H. R. Rackham (Cambridge, MA: Harvard University Press, 1942). All quotations from *De oratore* are from this translation. References to this work hereafter are cited in the text.
22. The Latin term *laudationes* seems to narrow and perhaps confuse Aristotle's conception of epideictic. See Hinks, "Tria Genera Causarum," 174–76. Undoubtedly much of the difficulty that Cicero and other Latin authors have with this genre stems from the fact that there is no very close equivalent to Greek epideictic oratory in the Roman tradition.
23. 2.71. The Latin text reads: *in duo genera solurn causarum*. The meaning of *causarum* here is not entirely clear to me. Sutton and Rackham translate it as "subjects" and note that it refers to the two types of issues, the thesis and hypothesis. The context indicates that this is a plausible conjecture. But *causae* is the term Cicero uses to name the Aristotelian genres. Thus, it may be that Catulus means the two genres—forensic and deliberative—which remain after eliminating epideictic from the scheme. If this is his meaning, then it is somewhat peculiar that he himself implies and Antonius clearly assumes that only one genre, forensic, is now under discussion. Yet, as I argue below, the logic of the entire passage is somewhat peculiar.
24. Additional evidence on this point emerges at 2.333–50, where, paradoxically, Antonius proceeds to give separate treatment to deliberative and epideictic. Yet he implies that the divisions he is following are really insignificant, since the conventional precepts allotted to these two genres really apply to forensic discourse or to the whole field of eloquence. Thus, he refers to a common store

of precepts (333) and stresses the fundamental unity of eloquence (337). And in respect to panegyric, he asserts that all its precepts are obviously relevant to legal argument (318–19).

25. My words here, and indeed my whole train of thought, reflect Burke's concept of irony.
26. Compare Michael McGee, "A Materialist's Conception of Rhetoric," in *Explorations in Rhetoric: Studies in Honor of Douglas Ehninger*, ed. Ray E. McKerrow (Glenview, IL: Scott Foresman, 1982), 23–48; with Roderick Hart, *Verbal Style and the Presidency: A Computer-Based Analysis* (New York: Academic Press, 1984). McGee explicitly connects his own position with Isocrates in "The Moral Problem of Argumentum per Argumentum," in *Argument and Social Practice: Proceedings of the Fourth SCA/AFA Conference on Argumentation*, ed. J. Robert Cox, Malcolm Sillars, and Gregg B. Walker (Annandale, VA: Speech Communication Association, 1985), 1–15.

The Topics of Argumentative Invention in Latin Rhetorical Theory from Cicero to Boethius

Rhetorical arguments generally deal with confused notions, with ideas and concepts that do not admit of a single, unequivocal meaning.[1] Consequently, rhetorical argumentation normally does not begin with fixed axioms in the manner of demonstrative reasoning. Instead rhetoricians must draw their starting points from accepted beliefs and values relative to the audience and the subject of discourse. When these beliefs and values are considered at a high level of generality, they become "commonplaces" or "common topics" for argumentation: the attempt to render a systematic account of such topics therefore has been a major concern of rhetorical theory from antiquity to the present.

Given the ambiguous nature of the subject of topical argument, it is hardly surprising that the concept itself proves to be a confused notion. Even when limited to its technical use in rhetoric, the term "topic"

From *Rhetorica* 1 (1983): 23–44.

incorporates a bewildering diversity of meanings. Hence, among modern authors we find conceptions of the topics ranging from recurrent themes in literature, to heuristic devices that encourage the innovation of ideas, to regions of experience from which one draws the substance of an argument. Nor do the ancient authorities provide a single consensus that helps clarify this confusion. The number of classical conceptions of topics rivals the Babel of modern scholarship, since classical rhetoricians are not very scrupulous in defining this key term. Aristotle, for example, makes the topics one of the central elements in *Rhetoric* without ever explicitly defining what they are. And other sources that do provide definitions are brief and vague. Traditional formulations tell us little more than that a topic is a resource for an argument, or a seat of an argument, or a region in which an argument resides. Further explanation, when it occurs at all, is not of much theoretical value. Normally it takes the form of an allegory, where, to cite the classic example, the rhetor is a hunter, the argument his quarry, and the topic a locale in which the argument may be found. In short, the classical lore of topics is as confused as the modern efforts to revive it.

Under these circumstances it would be futile to attempt to understand the topics as a single, coherent doctrine. The historian of rhetoric is better advised instead to isolate a single strand in this complex tradition and to follow its development carefully. This essay proposes just such an isotopic analysis. Specifically, I intend to investigate the topics associated with the person and with the act in Latin theory. There are a number of reasons to recommend these topics as a special object of study. First, they are easily isolated, since they belong to a discrete tradition that persists throughout the history of Latin rhetorical theory. (Owing to limitations of space, I end this study with Boethius, but the topics of the person and act continue to play a significant role in medieval and Renaissance texts.)[2] Second, of the various topical schemes used in antiquity, these two topics seem most intimately connected with the problem of argumentative invention. Some authorities designate them as the most important topics of argument, and among Latin rhetoricians they generally provide the clearest instances of artistic principles for constructing arguments. It is safe to assume, therefore, that these topics occupy a central position in the theory of argumentation. Finally, unlike the other major topical system in the tradition—the analysis of issues contained in *stasis* doctrine—the topics of the person and the act have received scant attention in modern scholarship.[3]

Before turning directly to the attributes of the person and the act, however, it might be useful to place this particular topical system into some kind of theoretical context. For this purpose, Aristotle's theory of topics offers a convenient touchstone, since it addresses similar issues from a rather different perspective.

For Aristotle, the topics (Greek, *topoi*) belong to both the related faculties of rhetoric and dialectic. In both faculties the topics deal with inference; thus in both faculties they prove opposite sides of an issue indifferently, and they consist in principles or strategies that enable an arguer to connect reasons with conclusions for the purpose of effecting a proof. The nature of inference in dialectic and rhetoric, however, differs significantly, and hence the topics proper to each of these faculties assume a different character. Dialectical argument is predicative, and its fundamental elements are the terms of a proposition. As Eleonore Stump observes, "arguing for a dialectical proposition" consists "in showing that a predicate is or is not a predicate of the subject at issue."[4] Consequently, dialectical topics provide a lore of predicables, and the key issue is the way in which terms relate to one another within the propositions of an argument.[5]

In rhetoric, however, it is the proposition and not the term which emerges as the atomic unit of discourse. Apparently, any attempt to refine analysis below the propositional level would badly distort the way that speakers present and audiences process rhetorical arguments. The predicables play no role in rhetorical invention, since inference depends upon perceived connections between propositions taken as whole units. Moreover, in rhetorical argumentation, the required connectives are relative to the audience addressed, and thus they arise from and are verified by social knowledge existing within a community.

Rhetorical topics are mechanisms for generating these connectives, and Aristotle divides them into two basic forms: first there are the special or subject specific topics, which actually take the form of propositions—propositions that express abstract, generally accepted beliefs and values; for example, the topical proposition, "What is rarer excels what is more abundant," functions as a warrant connecting the "premise," "Gold is rarer than iron," to the conclusion, "Gold is more precious than iron."[6] Second, there are the universal or common topics, which take the form of a word or short phrase expressing a highly abstract pattern of relationship relevant to any subject of argument whatsoever. Thus, the topic "from degree" includes, among other things, the principle that if something has happened where it is less likely, it will happen where it is more likely. And this principle warrants movement from the premise, "This man struck his father," to the conclusion, "This man is likely to have struck his neighbor."[7] In sum, the Aristotelian topics, whether dialectical or rhetorical, focus on the process of inference rather than on the subject proposed for argument; in dialectic, however, such inferences depend on the relationship between the terms of the propositions, while, in rhetoric, they rest on the more ambiguous ground of the relationship between propositions and audiences.[8]

Latin rhetorical theorists, strongly influenced by certain Hellenistic sources, depart from the Aristotelian concept of topics as inferential strategies. Instead, they base the topics of argument on a conception of the generic subject of rhetorical discourse. This topical system already appears in a rather elaborate form in Cicero's *De inventione*, where it is included under the heading of *confirmatio*, the fourth part of the oration. The elements of this system are said to constitute a universal, raw material for rhetorical argument, and they consist of the attributes of the person and of the act. All arguments, Cicero asserts, receive support from these attributes.[9]

Cicero does not explain the rationale for this approach to the topics, but certain later writers do, and their explanation is instructive. In the terms of this theory, an argument is that which creates belief about a doubtful issue. In a rhetorical *causa*, the issue must concern persons and their actions, for without these elements, there would be no material for dispute. Thus, when rhetorical argument is considered at the broadest, most general level, its subject matter consists of persons and acts. But since an argument must proceed from what is better known or more readily believed to that which is doubtful, the very subjects of the argument (the matters that are in doubt) cannot themselves furnish the resources of argument. Consequently, the argument must proceed from the attributes of persons and acts in order to resolve doubt about the particular person and act in question.[10]

In *De inventione*, Cicero divides these attributes into a complex set of categories. The attributes of the person are eleven in number and include such straightforward matters as the person's name, nature, manner of life, and the like.[11] The enumeration is not exhaustive (later authorities list more than twenty divisions), nor is there any apparent attempt to rationalize the items in this inventory into a coherent structure.

The attributes of the act receive a more systematic four-part analysis: (1) *Topics coherent with the act itself*: These are attributes which always adhere to the act and seem inseparable from it (*ea quae semper affixa esse videntur ad rem atque ab ea possunt separari*),[12] including the motive and summary statements representing the nature of the act. (2) *Topics involved in the performance of the act*: These involve what we would call necessary but not sufficient conditions for performing an act—such considerations as time, place, and occasion.[13] (3) *Adjuncts of the act*: These are mainly topics of relation in which the act in question is compared to, contrasted with, or somehow brought into relationship with another act.[14] (4) *Consequence*: These topics are based on things that follow from the performance of the act. Such arguments, however, do not arise from considerations of logical consequence or effect, but from public reaction to the act.[15]

This Ciceronian scheme and the Aristotelian theory of rhetorical topics differ in a number of obvious points. The "special" topics disappear altogether in Cicero. We no longer have topical principles that assume propositional form, nor is there any apparent interest in the proposition as a fundamental unit of rhetorical argument. All of the topics which Cicero places under the divisions of the attributes of person and act are expressed, in the manner of the Aristotelian universal topics, as single words or as short phrases. And while some of the topics under Cicero's category *adiuncta negotio* bear a resemblance to items in Aristotle's inventory, the others seem totally foreign to Aristotle's interests. More important, but perhaps less obvious, the two topical systems emerge from, and eventuate in, markedly different approaches to the process of invention itself. The nature of this distinction can be best appreciated when we understand the apparent origin of Cicero's theory.

The division of topics into the attributes of the person and act reflected the attempt of Hellenistic rhetoricians, most notably Hermagoras of Temnos, to come to grips with the difficult question of the subject matter of rhetoric. Hermagoras had divided the issues of rhetorical discourse into the *thesis* and *hypothesis*. The thesis was an abstract issue unencumbered by specific circumstances, while the hypothesis was a concrete issue that entailed a constellation of circumstances (*peristaseis*), and these were often expressed in the form of the following questions: who? (*qui*), what? (*quid*), when? (*quando*), where? (*ubi*), why? (*cur*), how? (*quern ad modum*), and with what resources? (*quibus adminculis*).[16] In the first substantive section of *De inventione*, where preliminary definitions were presented, Cicero had attacked Hermagoras for including the thesis within the domain of rhetoric, arguing that the material of rhetoric consisted entirely in the hypothesis. Moreover, a close examination of Cicero's enumeration of argumentative topics reveals that his first three major categories incorporate the seven circumstances that define the hypothesis and thus mark out the boundaries of rhetorical subject matter. The category *ex personis* obviously corresponds to the "who?" circumstance; topics coherent with the act subsume the "what?' and "why?" circumstances; while the topics related to the performance of the act include the remaining circumstances, with the "when?" circumstance subdivided into time and occasion.

Apparently, then, the use of the "person" and "act" as organizing principles indicates a preoccupation with the subject or matter of rhetorical discourse as the basis for the topics. The focus of the system shifts from the discovery of inferential connectives to the discovery of materials for argument. Perhaps this accounts for the fact that Cicero does not apply the term *loci* to the attributes until the end of his analysis,[17] and that he first refers to them as a sort of universal resource or material (*quandum silvam atque materiam universam*).[18] These resources achieve status as artistic topics, as common grounds for invention, since they do not consider the specific subject of any particular case, but rather the generic subject of all rhetorical arguments. Nevertheless, the result of this inventional process is discovery of a material element, a discrete bit of argumentative content, which then must be integrated into a larger argumentative structure. Thus, Cicero clearly distinguishes between his *loci* and the two other main components of inventional theory—necessary and probable inference, and induction and deduction. The latter two processes bear on the form and the elaborations of the argument; the *loci* provide the matter on which they operate.[19]

These "material" topics of invention make their closest approach to the process of inference when the rhetor considers the adjuncts of the act (*adiuncta negotio*). Topics in this category imply principles of comparison and relationship that go beyond material information and enter the domain of inferential connection. Cicero, however, treats these topics in a summary and somewhat confused fashion. For example, he includes the topics of genus and species, which seem more suited to definitional rather than comparative arguments. None of the topics are explained carefully, and there is no explicit attention to the possible strategies of inference they indicate. More important, Cicero does not even consider the possibility that the special characteristics of rhetorical arguments may require special principles of inference. In fact, the topics listed among the adjuncts of the act are almost certainly drawn from dialectical sources, and their placement here bears witness to a confusion between dialectical and rhetorical theories of invention that occurred during the Hellenistic period.[20]

In his mature works, *Topica* and *De oratore*, Cicero presented a significantly revised system of topics. This version deleted the topics associated with the seven circumstances, added a number of definitional topics, and generally placed greater emphasis on matters of logical relation. The interest here centered on forms of reasoning, and thus this system had a more "dialectical" cast than the theory contained in *De inventione*. But the position that Cicero assumed blurred the conventional distinctions between rhetoric and dialectic. In the first place, despite the references to Aristotle in the introduction to the *Topica*, there was little resemblance between Ciceronian and Aristotelian theory.[21] Aside from his analysis of a few Stoic concepts, Cicero totally ignored the proposition, and he did not use the predicables as the basis for organizing the topics.[22] Instead, his main divisions followed from the subject of the argument—some topics being inherent in the subject, others being closely connected with it, and still others being extrinsic. Thus, he omitted the grounds for the Aristotelian dialectical topics—the clearest feature that separated them from rhetorical topics. At the same time, Cicero did not further distinguish the subjects of argument into rhetorical and dialectical categories, and so he implicitly rejected the special, material criteria for rhetorical argument that informed the doctrine of *De inventione*. Thus, he refused to consider the topics based on the person and the act, since these topics referred to circumstances that defined a unique genre of argument for rhetorical theory. His theory of invention, then, was not divisible on either material or inferential criteria, and it emerged as a single, unified method. Cicero articulated this position most clearly in the *Topica* when he divided the whole art of argumentation (*ratio disserendi*) into invention and judgment, and identified the topics with the process of invention.[23] Holding consistently to this position, Cicero used precisely the same topics in both *De oratore* and *Topica*, and in the *Topica* itself he included such purely rhetorical matters as the *genera oratorum* and the *status* doctrine. In short, the rhetorician and the dialectician, the orator and the philosopher, drew their arguments from the same sources and possessed equally a common method of topical invention.[24]

Cicero's attempt to unify, rather than merely conflate, the topics of rhetoric and dialectic, was to be a source of inspiration to the Renaissance humanists who sought an integrated theory of practical argument.[25] Among Cicero's more immediate successors, however, the schematic approach of *De inventione* proved more influential than the complex, nuanced doctrine of *De oratore*. This held good not only for the purely technical treatises of late antiquity, but also for Quintilian's masterwork, the *Institutiones oratoriae*.

Quintilian presents a detailed and interesting analysis of the topics in the tenth chapter of book 5. Though, as is his custom, he seeks to disguise or avoid technical categories, a careful reading of the chapter reveals its dependence on the schema contained in *De inventione* 1.34–43. Beginning with the basic division between person and act as sources for argument, Quintilian proceeds from the topics relevant to the person to those attributes of the act most closely connected to the person.[26] This latter set of topics corresponds to the Ciceronian category of attributes involved in the performance of the act (*in gestione negotio*), and it includes the Hermagorean circumstances of motive, place, time, and resources. Then, in an apparent departure from Cicero, there is an analysis of a group of definitional topics: genus, species, property, and difference. (These topics obviously are related to the Aristotelian predicables, and their presence here further evidences the conflation between rhetorical and dialectical lore.) This section ends with a distinction, derived from the *Topica*, between definition by logical division of genus and species (*divisio*) and by enumeration of parts of a whole (*partitio*). Finally, Quintilian lists a large number of topics that are not subordinated under a single heading. It is apparent, however, that these topics of comparison, cause, and logical relation belong to the same cluster as Cicero's *adiuncta negotio*.

Quintilian makes no reference to the Ciceronian categories of topics coherent with the act (*continentia cum ipso negotio*) and the topics based on consequence (*consecutio*). Even in these respects, however, the differences between the two systems may not be as great as they first appear. Quintilian's definitional topics seem to substitute for Cicero's topics coherent with the act. The definition of an act, after all, would indicate attributes which would "always adhere to" and be "inseparable from" the act itself. This connection is further recommended by Cicero's inclusion of the "gist of the matter" (*summa facti*) as one of the topics coherent with the act, and by the practice of later Latin rhetoricians who replace this category with a cluster of definitional topics subsumed under the heading *in re*.[27] Consequently, Quintilian appears to use the topics of definition in place of the topics coherent with the act and to reverse the order of the first two categories under the attributes of act. In the process, he very logically moves genus and species from the adjuncts of the act to the category of definition, and he adds the dialectical topics of property and difference to the system. It is also likely that Quintilian employs a similar kind of substitution for the Ciceronian category of consequence. At the end of chapter 11, following his discussion of the example, Quintilian analyzes the topic of authority, which he identifies as an extrinsic source of proof.[28] The concept he invokes appears only marginally related to Cicero's consequence, and the distance in the text between "authority" and the other topics makes their connection seem remote. Nevertheless, we should recall that the last item in the divisions of the *Topica* is the extrinsic topic, and this category consists entirely of arguments from authority. And again we may refer to later Latin rhetoricians; both Julius Victor and Fortunatianus include judgment (*iudicatio*, a topic virtually identical to Quintilian's *auctoritas*) as one of the elements in the category *post rem*, which they use in place of Cicero's *consecutio*. All told, then, despite some refinements and much juggling of components, Quintilian's system of topics adheres very closely to the model provided in *De inventione*.

The real significance of Quintilian's discussion of the topics lies in his sensitive analysis of their use in rhetorical pedagogy. The topics, he implies, have limited value in and of themselves. Their authentic function is to help promote the argumentative skills of the student, to foster the development of natural talents and to sharpen insight into cases that arise in the public arena. For this reason, Quintilian disclaims any intention to devise a fully rigorous and exhaustive topical system. The effort would be futile and useless; it would cause the theorist to become prolix without being complete.[29] No system of classification can exhaust the possibilities of argumentative performance, since the demands placed on the orator are infinitely varied and intimately connected with the specific considerations of the case at hand.[30] Likewise, the student should not approach the topics as a system to be subjected to rote memory and applied mechanistically to various situations. Such a procedure would focus attention on artificial rules while obstructing perception of the source of the most numerous and powerful proofs, the special characteristics of individual cases.[31] Moreover, in practical situations, the arguer does not have time to run through a long list of topics until he discovers one that fits the particular situation.[32] Mere rules do not produce eloquence, and to possess nothing more than knowledge of a system of topics is to possess a dumb science (*mutam scientiam*).[33]

This is not to say that Quintilian believes topics lack practical value. They are, in fact, extremely useful as training devices. The student who examines the topics and applies them in practice compositions may develop habits of thought that spontaneously and naturally carry over into public debate. Approached in this spirit, the topics can enhance native ability and enlarge the capacity to recognize the argumentative possibilities in any case whatsoever. The topics, then, are less important as molds for producing a type of argument than as exercises for developing the intellectual faculty of making arguments in general. Quintilian summarizes these ideas through a series of striking metaphors:

> But it is only by constant practice that we can secure that, just as the hands of the musician, even though his eyes be turned elsewhere produce bass, treble, or intermediate notes by force of habit, so the thought of orator should suffer no delay owing to the variety and number of possible arguments, but that the latter should present themselves uncalled, and just as letters and syllables require no thought on the part of a writer, so arguments should spontaneously follow the thought of the orator.[34]

Thus, topics should lead through art to nature, and the genuine art of invention does not reside in the pages of the theorist's book, but in the mind of the speaker.

After Quintilian, at the end of the first century AD, up to the fourth century we have few Latin works on rhetorical theory and none that make a significant contribution to the doctrine of topics. From the fourth through the sixth centuries, however, a considerable revival of interest in Latin rhetorical theory occurs, perhaps because of the declining knowledge of Greek in the West.[35] Several treatises written during this era make extensive reference to the topics of rhetorical argument. These include (1) Marius Victorinus's *Explanationes in Ciceronis rhetorica*, the earliest extant commentary of *De inventione*, (2) a group of general surveys of the rhetorical art, and (3) Boethius's synthetic treatise *De differentiis topiciis*. These works variously simplify, supplement, and revise the earlier Latin tradition on the topics. Some of these changes are theoretically interesting; moreover, these works are certainly important as a major source for transmitting topical lore to the Middle Ages.

Victorinus's *Explanationes* is a lengthy, detailed commentary that proved to have a significant impact on medieval rhetorical theorists, particularly on the commentators of the late eleventh and twelfth centuries.[36] Victorinus duly reproduces the topical schema in *De inventione*, making extensive and sometimes very useful remarks about most points. For example, he carefully notes and explains the relationship between the Hermagorean *peristaseis* and the divisions in Cicero's system;[37] he illustrates various topical principles with appropriate examples, even as he clarifies a number of confusing and ambiguous passages in *De inventione*.[38] The *Explanationes* is an important work, and it deserves more serious attention from modern scholars than it has yet received.[39] For present purposes, however, it is enough to note that Victorinus preserves the original Ciceronian topical system and provides an apparatus that makes the system more accessible to later writers.

Three of the compendious rhetorics collected in Halm's *Rhetores Latini minores*, the *artes* of Fortunatianus and Julius Victor and the chapter on rhetoric from Martianus Capella's *De nuptiis Mercurii and Philologiae*, present an account of the topics of argument. All three use essentially the same quadripartite system, but there is one anomaly. Martianus, at different places in his chapter, reproduces virtually the same scheme that appears in Fortunatianus and another that obviously follows Cicero's *Topica*.[40] Martianus does not explain why he includes both systems, nor does he indicate how they might be related to each other.[41]

The four-part system enunciated in these treatises divides the topics into those that precede the act (*ante rem*), those that are in the act (*in re*), those that surround the act (*circa rem*), and those that follow the act (*post rem*).[42] This system is broadly similar to the categories in *De inventione*, but there are some notable points of departure. First, and most obvious, the attributes of the person no longer exist as an independent heading. All the categories are now arranged with reference to the act; the attributes of the person, along with the other Hermagorean *peristaseis*, fall under consideration of topics preceding the act. This first category (*ante rem*) collapses the Ciceronian headings *ex personis* and *in gestione negoti* and presumably would include the extensive subdivisions of the former. Second, the category *in re*, consisting of definitional topics, replaces Cicero's *continentia cum ipso negotio*. As I have noted, this maneuver has precedent in Quintilian. The topics subsumed under *circa rem* are very close to those in Cicero's *adiuncta negotio*, except that the late technical writers, like Quintilian, remove genus and species and include them among the topics of definition. Finally, Cicero's *consecutio* is replaced by *post rem*, which in turn is divided into arguments from outcome (*ab eventu*) and from judgments (*a iudicais*). The late Latin rhetoricians treat this system in a very schematic way; they simply enumerate the topics without much explanation or illustration. Nevertheless, the system itself evidently is the product of careful thought. Its components are arranged in a much clearer and more internally consistent order than those of *De inventione*.

In an almost literal sense, these late technical treatises complete the process of reifying the topics begun in *De inventione*. Not only are the topics subordinated to the act (*res*) which forms the subject of argument, but the main headings for these topics are developed and coordinated in terms of the successive temporal manifestations of that subject. The activity of topical invention thus consists in gathering materials relative to the generic subject of rhetorical argument. Equally important, the whole system of topics appears to have little practical application. There are no indications of how a speaker might apply various topics to actual cases argued in public, and nothing remains of Quintilian's sensible approach to the topics as pedagogical devices. The later handbooks simply list the topics as though they are elements in an autonomous system. The system itself is structured coherently, but it merely functions to occupy space within the theoretical text; the topics become first and foremost places to be ordered within that space, and their organization becomes an autotelic act of taxonomy. The system and its parts seem to be things existing for their own purposes.[43]

A much more subtle and complex theory of rhetorical topics appears in Boethius's *De topicis differentiis*. This work is an advanced study of topical reasoning divided into four books. The first three treat dialectic, while the fourth is reserved for rhetoric. My present concerns center on rhetoric, but since the doctrine of the fourth book follows from the earlier analysis of dialectical topics, it is necessary to begin with a rudimentary sketch of Boethius's dialectical theory.[44]

The first three books of the treatise attempt to explicate and synthesize the topical doctrines of Aristotle and Cicero. Consequently, Boethius engages both of the two major approaches to dialectical topics that we have already noted—the one based on types of inference relative to the terms of the proposition, the other based on the less technical ground of the subject of discourse. It is clear, however, that the former position has priority in Boethius's thought. He explicates the Aristotelian topics first, or at least the version of Aristotelian topics he has learned from studying Themistius's commentary. And he then turns to Cicero's *Topica* for the purpose of demonstrating that the topical categories in that work fit within the Themistian divisions. The effect is less to synthesize Aristotle's dialectic with the Ciceronian system than it is to collapse the latter into the former. Moreover, this position is consistent with Boethius's contention that an argument is "nothing other than the discovery of an intermediate."[45] In this view, argumentative invention is a process of finding a middle element to connect two extremes, and the topics serve as instruments for effecting this end.

For Boethius, as for Aristotle, the term is the basic unit of dialectical argument. Unlike Aristotle, however, Boethius does not rely on the predicables as the basis for categorizing the topics. Instead, he makes a division between two basic forms of topics. One of these is the topical maxim, a self-evident, indemonstrable proposition—the sort of proposition that Aristotle uses for his topics in dialectical theory, as, for example, "Where the matter needed for something is absent, that thing is also absent."[46] Such topical maxims are useful since they provide secure points of argumentative reference and yield inferential connectives applicable to a variety of different argumentative situations. Nevertheless, they are seemingly infinite in number, and thus defy systematic classification. To remedy this defect, Boethius introduces the second topical form, the topical *differentia*. The *differentiae* are mechanisms for grouping the maxims into coherent classes based on the way they differ from one another. Thus, for example, the topical maxim just quoted above is assigned to the *differentia*, "from cause." All maxims in this class exhibit a generic similarity that allows them to be distinguished from topics belonging to other *differentiae* (e.g., "from the whole," "from end"). Boethius identifies a total of twenty-eight *differentiae*.

Following Themistius, Boethius maintains that the *differentiae* themselves may be organized into three superordinate categories, and these categories depend on the relationship between the topic and the terms of the question set forth as the subject of argument. Thus, some *differentiae* incorporate topics intrinsic to the subject (i.e., the terms of the question); some incorporate extrinsic topics, and some intermediate topics. The intrinsic topics arise either from the substance of the terms, as in the case of definition or description, or from consequences intimately associated with the terms, as in the case of material or efficient cause.

Extrinsic topics involve considerations that go beyond the terms, as in arguments from similarities or contraries; intermediate topics, such as those based on inflection of the same word, are somehow related and somehow unrelated to the terms of the question.

Taken together, these distinctions allow for a synthesis of Cicero's *Topica* and the Aristotelian dialectical topics. The *differentiae* of Aristotle's maximal propositions are easily correlated with the Ciceronian topics. And the Ciceronian topics can be related to maximal propositions, since they are viewed as generic headings for such propositions. Furthermore, the subject-based categories of *Topica* prove compatible with propositional logic once the subject of argument is conceived as the question proposed for disputation. (The question, after all, becomes a proposition at the point that the dialectician takes a side on it and produces an argument.) Consequently, Boethius is able to make a point-by-point analysis that demonstrates the coherence of the Aristotelian and Ciceronian dialectical topics.[47]

When Boethius turns to rhetorical topics, he first summarizes and comments on the topical system found in *De inventione*, and he then attempts to prove that these topics fall within the same categories of inference that operate in dialectic. He argues that the Ciceronian categories of *ex personis*, *continentia cum ipso negotio*, and *in gestione negoti* all incorporate topics inseparably connected with the person and act that form the subject of argument; hence, these topics may be regarded as intrinsic. The topics of *consecutio* depend on matters outside the subject and are therefore extrinsic. Finally, the *adiuncta negotio* require the drawing of a relationship between something extrinsic to the act and the act itself, and in this sense, these topics are intermediate.

On the basis of this analysis, Boethius concludes that the similarities between rhetorical and dialectical topics are clear and that "both faculties use essentially the same topics."[48] There are, however, certain differences between the topics of rhetoric and dialectic, and these stem from the different subject matter (*materia*) proper to the two faculties. Dialectic deals with the abstract issue or thesis, rhetoric with the concrete issue or hypothesis, and their topics differ correspondingly, since dialectical topics, then, are broader in scope and prior in nature, since the principles of inference they specify encompass the circumstantial inferences associated with the rhetorical topics.[49] Dialectic treats the forms of inference, rhetoric the manifestations of those forms.

Boethius's theory obviously revives the Aristotelian interest in topics as principles of inference, but it also overpowers the delicate balance Aristotle strikes between rhetorical and dialectical invention. Where Aristotle regards the topics of the two faculties as counterparts, as related but independent sources of invention, Boethius places them in a hierarchical order; the rhetorical topics are subordinate, concrete instances of the purer forms of inference contained in dialectical theory. The conception allows for an orderly and elegant theory of topical invention, but it does so by ignoring the influence of the audience and the impact of social knowledge on the conduct of rhetorical argument. Such theoretical precision can occur only when one loses sight of the types of argumentative performance that Aristotle, Cicero, and Quintilian conceive as the subject of the rhetorical art.

The developments we have just reviewed in late classical theory are significant both as a sign of, and influence on, subsequent trends in the history of rhetoric. The major sources that transmit topical lore into the Middle Ages offer little scope for a viable independent theory of rhetorical inference. *De inventione*, Victorinus's commentary, and the late Roman handbooks all tend to limit the rhetorical topics to material aspects of invention. With the demise of the Roman courts, the relevance of the matter to which these topics refer becomes increasingly obscure—hence the tendency of the rhetorical texts to turn in on themselves. Lacking other outlets, the topics become modes of arguing about the organization and content of topical theory itself. As John Ward observes, this tendency emerges as an important feature of early medieval rhetorics,[50] and it is already apparent in Boethius's *De differentiis topicis*; Boethius's efforts center much more on the construction of a theoretically coherent art of rhetorical topics than on the application of topics to public argument. In other respects, of course, Boethius stands apart from and above his contemporaries. His stress on the inferential function of topics is especially important, but in rhetoric that function devolves from the more abstract principles of dialectic. The peculiar circumstances that are said to frame rhetorical argument become a vehicle for rationalizing the sprawling practices of rhetoric by reference to the more theoretically manageable categories of dialectic. No consideration is given to the possibility that the special circumstances impinging on the rhetorical act might require special forms of inference, that they might demand a logic of social inference generally similar to but specifically different from the propositional logic of dialectic. Thus, by the end of antiquity, the inferential approach to topics leads to a theory that overwhelms the material conditions relevant to the art, while approaches based on the matter of the art refer to categories and situations that are anachronisms.

When viewed at another level, the persistent tension between form and matter in topical invention raises an issue of considerable theoretical interest. The study of topics encourages attention to minute, technical analysis, but at the same time the use and organization of these technical elements raise fundamental questions about the subject matter and purpose of rhetoric. Perhaps the dimensions of this issue emerge most clearly in the first major section of the *Gorgias*, where Plato sets forth three different definitions of the subject matter of rhetoric. At various points in the text we are told that rhetoric deals with words, with the power of persuasion, and with justice and injustice.[51] The first definition leads us into the domain of tropes and figures and other matters far removed from the interests of this essay. The other two, however, seem to underscore a dichotomy that runs through the history of topical theory and leaves vestiges in even the most technical handbooks. When conceived primarily as the "power of persuasion," rhetoric becomes a neutral art, and argumentation draws its resources from the inferential process. Thus, Aristotle, who assumes one version of this position, rather sharply distinguishes between the art of rhetoric and the content of the issues addressed in rhetorical discourse. The topics arise not from the subjects discussed but from common beliefs and patterns of inference that audiences apply to these subjects. Other rhetoricians, however, resist splitting process from content in this manner and thus locate the topics in terms of "justice and injustice" or other categories based in the subject matter of discourse.

Both of these perspectives entail strengths and liabilities. The inferential perspective allows the art greater internal coherence and integrity. It distinguishes rhetoric from allied substantive arts, such as ethics and politics, and provides a basis for artistic precepts unique to rhetorical argumentation. Nevertheless, this approach tends to slight the special, material circumstances that surround issues of public debate, and unless tightly controlled, it gravitates toward a logical formalism wholly alien to practical argumentation. On the other hand the material perspective places the topics in closer contact with actual situations and calls attention to the circumstantial character of rhetorical inference. Nevertheless, it also tends to confuse the relationship between the art of rhetoric and the substance of issues treated by the art. Furthermore, unless the system refers to a well-established, conventional genre of discourse, it has great difficulty delimiting and ordering the relevant topics of argument.

In short, neither perspective is entirely satisfactory; both give only a partial account of the inventional process, and no one has yet succeeded in synthesizing the two approaches. Nevertheless, it would still seem wise to understand the grounds for this confusion, and this objective is best achieved through careful study of the history of topical theory.

NOTES

1. Concerning the role of "confused notions" in rhetoric, see Chaïm Perelman, "The Use and Abuse of Confused Notions," *ETC: A Review of General Semantics* 36 (1979): 313–24.
2. See, for instance, Sister Joan Marie Lechner, *Renaissance Concepts of the Commonplaces: An Historical Investigation of the General and Universal Ideas Used in All Argumentation and Persuasion with Special Emphasis on the Educational and Literary Tradition of the Sixteenth and Seventeenth Centuries* (New York: Pageant Press, 1962).
3. Perhaps the best account of these topics appears in the summary analysis by Josef Martin, *Antike Rhetorik: Technik und Methode* (Munich: C.H. Beck, 1974), 110–17.
4. Eleonore Stump, *Boethius's "De topicis differentiis": Translated with Notes and Essays on the Text* (Ithaca, NY: Cornell University Press, 1978), 178.
5. Stump, *Boethius's "De topicis differentiis"*, 159–78.
6. *Rhetoric*, 1364b.
7. *Rhetoric*, 1397a.
8. On this distinction, see Richard McKeon, "Aristotle on Language and the Arts of Language," in *Critics and Criticism: Ancient and Modern*, ed. R. S. Crane

(Chicago: University of Chicago Press, 1952), 222. The interpretation of the Aristotelian topics I present here obviously is a simplification of a very complex matter. My argument is not entirely consistent with the views of sophisticated commentators who argue that the topics of the *Rhetoric* may be divided into "formal" and "material" categories. See, for example, William Grimaldi, "The Aristotelian Topics," *Traditio* 14 (1958): 1–16; and *Studies in the Philosophy of Aristotle's Rhetoric* (Wiesbaden: F. Steiner, 1972), esp. 118–35. My position follows from the interpretation of topics as "warrants" developed by Thomas M. Conley, "'Logical Hylomorphism' and Aristotle's *Koinoi Topoi*," *Central States Speech Journal* 29 (1978): 92–98; and "*Pathe* and *Pisteis*: Aristotle II 2–11," *Hermes* 110 (1982): 300–315. Also see Michael C. Leff and Dean E. Hewes, "Topical Invention and Group Communication: Towards a Sociology of Inference," in *Dimensions of Argument: Proceedings of the Second Summer Conference on Argument*, ed. George Ziegelmueller and Jack Rhodes (Annandale, VA: Speech Communication Association, 1981), 770–89.

9. *De inventione* 1.34.
10. This analysis follows Boethius, *De differentiis topicis*, in *Patrologia latina*, ed. J. P. Migne, vol. 64 (Paris: published by the editor and his successors, 1891), cols. 1211C–1212B; and Marius Victorinus, *Explanationum in rhetoricam M. Tullii Ciceronis libri duo*, in *Rhetores Latini minores*, ed. C. Halm (Leipzig: Teubner, 1863), 213–14.
11. *De inventione* 1.34–37.
12. *De inventione* 1.37.
13. *De inventione* 1.37–41, and see Boethius, *De differentiis topica* 1213C for a note on the logical status of these topics.
14. *De inventione* 1.41–42.
15. *De inventione* 1.43.
16. On the relationship between these circumstances and the Ciceronian attributes of person and act, see Victorinus, in Halm, *Rhetores Latini minores*, 213; and Martin, *Antike Rhetorik*, 111. This list of circumstances in the form of questions has a long history. The English rhetorician Thomas Wilson expresses them as a rhyme: "Who, what, and where, by what helpe, and by whose. / Why, how and when, does many things disclose." *The Art of Rhetorique*, ed. G. H. Mair (Oxford: Clarendon Press, 1909), 17.
17. *De inventione* 1.44.
18. *De inventione* 1.34.

19. *De inventione* 1.44, 1.50. The latter passage makes a particularly strong case for the distinction between argumentative invention and the elaboration of argumentative form. Cicero maintains that he has paid special attention to the elaboration of argument so that *ad inventionem argumentandi ratio adiungeretur*. This same sort of distinction appears in 1.78, where Cicero deals with refutation. A very careful study on this and other related issues in Latin rhetoric is Gillian Evans, "*Argumentum* and *Argumentatio*: The Development of a Technical Terminology up to C. 1150," *Classical Folia* 30 (1976): 81–92.
20. See Martin, *Antike Rhetorik*, 111.
21. On the vexing question of Cicero's sources for the *Topica*, see H. M. Hubbell's introduction to the translation in the Loeb series (Cambridge, MA: Harvard University Press, 1949); Jorma Kaimo, *Cicero's "Topica": The Preface and the Sources* (Turku, Finland: Turun yliopisto, 1976); and B. Riposoti, *Studi sui "Topica" di Cicerone* (Milan: Universita Cattolica del S. Cuore, 1947) and the references cited in these studies.
22. On the contrast between Aristotle and Cicero, see Donovon J. Ochs, "Cicero's *Topica*: A Process View of Invention," in *Explorations in Rhetoric: Studies in Honor of Douglas Ehninger*, ed. Ray E. McKerrow (Glenview, IL: Scott, Foresman, 1983), 108.
23. Cicero, *Topica* 2.6.
24. Cf. *De oratore* 3.71–72, where Cicero urges the orator and philosopher to draw knowledge from a common source. Cicero's position on the topics seems thoroughly consistent with the main doctrine of *De oratore*, the union of wisdom and eloquence.
25. Concerning Renaissance theorists who attempted to synthesize rhetorical and dialectical invention, see inter alia, Walter Ong, *Ramus, Method, and the Decay of Dialogue* (Cambridge, MA: Harvard University Press, 1958); Cesare Vasoli, *La dialectica e la retorica dell'Umanisimo: "Invenzione" e "metodo" nella cultura del XV e XVI secolo* (Milan: Felrinelli, 1968); Quirinus Breen, "The Subordination of Philosophy to Rhetoric in Melancthon," *Archiv fiir Reformationsgescbichte* 43 (1952): 13–28; James R. McNally, "*Rector et Dux Populi*: Italian Humanists and the Relationship between Rhetoric and Logic," *Modern Philology* 67 (1969): 168–76.
26. *Institutiones oratoriae* 5.10.32, and see the note on this passage by Jean Cousin in his edition, *Institution oratoire*, vol. 3, *Livres IV et V* (Paris: Bude, 1976), 235. Cousin's notes are useful for this entire section. Martin, *Antike Rhetorik*, 115,

draws attention to the similarity between Quintilian's topoi and *De inventione*.

27. Fortunatianus, *Ars rhetorica*, in Halm, *Rhetores Latini minores*, 115–16; Julius Victor, *Praecepta artis rhetoricae*, in Halm, 396–403; and Martianus Capella, 5.557–60, in Halm, 488–90.
28. *Institutiones oratoriae* 5.11.44.
29. *Institutiones oratoriae* 5.10.100.
30. *Institutiones oratoriae* 5.10.101–3.
31. *Institutiones oratoriae* 5.10.103.
32. *Institutiones oratoriae* 5.10.122–23.
33. *Institutiones oratoriae* 5.10.119.
34. *Institutiones oratoriae* 5.10.125, translated by H. E. Butler in the Loeb edition (Cambridge, MA: Harvard University Press, 1921).
35. "By the fourth century, the linguistic break between East and West is nearly complete: Latin rhetorical handbooks flourish, soon to replace the traditional Greek technical manuals." Jacques Fontaine, *Isidore de Seville et la culture classique dans l'Espagne wisigothique*, vol. 1 (Paris: Etudes Augustiniennes, 1959), 212.
36. Mary Dickey, "Some Commentaries on the *De inventione* and *Ad Herennium* in the Eleventh and Early Twelfth Centuries," *Medieval and Renaissance Studies* 6 (1968): 29; and Karin Margareta Fredborg, "The Commentaries on Cicero's *De inventione* and *Rhetorica ad Herennium* by William of Champeux," *Cahiers de l'Institute du Moyen Age Grec et Latin* 17 (1976): 21.
37. Halm, *Rhetores Latini minores*, 213–14.
38. Compare, for example, *De inventione* 1.42 with Victorinus, in Halm, *Rhetores Latini minores*, 227, and *De inventione* 1.43 with Victorinus, Halm, 229–30.
39. The most important work on Victorinus is Pierre Hadot, *Marius Victorinus: Recherches sur sa vie et ses oeuvres* (Paris: Etudes Augustiniennes, 1971). Though Hadot is not primarily concerned with rhetoric, his analysis of Victorinus's commentary is extremely valuable (77–100). Hadot is probably correct in his assessment that Victorinus adds little to the properly rhetorical doctrine in Cicero. Nevertheless, owing to the great influence this commentary had on the Middle Ages, it deserves careful study from the perspective of technical rhetoric.
40. Compare 5.474–502, Halm, *Rhetores Latini minores*, 465–70, and 5.557–60, Halm, 488–90.
41. The explanation probably stems from the fact that Martianus's chapter preserves and gives separate treatment to two distinct traditions of rhetoric. See Fredrich

Solmsen, "The Aristotelian Tradition in Ancient Rhetoric," *American Journal of Philology* 62 (1941): 50.

42. On the sources for this division of the topics, see Martin, *Antike Rhetorik*, 116, and the references cited there.
43. This tendency anticipates developments in Renaissance theory noted by Ong, *Ramus*, esp. 199–202.
44. For a more detailed analysis of Boethius's dialectical topics, see Stump, *Boethius's "De topicis differentiis,"* 179–205. The general position I argue here concerning Boethius is developed at greater length in my paper "The Logician's Rhetoric: Boethius' *De differentiis topicis*, Book IV," in *Medieval Eloquence: Studies in the Theory and Practice of Medieval Rhetoric*, ed. James J. Murphy (Berkeley: University of California Press, 1978), 3–24.
45. Boethius, *In Ciceronis Topica*, in Migne, *Patrologia latina*, 1050C–D.
46. Boethius, *De differentiis topicis*, 1189D.
47. This analysis is conveniently summarized by three diagrams at the end of book 3, 1204A–1206B. It is significant that Boethius, unlike Martianus Capella, regards Cicero's *Topica* as a work on dialectical and not rhetorical argumentation.
48. Boethius, *De differentiis topicis*, 1215C.
49. Boethius, *De differentiis topicis*, 1215D–1216C.
50. John Ward, "*Artificiosa Eloquentia* in the Middle Ages," PhD dissertation, University of Toronto, 1972, 72–119.
51. Adele Spitzer, "The Self-Reference in the *Gorgias*," *Philosophy and Rhetoric* 8 (1975): 1–22, presents an interesting commentary on these definitions.

PART TWO

Contemporary Extensions of Classical Rhetorical Theory

An evolving interpretation of the Greco-Roman rhetorical traditions of antiquity grounded Leff's guiding vision of the purpose and distinctiveness of rhetoric study. And yet this vision advanced, became more complex, and found new audiences thorough its intimate connection to the social and political tensions of nineteenth and twentieth Century American public address and through its dialogue with philosophies of language and hermeneutics that he encountered in his early years as a scholar.

In "Piety, Propriety, and Perspective: An Interpretation and Application of Key Terms in Kenneth Burke's *Permanence and Change*" Leff and Thomas Rosteck bring each of these streams together to address a common objection to the extension of classical rhetorical thought into the present—namely, that such thought inevitably favors establishment speakers and dominant ideologies. The Isocratean-Ciceronian stress on "propriety" as a unifying goal of rhetorical performance, from this vantage, always threatens to freeze classical rhetoric into an elitist mold and thus, politically speaking, to align its adherents with the maintenance of the status quo over its critique and transformation. Leff and Rosteck see the threat but then turn to a contemporary source of inspiration, the work of Kenneth Burke, and to one of his favored eras of rhetorical production—the history of labor struggle in the United States during the late 1800s—not only to disarm his critics but to reveal the mistakenness of their assumptions about the very nature of rhetorical invention. Leff and Rosteck link Burke's observations on "piety" as a principle of order present in *any* social context irrespective of ideology to the classical idea of "decorum" as an inherent principle of order governing form and content within a discourse and among a discourse, speaker, and occasion. Centering his analysis on how the atheist, anarchist Voltairine de Cleyre's "The

Fruit of Sacrifice" speech from 1895 negotiates the tension between her materialist worldview and the transcendent poetic metaphor she deploys, Leff challenges the notion that classical rhetoric's stress on propriety translates into a recipe for quiescence.

"Piety, Propriety, and Perspective" continues a trend exemplified earlier in "Topical Invention and Metaphoric Interaction," in which Leff draws from the scholarship of Burke and others to explain otherwise hidden connections between argument and style, classical and contemporary theory. Beginning with a comment from Burke that argument and style are in fact closely related, Leff notes that despite this fact the classical tradition kept them apart (the exception, of course, is the later Cicero, whose distinctive treatment of this question Leff will emulate throughout his career). Bringing topics and tropes together, Leff notes how topical argument deals with the development of an argument across time, while metaphor locates it in space. Drawing on Max Black's interactionist view of metaphor, the practice of classical rhetorical education, and his own work on the topics, Leff shows how argument and imagery themselves interrelate during the development of a discourse to produce a locally stable meaning. Leff then tests his thesis in a short rhetorical analysis of Loren Eiseley's essay "The Bird and the Machine." The theoretic groundwork of "Topical Invention and Metaphoric Interaction" informs all of Leff's subsequent criticism and work in theory. At the same time, the next essay in this section, "Up from Theory: Or I Fought the Topoi and the Topoi Won," which was published more than two decades later, is easily Leff's most accessible on this question. We refer readers to our extensive comments on this retrospective piece in our introduction.

The next two essays in this section—"The Habitation of Rhetoric" and "Decorum and Rhetorical Interpretation: The Latin Humanistic Tradition and Contemporary Critical Theory"—cover similar theoretic ground in pursuit of slightly different questions. "The Habitation of Rhetoric" rehearses a history, also developed in other Leff essays, of the form/content divide which he and Mohrmann alike had argued kept rhetorical critics from more closely approaching the object of their inquiry. Working through Paul Ricoeur's reading of Aristotle's *Poetics*, which has as its object the poem, and the *Rhetoric*, which, while about the process of persuasive inference, has no similar concrete product, Leff uses a brief synthesis of Ricoeur and contemporary argumentation theory to show how the ontological claims Ricoeur has no trouble extending to poetry can also be extended to rhetoric. Establishing a parallel between rhetoric and poetry, Leff shows how a proper understanding of Aristotle on argument is capable of freeing rhetoric from the limits of Ricoeur's perspective. In turn, the locus of rhetoric would be a speech that, like a poem, offers an invitation to share a perspective on the real while at the same time anchoring the auditor in time, place, and circumstance.

While "The Habitation of Rhetoric" focuses on the individual speech as the locus of rhetoric, "Decorum and Rhetorical Interpretation" addresses the global ideological issue of why the modes of thinking characteristic of classical rhetoric have so completely disappeared from the modern intellectual horizon. "Decorum and Rhetorical Interpretation" explores in great detail the theoretic challenges that keep even outstanding readers, such as Ricoeur and Tzvetan Todorov, from recognizing how rhetoric can draw together (or sometimes place into exquisite tension) the substantive, the aesthetic, and the practical. Leff both commends Ricoeur's postmodern view of poetry and cautions readers about the dated modernist assumptions about the instrumentality of argument that prevent Ricoeur from realizing that "theory" (in the high sense of the term he reads Aristotle as using) cannot supervise rhetoric. Likewise, Leff critiques Todorov for a rigid periodization which ignores the abiding functional realities of rhetorical practice that transcend periods. Leff tracks the central error of postmodern thinking through Todorov's generally sensitive account of the history of rhetoric through antiquity. Turning to the analysis of Ricoeur that he used to identify the speech as the proper habitation of rhetoric and also drawing on Cicero's union of form and content in *De Oratore*, Leff focuses on "decorum" as a master term capable of bridging the modern/postmodern form/substance divide and thus mediating the individual, community, discourse and the world.

The closing essay of this section, "In Search of Ariadne's Thread: A Review of the Recent Literature on Rhetorical Theory," shows Leff to have been as astute a chronicler of the recent history of rhetoric as he was, in his dissertation and his several subsequent publications, of its first thousand years. Against the backdrop of an emerging consensus about rhetoric's "epistemic" function, Leff notes how two types of essays—metarhetorical and historical/textual—recur throughout the late 1970s scene of rhetorical scholarship. While the metarhetorical essays are full of points of theoretic interest, and while they occasionally gesture toward traditional authorities or examples, they demonstrate no sustained engagement in cases. Conversely, the historical/textual studies are as theoretically underfunded as their metarhetorical opposites are impoverished in instantiating particulars. Leff situates this trend in terms of what he sees as broader uncertainty unleashed by rhetoric's confrontation with postmodernism. Epistemic rhetoric raises ethical questions and questions about the scope of rhetorical theory that rhetoricians struggled both to define and to make relevant for their critical practices. And yet Leff finds "a virtual silence about the middle-level issues that form the content of a theory. Thus, the literature leaves us in a state of limbo; we have a past and a future, but no present." In other words, the problem of the field as Leff saw it went deeper than having the wrong theory. Nor was the problem to be fixed by overturning the modernist past and giving a positive valence to what it had assigned a negative one. The problem was: What constituted the kind of explanation that would provide an appropriate basis for rhetorical analysis and set proper expectations for rhetorical "theory"?

FURTHER READING

"Acting and Understanding: A Note on the Relationship between Classical and Contemporary Rhetorical Theory." *Federation Review: The Journal of the State Humanities Councils* 8 (1985): 6–10.

"Burke's Ciceronianism." In *The Legacy of Kenneth Burke*, ed. Herbert Simons and Trevor Melia (Madison: University of Wisconsin Press, 1989), 115–27.

"The Idea of Rhetoric as Interpretative Practice: A Humanist's Response to Gaonkar." In *Rhetorical Hermeneutics: Invention and Interpretation in the Age of Science*, ed. Alan Gross and William Keith (Albany: State University of New York Press, 1996), 89–101.

"Modern Sophistic and the Rhetoric of Inquiry." In *The Rhetoric of the Human Sciences: Language and Argument in Public Affairs*, ed. J. Nelson, A. Megill, and D. McClosky (Madison: University of Wisconsin Press, 1987), 19–37.

"Perelman, ad Hominem Argument, and Rhetorical Ethos." *Argumentation* 23 (2009): 301–11.

"The Relation between Dialectic and Rhetoric in a Classical and Modern Perspective." In *Dialectic and Rhetoric: The Warp and Woof of Argumentative Analysis*, ed. F. van Eemeren and P. Houtlosser (Dordrecht, Netherlands: Kluwer, 2002), 53–64.

"Rhetoric and Dialectic in the Twenty-First Century." *Argumentation* 14 (2000): 241–54.

"Rhetorical Theory in the Twentieth Century," with Margaret Organ Procario. In *Speech Communication in the Twentieth Century*, ed. Thomas W. Benson (Carbondale: Southern Illinois University Press, 1985), 3–27.

"Serious Comedy: The Strange Case of Dr. Vitanza." *Rhetoric Review* 6 (1988): 237–45.

"Topical Invention and Group Communication: Towards a Sociology of Inference," with Dean Hewes. In *Dimensions of Argument: Proceedings of the Second Summer Conference on Argumentation*, ed. George Ziegelmueller and Jack Rhodes (Annandale, VA: SCA, 1981), 770–789.

Piety, Propriety, and Perspective: An Interpretation and Application of Key Terms in Kenneth Burke's *Permanence and Change*

In the second main section of *Permanence and Change*, near the end of the chapter entitled "The Range of Piety," Kenneth Burke presents us with an unlikely vision. Imagine, says Burke, a scene where Matthew Arnold is found "loafing on the corner with the gashouse gang." Picture Arnold studiously trying to ape the style of his buddies—the casual lean on the lamppost, the cut of a cap across the eyes, the demeanor of calculated indifference. It is a wildly implausible scene, and Arnold emerges as a hapless figure. Witness, says Burke, "the crudeness of his perception as regards the proper oaths," his awkward and embarrassing comments about passersby, his ignorance of the "etiquette of spitting." Indeed, the very characteristics that make Arnold a paragon of literary gentility render him a buffoon on the street corner: "Everything about him would be inappropriate: both what he said and the ways in which he said it."[1]

With Thomas Rosteck, from *Western Journal of Speech Communication* 53 (1989): 327–41.

This passage certainly illustrates Burke's comic touch, but here, as elsewhere in his work, the comic attitude manifests itself in an ironic and potent realignment of terms. In Burke's idiosyncratic lexicon, piety is transferred from the religious orbit where it normally appears and applied to a secular context. The term still retains an ethical valence, since it represents a principle of coherence, a standard against which to judge all aspects of speech and behavior. Yet Burke extends the term so that it encompasses *any* impulse toward order and system. Piety thus functions to sustain the coherence of a perspective, but it now attaches itself to all levels of human experience, to the mundane as well as the divine. Moreover, while the function of piety remains constant, in substance pieties are diverse, since their content shifts in accordance with changing perspectives.

This perspectivism entails a second and somewhat more subtle distillation of terms. Note that Arnold's impious behavior is described as "inappropriate," and this implicit but clear equation between piety and appropriateness strains against our conventional usage of the two terms. Piety, in our normal way of thinking, describes a profound moral or religious commitment; propriety connotes the artificial conventions of a social elite. For Burke, however, standards of appropriate social behavior always rest upon some principle of order, and hence they are symptoms of a piety. This attitude dislocates our normal conception of the distinction between the "proper" and the "improper," since it cuts across the bias of our category system. The difference between refinement and vulgarity, for example, dissolves within a more encompassing functional orientation. Vulgarity is not simply the absence of culture. It is a competing perspective, a rival version of piety. Thus, the systematic rejection of one perspective does not yield an absence, but generates adherence to a new and equally systematic principle of order. The distance between Arnold and the gashouse gang does not separate the appropriate from the inappropriate. It reveals the difference between standards of decorum defined in opposition to one another. Or, as Burke ironically puts the point, "Vulgarity is pious" (77).

Burkean piety, then, incorporates a conception of propriety, and even though this conception is unorthodox, it still invites comparison to the older rhetorical tradition. Within that tradition, propriety held a persistent and important place. Aristotle listed appropriateness among the constituents of rhetorical style,[2] and his Hellenistic successors canonized it as one of the "four virtues of style."[3] The Romans inherited this technical sense of the term, but Cicero altered and greatly enlarged its significance. For him, propriety or decorum was not only the central concern in rhetoric, but it also functioned as a guiding principle in ethics.[4] And in one form or another, propriety or decorum continued to maintain a presence in rhetorical doctrine through the eighteenth century.[5] More recently, however, the concept has faded to the point of almost total obscurity. Its demise followed from the advent of modernist sensibilities that have stressed individuality, spontaneity, and cultural egalitarianism. Propriety and decorum have been discarded as remnants of an aristocratic era, as stultifying conventions of the dead past.

Burke's invocation of propriety, however, does not disclose a reactionary bias. Instead, piety and propriety become terms that uncover order within a relativistic social universe. They allow us to understand how the elements of rhetoric cohere within discourses spawned by a multitude of differing perspectives. In this sense, propriety becomes a principle of local integration—the agency that coordinates what is said with how it is said within some particular context. Thus, in *Permanence and Change*, Burke suggests a way to refurbish the classical notion of propriety and to place it again near the center of the rhetorical process.

Our purpose is to pursue this task of rehabilitation through an interpretation and application of two key terms in *Permanence and Change*—piety and perspective by incongruity. Our objective is to sustain a kind of dialogue between Burke and the older tradition, and for this reason, our interpretative work will proceed simultaneously at two levels. On the one hand, we hope to clarify Burke's complex and idiosyncratic use of terms by reference to the larger rhetorical tradition. Specifically, we will stress the affinities between "piety" and "propriety" and between "perspective by incongruity" and "metaphor." On the other hand, we hope to counter the stabilizing force of the tradition by stressing the way Burke expands and reconfigures its elements and their relationship to one another. In this respect, the interaction that Burke posits between his key terms seems especially important. We will argue that "propriety," when aligned with "piety," represents a principle of symbolic order, and that "metaphor," when aligned with "perspective by incongruity," represents a mode of breaking down existing pieties and establishing new ones. On this view, rhetorical action is at once subversive and constitutive, and if "metaphor" functions to convey this action, it does so under the aegis of some stable or emerging conception of "propriety." Propriety, in other words, becomes the master term, the term of completion.

After we explicate these connections in Burke's text, we then wish to illustrate the practical use of the position we outline. For this purpose, we present an analysis of a rhetorical text. This case study also suggests some general observations about the range and significance of propriety, and we will conclude by considering them briefly.

Piety and Perspective by Incongruity

For Burke, piety refers both to a certain kind of product—an orientation, a frame, or a way of organizing things—and to a certain kind of process—a process by which we generate orientations, frames, and ways of organizing things. As systems, pieties are schemes of orientation (76). They consist of what Burke calls a "sense of what goes with what," and they work to "round things out." Ultimately, Burke claims, "Pious linkages may have brought all the significant details of the day into coordination, relating them integrally with one another by a complex interpretative network" (75). Pieties, then, function as stable frames of reference which direct human perception and determine our judgments about what is proper in a given circumstance. In this respect, a piety is an orientation that governs our sense of propriety. Nevertheless, pieties are not immutable or inert givens; they are created by human makers as they interact with their fellows and with the world. So, pieties are processes as well; they come to be, change, and pass out of existence in accordance with the situated interests of human communities.

Burke illustrates this dual operation of piety by examining modern attitudes toward the machine. Our century, he argues, tends to ethicize the machine. Modern man tends to regard machinery as intrinsically good because of its apparent connection with progress. This linkage, when fully ramified, yields a systematic orientation—a piety that we might call the "Piety of the Machine." In certain contexts, its results are impressive, so much so that we are tempted, perhaps unconsciously, to extend its reference and to invest the Piety of the Machine with a universal interpretative value. Hence, we may come to gauge biological behavior against the standard of the mechanistic behavior (207). As this process occurs, the pieties of traditional religion and philosophy are displaced, and we arrive at new conceptions of ourselves and our world.

Burke suggests that all pieties arise out of the impulse for order, but as interests diverge or change, principles of order come into conflict. Within this zone of competition, pieties struggle to organize matter at the expense of rival perspectives. It is here, of course, that we enter the domain of persuasion, but at an angle somewhat different from the more traditional approaches. Burke does not focus his attention upon specific, local issues; rather, for him, persuasion implies a tension between differing ways of organizing and understanding the particular circumstances that engage us.

In this global sense, persuasion is at once subversive and constructive; old pieties must fall to provide space for new ones. Burke compares the struggle over this working out of linkages with the two-step movement of "conversion"—first there is a "reduction of scale" effected through a deliberate misnaming, and then the construction of new order begins through the development of a replacement terminology (126–28). Persuasion, in this new key, leads us from piety through an impiety to a new piety.

The midpoint in this progression constitutes what Burke calls a "perspective by incongruity." Perspective by incongruity is a linguistic impiety, an upsetting of normal patterns of association, and it operates by "attaching to some name a qualifying epithet which heretofore has gone with a different order of names" (90). Perspective by incongruity, in other words, is the wedge that pries apart established linkages. Yet, at the same time, it prepares for a new fusion. Burke views this whole process as an instrument of human motivation. It is our interests that prompt us to merge things or events in terms of a potential similarity despite the important differences among them in other respects (as, for instance, when one places fire and acid in the same category because of their burn-character). The classification system is not an objective report on the state of the world; it is a manifestation of our attitudes about that world.

When our point of view shifts, we "approach events with a new ideality, reclassifying them, putting things together that were in different classes, and dividing things that had been together" (106). Pursuing this notion, Burke identifies metaphor with perspective and characterizes perspective by incongruity as a lens that focuses or refocuses our encounters with the world in a way consistent with our interests (141)

The reference to metaphor is especially interesting, since Burke's perspective by incongruity rehearses an orientation that would later inform the "interaction" theory of metaphor.[6] In the terms of this theory, metaphor works by breaking down and reconstructing semantic fields associated with terms as these terms are brought together in novel relationships to one another. Thus, to say "Man is a wolf" is to utter a sentence that is nonsense at a certain level; the subject and predicate terms literally do not belong in the same category. Yet we readily understand the meaning of this utterance, since we are able to discover attributes of the term "wolf" that do go with man (e.g., rapacious, aggressive, destructive) even as we overlook those that do not (e.g., four-legged, having a tail).[7] At the literal level, the sentence is inappropriate, but at another level it creates a propriety of its own. Thus, metaphor is, to use Paul Ricoeur's formula, a semantic impertinence that gives rise to a new semantic pertinence.[8] Like perspective by incongruity, metaphor represents a point of coalescence between the logic of categorization and the imaginative play of language action.

While interaction theorists stress the generative power of metaphor and acknowledge the intimate connection between ideas and images, they concentrate on meaning as it occurs at the sentence level. Burke is far more expansive. Perspective by incongruity aligns and reorders entire domains of experience, not just word meanings. Moreover, while Burke fully recognizes the force of semantics, he places semantic interaction within a broader context. His equations link metaphor with perspective and perspective with human interests. Consequently, symbolic activity incorporates both the intrinsic properties of the symbol system and the motives of the agents who use it. The processes of naming and attributing are shot through with human purposes, and, in this sense, they are fundamentally rhetorical. For Burke, symbolic action always incorporates the rhetorical motive that leads us to round out, coordinate, and rearrange things in keeping with our expectations and desires. Or, to put our point in Burke's own vocabulary, metaphor organizes pieties; pieties reflect our varying interests and perspectives, and the disorder caused by the inevitable conflict of pieties can be resolved only by reference to strategies that realign old perspectives into new orders of propriety.

This brief explication simplifies the long argument that occupies Burke through the middle section of *Permanence and Change*. But if we are unable to do justice to the nuances of his argument, we hope that our summary reveals its basic architecture. In our judgment, Burke's fundamental insight is a complex understanding of the coordinating function of persuasive discourse. This function operates simultaneously at three interrelated levels. Within a given text, it generates a perspective and a network of internally consistent entailments in order to establish the coherence necessary to sustain belief. At this level, propriety becomes a constructive vehicle for organizing the elements of discourse into a unified whole. At the intertextual level, however, the piety of a discourse functions competitively as it seeks to undermine the integrity of rival perspectives. Propriety here becomes an instrument for subversion and reconstruction, just as metaphor is an instrument for breaking apart and reconstituting established fields of meaning.

Finally, persuasive discourse aligns the relationships between texts and contexts; this entails a coordination between the intrinsic and extrinsic dimensions of discourse, so that a discourse can appropriately mediate between its own internal structure and the situated events and interests that it seeks to encompass. All three functions work together as the text sustains its authority, struggles against the authority of other texts, and strives to render an authoritative account of some region of public experience. Each phase of this process responds to the demands of propriety, and thus propriety becomes the master term—the term of completion.

The Piety of an Anarchist

To this point, we have used Burke's thought to redefine propriety, to outline its elements, and to indicate the complex relationships that exist among these elements. Abstract analysis, however, leads to a rather schematic and somewhat distorted view of the process. Propriety demands situated, qualitative judgment, and its dynamics become real only when they are embodied in a discursive act. An adequate explication of the concept, therefore, requires attention to discursive practice; that is, it must emerge from a critical understanding of specific rhetorical transactions. Moreover, the claims that follow from Burke's position are very general, and their application to public address is not immediately obvious. For these reasons, we now want to turn to an oratorical text and attempt to establish a more concrete ground for our position. We would emphasize, however, that the issues involved are broad in scope, and, in this short paper, we cannot explore all of their ramifications. Our objective, therefore, is to use a single case study to illustrate our approach and to offer some initial justification for its plausibility and its potential as a mode of critical practice.

For these purposes, we have selected a short but intriguing oration entitled "The Fruit of Sacrifice." Delivered on November 17, 1895, by Voltairine de Cleyre, "The Fruit of Sacrifice" was the first in a series of annual addresses Cleyre presented to memorialize the execution of the anarchists convicted in the Chicago Haymarket incident.[9] Cleyre was a prominent leader of the anarchist movement, a practiced advocate for the cause, and in the judgment of Emma Goldman, "the greatest woman Anarchist of America."[10]

"The Fruit of Sacrifice" seems directed primarily toward adherents of the anarchist cause, for it addresses the question of how the movement should understand the significance of the Haymarket affair and the loss of five martyrs to the cause. Yet, as Cleyre deals with this theme, she faces a number of problems that place both the occasion and her mode of addressing it in an apparent tension with a crucial tenet of anarchist doctrine. Thus, the speech offers a particularly clear example of the way that a radical and seemingly "impious" doctrine strives to achieve an internal coherence on its own terms and to encompass anomalies within a region of shared experience.

To a contemporary reader, both the manner and matter of the speech seem curious. The style is the more immediately notable feature. Cleyre speaks in a florid, poetic idiom. Even taking into account the different tastes and oratorical practices of her time, the speech is extravagant. Witness this passage from the introduction:

> Eight times has our Mother Earth bared her scarred breast to the hitter blast—eight times laid naked this unhealing wound whence blood still issues. . . .
>
> Eight weary years have the women wept, and the orphaned children placed upon their father's tomb their wreaths of tear-wet flowers.
>
> Eight slumbrous years has the powerful silence lain upon those lips that, living, never unclosed save to utter defiance to the tyrant that strangled but could not subdue. . . .
>
> Eight rain-breath'd springs have the graves grown green, eight withering autumns turned old and white.

This sort of rhapsodic syntax and diction is not sustained throughout, but Cleyre's language consistently retains a strong poetic coloration, and almost every paragraph includes a romantic outburst. Thus, as she establishes the grounds of her argument, she presents a paean to martyrdom: "Not a corner of the populated world so isolated, not a people so barbarous, not a religion so rude, but has had its Hofers, its Cranmers, its Savonarolas, breathing defiance under the mouths of guns or singing glorias from the centre of the smoke." Likewise, her account of the effects following from the executions concludes with an almost frenzied vision:

> Whenever in the horrible conflict between laborers and soldiers, a shredded striker is borne away by his comrades, who looking on his blood hate deeper, there walks the mangled corpse of Louis Lingg, that brave, beautiful boy, who, tossing his proud head, "with his tawny hair like a lion's mane," and gazing with dauntless eyes full at the court about to sentence him, exclaimed: I do believe in force, hang me for it.

And, as might be expected, the peroration returns to the overblown style of the introduction: the funerary monument at Waldheim is made to "stand with great, sorrowful stem eyes" and drop "the laurel on her slaughtered child" while the voices of the five martyrs rise from the grave.

The passages just cited are among the most extravagant in the text, but they provide a reliable indication of the tone of the speech as a whole. This tone seems hardly consistent with the perspective Cleyre adopts as the basis for her argument. Adhering to a fundamental tenet of anarchism,

Cleyre commits herself to an unforgiving materialism.[11] She rejects any appeal to the mythical or supernatural and insists upon "a scientific basis" for her reasoning. "That is," she explains, her argument must "not contradict any well-grounded statement of the processes of nature (or as we commonly say natural law)." How, then, can one reconcile this cold, detached, scientific materialism with the emotionally charged, romantic language that is displayed throughout the text? As the speech unfolds, we discover that Cleyre is well aware of this problem, and her argument works to resolve it through a creative realignment of terms.

The argument begins as Cleyre articulates a tension between materialist philosophy and the very nature of the occasion—a memorialization of men who sacrificed their material existence for an idea. Martyrdom, Cleyre asserts, is a common phenomenon through history. In the past, however, such sacrifice was founded upon a trust in an intangible spiritual force governing human destiny: "At the heart of these ecstatic triumphs over death, has ever been the idea of a compensating God who for pains suffered here will grant reward of eternal bliss." Thus, martyrdom is explicable through a calculus that values the spiritual over the material and gauges the concerns of the body against the welfare of the soul.

This spiritual reduction, however, offers no solace in the anarchist scheme of things. "Modern science," Cleyre confidently announces, "has proven this God does not exist; nowhere in sky or earth or sea can any trace of him be found. On the contrary, telescope, microscope, spectroscope, all enter the protest that cannot be gainsaid against a belief in the existence of any mythical power which troubles itself about an individual's life or death." Consequently, "the old belief, which sustained the martyrs of the past . . . plays no part" in assessing the case at hand. Another "piety," one which accords with material fact, must be found to warrant an act by which a human being becomes "a handful of senseless ashes for the sake of an idea." The issue, then, becomes how one can place a positive value on self-sacrifice in a world of thoroughgoing materialism.

Cleyre attacks this issue through a series of indirect and rather skillfully arranged steps. She first affirms that the Haymarket martyrs were orthodox anarchists; they were men spawned by the nineteenth century and were not deceived by the promise of a hereafter. They understood, therefore, the measure of their sacrifice. Next, Cleyre carefully presents evidence to prove that these men suffered execution willingly and without reservation. Thus, she can emphasize their heroic stature and can balance their deaths against the forward impulse they imparted to the movement. While the government sought to silence them, their resolute action "sent their words on wings of flame in many tongues and many lands. . . . And tonight ten thousand, nay thrice ten thousand repeat in reverence the names of Parsons, Fischer, Engel, Lingg, and Spies." They are not lost to the cause, since, by their death, the cause has "gained a thousand fold." Finally, Cleyre ends this section with the bold vision of Lingg's specter marching through the ranks of future anarchists.

The emotional intensity of the passage, however, cannot overcome its argumentative deficiency within the terms set out earlier by the speaker. To this point, Cleyre has pursued a thoroughly conventional justification for martyrdom. The sacrifice of the individual to the more general good of the cause obviously fits within the piety of mainstream thought. Yet to speak of a cause is to become caught up in an abstraction, an idea or a network of ideas. Thus, this conventional appeal to heroic sacrifice, however fervently Cleyre might make it, still does not satisfy the goal of memorializing the Haymarket anarchists in conformity with her materialistic perspective.

The turning point occurs as Cleyre locates this problem and corrects her course. Adopting a self-reflexive stance, she gives voice to an objection bearing upon both the style and argument of her previous remarks: "Ah, you say, 'you are talking poetry.'" Evidently, poetic "talk" diverts the speaker from the real issue, since it seems to entrap her in the spiritual idiom of the perspective she would discard. Thus, Cleyre quite consciously equates her own performance with the substance of the issue at hand. That performance is itself "impious" on anarchist terms, unless she can simultaneously reconcile the martyrdom of the Haymarket victims within a materialist frame and the use of poetic utterance within a world governed by scientific fact. Every facet of the situation must be aligned in systematic consistency—the subject, the occasion, the matter, and manner of the speech itself are all bound together. The function of the speech is to vindicate the Haymarket martyrs, but the speaker now places herself at hazard; for she must achieve this goal in order to vindicate her own practice.

The dramatic point of this maneuver is highlighted by contrast to Cleyre's initial and more conventional justification of martyrdom. Viewed from the abstract perspective of the "cause," the speaker judges from a historical and conceptual distance; she measures the concrete event against its later and somewhat intangible consequences. But as she openly reflects about her performance, her verbal action becomes consubstantial with the passion of her martyred comrades. The action of the speech, in other words, is required to do what the speech says about the event it describes.

Cleyre seeks to achieve this dual vindication through a "scientific" appraisal of the relationship between body and soul. Science teaches that the body is no more than "so much lime, so much iron, so much sulfur, so much carbon, and so on, which disappear at death and pass into other forms but cannot be destroyed." What, then, is soul? Again the answer is found through science, which defines the soul as a compound. It is "an organism of certain psychological elements, just as much facts as the physical elements that accompany them. The soul of man is so much courage, so much energy, so much prudence, so much daring, so much poesy, so much fear, and so on through the qualities that make a man." In short, the soul consists of elements that are as thoroughly material as those that constitute the body.

This analogy establishes the perspective by incongruity that is essential for Cleyre's purposes. The coherence of anarchist sentiments and the integrity of her speech are secured by reversing the terms of the theological perspective. That older perspective assimilates the material into the spiritual and thus promotes values that gauge the body against the welfare of the soul. Cleyre retains the same terms but reverses their relationship. The Piety of Materialism systematically "misnames" the elements formerly associated with spiritual values and relocates them within a materialistic vocabulary, and as it displaces the rival perspective, it simultaneously establishes its own coherence.

In the immediate context, Cleyre's task is to extend the Piety of Materialism to encompass martyrdom—a subject traditionally understood only from a theological or spiritual perspective. Her perspective by incongruity achieves this end by reconfiguring the psychological qualities associated with martyrdom and defining them as material elements. Thus, as the

Haymarket anarchists willingly faced death, their "nobler elements" were enlarged, presumably in a quite material fashion. Moreover, as physical death means only "a setting free of original elements to form new combinations," so also is the death of the soul part of an ongoing chemical process. "But the soul-elements, like the body-elements, are common to all mankind, and at death nothing is lost in the one case any more than the other—only transmuted." Thus, even in the most severely materialistic terms, the fate of the anarchist martyrs "meant only an intenser, larger life." Cleyre now has rescued the occasion and her purpose: an encomium on martyrdom is appropriate within the anarchist frame, since, through suffering execution, the martyrs ennobled and bettered themselves, while they also materially improved the common fund of "soul-elements" available to the human race.

There remains the justification of the style of the speech. On this point, Cleyre does not draw a stated conclusion, but her closing argument clearly implies a solution to the problem she acknowledged earlier. Throughout "The Fruit of Sacrifice," Cleyre attributes a poetic heroism to the Haymarket martyrs, and the attribution depends not only on what she says, but the poetic manner used in saying it. In this respect, we should note that "poesy" is one of the items listed among the material "soul elements." Consequently, we understand that Cleyre's sentimental and romantic style is neither self-indulgence nor a residue of a false, "spiritualist" consciousness. Instead, it consistently represents events as they must exist within the piety of the anarchist perspective. The poetic style of her speech transmits a sensibility that is part of the enduring heritage of the Haymarket martyrs. It is appropriate to the subject, since it embodies one of the material elements inherent within that subject.

Conclusion

Judged by the analytic standards of traditional criticism, the "Fruit of Sacrifice" must be regarded as an inappropriate and ineffective rhetorical effort. The overwrought style of the speech does not seem to mesh with its doctrine, and it often violates the boundaries of conventional oratorical prose. The argument seems circuitous, and its crucial premise depends upon a tenuous and inadequately developed analogy. In fact, these considerations might enter into any evaluation of the speech. Even when read from within the anarchist frame, Cleyre's argument sometimes appears forced and incomplete, and in many passages, her idiom is awkward and yields something closer to bathos than genuine emotional power. The problem with the traditional analytic approach, therefore, is not that its standards are wholly irrelevant to the text. Rather, its deficiency is the inability to connect relevant general categories of analysis with the symbolic action indigenous to the text itself; thus it encourages misinterpretation because it fails to comprehend the horizons that define the effort at rhetorical synthesis.

But the Burkean concepts of piety and perspective by incongruity offer an important corrective, since they allow us to approach the text as a field of action rather than as a static ground for the application of externally conceived standards of propriety. Viewed from our "neo-Burkean" perspective, "The Fruit of Sacrifice" seems as much an exercise in propriety as a Fourth of July oration or a memorial delivered at the Tomb of the Unknown Soldier. Indeed, the radical character of Cleyre's ideology underscores the effort to achieve the piety afforded by rhetorical coherence. Strategies that are often implicit in mainstream discourse become more transparent within Cleyre's rhetoric. The text consciously struggles with the problem of sustaining its own authority, since the orator must somehow reconcile the conventions of memorialization with anarchist doctrine, and this dilemma bears both on the internal consistency of argument within the speech and on the coordination of what is said with the way it is said. Moreover, the "intertextual rivalry" of other perspectives becomes the conscious basis for resolving these apparent tensions; the speech pivots on its subversive redefinition of terms found in the "spiritualist piety." Finally, the alignment between text and context emerges in a rather clear form that seems to embody the "materialist piety." The speaker implicitly seeks to demonstrate that her own performance is a material act coherent with the actual events to which it refers. Thus, the speech is not just talk, but action that explains and manifests the character of the world as anarchists experience it.

Beyond clarification of the critical orientation we have sketched earlier, we believe that this analysis suggests two additional conclusions.

First, Cleyre's speech seems sufficiently radical and sufficiently resistant to conventional analysis that its explication blunts the charge of conservatism often associated with the doctrine of propriety. Insofar as our critique is successful, it demonstrates that propriety, as we conceive it, is not limited to mainstream political discourse. On the contrary, it appears as an especially useful concept in interpreting discourse that is radical and apparently subversive in character. In fact, the main benefit derived from the invocation of propriety is that it allows the critic to engage a text systematically but without reducing it to categories alien to its own rhetorical purposes.

Viewed from this perspective, the rhetorical economy of the "Fruit of Sacrifice" exhibits a special characteristic that seems to *mark* it as "radical" discourse. The speech maintains its balance by coordinating the occasion, the subject, and the stance of the speaker against the standard of an explicitly articulated ideology. Cleyre makes little effort to adapt to the audience, and thus, as opposed to most mainstream oratory, her speech appears as a more nearly self-contained unit, something more nearly perfected within its own conceptual horizons. Conventional epideictic discourse (any of Webster's efforts in this genre, for example) draws its material from the received values and attitudes of the audience; its balance occurs within what Farrell aptly calls the semi-choate medium of social knowledge,[12] and the integrity of the discourse depends upon accommodation to existing beliefs that are not consciously organized into a consistent or comprehensive system. This contrast not only indicates that radical discourse avoids adaptation to the audience, but that it often must construct its own standard of propriety. That is, such discourse, as it departs from taken-for-granted beliefs, must specify its own terms of completion and explicitly round out a perspective, since the perspective itself turns against conventional assumptions. Or, in other words, radical discourse becomes radical as it reconstructs rather than adjusts itself to the standards of propriety accepted by an audience.

We recognize, of course, that this speculation rests upon examination of only one case, and so we submit it only as a crude and provisional hypothesis. Nevertheless, this hypothesis seems consistent with the well-established view that radical discourse finds its end in confrontation instead of accommodation,[13] and we believe that an expanded conception of propriety may help to deepen our understanding of how confrontation and accommodation operate within rhetorical discourse.

Our second conclusion raises an issue of more general theoretical concern. Traditional rhetorical criticism has experienced much difficulty because it does not supply a focal point adequate to synthesize its own apparatus. Consequently, distinctive rhetorical features (e.g., stylistic devices or forms of argument) are more readily isolated and identified than they are integrated into an account of rhetorical action per se.[14] This bias obstructs perception of the rhetorical text as a unified effort since persuasive discourse seems unable to sustain an integrity of its own.

We can illustrate this problem briefly by referring to Paul Ricoeur's recent analysis of Aristotle's *Rhetoric*. Ricoeur argues that Aristotle's theory is disjointed since it lacks a mechanism sufficient to link argumentation and style. As Ricoeur conceives it, moreover, this problem is inherent in the rhetorical project. Argument must maintain its identification with logic, and thus it aims at proof in some reasonably objective sense of the word. Style, however, aims at pleasing, a function that is relative to the audience and distinct from the realm of objective argument. Consequently, Ricoeur concludes that the *Rhetoric* is a bifurcated work, torn by an unavoidable contradiction between its two main components.[15] It is possible, of course, to quarrel with Ricoeur's interpretation of Aristotle, but his position certainly underscores an issue that consistently plagues rhetorical theorists and critics. Received views of argument and style seem to set the two in isolation, and we are forced either to subordinate one to the other or to accept a disastrous schism between the cognitive and aesthetic functions of the rhetorical process. In either case, we are ill-equipped to deal with any particular rhetorical discourse as an independent and integrated field of action.[16]

As our reading of Cleyre's speech indicates. Burke implies a doctrine of propriety that helps to resolve this problem. This doctrine enables us to view an oratorical text as a local achievement without dissolving it into the immediate historical context. Viewed as a term of rhetorical completion, propriety allows us to identify the text *as* something constructed for a specific purpose but which retains an artistic integrity. Propriety assimilates style and argument to a common goal intermediate between the internal resources of the text and its extrinsic purpose. Under the aegis of propriety, all the elements of rhetoric function to round things out within a discourse and to maintain the coherence of a perspective against the claims of rival perspectives. This operation always yields a preferred view of the world that surrounds the discourse, and thus propriety becomes the agent that holds a persuasive discourse together internally even as it extends the force of that discourse outward into the public domain of shared beliefs and actions.

NOTES

1. Kenneth Burke, *Permanence and Change: An Anatomy of Purpose*, 3rd ed. (Berkeley: University of California Press, 1984), 77. Subsequent citations all refer to this edition and are noted in the text.
2. Aristotle, *Rhetoric*, 1404b1–8. Also see 1408a10–11, a passage which sometimes has been interpreted as granting an expanded role to propriety as agent for coordinating the modes of proof within a discourse. This argument is advanced in detail by William Grimaldi, *Studies in the Philosophy of Aristotle's Rhetoric* (Wiesbaden: Hermes, 1972), 51.
3. George Kennedy, *The Art of Persuasion in Greece* (Princeton, NJ: Princeton University Press, 1963), 273–76.
4. For *decorum* as a rhetorical principle, see *De oratore* 1.132, and 3.212. The centrality of *decorum* in rhetoric is most fully developed at *Orator* 69–74. On this crucial passage, see A. E. Douglas, "A Ciceronian Contribution to Rhetorical Theory," *Eranos* 55 (1957): 18–26; and Elaine Fantham, "*Orator* 69–74," *Central States Speech Journal* 35 (1984): 123–25. *Orator* 70 indicates that *decorum* applies to life in general as well as to oratory: *Ut enim in vita sic in oratione nihil est difficilius quam quid deceat videre*. In *De officiis*, Cicero's most influential work on ethics, the same point is made through an analogy between orderly and balanced conduct and a finished work of oratorical art (1.144). Moreover, Cicero's continual parallels between art and life (e.g. 1.93–95 and 1.1) rest upon this expansive conception of *decorum*. For the general significance of this doctrine, see P. Kukilca, "Ciceros aesthetique Ansichten," *Grecolatina et Orientalia* 11–12 (1979–80): 17–29.
5. Concerning decorum as a rhetorical standard in the eighteenth century, see W. R. Keast, "The Theoretical Foundations of Johnson's Criticism," in *Critics and Criticism: Ancient and Modern* ed. R. S. Crane (Chicago: University of

Chicago Press, 1952), 389–407; and James Biester, "Samuel Johnson on Letters," *Rhetorica* 6 (1988):145–66. The atrophy of this concept, however, is indicated by its absence in the major rhetorical treatises (e.g., Campbell, Blair, Whately) of the late eighteenth and early nineteenth centuries. But in America, decorum retains a position of central interest well into the nineteenth century, a point copiously documented by Robert Ferguson, *Law and Letters in American Culture* (Cambridge, MA: Harvard University Press, 1984).

6. See I. A. Richards, *The Philosophy of Rhetoric* (Oxford: Oxford University Press, 1936); Max Black, *Models and Metaphors: Studies in Language and Philosophy* (Ithaca, NY: Cornell University Press, 1962); and "More on Metaphor," in *Metaphor and Thought*, ed. Andrew Ortony (Cambridge: Cambridge University Press, 1979), 19–43; and Monroe Beardsley, "The Metaphorical Twist," *Philosophy and Phenomenological Research* 22 (1962): 293–307. Interaction theory has been applied widely within the critical literature of our discipline. One of the earliest and most influential efforts in this direction is Michael Osborn and Douglas Ehninger, "The Metaphor in Public Address," *Speech Monographs* 29 (1962): 223–34. For more recent applications of this approach see Robert Ivie, "Metaphor and the Rhetorical Invention of Cold War 'Idealists,'" *Communication Monographs* 54 (1987): 165–82, and the references cited therein.
7. Our example follows Black, *Models and Metaphors*, 39–41.
8. See Paul Ricoeur, *The Rule of Metaphor: Multi-disciplinary Studies of the Creation of Meaning in Language*, trans. Robert Czerny (Toronto: University of Toronto Press, 1977), 65–100.
9. The text is found in Voltairine de Cleyre, *The First Mayday: The Haymarket Speeches, 1895–1910*, ed. Paul Avrich (Sanday, Orkney: Cienfuegos Press; New York: Libertarian Book Club, 1980), 1–5. All subsequent references and quotations are from this edition. For the background to this speech and the others in the series, see Avrich's introduction to this volume, and his biography, *An American Anarchist: The Life of Voltairine de Cleyre* (Princeton, NJ: Princeton University Press, 1978).
10. Quoted by Avrich in *The First Mayday*, ii. See also Emma Goldman's biography, *Voltairine de Cleyre* (Berkeley Heights, NJ: Oriole Press, 1932).
11. Concerning anarchist doctrine, the standard works include Sir Herbert Read, *Anarchy and Order: Essays in Politics* (Boston: Beacon Press, 1971); James Joll, *The Anarchists* (Boston: Little, Brown, 1965); and George Woodcock, *Anarchism: A History of Libertarian Ideas and Movements* (Cleveland: Meridian Books, 1962).

12. Thomas B. Farrell, "Knowledge, Consensus, and Rhetorical Theory," *Quarterly Journal of Speech* 62 (1976): 1–14.
13. See, for example, Robert L. Scott and Donald K. Smith, "The Rhetoric of Confrontation," *Quarterly Journal of Speech* 55 (1969): 1–8.
14. The problem, in general terms, is outlined in, for example, Gerry P. Mohrmann, "Elegy in a Critical Graveyard," *Western Journal of Speech Communication* 44 (1980): 265–74; and Edwin Black, "A Note on Theory and Practice in Rhetorical Criticism," *Western Journal of Speech Communication* 44 (1980): 351–56. The specific issue mentioned above is elaborated by Michael C. Leff, "Topical Invention and Metaphoric Interaction," *Southern Speech Communication Journal* 48 (1983): 214–28; and "Textual Criticism: The Legacy of G. P. Mohrmann," *Quarterly Journal of Speech* 72 (1986): 377–89.
15. Ricoeur, *Rule of Metaphor*, 27–43.
16. This argument is developed more fully in Michael C. Leff, "The Habitation of Rhetoric," in *Argument and Critical Practices: Proceedings of the Fifth SCA/AFA Conference on Argumentation*, ed. Joseph Wenzel (Annandale, VA: Speech Communication Association, 1987). For evidence of the recent revival of interest in propriety and decorum, see Wesley Trimpi, *Muses of One Mind: The Literary Analysis of Experience and Its Continuity* (Princeton, NJ: Princeton University Press, 1983) 87–240; James L. Kinneavy, "*Kairos*: A Neglected Concept in Classical Rhetoric," in *Rhetoric and Praxis: The Contribution of Classical Rhetoric to Practical Reasoning*, ed. Jean Dietz Moss (Washington, DC: Catholic University of America Press, 1986); James S. Baumlin, "Decorum, *Kairos*, and the 'New' Rhetoric," *PRE/TEXT* 5 (1964): 171–83; Michael Carter, "Stasis and Kairos: Principles of Social Construction in Ancient Rhetoric," *Rhetoric Review* 7 (1988): 97–112; Helen De Witt, "*Quo Virtus*? The Concept of Propriety in Ancient Literary Criticism," PhD dissertation, Oxford University, 1988; Michael C. Leff, "Burke's Ciceronianism," in *The Legacy of Kenneth Burke*, ed. Herbert Simons and Trevor Melia (Madison: University of Wisconsin Press, 1989).

Topical Invention and Metaphoric Interaction

In the course of his analysis of traditional principles of rhetoric, Kenneth Burke makes the curious remark that "the Aristotelian topics shift so imperceptibly between ideas and images that you wonder how the two realms could ever come to be at odds."[1] The remark is curious, perhaps even subversive, since it associates two domains that both ancient and modern theorists generally have kept apart. In classical rhetoric, of course, images belong to the office of style and function to ornament the language of oratory. Topics, on the other hand, refer to matters of thought and to the office of invention. Certain authorities, Cicero and Isocrates most notably,[2] object to a rigid dichotomy between style and argument, but no classical rhetorician seriously considers possible interrelationships between the technical devices allotted to these two domains. So strict is the separation that where a term such as "analogy" is used both

From *Southern Speech Communication Journal* 48 (1983): 214–28.

in inventional and stylistic theory, authors either pass over this fact in silence or caution the reader not to confuse the different referents for the same term.[3] Among contemporary theorists, the line of demarcation is sometimes even more pronounced, since the distinction between topics and tropes has come to designate two entirely different rhetorics. Thus, one school of thought defines rhetoric as the means of securing or intensifying adherence to theses, while another contends that rhetoric is the study of those deviations from the norms of usage that render language opaque.[4] In short, whether we are dealing with the rhetorical divisions of antiquity or the divided rhetorics of contemporary theory, we still regularly encounter a wall of separation between topic and trope.

Consequently, when Burke suggests that topics partake of ideas and images, he is challenging a fundamental and enduring assumption of technical rhetorical theory. Since Burke's own interests center on matters that are larger and more general than the techniques of the art, he himself does not expand on this matter. But it does demand careful consideration, all the more urgently because of recent studies of figurative language that seem both to support and to undermine conventional distinctions between style and argumentation. Put simply, the question is this: when viewed as a technical element in rhetoric, does topical invention encompass or preclude the cooperative interaction of ideas and images? This is an enormously complex question, and it is obvious that no definitive answer can issue from this short essay. My objective, then, is to select a few aspects of the problem and to indicate a plausible approach to its solution. The line of inquiry will begin with the case for retaining the distinction between argumentative and stylistic rhetoric, a case grounded in the differences between the temporal and spatial axes of language. I will then turn to the interaction theory of metaphor in order to establish a basis for understanding the technical operation of metaphor and to examine the way in which this understanding might modify the initial distinction between metaphor, the master trope, and argumentation. Third, I will briefly outline an Aristotelian approach to topical invention and indicate some affinities and differences between the operation of the topics and metaphor. Finally, I will argue that consideration of these matters encourages a reconception of the role that topics play in the rhetorical process.

We can begin with Roland Barthes's synoptic essay "L'ancienne rhetorique," since it provides a clear rationale for the division between the rhetoric of style and argument. Barthes separates the rhetorical tradition into two parallel streams, the one called syntagmatic, the other paradigmatic. Syntagmatic rhetoric deals with the linear and sequential aspects of discourse—with the progressive arrangement of the parts of the oration and with such mechanisms of argumentation as topics and enthymemes. Paradigmatic rhetoric deals with the aesthetic dimensions of discourse, most particularly with tropes and figures.[5] This distinction follows from Saussurean linguistics, which separates language along two axes: (1) the horizontal, syntagmatic axis of combination, governing the diachronic arrangements of linguistic units, and (2) the vertical, associative (or paradigmatic) axis of selection, governing the synchronic choice of linguistic units.[6] Or, to state the matter in simpler terms, language operates in time through the combination of signs and in space through the selection of a sign to occupy a certain place within an utterance.

By pursuing this distinction, we can arrive at a general characterization of topical argument and metaphor as distinct rhetorical processes. Topical argument proceeds through a sequence of propositions in order to arrive at a conclusion. Its structure, then, is sequential, and it produces its effects in terms of the auditor's sense of temporal or logical progression. Metaphor operates by fixing attention within a linguistic space, and it produces its effects in terms of the synchronic associations and images it evokes in the auditor. Topics orient us rhetorically in and through time; metaphors orient us rhetorically in and through space. The topical method enables us to anticipate and appreciate a denouement; metaphor gives us a seat in the theater.

The position I have just sketched devolves from structuralist theory, and it presumes that metaphor is purely a matter of lexical selection. A very different conception of metaphor emerges when we examine the so-called interaction theory. First suggested by I. A. Richards and later developed by Max Black and other American scholars,[7] interaction theory posits that metaphor consists of a juxtaposition of two terms normally regarded as belonging to different classes of experience. On this view, metaphor involves an act of prediction joining together' two distinct subjects—a principal subject (or tenor, or focus) and a secondary subject (or vehicle, or frame). Metaphorical meaning emerges as these two subjects interact with one another, and various aspects of these subjects are selected, emphasized, suppressed, and ordered as they come into contact. Take, for example, a simple metaphor that might have been uttered long ago by a Greek embarking for Troy: "Helen is a fox." Helen is the principal subject (tenor), fox the secondary subject (vehicle), and the two belong to different classes (human vs. animal). Interaction between these two terms, and thus metaphorical meaning, is possible since they do not refer to simple, univocal subjects, but rather to complex, multifaceted aspects of experience. The term "fox," for example, incorporates a large number of "associated commonplaces"—commonly accepted ideas and feelings that people in a given speech community understand when the term is uttered. In different contexts, some of these commonplaces occupy one's attention and others recede. In the presumably sexist speech community we have imagined in ancient Greece, as soon as the term fox is mentioned in connection with a woman, commonplaces such as "sleekness," "attractiveness," and "desirability as object of a hunt" rise to the foreground, while others, such as "wily," "four-footed," and "predator," fade into the back ground. The whole process works in two stages; the juxtaposition of the two terms first causes the vehicle to assume a pattern of foreground associations, and then this pattern serves to direct our understanding of the tenor. The mutual attraction of terms belonging to different classes causes a response that decomposes the elements associated with these terms and then recombines them into a new structure of meaning.[8] And in the case of rich metaphors, the reverberation between subjects may continue to move back and forth in a very complex manner.

Interaction theory offers a useful account of metaphoric structure, and it obviously forces modification of a purely synchronic or paradigmatic view of metaphor. Metaphor does not consist solely in word choice, or in the substitution of one word for another, since it also involves a relationship between words linked together in a diachronic sequence. In other words, interaction theory proves that metaphors, or at least some metaphors, depend upon predication, upon the temporal relationship of items within the horizontal axis of language. This fact, as Ricoeur notes in his critique of structuralist theory, upsets the basic foundation of a purely semiotic conception of metaphor.[9]

Nevertheless, it is one thing to deny that metaphor is entirely confined to the axis of selection and quite another to reject the view that the rhetorical operation of metaphor is dominantly synchronic or paradigmatic. In fact, the very notion of metaphoric interaction seems to sustain this modified position. As an act of predication, metaphoric utterance moves forward in time, and the temporal sequence is necessary to initiate the production of meaning. The meaning itself, however, emerges in the space between the two terms, for as these terms, belonging to different constellations of literal meaning, come within each other's orbit, various elements are detached from each and then recomposed into a new structure. The diachronic progression of the utterance is interrupted as some of its lexical units collapse against each other. Consequently, the interpretation of metaphor forces us into the paradigmatic axis, since we are required to select and organize the various ideas, images, and feelings associated with the tenor and vehicle that allow for a connection between them. Metaphoric meaning is apprehended in the linguistic space between the tenor and vehicle.

In sum, metaphor converts utterances that are problematic at the syntagmatic level into structures stable at the paradigmatic level within a given context. These structures arise from a complex, almost bewildering, sequence of psychological, sociological, and linguistic interactions. The rhetorical effects of this process, however, may be less difficult to appreciate. Since metaphoric structure limits and organizes our perception of a situation, it seems to establish the ground for viewing that situation; it creates a perspective and hence defines the space in which we encounter the situation. As metaphoric meaning localizes our attention, it produces a frame within which we can synthesize our reactions to the ongoing flow of events in time.

Finally, the interaction theory not only enhances our understanding of the effect of metaphor, but it also suggests that many features of the metaphoric process are fundamentally rhetorical. In the first place, the grounds for constructing and interpreting a metaphor consist in commonly accepted notions. Metaphorical communication, then, depends upon social knowledge and the intersubjective connections that exist within a speech community. Furthermore, the connections must be supplied by the auditor himself or herself, and thus the auditor directly and actively participates in the creation of meaning. Third, metaphor eventuates in partial structures.[10] That is, the new meaning arises from the selection and identification of elements belonging to complex subjects, and the resulting structure exhibits a stability of its own without overwhelming the independence of its constituent subjects. The metaphorical value of a term is unstable in and of itself and will shift considerably depending on the context in which it is used. (Witness that not long ago D. H. Lawrence wrote a short story entitled "The Fox: Symbol of the Male.")[11] Thus, while metaphor may guide perception of a situation, it is itself intimately connected with the situation in which it is uttered. Metaphor draws its materials from communal knowledge, achieves its effects through the active cooperation of the auditor, and assumes its form in relation to a particular context; and all of these features surely apply to a description of the rhetorical process itself.

We may now turn to the second of our major rhetorical forms, topical argument. The term "topic" is notoriously ambiguous, and even in its technical uses, its meaning ranges from recurrent themes appearing in a certain kind of discourse to abstract patterns of inference. In this short essay, it is not possible to disentangle the various senses of the term, and so, for present purposes, I will merely stipulate a definition. Topics are resources for constructing arguments, and an argument is a series of propositions offered as reasons to support a conclusion about a doubtful issue. The propositions that serve as reasons may be divided into two classes: those that establish the data of an argument, and those that warrant the connection between the data-establishing propositions and the conclusions. Topics may provide assistance in discovering propositions of either type, but only those related to the second category, the "warranting propositions," seem distinctively rhetorical, and so I will concentrate exclusively on them in this essay. All told, this leads to the conception of a topic as a source for discovering a middle element in an argument, that is, for discovering propositions that link the extremes, and these extremes in a rhetorical argument are the data from which the argument begins and the conclusion with which it ends.[12]

Following the authority of Aristotle, we must divide these warranting or inferential topics into two distinct forms.[13] The first is the universal topic, an abstract category of inference designated by a word or phrase, for example, "consequence," "logical division," "from opposites," "from degree," and the like. These categories suggest principles of inference capable of generating warrants relevant to any subject of rhetorical discourse whatsoever. The second form is the special topic, and these topics consist of an inventory of propositions expressing abstract beliefs and values generally accepted by the public. These propositions apply only to a particular subject or type or rhetorical discourse, and thus, for deliberative oratory, topics take the form of propositions such as the following:

- That is good the contrary of which is bad.
- That is good on which much labor or money is spent.
- That is good which men deliberately choose to do.
- What is rare is a greater good than what is more plentiful.
- The hard thing is better than the easy.[14]

Here I will deal only with the special topics in illustrating the way that these topical warrants operate.[15] Like the common grounds that effect connection in metaphor, these topics draw their material from commonly accepted opinion within the community. Stated in the form of a premise, these common notions provide the inferential binding necessary for argumentative inference. For example, we have the topical proposition: "That is good on which much labor or money has been spent." We can use this as a connective linking an established belief about a subject (e.g., many famous men exerted much labor and money to possess Helen) to a desired conclusion (e.g., Helen must have been good).

We should note that these topics only create partial structures. This is true in respect to the internal form of the topical argument, since it provides a pattern of deductive reasoning that falls short of demonstration. Not only are the premises of topical argument based on probabilities, but the argument normally does not express all the steps required for necessary entailment. Perhaps more important, the external configuration of the topics as a system is unstable and incomplete. The special topics defy arrangement into neat, hierarchical categories, and the application of a given topic is always contingent on the rhetorical context. These limitations follow from the source of the topics, social knowledge, for one of the distinguishing features of social knowledge is its lack of full coherence.[16] Common beliefs, attitudes, and values are mutable and volatile, and they take clear form only as they come into contact with particular situations. The more abstract items in the repertoire of social knowledge are often inconsistent with one another; some of them are flatly contradictory. Thus, some topical premises are so unstable that, depending on the context and the purpose of the rhetor, they may me reversed completely. Witness this passage from the *Rhetoric*:

> Again what is rarer excels what is more abundant. So gold though less useful than iron is more precious. . . . On the alternative side, the abundant is a greater good than the scarce since there is more use of it; frequent use excels rare—whence the saying "Best of all is water." In general, the more difficult of two things is the better, as being rarer. But, on the alternative side, the easier is a greater good than the more difficult, as conforming to our wishes.[17]

Analysis of metaphor and topical argument suggests some general points of resemblance between the two processes. Both involve the organization of belief, the partial structuring of commonly held attitudes and values. Both also function through a process of mediating between extreme elements; in metaphor the commonplaces associated with various terms provide the ground for connection, and in topical argument, propositions expressing abstract values provide the necessary link. Finally, both require the invention of verbal strategies in circumstances where diverse elements compete for attention. Metaphor and topical argument alike highlight certain aspects of a situation even as they suppress others.

The differences between these processes, however, seem equally obvious. The special topics are statements joining together at least two other statements. The common grounds of metaphor are much more vague, much less choate items of social knowledge, and they join together two terms within the same statement. The topical commonplace operates as a part of an argument, and the argument moves forward through the place to a conclusion. Apparently the whole process is a linear sequence, the commonplace acting as a mediating station through which one passes to reach a final destination. Metaphorical common grounds, of course, do not produce an argument at all, but only a meaning, and this meaning emerges in the middle of the structure. Since metaphor involves predication, its utterance exhibits some type of linear sequence, but the meaning of the metaphor primarily results from a reverberation between the extreme elements.

At this point in our inquiry, then, there seems good reason to adhere to some form of the distinction between a syntagmatic rhetoric of invention and a paradigmatic rhetoric of metaphor. The similarities between the two processes appear very broad and do little more than indicate that both are rhetorical. The differences are more concrete, and they underscore important distinctions in the structure and effects of topics and metaphors. Topical invention works within the isotopy of a context to produce an effect in time; the object of invention is to bridge ideas belonging to the same essential class. Metaphor, on the other hand, fuses elements that are not isotopic, and thus it negotiates meaning through the reconfiguration of a statement. Metaphor frames rhetorical situations; topics order the elements within the frame.

This position offers an elegant symmetry, and in abstract, theoretical terms, its rationale seems plausible. Yet when we move outside the realm of pure theory and consider rhetorical discourse as it is actually practiced, Burke's speculation about the confluence of ideas and images demands attention. The more closely we contemplate the workings of specific rhetorical transactions, the less obvious is the dichotomy between metaphoric frames and argumentative contents. Rhetoric as we actually experience it may force a reconsideration of this dichotomy, or, at the least, force us to exercise great caution developing its implications.

In order to illustrate this problem, let me refer to Loren Eiseley's "The Bird and the Machine," an essay that uses topical argument and metaphor in a very complex and interesting way.[18] Eiseley begins by expressing concern about articles he has read connecting the human mind with the operation of machines. The articles tell him that machines are becoming more like humans every day and that the brain is "just another type of more complicated feedback system." This image disturbs Eiseley, leads him to think of "the little purr of the cogs in my head and the tubes flaring and dying as the messages go through them and the circuits snap shut or open." And he rejects these thoughts, since "it's human life I believe in, not machines."[19]

Eiseley's proof is formed as a narrative, a reminiscence of an event that occurred in his youth. Commissioned to capture animals for a zoo, Eiseley had come across a pair of sparrow hawks. He captured the male bird, but it had attacked him and allowed the female to escape. After caging the bird, Eiseley went to sleep. The next morning, thinking better of what he had done. Eiseley released the mare hawk, and as it flew away, something remarkable happened:

> Then from far up somewhere a cry came ringing down. . . . Straight out of the sun's eye, where she must have been restlessly soaring above us for untold hours, hurtled his mate. And from far up, ringing from peak to peak of the summits over us, came a cry of such unutterable and ecstatic joy that it sounds down across the years and tingles among the cups on my quiet breakfast table.
>
> I saw them both now. He was rising fast to meet her. They met in a great soaring gyre that turned to a whirling circle and a dance of wings. Once more, just once, their two voices, joined in a harsh wild medley of question and response, struck and echoed against the pinnacles of the valley.[20]

Eiseley has read: "It does not seem that there is anything in the construction, constituents, or behavior of the human being which is essentially impossible for science to duplicate and synthesize." But, on the other hand, he knows: "The machine does not bleed, ache, hang for hours' in the empty sky in a torment of hope to learn the fate of another machine, nor does it cry out with joy nor dance in the air with the fierce passion of a bird."[21]

The whole essay displays an almost poetic tone of reverie, but it is also an argument. In fact, without expending too much analytical effort, we can reduce its basic argumentative content to a sequence of propositions, what a logician would call a sorties:

- Al Machine intelligence is entirely rational.
- A2 Passion is the contrary of reason.

- A3 Therefore, machine intelligence lacks passion.
- B1 But human intelligence involves passion.
- B2 Therefore, human intelligence is not the same as machine intelligence.

Some of these propositions are not stated in Eiseley's argument, but they do lurk at the margins and seem necessary if we are to account for its rhetorical force. Moreover, the two "warranting propositions" (what I have labeled "A2" and "B1") clearly instantiate the topic of contraries, for they make the argument turn on the belief that an attribute contrary to the character of machines exists as an important characteristic of human intelligence.

Obviously, however, this analysis is incomplete, since it does *not* explain how Eiseley establishes the crucial premise that human intelligence incorporates passion. This is the one controversial premise in the argument, and it is to support this premise that Eiseley presents the story of the two sparrow hawks. Now it is possible to give some account of how the story performs this function in the terms of topical method. We can view the whole process as a subsidiary argument based on the topics of genus and degree (i.e., a fortiori). Thus, we reason that, because humans and birds belong to the same essential class (living creatures as opposed to machines), if birds are motivated by passion, then so are humans, and this is all the more true since humans represent a higher level of development in the order of life. Yet even if we restrict our attention to the linear aspects of the argument, this account is hardly satisfactory. The metaphoric dimension is also at work here, and in a vitally important way. Eiseley does not argue that humans and birds belong to the same class so much as he invites us to view the two sparrow hawks as human. The entire structure of the narrative encourages this vision, and it is subtly supported by metaphorical expressions that attribute human characteristics to the two hawks. The male hawk is attributed with gallantry and despair, the female with hope and anxiety, and the two together do not simply fly; they join in a dance of passion. They do not simply utter cries, but give voice in question and response.

From my perspective, the most remarkable feature of this metaphorical structure is the way that it embeds itself within and merges with the development of propositional argument. As the analysis above suggests, the central metaphor does some of the same work as topical argument, but does it in a more comprehensive and efficient manner. The symbolic association of man and bird is not a mere frame for the movement of topical reasoning. It serves as a link connecting the two major clusters of propositional argument, and even more important, the metaphor fills out and completes the tendencies of the propositional logic. Passion, the metaphor implies, is an essential characteristic of the way living beings think, and its existence not only distinguishes them from, but also marks them as superior to, mechanical devices. The first of these implications is logically necessary for Eiseley's argument, for without it he might appear to be arguing on the basis of an accidental or irrelevant distinction. The second is necessary to convert the distinction made by the logic of contraries into an idea that imparts an attitude to the reader. It urges the reader to participate in Eiseley's revulsion against being compared to a machine, and the metaphor which concludes the essay recalls the reverie with which it began. In the opening paragraph, we find Eiseley seated at breakfast, wondering how an article on machine intelligence could elicit seemingly unrelated memories of the distant past. "It is a funny thing," he writes, "what the brain will do with memories and how it will treasure them and finally bring them into odd juxtapositions with other things, as though it wanted to make a design, or get some meaning out of them, whether you want it or not, or even see it."[22] The mind's powers of effecting connections are a mystery not even fully known by the mind itself, let alone capable of reduction to mechanical operations. The essay stands as proof of this conclusion, for it embodies the author's distinctly human capacity to reason metaphorically. A machine, after all, cannot feel empathy for a creature of a different species, cannot connect emotions experienced in the past to logical problems in the present, cannot fathom the universal consequences that flow from a single concrete experience.

The metaphoric process, as Eiseley's essay both states and illustrates, encompasses principles of classification and categorization strikingly similar to those we attribute to the activity of reasoning. Through the interaction of terms in metaphor, we are able to sort out the diverse items of our experience and group them into coherent patterns. As Lakoff and

Johnson argue, "Metaphor unites reason and imagination. Reason, at the very least, involves categorization, entailment and inference. Imagination, in one of its many aspects, involves seeing one thing in terms of another kind of thing. . . . Metaphor is *imaginative rationality*. Since categories of everyday thought are largely metaphorical, and our everyday life involves metaphorical entailments and inferences, ordinary rationality is therefore imaginative by its very nature."[23] These considerations prompt a revision of our traditional conception of metaphor and encourage the attempt to assimilate principles of metaphoric action into our model of reasoning and argument. And, in fact, several scholars have already begun work in this direction.[24] This approach seems especially useful in respect to rhetorical invention. Though rhetorical scholars have been slow to recognize the point, the synchronic interactions characteristic of metaphoric thought seem to play an important role in topical argumentation.

The imaginative rationality hypothesis has little effect on the distinction between metaphor and rigorous apodeictic inference, since pure demonstration does not involve imaginative connection between different classes of things.[25] Yet, as we have noted, topical reasoning is not pure demonstration; the topical method is not sufficiently rigorous to erect categories fully including or excluding classes of things in relation to one another. At best, the topics work in a given context to produce contingent entailments. They effect a partial structuring of attitudes in the unstable domain of everyday thinking. Consequently, topical arguments do not seem entirely removed from the imaginative inferences that operate in metaphor.

Let me try to rephrase this point in the terminology I have used earlier in the paper: Since a topical warranting proposition does not completely subsume the data-establishing propositions, the relationship between data and warrant is not strictly linear. The two generally interact as they proceed to highlight and obscure various aspects of a problematic situation. The selection of a data-establishing premise affects our judgment about the proper warrant to cover the situation, and the selection of a warranting premise conditions our conception of the situation and hence the choice of propositions we use to describe it. The two processes are not discrete steps in a temporal sequence; nor do they proceed in a single, unobstructed direction toward the conclusion, since each one intrudes on the other as the argument is produced or interpreted. Topical reasoning, then, involves a reverberation in argumentative space, and the conclusion is, at least to some degree, a product that emerges between the data and the warrant.

This perspective encourages us to regard both topics and metaphors as forms of invention that rely on imaginative rationality. It does not, however, obliterate all of the distinctions between the two that I sketched earlier in this paper. As a matter of tendency and degree, metaphor does seem to stress synchronic connections, while the topics stress diachronic movement. Topical arguments normally obscure the imaginative and selective nature of their constituent propositions, whereas some metaphors, especially fresh metaphors, depend upon an initial recognition that the elements combined do *not* belong to the same class. Furthermore, metaphor coordinates terms, while topics coordinate whole statements, and the diachronic value of these two units is significantly different. The sheer temporal duration of a series of propositions imparts a linear appearance to topical argument.[26] It is possible to exploit these relative differences and to imagine "pure forms" where topics depend solely on temporal combination and metaphors solely on synchronic association. In practice, however, the distinction is not absolute, and both rhetorical forms exhibit broadly similar processes of tension and attunement within the matrix of their constituent elements. Consequently, a rigid dichotomy between topical argument and metaphor seems unjustified, whether the separation involves a division between two arts or divisions within the same art. Moreover, the modification of this traditional dichotomy should prove congenial to the interests of American rhetoricians who have defined their art in terms of the interaction between speaker and auditor. We now have reason to argue that interaction not only determines the external configuration of the art, but that it also informs the internal structure of the two most distinctive devices belonging to that art.

NOTES

1. Kenneth Burke, *A Rhetoric of Motives* (Berkeley: University of California Press, 1969), 86.
2. For Isocrates, see *Nicocles*, 5–9, *Against the Sophists*, 16–17, and *Antidosis*, 46–47.

For Cicero, *De oratore* 3.19 and 125.

3. Compare Quintilian 5.11.5 and 8.3.72–81. Also see Marsh H. McCall Jr., *Ancient Theories of Simile and Comparison* (Cambridge, MA: Harvard University Press, 1969), 191–92.
4. Compare Chaim Perelman and L. Olbrechts-Tyteca, *The New Rhetoric: A Treatise on Argumentation*, trans. John Wilkinson and L. Purcell Weaver (Notre Dame, IN: University of Notre Dame Press, 1969), 4; and J. Dubois et al., *A General Rhetoric*, trans. Paul B. Burrell and Edgar M. Slotkin (Baltimore: Johns Hopkins University Press, 1981), 16–21.
5. Roland Barthes, "L'ancienne rhetorique, aide-memoire," *Communications* 16 (1970): 175–76.
6. See Terrence Hawkes, *Structuralism and Semiotics* (Berkeley: University of California Press, 1977), 76–80.
7. The major works in the tradition include I. A. Richards, *The Philosophy of Rhetoric* (Oxford: Oxford University Press, 1936); Max Black, *Models and Metaphors* (Ithaca, NY: Cornell University Press, 1962); and "More on Metaphor," in *Metaphor and Thought*, ed. Andrew Ortony (Cambridge: Cambridge University Press, 1979), 19–45; and Monroe Beardsley, "The Metaphorical Twist," *Philosophy and Phenomenological Research* 22 (1962): 293–307. For an excellent analysis of interaction theory and its significance, see Paul Ricoeur, *The Rule of Metaphor: Multi-disciplinary Studies in the Creation of Meaning in Language*, trans. Robert Czerny (London: Routledge and Kegan Paul, 1978), 65–100.
8. This analysis follows Black, *Models and Metaphors*, 39–42. Black presents a detailed analysis of the metaphor "Man is a wolf," and it greatly clarifies the theory of interaction.
9. Ricoeur, *Rule of Metaphor*, 168–72.
10. I borrow the phrase "partial structure" from George Lakoff and Mark Johnson, *Metaphors We Live By* (Chicago: University of Chicago Press, 1980), 52–55.
11. In the story, the fox comes to symbolize the predatory, intrusive male. The contrast between this metaphor and the one in the statement "Helen is a fox" is an excellent example of the way that the tenor selectively emphasizes various commonplaces associated with the vehicle.
12. For a more detailed explanation of this position, see Michael C. Leff and Dean E. Hewes, "Topical Invention and Group Communication: Towards a Sociology of Inference," in *Dimensions of Argument: Proceedings of the Second Summer Conference on Argumentation*, ed. George Ziegelmueller and Jack Rhodes

(Annandale, VA: Speech Communication Association, 1981), 773–75.

13. *Rhetoric*, 1358a. In this paper, all citations and quotations from the *Rhetoric* refer to the translation by Lane Cooper (London: Prentice Hall, 1932).
14. *Rhetoric*, 1363a–1365b.
15. The common or universal topics present a somewhat more complex problem for analysis in comparison with metaphor. It is unclear whether the universal topics function as containers for various special topics or as abstract patterns of connection (See Leff and Hewes, "Topical Invention," 780). If we accept the latter interpretation, the universal topic becomes a sort of inferential form, and its relationship to the proposition is not obvious. Furthermore, viewed as forms, these topics might be compared to the forms indicated by the tropes. Perhaps this is the sense in which Burke understands the relationship between image and idea in the Aristotelian topics. This issue, however, is extremely complex and would demand lengthy analysis. In this paper, I wish to concentrate on the structural relationships between metaphor and propositional argument in rhetoric, and so my remarks are limited to special topics or to propositions derived from universal topics.
16. Thomas Farrell, "Knowledge. Consensus and Rhetorical Theory," *Quarterly Journal of Speech* 62 (1976): 9.
17. *Rhetoric*, 1364a.
18. Loren Eiseley, "The Bird and the Machine," in *The Immense Journey* (New York: Time Inc., 1962), 130–40. I would like to thank Diane Dowdy for bringing this essay to my attention and for indicating some of the problems it poses. Ms. Dowdy is currently writing a dissertation on the rhetoric of the popular scientific essay that promises to shed considerable light on problems of the sort I have addressed in this paper.
19. Eiseley, *The Immense Journey*, 131.
20. Eiseley, *The Immense Journey*, 239.
21. Eiseley, *The Immense Journey*, 140.
22. Eiseley, *The Immense Journey*, 130.
23. Lakoff and Johnson, *Metaphors We Live By*, 193.
24. See Lakoff and Johnson, *Metaphors We Live By*, 115–222; Black, "More on Metaphor," 32–41; and Mark Johnson, introduction to *Philosophical Perspectives on Metaphor* (Minneapolis: University of Minnesota Press, 1981), 35–42.
25. I am referring here to the operations of a demonstrative system after it has been set in motion. Metaphor, however, may play an important role in establishing the

first premises of such a system. On this point, see Ernesto Grassi, "Rhetoric and Philosophy," *Philosophy and Rhetoric* 9 (1976): 200–202.

26. This effect, however, may be modified when the sequence of propositions is not presented in linear order.

Up from Theory: Or I Fought the Topoi and the Topoi Won

When I first began to study rhetoric, some forty or so years ago, the terms "substance" and "theory" occupied privileged positions in disciplinary consciousness. "Substance" referred to content or subject matter, and in this pre-postdisciplinary scheme of things, scholars were supposed to work within bounded and clearly differentiated domains of inquiry. A discipline, that is, needed to have a proper subject, and since scholarship demanded rationally refined, systematically organized abstract principles that stood above and apart from particulars, the study of an academic subject required the use of "theory." In the quasi discipline then known as speech (*requiescat in pace*), the need to get theoretical became an urgent mantra. It was regarded not only as a protection against individual biases and a means to enforce scholarly rigor, but it also seemed to open the sole path available for rhetoric to

From *Rhetoric Society Quarterly* 36 (2006): 203–11.

escape from its marginal status and attain a place of orthodox respect in the academy.

As I now review these terms and the commonplaces associated with them, they seem so quaintly misdirected and antirhetorical that I can hardly believe I once accepted them. No doubt, this change of attitude largely results from the revolution in academic fashion that has occurred during the past several decades. Because of causes centered far outside the orbit of rhetorical studies, most of us no longer think of substance, theory, or even rhetoric in the same way that we did in the days when speech departments still roamed the academic planet. But these external forces don't tell the whole story. At least some of my revisionism follows from, or at least correlates with, my own experience working inside the comparatively narrow boundaries of traditional rhetoric. So I think it might serve some purpose to reconstruct part of this experience and to consider its relevance for studying and teaching the history of rhetoric in the twenty-first century.

In the year I entered graduate school, Karl Wallace published an article entitled "The Substance of Rhetoric: Good Reasons."[1] Although I had to take some time and care to understand the specifics of Wallace's argument, its conceptual underpinnings seemed immediately clear to me. Having spent most of a semester reading about the early history of speech departments, I sensed that Wallace's article embodied a line of thought that stretched back to disciplinary origins and that proceeded as follows: In order to achieve a substantive conception of rhetoric, we would have to set aside modes, techniques, and styles of presentation and concentrate upon invention, which was the process of finding and making arguments. But many other disciplines studied argumentation, and so we needed to hit upon a distinctively rhetorical type of argument. Through most of the tradition, the topics had served as the primary source for rhetorical invention, and hence the recovery of the topics, in some form or another, represented our best hope for developing a substantive theory of rhetoric.

In the effort to resurrect topical invention, earlier scholars had adopted a variety of different strategies, all of them involving a conscious effort to adapt some aspects of classical lore to contemporary circumstances. I conceived a more straightforward foray into the historical record: The history of topical invention, I believed, had not been studied adequately, and so if the lore was examined more carefully, we might be able to discover a system of invention already in place and capable of more or less direct application to current theoretical interests.

Before too long I discovered that I had sent myself on a fool's errand. In the first place, "topical invention" proved to be an ambiguous and multifaceted concept. Topics sometimes referred to modes of inference, sometimes to aspects of the subject under consideration, sometimes to the attitudes of an audience, sometimes to types of issues, sometimes to the generic headings for rhetorical material, and sometimes to several of these alternatives. It was possible to sort out some of these strands and recognize them as coherent resources for an aspect of argumentation, but it was difficult to understand how any or all of them could provide a unified theory.

Eventually I focused on one of most common and enduring topical systems in the tradition—the attributes of the person and the act.[2] These topics were connected with a generic conception of the subject matter of rhetoric (i.e., all rhetorical cases necessarily involved people and their actions), and both the nature and the organization of these topics seemed to call for theoretical explanation. But, for the most part, the classical authors displayed little interest in theoretical issues; sometimes they modified or rearranged categories in the system, and occasionally they quarreled about small issues of classification, but mainly they treated the topics like so many tools on a shelf—as long the rhetor knew how to get hold of a topic and use it, there was not much need to fuss about abstract considerations.

The most notable exception to this tendency appears in Boethius's *De topicis differentiis*, a work that treats the topics of both rhetoric and dialectic in a relentlessly systematic and theoretical fashion. In the fourth book of this treatise, Boethius turns his attention from dialectic to rhetoric, and just as we would expect from a rigorous theorist, he begins by distinguishing the two disciplines.

The most important of these distinctions has to do with subject matter (*materia*). Dialectic, in Boethius's account, deals with theses, abstract questions that have no connection with particular circumstances. Rhetoric deals with hypotheses, questions that do entail circumstances (i.e., persons and acts). Dialectic, in other words, engages the genus of argument qua argument, while rhetoric limits itself to arguments embedded in particular cases, and this distinction in the conceptual ambit of the two makes clear their hierarchical alignment:

> For as the disciplines are distinguished from one another by the universality of the one and particularity of the other, so their Topics differ in range and restriction, because the range of dialectical Topics is greater. Since they are independent of circumstances, which produce individual cases, they are useful not only for theses but also arguments put forward in hypotheses, whose Topics, composed of circumstances, they include and range over. (1215D)[3]

This arrangement allows Boethius to contain rhetorical topics within theoretically rigorous boundaries, but he can do so only by subordinating rhetorical invention to an abstractly conceived system of dialectical argument.

Even if rhetoricians were willing to accept this humble but tidy placement of their discipline, they could hardly find much use for the topical system that Boethius produces. He reduces arguments grounded in circumstances to static categories that have no connection with the flux of circumstance, and thus his theory achieves coherence at the expense of alienation from the defining characteristic of the phenomenon being studied. His topical schematic offers little help for those who seek to practice or evaluate arguments that occur in the contingent world of rhetorical practice, and so the value of his theory seems to consist in its elegantly self-contained structure. It is a scholastic rhetoric. Once I understood the autotelic nature of Boethius's theory, its contrast with the earlier, more humanistic version of Latin rhetoric emerged with some force. The dissimilarity is striking even if we use Cicero's most technical and schematic work, the *De inventione*, as the object of comparison. In *De inventione*, Cicero classifies rhetoric as a part of politics; Boethius (perhaps consciously deviating from the antecedent work) asserts that the genus of rhetoric is discipline (*disciplina*).[4] This is the difference between viewing rhetoric as an activity conducted in public and rhetoric as a subject to be learned in school. And the significance of this distinction unobtrusively but dramatically surfaces in a passage where Cicero reflects on his critique of a rather technical point made by the Hellenistic rhetorician Hermagoras of Temnos:

> Not that I think the text-book which he wrote is very faulty, for he seems to have done well enough at arranging topics which he chose with ingenuity and care from earlier authors, and to have added something new himself; but for an orator it is a very slight thing to talk about his art, as he has done; by far the most important thing is to speak in accordance with the principles of the art, which as we all see he was wholly incapable of doing. (*De inventione* 1.8)[5]

Thus, while Cicero's treatise examines the technical apparatus of the art in great detail, he clearly regards that apparatus as equipment for use rather than as something to be learned for its own sake.

Quintilian provides an explicit justification for this perspective when he considers the placement of rhetoric among the various types of arts. One class of arts, he notes, is contemplative and based upon knowing and appreciating what they study; such arts do not call for action but only for understanding, and he calls such arts "theoretical" and cites astronomy as an example. Other arts, however, are concerned with and find their end in action, so that once the action is "performed nothing more is left to do." These arts, Quintilian tells us, are "practical," and dance is an example. Third, and finally, some arts have to do with production and achieve "their end in completion of a visible task," and painting illustrates this type. Rhetoric, in Quintilian's judgment, has theoretical and productive dimensions, but it is mainly "concerned with action; for in action it accomplishes that which it is its duty to do" (2.17.43).[6]

In book 5, chapter 10 of his *Institutes*, Quintilian deals with the topics related to the person and the act, the same subject that occupies book 4 of Boethius's *De topicis differentiis*. Like Boethius, Quintilian treats these topics in detail and at great length, and he frequently considers rather technical issues about the definition, classification, and arrangement of the elements in the system. As his analysis draws to a close, however, Quintilian adds some general remarks that reveal an entirely different attitude about the status and function of topical invention.

Having surveyed "the usual topics of proof as specified by the teachers of rhetoric," Quintilian warns that this classification does not and cannot satisfy the task of rhetorical instruction. The arguments associated with these topics are infinite, and hence it is impossible to locate and index all their "individual species." Any attempt to do so condemns the teacher to the unhappy fate of simultaneously "saying too much and yet failing to cover the whole ground" (5.10.100). In fact, Quintilian adds, the main resource for rhetorical invention arises from the specific case at hand, since "the majority of proofs are to be found in the special circumstances of individual cases and have no connexion with any other dispute" (5.10.103). These proofs are at once the strongest and the most difficult to discover since they are so embedded in particulars that general principles cannot bring them to light. Moreover, the task of deciding when and how to deploy one of these proofs also requires a situated judgment that cannot be governed by formal rules (5.10.109). Thus, rhetorical invention demands painstaking attention to the particular case and the unique circumstances associated with it, and Quintilian illustrates this point through an extended example (5.10.113–19).

Given this emphasis on the particular, why does Quintilian bother to deal with the topics at all? The reason, he explains, is that topics have their use, but it is imperative "to prevent those who have learnt these rules . . . from regarding themselves as having a perfect and absolute knowledge of the whole subject, and to make them realize that unless they acquire a thorough knowledge of the remaining points . . . , they will be the possessors of what I can only call a dumb science (*mutam quondam scientiam*)" (5.10.119). But if the topics in and of themselves are of little value, they can serve an important role as part of the educational process. Just as gymnastic training prepares the body for physical performance, so can exercises in topical reasoning prepare the mind for verbal performance. The goal is not mechanistic application of the theoretical apparatus to particular cases, but the cultivation of an ability to encounter cases as circumstances demand:

> It is only by constant practice that we can secure that, just as the hands of the musician even though his eyes be turned elsewhere, produce bass, treble or intermediate notes by force of habit, so the thought of

> the orator should suffer no delay owing to the variety and number of possible arguments, but that the latter should present themselves uncalled and, just as letters and syllables require no thought on the part of a writer, so arguments should spontaneously follow the thought of the orator (5.10.125).

Viewed from this perspective, topics are not theoretical principles. They are precepts that have potential application to actual cases, and their most important function is as a training device. Proper use of the topics helps develop a capacity for arguing in precisely those situations where theory offers the least guidance. Consequently, the effort to discover or produce a theory of topics seems totally misdirected, and more generally, the whole program of turning rhetoric into a theoretical discipline has lost it appeal. To train rhetoricians as theorists is much like attempting to train basketball coaches not to pay attention to the game as it is actually played but to prepare them to produce treatises on the theory of the jump shot.

The story I have just told is personal, and its details are peculiar to my own interests and experiences. But unless I am very badly deceived, the general outline of the plot corresponds with a good many other stories that rhetoricians have to tell nowadays. As the reports from the ARS Conference in Evanston and the other papers in this issue demonstrate, a major shift in the rhetoric wind is in progress. The terms "substance" and "theory" are being revised and/or displaced, and terms like "performance" and "action" are gaining prominence. As the theoretical impulse fades, interest in teaching has intensified both as a means of preparing students for practice and as a form of practice in and of itself. And all these developments reflect and encourage a reassessment of the history of rhetoric that has gradually placed more stress on social/political developments or on teaching traditions than on theoretical constructs.

In some respects, these changes have had a direct and obvious impact on the way that I teach the history of rhetoric. Aristotle's *Rhetoric*, the central text of the theoretical paradigm, receives less attention than it once did, and the Sophists and Isocrates get more time and respect. Cicero, Quintilian, and other authors in the Latin tradition are the subject of a separate course. In all courses, I include more texts of speeches, plays, and other literary forms so that students can study rhetoric-in-use along with the canonical authors of the "theory" tradition. I am also now more interested in handbooks such as *ad Alexandrum*, the *ad Herennium*, and progymnasmata recently translated by George Kennedy, since they provide us with the best information available about how rhetoric was actually taught in Greco-Roman antiquity.

These amendments, however, are not fundamental, and the outward appearance of the classical rhetoric courses I teach has not changed greatly over the years. Yet, as I have explained, my attitude about the subject has changed quite dramatically, and so have my research interests. I wonder whether this is consistent. Is it reasonable to teach most of the same texts after the fall of the theoretical paradigm? Is it enough to reinterpret these texts and to alter the relative weight assigned to them? Or is a more basic and dramatic change necessary to break from the inertia of the older pattern?

Recently, I have begun to think that these questions, centered on the way we teach particular courses, may not take us to the heart of the matter. Our key problem might reflect institutional arrangements rather than individual practices. If we view the history of rhetoric as a teaching tradition in which we now actively participate, we conceive our subject in a way that runs against the bias of the contemporary research university where teaching and research are put into separate and very unequal bins. And if we think that our tradition seeks to promote the faculty of doing things with language,[7] we find ourselves struggling against the current of a curriculum designed to promote knowing rather than doing. Even the most radical alterations in particular courses can have little effect in dealing with problems at this level.

So perhaps the main task before us is to establish a curriculum for rhetorical studies. Some years ago, David Fleming observed that the interdisciplinary revival of rhetoric as a research area had not been accompanied by a revival of rhetoric as a discipline.[8] We are now witnessing some effort in that direction. Leading figures in composition studies are urging their colleges to generate "a robust curriculum" in rhetoric.[9] Rhetoricians in departments of English and communication are talking together more often than in the recent past, and some of this talk has raised the possibility of a rhetoric discipline that crosses (or even erases) departmental lines. At several universities, independent programs in rhetoric are struggling to the surface, and the concept of "rhetoric education" has gained currency as part of an effort to open curricular space for rhetoric.[10] As these developments unfold, revisionist attitudes toward the history of rhetoric just might blend into an effort to revise the current academic environment.

NOTES

1. Karl Wallace, "The Substance of Rhetoric: Good Reasons," *Quarterly Journal of Speech* 49 (1963): 239–49. Wallace's position is further developed in two later papers: "Topoi and the Problems of Invention," *Quarterly Journal of Speech* 58 (1972): 387–95; and "The Fundamentals of Rhetoric," in *The Prospect of Rhetoric: Report of the National Developmental Project*, ed. Lloyd F. Bitzer and Edwin Black (Englewood Cliffs, NJ: Prentice-Hall, 1971), 3–20. These papers develop issues that already had a long history in the field of speech, and to appreciate this background, see E. L. Hunt, "Adding Substance to Form in Public Speaking," *Quarterly Journal of Speech* 1 (1915): 185–93; Hoyt Hudson, "Can We Modernize the Study of Invention?," *Quarterly Journal of Speech* 7 (1921): 325–34; "The Field of Speech," *Quarterly Journal of Speech* 9 (1923): 167–80.
2. For more detail about these topics, see my paper "The Topics of Argumentative Invention in Latin Rhetorical Theory from Cicero to Boethius," *Rhetorica* 1 (1983): 23–44.
3. Eleonore Stump, trans., *Boethius' "De topicis differentiis": Translated with Notes and Essays on the Text* (Ithaca, NY: Cornell University Press, 1978).
4. See Stump's note in *Boethius' "De topicis differentiis"*, 1207B3, 143.
5. Cicero, *De inventione*, trans. H. M. Hubbell in the Loeb edition (London: William Heinemann, 1960).
6. All passages from Quintilian are translated by H. E. Butler in the Loeb edition, *Instituto oratoria of Quintilian* (London: William Heinemann, 1960).
7. I borrow the phrase "doing things with language" from Cheryl Geisler, "How Ought We to Understand the Concept of Rhetorical Agency? Report from the ARS," *Rhetoric Society Quarterly* 34 (2004): 9–18.
8. David Fleming, "Rhetoric as a Course of Study," *College English* 61 (1998): 169–91.

9. Andrea Lunsford, "Afterwords: A Dialogue," *Rhetoric Society Quarterly* 34 (2004): 56.
10. See Joseph Petraglia and Deepika Bahri, eds., *The Realms of Rhetoric: The Prospects for Rhetoric Education* (Albany: SUNY Press, 2003).

The Habitation of Rhetoric

The problem I want to engage is both fundamental and ancient. When Cicero wrote his *De inventione*, it already had had a long history. Yet his comments on that history still retain a lively theoretical interest for students of rhetoric and argumentation. Consequently, they can serve as an appropriate text for introducing and locating the issues addressed in this paper.

As part of the standard *accessus* to the technical precepts of the art, Cicero considers the definition of rhetoric and its placement relative to other disciplines. One aspect of this task is to understand the material of rhetoric, by which he means "those subjects with which the art and power of rhetoric are concerned." He then explains that "some have thought

From *Argument and Critical Practice: Proceedings of the Fifth AFA/SCA Conference on Argumentation*, ed. Joe Wenzel (Annandale, VA: Speech Communication Association, 1987), 1–8.

that there are more and some less of these subjects. To cite one example, Gorgias of Leontini, almost the earliest teacher of oratory, held that the orator could speak better than anyone else on all subjects. Apparently he assigned to the profession a vast—and in fact infinite material. Aristotle, on the other hand, who did much to improve and adorn this art, thought that the function of the orator was concerned with three classes of subjects, the epideictic, the deliberative, and the judicial." This commentary leads immediately to a judgment: "According to my opinion, at least, the art and faculty of the orator must be thought of as concerned with this threefold material."[1] This judgment, moreover, is consistent with Cicero's earlier definition of rhetoric as a "part of political science" (*civilis scientiae partem*).[2] That is, Cicero here assumes that the Aristotelian genres exhaust the boundaries of political discourse.

This assumption becomes more explicit in the next section of the text, where Cicero considers another aspect of the tradition. The Hellenistic rhetorician Hermagoras of Temnos divides the material of rhetoric into two types of issues, the special and the general. The former (often called the hypothesis) refers to controversies that involve specific circumstances, and Cicero identifies such issues with the subjects indicated by the three Aristotelian genres. The latter (often called the thesis) refers to disputations about abstract issues unconnected with specific circumstances—such questions as "Is there any good but honor?" or "Can the senses be trusted?" Hermagoras, Cicero argues, errs in assigning such issues to rhetoric, since "everyone understands that these questions are far removed from the business of the orator."[3] The scope of rhetoric, then, is limited to the hypothesis, which, in turn, draws its materials from the conduct of civic affairs.

This position obviously arises from a schematic and oversimplified version of the tradition. In fact, Aristotle's conception of the matter is much more complicated and ambiguous than its representation in *De inventione* suggests. And as Cicero realized in his later works, the whole issue demands careful inquiry and sophisticated reflection on the tradition rather than mere schematization.[4] Nevertheless, whatever the defects of our text, its bald simplicity has symptomatic value. The dichotomy between a "restrained rhetoric" and a "liberated rhetoric," sketched here in such consciously emphatic terms, recurs throughout the later history of rhetorical theory, normally in forms that are better disguised though no less potent. Certainly, as he embodies this dichotomy by reference to the opposition between "neo-Aristotelian" and Gorgianic (or "neosophistic") approaches, Cicero anticipates one of the main problems lurking just beneath the murky surface of twentieth-century rhetorical scholarship.

Before turning to these contemporary applications, however, I want to add one more note about the text. *De inventione*, consistent with most other rhetorical treatises, deals with the scope and location of the art as though these issues raised problems of strictly logical classification. But a slight adjustment of perspective might lead us to view the matter as a rhetorical operation, as an exercise in metonymy. In moving through one side of this metonymic process, the neo-Aristotelians regard rhetoric as a thing contained; it is an art domiciled within the territory of politics and domesticated by this political confinement. Moving in the opposite direction, the neosophists attempt to liberate rhetoric by conceiving it as a container, or, more properly, as a containing force. Unfettered by any particular subject matter, rhetoric becomes a power that ranges across the entire domain of human discourse, containing whatever matter it encounters. Since it is pure force, it is a container that constantly shifts its own configuration as it responds to circumstances, social interests, or the free play of linguistic whimsy.

In their modern incarnations, these two approaches yield results so different that their opposition seems total. Yet, viewed within a somewhat broader context, both share at least one important characteristic. While neo-Aristotelians seek to constrain the range of the rhetorical process and the neo-Sophists seek to expand it, both alike center attention in process. Rhetoric is either process confined within some larger domain from which it draws substance, or it is the unbounded action of process itself. In either case, rhetoric per se is not substantive, since it is a form of action that generates or manages material without ever resting in a material embodiment. This attenuation between activity and production is obvious in respect to the neosophistic position, but it may seem puzzling or even paradoxical when attributed to neo-Aristotelianism, since that position is so clearly centered around the oration itself. Nevertheless, especially when the interest is dominantly critical rather than pedagogical, neo-Aristotelianism tends to bracket the oratorical text as a product with an integrity of its own. The oration simply establishes a referent for studying contexts or for locating processes which are to be gauged in terms of their extrinsic effect. The text becomes a medium or an instrument rather than a substantive product.[5]

Consequently, the metonymic strategies in neo-Aristotelianism and neosophistic yield diametrically opposed conceptions of the scope of rhetoric, but they both encourage a similar preoccupation with action as opposed to substance. When either of these extremes is isolated, or when the two are set in unmediated opposition, the result is to weaken or sever the connection between action and production.

Throughout most of the history of the discipline, certain forces have militated against this kind of metonymic reduction. Most obviously, there is the pedagogical tradition that links rhetorical scholarship with the teaching of composition. So long as that connection holds, the tendency of abstract definition is checked against the concrete problems involved in teaching students how to *make* discourses, and it is only in our century that rhetorical scholarship has become dearly dissociated from its pedagogical orientation. More important, however, amid its technical clutter, the pedagogical tradition also houses a humane philosophy concerning practical discourse and its implications. This humanistic impulse traces itself in a line that moves from Isocrates to Cicero and Quintilian and from there forward to the Renaissance; its integrity consists in the effort to balance the aesthetics of production and the requirements of ethical action within the texture of practical discourse. Perhaps the key term informing this ideal is propriety, the flexible measure that unifies the elements of a discourse even as it adjusts them to the fluid ethical and political contexts in which it appears. Approached from this angle, a rhetorical discourse can be substantive, not because rhetoric commands a particular subject matter, but because the discourse commands attention as a thing made. Rhetorical discourse, thus, assumes an ontological solidity different in degree but not in kind from the products of the poetic art.

Humanistic rhetoric entailed a delicate balance that was always difficult to understand, let alone realize. And it always remained open to attack because of the way it blurred categories by treating them not as stable abstract entities, but as principles manifested in production and practical action. Hence, the humanistic perspective often was eclipsed by more technical conceptions of rhetoric and by more purely theoretical schemes for conceiving the placement of the arts in general. The most dramatic of these setbacks occurred during the Enlightenment, when the mainstream of philosophical thought collapsed the space needed to sustain the humanistic position. The Enlightenment liberated the aesthetic from the perturbations of all other forms of experience—set it in a zone of free and autonomous experience where it was to remain innocent of any prudential or teleological concerns. From this perspective, oratory was an inherently dubious business, since it conflated the aesthetic with matters of practical interest. More generally, Ciceronian rhetorical philosophy became a pseudophilosophy, a jumble of category errors which undermined the necessary separation among ethical judgment, the operation of the intellect, and the impulse of the artistic spirit.[6]

One of Jacques Derrida's best-known principles is that erasures always leave their traces. In this instance, however, we should remember that traces are often difficult to find and that erasures are sometimes effective in removing items from cultural awareness. That is, we need to understand current rhetorical scholarship against the background of what the Enlightenment blocked from direct perception. By the dawn of this century, oratory and composition had lost respectability within the academy, and rhetoric, insofar as it existed at all, was reduced to the mechanics of elocution or the taxonomic classification of tropes and figures. The humanistic conception of rhetoric was not simply rejected; it had been forgotten, or at best, distorted through the alien lens of Enlightenment thought. It was inconceivable that substantive art could arise from local adjustments to practical circumstance. Thus, subsequent efforts to revive rhetoric proceeded without much regard for the density of rhetorical products. The ballast that had kept premodern rhetoric close to the ground had been jettisoned, and the way was opened for the free action of the metonymic process.

In that twentieth-century innovation called the American Department of Speech, the history of rhetorical scholarship is, in considerable measure, the story of competing metonymic perspectives. The general direction of this conflict is reasonably clear; it is a movement from the neo-Aristotelian toward the neosophistic pole, from rhetoric contained to rhetoric as container. The details of this story are well known, and I want to pause here only long enough to indicate how they adhere to the pattern I have just sketched. And mindful of the contemporary interest in narrative, I will try to tell the story as a story.

Once upon a time, but not very long ago, there was a poor waif named Rhetoric. Though once the ruler of the arts, he had been banished from Europe and had found an academic home only in a new and unstable fiefdom known as the American Department of Speech. The people who lived in this fiefdom were concerned to define its boundaries so that it would not be annexed by powerful neighbors. Most of all, they feared the Duchy of English, which might try to enslave Rhetoric and commandeer his sections of the public speaking course. The great lords of English, moreover, disdained Rhetoric, since they regarded his teachings as impure and his bearing as too ordinary and insufficiently handsome. And so the leaders in the fiefdom of Speech, who were later known as the neo-Aristotelians, undertook a defense of Rhetoric which celebrated his individuality and modest respectability. They did so in words that echoed the sentiments of Cicero's *De inventione*. Rhetoric, they maintained, was confined to a particular kind of discourse—the political oration, and the rhetorical perspective was "patently single." Rhetoric cared not a whit for "permanence, nor yet . . . beauty." Instead, he was preoccupied 'with effect" and taught us to regard a "speech as a communication to a specific audience."[7]

As it turned out, the lords of English were concerned with their own squabbles and had no time to invade other territories. So the fiefdom of Speech survived and held its turf. But eventually it suffered from its own internal dissensions. A new generation of scholars arose and challenged the authority of the neo-Aristotelians. They complained that the older generation had committed the high crime of being atheoretical, and besides, it had neglected forms of discourse other than the oration. They broadcast these charges in all the journals of the fiefdom and gradually won adherents. Rhetoric was no longer viewed just as a modestly respectable actor in the political arena. He now seemed a great and powerful leader of the arts whose force had to be acknowledged in all the fiefdoms of the academy.

The point of this story is nicely summarized by comparing Donald Bryant's two well-known definitions of rhetoric. The first formulation appeared in 1953 and designated rhetoric as "the rationale of informative and suasory discourse." The amended version, published twenty years later, defined rhetoric 'as the rationale of the informative and suasory in discourse.'[8] The shift here is from a kind of discourse to a dimension in discourse, from an emphasis on certain products to an emphasis on a certain kind of activity. Though Bryant remained conservative in his attachment to public address, this rearrangement of priorities implicitly indicated a broader and more theoretical conception of rhetoric, and others have pushed this position in more radical directions. Much the same kind of progression has occurred within the area of argumentation. As Cox and Willard observe, "Historical-critical studies of particular orators, debates, or documents—long the dominant focus of argumentation scholars—have been gradually replaced by philosophical and theoretical examinations of the field's assumptions and methods." In the process, argument itself has come to be viewed as "a distinct form of human communication"[9]—that is, as a kind of activity that transcends any particular area of application. Moreover, this tendency in our discipline reflects the more general developments in the interdisciplinary revival of rhetoric. LaCapra, after surveying a number of apparently disparate forms of this revival, locates their common ground in "the idea that rhetoric is a dimension of all language use rather than a separable set of uses or a realm of discourse."[10]

Consistent with this orientation, the recent scholarship has centered around theories, models, and organizing conceptions that generally inform the process of arguing and persuading. The number of alternatives found here is striking—cognitive processing, constructivist psychology, narrative, ideology, cultural theory, symbolic interactionism, and the like.[11] Yet all of them are informed by a common interest in conceiving rhetoric as an activity conducted at the level of discourse. This interest implies a tension between process and product, and in the earlier phases of this development, that tension manifests itself rather forcefully.

Two entries in the report of the 1970 National Developmental Project on Rhetoric illustrate my point. In his essay "Rhetorical Studies for the Modern World," Samuel Becker presents a running critique of traditional scholarship in rhetoric and public address. Becker argues that "single message encounters" are an inadequate basis for drawing conclusions about how messages influence audiences. Consequently, he concludes that "our traditional concept of the message has severely limited usefulness for understanding contemporary communication. The emphasis of rhetorical studies should probably remain upon the message, but we must define message in a more fruitful way, in a way that is more descriptive of what man as receiver is exposed to, rather than what man as source creates."[12] Wayne Brockriede supports and extends this line of argument. He emphatically rejects "the idea that the most appropriate unit of rhetoric is the 'speech,' a one-shot attempt at persuasion, the idea that a rhetorical transaction is bounded by a speaker's introduction and his conclusion." In his view, Becker "argues convincingly that the speech is not an appropriate unit of analysis." Moreover, this position cannot be "assimilated as a minor modification of a traditional concept of rhetorical communication. It is revolutionary."[13]

Hence, we achieve a nearly total, a revolutionary, disjunction between the study of the rhetorical process and a serious interest in any particular rhetorical product. This sort of argument rarely appears in the more recent literature; but I suspect the reason is that the issue seems resolved. Neo-Aristotelianism is now only a historical curiosity, not a live option, and the placement of rhetoric at the abstract level of process has become a largely unconscious but well-established orthodoxy.

Yet I think that the issue calls for reconsideration. The position outlined by Brockriede and Becker has real force when applied to neo-Aristotelianism and its presupposition that rhetoric deals solely with extrinsic effect. If rhetoric concerns itself only with the way auditors process "messages," then attention to isolated "messages" has limited utility. Viewed from a broader perspective, however, the neo-Aristotelian doctrine itself appears as an aberration negatively informed by the Enlightenment's antirhetorical presuppositions.

In this important respect, the position described by Becker and Brockriede is not revolutionary. Rather, it reverses the focus of attention within an existing frame of reference and corrects the older position by driving its assumptions to their ultimate conclusion. The neo-Aristotelian conception of rhetoric is largely a defensive gesture which accommodates the strict dichotomy between fine and practical arts simply by yielding to its demands. Since it is a practical art, rhetoric produces nothing intrinsically interesting, and so its products offer no more than an occasion for studying a process. In another intellectual environment, it might seem apparent that the power of a practical art would emerge from a qualitative study of its products. But the burden of the Enlightenment forces attention toward purely extrinsic standards, toward the process triggered by the product. From here it takes only a small step to bracket the product altogether. Becker's term "message" captures this reduction perfectly, since, in a way wholly consistent with the neo-Aristotelian technical psychosis, it suggests a concern for what is in and what is conveyed by a discourse without much concern for the discourse itself. A message is an abstracted thing, distanced from the voice of the speaker or the hand of the writer, embedded only at the point of its impact. Ironically, the neo-Aristotelian commitment to the particular perfects itself in the abstract study of message processing.

Brockriede clearly summarizes these tendencies when he asserts that the "speech is not an appropriate unit for analysis." On its surface, this position seems curious. Presumably, a critical study of one of Lincoln's speeches, motivated by an interest in the design of the speech per se, engages an inappropriate unit for rhetorical analysis. Imagine, if you will, a poetic theorist arguing that a Shakespearean sonnet is not an appropriate unit for poetic analysis.

Perhaps, however, the analogy makes Brockriede's point seem not so curious. Even the most ardent apologist for rhetorical art must admit that rhetoric's status as a productive discipline is much less apparent than that of poetic. The basic terminology associated with the two arts aptly illustrates the difference. In one instance, we have the terms "poet," "poem," and "poetic," which nicely distinguish the maker, the thing made, and the process of making. In the case of rhetoric, as Bryant has observed, "We are in something of a mess."[14] The term rhetor serves as analogue for poet, as does rhetoric for poetic. But we have no word that indicates a rhetorical product in the generic sense that poem designates a poetic product. Instead, we are forced to refer to some species of rhetorical artifact—an oration, an editorial, or a pamphlet.

This lexical gap is hardly an accident. On most accounts, the distinctive feature of the rhetorical art is the way that it embeds itself in and responds to specific, public circumstances. Moreover, in accepting persuasion as its goal, rhetorical discourse strives to efface its status as a constructed thing, since it calls for prudential judgments rather than judgments about its own integrity as a product. As it blends into the fabric of events and actions, such discourse seems to become a form of action, an embodiment of processes immediately connected with the referent of the discourse. By contrast, the poetic suspension of disbelief weakens this connection and focuses attention more sharply on the fabric of the discourse itself. Thus, if as McKeon has done, we group rhetoric and poetic together as practical/productive arts, they gravitate toward different margins in the category. Rhetoric emerges most clearly at the practical margin, because of its emphasis on efficient cause and on the exercise of productive powers. Poetry emerges at the productive margin, because of its emphasis on material cause and its obvious concern with the objects produced by the art "as composite wholes."[15] This contrast suggests the problematic status of rhetoric as a productive art and the difficulty involved in attaching rhetoric to distinctive products of its own making.

Consequently, the current tendency to view rhetoric as coherent only at the global level of discursive process reflects inherent problems and not just confusions associated with the recent history of the discipline. Yet current theory too often overcomes these problems simply by refusing to acknowledge their existence. Moreover, such innocence survives only through adherence to a systematic and fundamentally antirhetorical dichotomy between the prudential and the aesthetic. A far richer conception of rhetoric, especially with regard to its argumentative function, arises from the effort to confront the problem and grapple with the ambiguous relationships between action and production.

At this point, I hope to have shown that the placement of rhetoric is not merely an ancient topos but a persistent and fundamental issue. The problem initially surfaces in terms of categories that define rhetoric's place within the orbit of human arts and activities, but the latent territorial imagery involved here encourages a metonymic perspective. In turn, the metonymic process yields a dichotomy between rhetoric as an art contained within some substantive domain or rhetoric as a power that ranges over various domains. The epistemological implications of this division are relatively straightforward. From the contained perspective of neo-Aristotelianism, rhetoric tends to become a domestic art that arranges and communicates the materials of the domain which subsumes it. From the liberated perspective of neosophistic, rhetoric tends to become a generative force actively engaged in the acquisition and formation of knowledge. Both perspectives commonly stress the nature of rhetoric as process or activity and deflect attention from its relationship to finished products. Once recognized, this bias in the metonymic process leads us to a second question about the "placement" of rhetoric. We are forced to consider not just the domain of rhetoric, but the level of its manifestation. Is the habitation of rhetoric found at the level of discourse per se or at the level of a discourse? Does rhetoric exist only as an abstract activity or does it also exist in concrete embodiments? As the terms "manifestation" and "existence" imply, these questions have an ontological rather than an epistemological bearing.

As I have just framed it, this ontological issue implies a departure from previous attempts to locate the "substance of rhetoric." In the familiar tradition that proceeds from Hoyt Hudson through Karl Wallace, substance is found in the argumentative or inventional aspect of the rhetorical process.[16] The alternative I am now suggesting defines rhetorical discourses as substantive in themselves. The substance of rhetoric, that is, does not arise from processes attached to the logical, ethical, or psychological coordinates of discourse; instead it arises from the way such processes congeal within a particular rhetorical artifact. On this view, the essence of rhetoric becomes the constructed rhetorical thing-in-itself.

Yet, for reasons outlined above, even when we set Enlightenment prejudices to the side, the task of understanding polemic discourse as "substantive" raises some exceedingly difficult problems. To approach these problems, we must develop a better-refined conception of how action and production interrelate in practical discourse, and to accomplish this end, we are faced with a reconception of the basic relationships among persuasion, argument, and aesthetics.

Obviously, these matters are far too complex to be resolved in this presentation, but it does seem to me that the elements needed for the reconstruction already exist in the current literature. The defect in that literature, from my perspective, is that it divides itself into two arenas—the one concerned with the linkage between persuasion and argument, and the other concerned with persuasion and aesthetics. The two remain largely unconnected with one another, and hence a full synthesis has yet to emerge. In order to illustrate this problem and to suggest a possible resolution, I now want to tum to the first study in Paul Ricoeur's important book *The Rule of Metaphor*. Despite the complexity and erudition of that study, its main argument clearly reveals the imbalance that occurs when modernist assumptions about aesthetics are corrected without reference to recent thought concerning argumentation. At the same time, however, Ricoeur connects poetry with ontology in a way that suggests an important expansion of current thought about rhetorical argument.

In general, Ricoeur seeks to establish the ontological significance of metaphor. He does so by tracing its operation at its various levels of manifestation–the word, the sentence, and the discourse (i.e., the poem, narrative, essay, etc.). As analysis moves through each of these stages, metaphor assumes increasing potency, until, at the hermeneutic level of discourse, it becomes the prime vehicle for redescribing reality. Yet, for Ricoeur, metaphor does not come to rest at this final level, since its place, "its most intimate abode, is neither name, nor sentence, nor even discourse, but the copula of the verb to be."[17] In short, the power of metaphor consists in its capacity to align the different levels of discourse while connecting discourse itself to the contexts in which it appears. And as it effects this extraordinary negotiation, metaphor becomes the nexus between language and world that is basic to all our ontological conceptions.

His first study presents an extended analysis of this conception as it applies to Aristotle's thought. This analysis requires consideration of both the *Rhetoric* and the *Poetics*, the two loci of his theory of metaphor. On Ricoeur's account, Aristotle assigns a single operation to metaphor in both domains; it consistently works to transfer meaning. Yet it functions differently in the two arts, and the difference follows from the goals proper to each.[18] Ultimately, this distinction leads Ricoeur to affirm the ontological solidity of poetic discourse while denying a similar status to rhetorical discourse.

The goal of poetic is mimesis, and all poetic discourse must find direction from this mimetic function. Thus, all dements of the poetic art cohere in service to this single, overarching goal. Moreover, these elements—*muthos* (plot), character, *lexis* (diction), thought, spectacle, and melody—are themselves placed in a hierarchical order, since *muthos* structures the other five in respect to their poetic operation. *Muthos*, then, is the fulcrum of the poetic act; it is the principle that organizes the other aspects of the act into a coherent internal form, while it simultaneously draws the whole apparatus toward its mimetic goal. The relationship between *muthos* and mimesis is intimate, and the complex function of *muthos* holds sense and reference together within the fabric of the poetic text. The plot, in other words, retains its integrity as a linguistic product even as it sustains reference to the world that extends beyond its self-constituted limits. As it thus wavers constructively between submission to the reality of human action and the creative action of "poetry as such," *muthos* imparts an ontological density to poetic discourse.[19] The poem, like the metaphor, both is and is not "real," and yet always remains like the real.

In the case of the *Rhetoric*, Ricoeur cannot discover any analogous principle of complex structural integrity. The goal of rhetoric is persuasion, and its proper habitat is the arena of political power. Within this space, discourse is neither free to develop its own possibilities nor subject to the philosophical demand for truth. Hence, in Ricoeur's view, Aristotle's purpose is to domesticate or institutionalize rhetoric,[20] and he does so by devising a means whereby philosophy can "watch over rhetoric."[21] To achieve this purpose, Aristotle constructs a theory of probable reasoning which delimits the operation of rhetorical discourse and which, through the link with dialectic, places rhetoric in some contact with first philosophy. In this way, Aristotle finds a point of equilibrium between the conflicting claims of power and truth.[22]

Yet, as Ricoeur understands the matter, this equilibrium is fragile and incapable of sustaining a coherent realm of discourse. Owing to its connection with common opinion, rhetoric cannot become a purely formal discipline, and its content sprawls throughout the entire range of human affairs. Thus, the rhetorical art seems doomed by an "overburdening content" that leaves its elements scattered and uncoordinated.[23] This problem manifests itself most obviously when Ricoeur considers the rhetorical function of metaphor.

That function is difficult to apprehend, since the connection between style and argument in the *Rhetoric* is rather tenuous. Whereas, in poetry, form and meaning blend in a way similar to sculpture, the public use of speech encourages a dissociation between style and proof. Manner in oratory appears "extrinsic" and "variable." For this reason, the devices of style in rhetoric require special adaptation to the larger purposes of the art; they cannot develop according to their own impulses, but must respond to probative ends which they do not shape. Metaphor, in this context, does not generate contact between discourse and world, but is bent in the direction of "creating the right impression." This process, Ricoeur explains, entails its own complexities, and it does involve a certain cognitive element. Metaphor and the other aspects of *lexis* enter into rhetoric as a manifestation of a kind of thought concerned not with proof alone but with proof relative to a hearer.[24] Yet Ricoeur holds that this persuasive function of metaphor exists in a state of unresolved tension with the requirements of proof, and hence rhetorical metaphor becomes something added to rather than embedded within the discursive formations of the art.

This tension reveals the divided condition of the rhetorical art as a whole and accounts for its incapacity to describe or generate discourses that preserve an independent integrity. Moreover, Ricoeur implies that this defect is inherent in rhetoric per se and not the result of Aristotle's particular construction of the art.

> The lack of consistency in the link between a treatise on argumentation and a treatise on style reveals contradictions within the very project of persuasion. Set between two limits exterior to it—logic and violence—rhetoric oscillates between its two constitutive poles—proof and persuasion. When persuasion frees itself from the concern for proof, it is carried away by the desire to seduce and please; and style itself ceases to be the "face" (figure) that expresses and reveals the body, and becomes an ornament in the cosmetic sense of the word. But this possibility was written into the origins the rhetorical project.[25]

To sum up Ricoeur's argument, it is apparent that poetic holds an ontologically privileged status because of its capacity to connect the resources of language with our fundamental experience of life in the world. Poetic accomplishes this fusion through the mediating force of *muthos*, an element of the poetic process that simultaneously attunes the internal constituents of poetic discourse and directs them toward the final goal of mimesis. Rhetoric, however, is a divided business, since its goal—persuasion—entails the seemingly incompatible demands of objective proof and aesthetic appeal. Lacking a principle that would coordinate these elements, rhetoric fails to achieve ontological significance at the level of discourse.

The main flaw in this analysis requires little explanation before this audience. Although Ricoeur carefully distinguishes between the rhetorical and poetic functions of style, he is curiously unaware of any functional distinction between argumentation and apodeictic proof. For him, rhetorical proof is little more than formal logic in mufti. As a consequence, he couples a strikingly postmodern defense of metaphor and poetry with an outmoded interpretation of Aristotle's *Rhetoric*[26] and a general view of the relationship between logic and argument that slights the main developments in the scholarship over the past three decades.[27]

Nevertheless, when Ricoeur notes the tenuous connection between argument and style in Aristotle's *Rhetoric*, he certainly stands on firm ground. Moreover, the same problem persists in the recent scholarship, where, as the contrast between Perelman and Group Mu indicates, the two aspects of the tradition sometimes have been severed completely from one another. Thus, I believe that Ricoeur accurately diagnoses the main obstacle to a conception of rhetorical discourse as substantive. Moreover, once we abandon his questionable distinction between proof and persuasion, his method suggests how we might resolve this problem.

Ricoeur observes that rhetorical style achieves its distinctive characteristics because of the way it is attracted to the goal of persuasion. Rhetorical *lexis*, that is, responds to the requirements of proof relative to a specific group of auditors and a specific set of public circumstances. It thus must balance the mode of expression against the occasion, the subject, and the interests of those who render judgment. In the terms of classical humanism, the point of balance is called decorum or propriety, and the flexible standard of decorum becomes the measure for assessing the rhetorical quality of expression.

Recent conceptions of argumentation exhibit a similar concern for proof in relation to specific circumstances and audiences. To cite just one example, Blair and Johnson distinguish argumentation from the logic of implication precisely because argument presupposes interlocutors, finds its end in persuasion, and develops "against the background of heterogeneity of point of view and of other arguments."[28] Conceived in this way, persuasion and proof are not antithetical, but rather persuasion is intimately and necessarily connected with one important type of proof—the proof that operates in public deliberation. Likewise, persuasion does not function in a way that is external to the subject, but as part of an adaptive mechanism vital to any reasonable understanding of public events themselves. Consequently, formal deductive logic cannot watch over or control the argumentative practice, since its abstracted principles have "little light to cast on the appropriate standards of argument."[29] Instead, these standards arise from the historically grounded context of argument and the community of interlocutors involved in the deliberative process.[30]

This flexible, socially grounded, and audience-centered conception of argumentative proof demands that arguers exercise a form of balanced judgment. In this important sense, argumentative practice seems to engage principles that are strikingly similar to the traditional notion of decorum or propriety. Yet, to my knowledge, no contemporary theorist has invoked these terms in respect to argumentation. The reason, I suspect, is that, in its contemporary usage, decorum has become associated exclusively with style. But this restriction is not necessary, and as Wesley Trimpi has shown, premodern rhetorical theory grants a much wider application for decorum—one that embraces cognitive as well as stylistic concerns.[31] The grounds for this broader conception have a strong bearing on current argumentative theory and its relation to rhetorical style in the sense that Ricoeur describes it.

Rhetorical discourse occurs in contexts where judgments must be rendered about specific matters of communal interest. Such judgments normally invoke the general principles that categorize and direct our response to public events. Yet the application of these principles is open to question, and, in their abstract state, they are insufficient to allow for an adequate decision in any given case. Moreover, these principles themselves are subject to revision in light of our concrete experience. Consequently, rhetorical judgment cannot suffer reduction to strictly formal or methodical procedures. It always engages qualitative considerations that balance the particulars of occasion and circumstance against the more general rubrics that inform our thinking.[32] This adjustment, moreover, does not simply concern the external form of a persuasive discourse, but also enters into our very mode of understanding the subjects of such discourse. In other words, both understanding and representation entail a mediation between concrete circumstances and principles of intelligibility. Moreover, whenever discourse addresses complex circumstances and heterogeneous interests, a clear separation between expressive form and argumentative content becomes virtually impossible. Our mode of representing situations and our assessment of their nature and moral significance coalesce within the structure of rhetorical judgment. And, in fact, the most skillfully constructed rhetorical discourses blend these elements so as to render them indistinguishable. This artistic skill is neither cosmetic nor deceptive. Instead, it reflects the unity of thought and expression necessary for the comprehension and direction of life in the pluralistic space of public experience.

Decorum is the term that best describes the process of mediation and balance connected with qualitative judgment. It is the principle of decorum that allows us to comprehend a situation as a whole, to locate its meaning within a context, and to translate this understanding into a discursive form that becomes an incentive to action. As it applies to the rhetorical act, decorum orders the elements of a discourse and rounds them out into a coherent product relative to the occasion. That is, it works to align the stylistic and argumentative features of the discourse within a unified structure while adjusting the whole structure to the context from which the discourse arises and to which it responds. The locus of decorum always depends upon the particular case, and so, although it directs artistic production, it is incapable of being formulated in terms of abstract, artistic precepts. It manifests itself only as embodied in particular discourses, and it governs the integrity of the discourse as a whole. Decorum, then, is a principle of action that accounts for the adaptive power of persuasive discourse, and it also establishes a flexible standard for assessing the intrinsic merit of a rhetorical product. Thus, decorum functions as the rhetorical counterpart of poetic *muthos*, for like *muthos*, decorum mediates between internal sense and external reference in a certain kind of discursive product, and it does so in a way that maintains a consistent link with the subjects and goals proper to the domain where it operates.

Finally, referring back to the point from which this analysis began, decorum seems a peculiarly rhetorical principle because of its ambiguous placement between action and production. Decorum has no substantive stability across situations, since it represents a constantly moving process of negotiation. It is, as Trimpi says, "an activity, rather than a possession, of the consciousness."[33] Nevertheless, the achievement of decorum in a given situation establishes a point of maximum balance and stability. At the global level, decorum is pure process, but its local manifestations are products that display a powerful solidity. So also is rhetoric a universal activity that finds its habitation only in the particular. Since it is the art of the persuasive dimension in discourse, rhetoric finds no rest at the theoretical level. Its adaptive genius cannot be circumscribed by the fixed boundaries of theoretical constructions. As a form of activity, it must retain the freedom to encounter subjects, occasions, and audiences as each situation demands. Yet, within the particular situation, this adaptive process achieves productive closure; its mobile resources of argument and expression coalesce and become embodied as they grasp the matter of an actual case. Viewed at a distance, the principle of adaptation to situations becomes a nomadic process, a constantly changing program for action. Viewed within some specific situation, this principle manifests itself as a product, as a discourse possessing the density and integrity demanded by that situation.

NOTES

1. Cicero, *De inventione* 1.7, trans. H. M. Hubbell (Cambridge, MA: Harvard University Press, 1960). All subsequent quotations from *De inventione* are taken from this translation.
2. *De Inventione* 1.6.
3. *De Inventione* 1.8.
4. See Wesley Trimpi, *Muses of One Mind: The Literary Analysis of Experience and Its Continuity* (Princeton, NJ: Princeton University Press, 1983), 247–52.
5. For a more detailed argument concerning this point, see Michael C. Leff,

"Textual Criticism: The Legacy of G. P. Mohrmann," *Quarterly Journal of Speech* 72 (1986), 383–85.

6. Concerning these trends in enlightenment thought, see Hans-Georg Gadamer, *Truth and Method* (New York: Crossroads, 1984), 39–73.
7. The quotations are all from Herbert A. Wichelns, "The Literary Criticism of Oratory," in *Methods of Rhetorical Criticism*, ed. Bernard L. Brock and Robert L Scott (Detroit: Wayne State University Press, 1980), 67.
8. Compare Donald Bryant, "Rhetoric: Its Functions and Its Scope," *Quarterly Journal of Speech* 39 (1953): 401–24; and "'Rhetoric: Its Functions and Its Scope,' Rediviva," in *Rhetorical Dimensions in Criticism* (Baton Rouge: Louisiana State University Press, 1973), 3–23.
9. Robert Cox and Charles A. Willard, "Introduction: The Field of Argument," in *Advances in Argumentation Theory and Research* (Carbondale: Southern Illinois University Press, 1982), xiii–xiv.
10. Dominick LaCapra, *History and Criticism* (Ithaca, NY: Cornell University Press, 1985), 17.
11. Cox and Willard, "Introduction," xiv, enumerate some of the approaches in the literature on argumentation.
12. Samuel Becker, "Rhetorical Studies for the Modern World," in *The Prospect of Rhetoric: Report of the National Developmental Project*, ed. Lloyd F. Bitzer and Edwin Black (Englewood Cliffs, NJ: Prentice Hall, 1971), 31.
13. Wayne Brockriede, "Trends in the Study of Rhetoric: Toward a Blending of Criticism and Science," in Bitzer and Black, *The Prospect of Rhetoric*, 125–26.
14. Bryant, *Rhetorical Dimensions in Criticism*, 3.
15. Richard McKeon, "Rhetoric and Poetic in the Philosophy of Aristotle," in *Aristotle's "Poetics" and English Literature: A Collection of Critical Essays*, ed. Elder Olson (Chicago: University of Chicago Press, 1965), 207–8.
16. See, inter alia, Hoyt H. Hudson, "Can We Modernize the Study of Invention?," *Quarterly Journal of Speech* 7 (1921): 325–34; and Karl R. Wallace, "The Substance of Rhetoric: Good Reasons," *Quarterly Journal of Speech* 40 (1963): 239–49.
17. Paul Ricoeur, *The Rule of Metaphor: Multi-disciplinary Studies of the Creation of Meaning in Language*, trans. Robert Czerny (London: Routledge and Kegan Paul), 5.
18. Ricoeur, *Rule of Metaphor*, 12.
19. Ricoeur, *Rule of Metaphor*, 39.

20. Ricoeur, *Rule of Metaphor*, 10.
21. Ricoeur, *Rule of Metaphor*, 28.
22. Ricoeur, *Rule of Metaphor*, 10.
23. Ricoeur, *Rule of Metaphor*, 30.
24. Ricoeur, *Rule of Metaphor*, 31.
25. Ricoeur, *Rule of Metaphor*, 32.
26. See my review essay, "Recovering Aristotle: Rhetoric, Politics, and the Limits of Rationality," *Quarterly Journal of Speech* 71 (1985): 363; and Thomas M. Conley, "The Enthymeme in Perspective," *Quarterly Journal of Speech* 70 (1984): 168–72, and the references cited in both of these papers.
27. See Cox and Willard, "Introduction"; and J. Anthony Blair and Ralph H. Johnson, "Argumentation as Dialectical," *Argumentation* 1 (1987): 41–56.
28. Blair and Johnson, "Argumentation as Dialectical," 48.
29. Blair and Johnson, "Argumentation as Dialectical," 48.
30. Blair and Johnson, "Argumentation as Dialectical," 51–53.
31. Trimpi, *Muses of One Mind*, 87–240.
32. My argument here owes much to Ronald Beiner, *Political Judgment* (Chicago: University of Chicago Press, 1983).
33. Trimpi, *Muses of One Mind*, 234.

Decorum and Rhetorical Interpretation: The Latin Humanistic Tradition and Contemporary Critical Theory

I want to begin with an unlikely text, Jonathan Valin's novel *Day of Wrath*, a crime novel, in fact a work belonging to that unrefined subgenre known as the "hard-boiled" detective story. The novel's protagonist and narrator is named Harry Stoner, and the name aptly suggests the qualities of a detective-hero. Stoner, of course, has a hard and tough exterior, but more than that, his name defines a set of psychological traits which set him apart from his environment. He is self-contained, independent, resistant to the corruption that surrounds him, and impervious to social pressure. A rugged individualist and an idealistic loner, Stoner acts according to his own conscience and in disregard for what others might think of, or even do to, him. Paradoxically—though the paradox is itself a convention of the genre—Stoner also has a soft side, a sense of compassion which expresses itself as he ruminates about the social victims he is hired to protect. In *Day*

From *Vichiana*, 3rd series, 1 (1990): 107–26.

of Wrath, his thoughts revolve around his client, Mildred Segal, a middle-aged widow whose life is a desperate and compulsive effort to retain the emblems of middle-class respectability. Mildred is the foil to Stoner; she is the victim of the decorum against which he rebels; her behavior is other-directed, motivated not by an authentic self, but by conventions of status, neighborliness, and accommodation. From his position of sympathetic detachment, Stoner quickly realizes that her gestures are directed toward "Eastlawn drive and its nervous air of respectability," toward "the world at large, which in this deeply fugitive city prizes nothing more than the show of propriety and the concealment of shame."[1] Stoner understands this "fierce sense of propriety" (127), for he was raised in its ambience and had fought—"mostly successfully"—to escape it—that is, to escape "a life in which you're told the cost of every thought or act in advance, in which every idea is a received idea and every impulse is carefully weighed on the scale of public opinion before being acted upon" (92).

Here, in a compact and simplified form, we can locate the dominant modern attitude toward propriety and recognize the gulf that separates us from the sociability that informed the rhetorical culture of the past. For Cicero, decorum was a principle that operated to civilize our lives as well as our speech.[2] For Milton, decorum represented the "grand master peece to observe."[3] And as late as the early nineteenth century, William Hazlitt could write that "propriety is one great matter in the conduct of life; which, though like a graceful carriage of the body it is neither definable nor striking at first sight, is the result of finely balanced feelings and lends a secret strength and charm to the whole character."[4] But for Harry Stoner, as for most products of the modern world—whether fictional or real—propriety represents imbalance, a radical dislocation of the self.

To act or speak decorously is to yield to appearance, to adhere to the mere surface, and to capitulate to the tyranny of a hollow and artificial social exterior. Matters of substance and depth are found in the interiority of the self, separated from the charms of social discourse and linked to a healthy, scientific skepticism about the opinions of others. The path to Truth is a hard and lonely monologue which leaves no space for received ideas.

This "hard-boiled," solitary rationalism assumes more systematic contours as we move from popular to academic discourse. Modern philosophy, to cite a crucial example, takes shape through what Timothy Engstrom calls its "politics of separation." The identity of philosophy arises through the opposition between epistemology and rhetoric, and epistemology—that is, true knowledge—must purify itself of all literary flourish, all forms of mere opinion, and all considerations of local or social interest.[5] Thus conceived, philosophy exists in splendid isolation, devoted to truth and divorced from any political disturbance. As opposed to rhetoric, which is par excellence the art of social accommodation, philosophy must voice only "pure speech" and become "an objective science of truth, . . . of necessity, conceiving knowledge, and neither opinion nor the spinning out of opinions."[6] Such rigor, Hegel insists, applies even to the history of philosophy, which must not be reduced to a narration of "philosophical opinions as they have arisen and manifested themselves in time." To follow this course is to produce mere literary history, an "idle tale" of the kind told by Cicero, which treats the "ideas of philosophy as if they were opinions."[7] In short, the neighborhood of philosophy is no place for a social gathering; it is located in those detached and rarified precincts where the residents have no stories to tell each other, for they speak only in monologues addressed to the spirit of objective ideas.

The disjunction between philosophy and rhetoric is not a distinctively modern notion. While nineteenth- and twentieth-century thinkers have accepted it more generally and more thoroughly than their predecessors, the idea itself has a long lineage which can be traced at least back to Plato. What is more peculiar, however, is the way modernism has "purified" disciplines that engage more obviously grounded human activities. The fate of political studies is especially striking and ironic, for, as Terry Eagleton puts the point, modernism has led to "the emergence of a political science relatively sealed from the turmoil of political practice."[8] Traditional political theory—most of it produced by practicing politicians—typically sought to comprehend the interested and partisan scenes in which the political drama unfolded, and thus it encompassed such situated concepts as judgment, prudence, and decorum; these concepts offered avenues for exploring the complexity of practical action and recognized the overlapping functions of politics, ethics, and rhetoric within the metabolism of the community. Modernist political theory—most of it produced by academic specialists—seeks distance and independence from these impurities and strives for the objectivity characteristic of "philosophic" thought or scientific research. As science replaces prudence, it brackets the local perturbations of political action and operates by algorithmic deduction from abstract principles or by objective measurement of the effects on policy.[9] Thus, through a planned incongruity, the discourse of political theory alienates itself from the discourse of political practice.

Modernism, however, is not all hard surfaces. Like Harry Stoner it has its soft side. Across the divide from the "real world" of philosophy and politics, the modernist locates another domain—the domain of art where imagination is left free to pursue its own career. And it is from within the boundaries of this open space that the modernist contemplates literature. Thus, literary criticism achieves an autonomous, disinterested subjectivism that precisely matches the autonomous, disinterested objectivism of philosophy and science. Obviously, this purification works equally well to ward off the demands of propriety and seal the literary imagination from pedestrian traffic with specific occasions and interested motives. The result, as Stanley Fish observes, is to disinfect literary criticism from "anything that might recommend it to the community at large. It does not report on the 'moral content' of literature; it is unconcerned with the lives of authors, or with literature's relationship to science, politics, the law, or geography," and "above all," it cannot countenance any view that would allow a public function for literary products. Even high moral designs are "tarred by association with the brush of vulgarity; they are just another version of box-office designs because the intention of those who have them is to move others to this or that action in relation to this or that quotidian concern. Poetry, by contrast, is an effort deliberately abstracted from such concerns."[10] A literary work, then, is apolitical, arhetorical, and acontextual; it is an autonomous morsel of the imagination, properly digested only by those who know how to let it stew in its own juices.

In sum, the fearful symmetry of modernism frames the academy between the hard place of scientific realism and the soft spot of artistic imagination. Between these zones of purity there is no space for accommodation to situated interests or politically motivated dialogue—no space for the neighborly exercise of propriety and decorum, and hence no space for rhetoric.

But this is an old story, now already told in many different variants. Within the academy, modernism has become passé and has suffered withering critique from nearly every outpost of revisionist thought—from phenomenology and feminism, from communitarianism and deconstructionism, from reader-response criticism and speech act theory, and so on through the tribes of academia loosely and uncomfortably clustered under the banner of "antifoundationalism." Moreover, the demise of modernism corresponds precisely with a renewed interest in rhetoric.

In my version of this tale of decline and resurrection, "propriety," or decorum, emerges as the pivotal concept which divides the old rhetoric from modernism and links rhetoric to the postmodern temperament. The story, of course, is partial and incomplete. I have assumed that decorum is a central feature of the old rhetoric—a point which is disputable, and I have arranged things so that the rejection of decorum becomes a much more crucial feature of modernism than a full and balanced account might justify. Nevertheless, I hope to have said enough to give presence to a "decorum version" of the story and prompt interest in exploring the role of decorum as a mediating force between traditional rhetoric and emerging conceptions of rhetorical interpretation.

This matter, I believe, deserves more careful attention than it has yet received. The revival of rhetoric has encouraged some notable efforts to reassess the importance of decorum: Wesley Trimpi, Eric Charles White, and James Kinneavy have produced seminal works that argue for the significance of decorum both as an element in Greco-Latin rhetoric and as an aspect of the rhetorical process generally.[11] Victoria Kahn and Eugene Garver have provided detailed accounts of the centrality of decorum in Renaissance humanism,[12] and Eugene Garver and Janel Mueller have illustrated the use of decorum for critical practice.[13] But studies of this kind are the exception; for the most part, propriety remains a marginal concept in rhetorical scholarship, far less significant than the fascination with tropology or the effort to refurbish traditional strategies of argumentation.[14]

The reasons for this neglect are complex, and in some measure, result from confusions indigenous to the rhetorical tradition, where the placement of decorum is equivocal. On the one hand, decorum sometimes assumes a broad, nontechnical (or even antitechnical) function. Here it becomes an architectonic force, the point at which thought and action, form and content, and wisdom and eloquence coalesce. Thus, decorum represents the goal of rhetorical culture—the adaptation of all the available resources to encompass concrete situations. Since this goal must change in the face of changing situations, it cannot suffer reduction to formal rules, and so it is set in opposition to any attempt to control discursive practice through abstract, technical standards. On the other hand, decorum also occupies a technical place within the morphology of the art of rhetoric. Canonized along with purity, clarity, and ornamentation as one of the virtues of style, decorum becomes isolated as a subdivision of one of the main divisions of the art and serves as a heading for a number of seemingly formal precepts, as, for example, that the rhetor should not use exalted metaphors when describing a mundane subject.[15]

The first and broader of these conceptions of decorum, precisely because of its radically nontechnical character, is difficult to describe or apprehend in theoretical terms. In fact, its appreciation demands careful and sympathetic interpretation of the major texts in the tradition. Under the regime of modernism, however, such reading was impossible, since it was incomprehensible that decorum could occupy a central and serious role in the organization of cultural experience. Consequently, the traditional texts could be approached only in relation to their technical form—a form that indicated a sharp distinction between the argumentative and stylistic precepts subsumed within the art. That is, as the idea of a rhetorical culture passed from consciousness, the mediation of form and content through decorum was lost even to historical understanding. Moreover, modernist assumptions about the history of rhetoric have survived the decline of modernism itself and have informed the perceptions of those who have turned against the modernist program. Thus, even so disciplined and sensitive a reader as Paul Ricoeur concludes that Aristotle's *Rhetoric* is torn by an "internal contradiction" built into the very nature of the rhetorical project—a rift between persuasion as "arguing" through proofs and persuasion as an effort to "seduce and please" through the devices of style.[16]

For Ricoeur, this divided heritage leads to skepticism about the possibilities of rhetoric.[17] Others, however, implicitly or explicitly accept this view of the tradition and proceed to devise new rhetorics based on some part of the old rhetoric. Perelman, for example, seeks to revive rhetoric as a mode of adaptive, audience-centered argumentation, and the association between rhetoric and style is an embarrassment which he ruthlessly suppresses[18] (even such traditional tropes as hyperbole and metaphor receive treatment solely as argumentative structures with no consideration of their aesthetic appeal).[19] Working from an entirely different perspective, Barthes, de Man, Todorov, and other students of language and literature construct rhetorics centered in the tropes. Here rhetoric is conceived as a textual practice grounded in the tropological possibilities of language per se. The rhetoric of tropes, thus, is set free from the constraints of argument and immediate, practical situations.[20]

This literary/linguistic approach now exercises great influence on the academic conception of rhetoric. Rhetoric has gained currency in philosophy and the other "human sciences" as it has rubbed up against the tropology of postmodern literary theory, and thus, as Engstrom explains, it has developed "not due to any systematic reengagement with the history of rhetoric but as narrative theory."[21]

The impetus for this rhetoric is largely negative, since it operates to undermine the foundationalist assumptions of modernism, and it does so by appropriating the "restrained rhetoric" of modernism (i.e., rhetoric as mere ornament), which it uses to expose the internal contradictions of modernist texts. In this sense, while the valence attached to rhetoric changes, the conception of its domain remains constant: argumentation is still bracketed. Nevertheless, advocates of this sort of new rhetoric are well aware of the history of rhetoric and the more expansive range of its premodern incarnation. As a consequence, they have attempted to establish their own readings of the history of rhetoric that justify a bifurcation between tropology and practical argumentation.[22] Perhaps the most interesting of these efforts is Todorov's brilliant essay "The Splendor and Misery of Rhetoric," and by considering it in some detail, we can better understand the obstacles involved in refurbishing decorum for contemporary use.

Todorov divides the history of rhetoric into three periods: the first extending from its origins to the end of the Roman Republic, the second continuing until the eighteenth century, and the third marking the death of rhetoric in the post-Enlightenment era. This periodization is conventional, derived from the orthodox modernist histories, but Todorov reconfigures this narrative sequence by invoking a linguistic typology—binary opposition between the functional (extrinsic) and formal (intrinsic) dimensions of semiotic use. Sprung from the conditions of the Greek polities, rhetoric originates as a form of political action. As such it is functional, designed solely to do work in the external environment. Functional rhetoric, for Todorov, "grasps language not as form—it is not concerned with utterance as such but as action. . . . Rhetoric deals with the functions of speech, not its structures. Its one constant is the objective it seeks to achieve: to persuade."[23] Conceived in this way, rhetoric becomes pragmatic in spirit, "and by that token immoral: whatever the circumstances or the cause defended, one must be able to achieve one's end." And so rhetoric does not give preference to "one type of speech over others," since "any speech may be efficacious; it must simply be used toward an appropriate end."[24]

At this point, Todorov quite rightly seizes upon propriety as the organizing conception within this view of rhetoric. Noting that functional rhetoric "teaches its practitioners to use the type of discourse suited to each particular case," he concludes (here following Albert Von) that "the key notion of rhetoric is therefore the notion of suitability, appropriateness (*prepon, decorum*)." Appropriateness, Todorov adds, "is the basis of efficacy," and to secure his point, he quotes the following passage from Cicero's *Orator*:

> This indeed, is the form of wisdom that the orator must especially employ—to adapt himself to occasions and persons. In my opinion one must not speak in the same style at all times, nor before all people, nor against all opponents, nor in defense of all clients, nor in partnership with all advocates. He, therefore, will be eloquent who can adapt his speech to fit all conceivable circumstances. (123)

In brief, this original rhetoric "is above all functional; to be functional is to be fitting."[25]

This kind of rhetoric, however, could not outlive the social and political institutions that spawned it, and thus with the collapse of republican government in the first century AD, rhetoric necessarily changed. Denied outlet into the practical world of politics, rhetoric distanced itself from functionalism and gravitated toward the formal side of the semiotic typology. The "instrumental" character of the old rhetoric, its preoccupation with "serving an external purpose," was abandoned in favor of a perspective grounded in the "beautiful" and the "ornamental." Discourse was to be appreciated "for itself, for its intrinsic qualities."[26] And so, Todorov maintains, rhetoric no longer found its end in utility but in the "useless, inefficacious" speech that drew attention only to itself, and rhetoric became "the theory of language admired in and for itself."[27] Under the circumstances, the lore of figures became increasingly prominent, while the other elements of the art suffered atrophy: "In the old instrumental perspective, these five parts [of rhetoric] are in principle . . . on an equal footing: they correspond to five aspects of the linguistic act, which were all subject to an objective exterior to themselves. Now that the exterior objective has disappeared, we find that elocution—that is figure, ornament—occupies an increasingly large place, since the new objective—that of speaking (or writing) artfully, of creating beautiful speeches—is best realized by this means."[28]

Nevertheless, Todorov quickly adds, the transformation remained incomplete. This "second rhetoric" could perfect itself only through a liberation of linguistic form such that language could be offered up as a spectacle, as a celebration, a festival of its own possibilities. But this sort of liberation was impossible in the authoritarian environment that stretched from late antiquity to the eighteenth century, for it did not offer the space needed to tolerate unsuppressed individualism in expression. Sadly, then, through the long second phase of its history, rhetoric became a stagnant, almost neurotic, enterprise, attracted to the lure of form for its own sake but inhibited by dogmas that suppressed form in favor of "content." So rhetoric went about its business reluctantly and with a guilty conscience, and when, in the eighteenth century, conditions changed again and the doors of the carnival of language swung open, rhetoric had become codified into a system of verbal and social regimentation that could command no respect—hence its death in the wake of bourgeois individualism and Romantic aesthetics.[29]

As I noted earlier, the surface of Todorov's narrative follows a familiar path: the career of rhetoric is plotted through changes in the external political and cultural environment; hence its rise as a judicial and political art in the Greek polities, its conversion into a literary art after the fall of democratic politics, and its eventual expulsion from the orbit of literature with the emergence of the Romantic consciousness. But unlike the conventional histories, Todorov's account treats the external stimuli merely as triggers which set in motion the binary possibilities intrinsic to rhetoric as a language system. His history, then, is one of oscillation between the poles of functionalism and formalism: Rhetoric as a discipline strains to place itself purely and entirely at one or the other end of this axis. Thus, while Ricoeur finds rhetoric divided against itself, Todorov finds it separated into two independent manifestations. But in both cases, rhetoric seems incapable of encompassing contrary impulses—the outward turn toward action in the political world and the inward turn toward self-reflexive aesthetic production.

Todorov significantly departs from the mainstream when he establishes decorum as the point of unification in classical rhetoric; here his position differs markedly from Ricoeur, or Perelman, or modernist historians who regard the classical system as merely taxonomic.[30] Nevertheless, Todorov, in effect, preserves the older dichotomies by sealing decorum within a narrow conception of functionalism. From Corax to Cicero, propriety acts as a simple, unitary force isolating rhetoric from all ethical or aesthetic considerations. Moreover, this conception of decorum rests upon the interpretation of a few passages selected from a large corpus of relevant works. Since Todorov is a skillful reader, he extracts striking insights from these passages and blends them together in a way that elegantly supports his binary semiotic typology. But he achieves this elegance at the price of neglecting or distorting the historical record, and as a result, I believe he misjudges the scope of propriety and its potential significance as a locus for rhetorical interpretation.

Helen de Witt, who, to my knowledge, has written the most comprehensive study of the classical conception of decorum, provides ample evidence that the subject is far more complex and much less purified than Todorov supposes. She notes that the consensus about persuasion as the end of rhetoric might seem to stabilize the operation of decorum.

Given that the speaker seeks to "command whatever means are in fact most effective in bringing an audience around to his point of view," it would appear that rhetorical propriety would avoid reference to questions of "moral decency" or "good taste." "But," she adds, "this is not altogether the case." Classical rhetoricians sometimes question whether certain techniques "are morally acceptable, regardless of their effectiveness," and the issue of

> whether certain types of oratory are in good taste is even more common. . . . There seems, then, to be an important confusion surrounding the criterion of propriety in ancient rhetoric. A wide variety of types of propriety is sought for the purpose of accommodating one's speech to one's audience; but one can apparently be extremely successful and still guilty of impropriety.[31]

Matters are further complicated by the fact that, contrary to modernist sensibilities and Todorov's suppositions, the classical theorists did not sustain a sharp, categorical distinction between literature and oratory. Thus, as De Witt observes, their conception of propriety "tried to combine both aesthetic and practical standards," and they "aimed at oratory which was both good as persuasion and good as literature."[32]

In other words, even during the heyday of functionalist rhetoric, propriety was not conceived as solely regulated by the persuasive "exterior" of discourse. This point is underscored and specified by Elaine Fantham, who locates two different headings for the treatment of propriety in the early Roman tradition. The first is indicated by the phrase *apte* or *accomodate dicere*, which refers to extrinsic accommodation—the "adjustment of thought and style to context and circumstance," the type of propriety that Todorov describes. The second is indicated by the verb *decere* and its nominal and adjectival variants (*decorum*, *decorus*, *decus*), which refer to intrinsic merit—an absolute standard of aesthetic worth "at which the speaker should aim."[33] In the *Orator*, Cicero, apparently for the first time in Latin literature, explicitly links these two dimensions of propriety, subsuming both under the heading of *decorum*. In this way, Cicero makes *decorum* equivalent to the Greek *prepon*, which already incorporated both aspects of the concept. But whether referred to through separate terms or subsumed under the same general term, the tension between these two sides of propriety persists throughout the classical period—a point copiously documented by De Witt.

This tension sometimes causes confusion among the classical authors, and we might view it, as does De Witt, as a confusion in principle—a category error that inevitably confounds clear thinking about rhetoric. On the other hand, we might view this tension as a productive complication—a problem whose recognition forces us to consider the various dimensions of language-use embedded in a functional rhetoric. From this perspective, propriety no longer appears as captive within the functional pole of an abstract dichotomy between form and function; it becomes a flexible principle that coordinates particular discourses as they simultaneously build internal coherence, refer to a context of facts and circumstances, and stretch outward to alter perception of that context. Decorum now seems to function within a field of concrete action which must engage both the immediate environment and the intrinsic appeals of language. It is this perspective, I believe, that Cicero adopts in his two most important rhetorical treatises, *De oratore* and *Orator*, and in them we can discover a productively complex notion of decorum.

In characterizing Cicero's attitude toward decorum, Todorov quotes an excerpt from *Orator* 123, which occurs in the midst of the second extensive and explicit discussion of the concept presented in that text. The passage Todorov cites does, indeed, place stress on the more clearly circumstantial aspects of decorum (on what might be called *accomodate dicere*). But in the immediately preceding and following portions of the text, the other side of decorum also surfaces. At 122, Cicero claims that it is treatment of the subject (*traetatio rerum*) which renders speech admirable; the facts themselves (*ipsaeres*)[34] are easily acquired, and as for the rules of art, Cicero dismisses them in a single (though very long) sentence that enumerates the conventional precepts relevant to each of the parts of the oration. He then observes that it is difficult to stipulate how these parts ought to be treated, since in actuality, "they are not always treated in the same way." And at this point (in the section quoted by Todorov), Cicero invokes decorum and refers to the requirements of the persons and occasions connected with the speaking situation (*ut sit tempo rum personarumque moderator*). Eloquence, therefore, depends upon the orator's capacity to accommodate the speech (*accomodare orationem*) to whatever will be appropriate (*ad id quodcumque decebit*). And once this matter is settled, the orator will speak each part (*quidque*) just as it ought to be spoken.

Thus far Cicero has behaved as on orthodox Todorovian functionalist. He refers the management of the parts of the speech (i.e., its internal form) not to formal rules but to the external circumstances that frame and motivate the case at hand. Decorum, then, governs the matter of the speech by pushing it toward accommodation to an "exterior" function. But, just where Todorov's quotation ends, the text takes an unexpected turn. Instead of simply leaving the orator to fit the subject matter (*res*) to the context, Cicero considers the ratio between subject (*res*) and "treatment" from a different angle, calling upon a doctrine normally located within the domain of style: the orator will speak appropriately by treating the subject in accordance with its magnitude. Propriety, that is, occurs when the speaker avoids treating a grand subject in a jejune fashion or vice versa, but instead speaks in a way equivalent to the demands of the subject. We are then escorted back through each of the parts of the oration and given a brief account of how different levels of style match different probative functions and how both vary in accordance with the importance of the subject (123–25). In the end, the orator will rule (*reget*), sway (*flectet*), and influence (*afficiet*) an audience to the extent that his effort comports with the nature of the cause (*natura causae*) and the demands of the occasion (*ratio temporis*). The verbs used in this final sentence clearly indicate that we are still in the orbit of functionalism; Cicero continues to look toward the external effect of a discourse. But the separation between *natura causae* and *ratio temporis* strongly suggests that some aspects of this effect are grounded in the nature of the subject itself: an efficacious treatment of the subject involves adjustment not just to constantly shifting circumstance but also to a more abiding relationship that influences the intersection of form and content.

All told, *Orator* 122–25 presents a very dense and complicated view of decorum. In a remarkably short space, Cicero manages to entangle proper treatment of a subject with internal form, the coordination of style and argument, the particular circumstances informing the subject, and the magnitude of the subject in itself. These complications remain unresolved in this passage, which has a condensed and elliptical quality.

Fortunately, however, in his earlier analysis of decorum (*Orator* 69–74), Cicero develops the same themes in somewhat greater detail, and here we can find some guidance in working our way through this maze.

The first thing to note about *Orator* 69–74 is the range that Cicero allots to decorum. He clearly does not regard it as a principle exclusively, or even mainly, relevant to the rhetoric of oratory. Decorum, he asserts, is a universal criterion that applies equally to the making of speeches and the conduct of life (71). Philosophers consider this matter when they deal with ethics, though not under the heading of absolute virtue (*de recta*), for in that case the objective is to locate a fixed and absolute standard (72) (the contrast here between *decorum* and *rectum* implies a direct connection between propriety and prudential ethics—a point Cicero already had made explicit in *De oratore* and would later reaffirm in *De officiis*).[35] Likewise, decorum operates in the fine arts: students of literature must consider it in poetry (72); poets themselves must accede to its requirements (74), and painters must observe it in making their compositions (73 and 74). In fact, decorum enters our lives at every point where we render judgment without reference to absolutes, for we say this is appropriate or that is inappropriate about everything we express or do, whether the matter is great or trivial (73).

Regarding rhetoric itself, decorum is a complex, multidimensional concept, embracing all the themes we have observed in 122–25. In the present passage, while these themes are still interwoven, it seems possible to sort them out by noting three strands that enter into the pattern: (1) decorum as accommodation to the circumstances that frame the rhetorical act; (2) decorum as the mediating link between the form and content manifested within the discourse—a link based on the relationship between the subject of the discourse and the rhetorical treatment of that subject; (3) decorum as an organizing principle governing the internal form of a discourse. As I list them here, these three themes move us progressively from the exterior of the rhetorical act toward its intrinsic form. The first establishes a simple ratio between the treatment or (to use a more contemporary term) the "representation" of the subject and the circumstances that determine the rhetorical context. The second deals with the ratio between thought and expression as elements of representation and establishes this ratio as a function of the relationship between the mode of representation and the nature of the subject being represented. The third takes us into what we might call the internal context of the discourse—the ratio of elements that unfold within the representation itself.

The first of these points requires little comment, for while Cicero evidently considers it important, he does not elaborate upon it, other than to list the constituent elements that enter into a rhetorical situation. The third point is more complex, but it has already received careful and expert attention from Elaine Fantham,[36] and I do not now have time to examine it. Thus, in the remainder of this paper, I will concentrate on the second aspect of decorum—the relationships among form, content, and subject. Since this issue bears most directly on the coordination of internal and external elements in the rhetorical process, it is the most important of the three for my purposes, and it raises problems that demand careful and detailed analysis.

In his seminal essay "A Ciceronian Contribution to Rhetorical Theory," A. E. Douglas demonstrates that *Orator* 69–70 effects a striking and apparently original synthesis of two constructs that were previously regarded as distinct—the functions of the orator and the typology of style.[37] At 69, Cicero sets forth the functions (*officia*) of the orator, which are to prove, to please, and to sway. These functions correspond with the Aristotelian modes of proof—logical, ethical, and emotional—and thus they represent the main components of inventional theory. Then, in an unconventional move, Cicero correlates these functions with the standard tripartite division of stylistic types: The plain style is proper for proof, the middle style for pleasing, and the grand style for swaying the emotions. This correlation, although very simple in schematic form, has dramatic implications. In a single stroke, it shatters the dichotomy between argument and style that had characterized Hellenistic and Roman rhetoric, and it opens the way for a conception of decorum as an agency mediating between the treatment of a subject and the subject per se. In the new Ciceronian scheme, style and argument come into a state of balance as they are mutually attuned to the subject, and the propriety of both together can be set on a scale of variation relative to the magnitude of the subject.

This position entails a special conception of subject. In the classical tradition, the nature of the subject often is included along with the speaker, the audience, and the occasion as one of the circumstances involved in a case. In the *Orator*, however, Cicero clearly separates the subject from the circumstances, distinguishing at 125 between the *causae natura* and the *ratio temporis* and at 71 between *in re de qua agitur positum* and *in personis et eorum qui dicunt et eorum qui audiunt*. The circumstances, then, consist in occasions and persons. The subject occupies a distinct and coordinate status. Moreover, Cicero also differentiates the subject from the "treatment of the subject"—a point which would seem to follow from his integration of argument and style. In general, classical rhetorics associate the subject with argument, and style is viewed as that which clarifies or embellishes the subject. But, as we have seen, Cicero overturns this arrangement when he connects the modes of proof with the levels of style. Style is now as much implicated with the subject as is argument, and at 122–25 this perspective emerges subtly but powerfully. According to the plan of the treatise as a whole, 122 opens the discussion of invention, and the first topic here is the "logical mode of proof," a topic often treated by reference to the parts of the oration. But recall that Cicero quickly dismisses the artistic precepts, invokes the doctrine of decorum, and then returns to the parts of the oration, this time commenting as much on the use of language as on argument. And this nexus between argument and style is emphasized again when Cicero turns to the next two components of traditional invention—the discussion of a general principle (*thesis*) and the amplification of a theme—for he calls both of them "ornaments" (*duplex ornatus*). In short, argument and invention emerge as cooperative modes of treating a subject; both work to represent that subject and both must be adapted to suit it, but the subject is itself distinct from its representation.

How, then, can the subject, which stands outside the treatment of the art, exercise such a decisive influence on artistic performance? Cicero never addresses this issue directly in the *Orator*, but the theory of *ornatus* he presents in book 3 of *De oratore* seems to have a bearing on this matter. And, in any case, the discussion there helps to clarify our understanding of Cicero's functionalism and its relationship to decorum.

In *De oratore* 3, Cicero, through the persona of Crassus, attempts to demonstrate that wisdom and eloquence are intimately linked, and thus the consummate orator must command philosophical knowledge. This issue hinges on the relationship between words (*verba*) and things (*res*), and Crassus develops a series of arguments designed to prove that eloquent language naturally emerges from an understanding of the subjects it treats. At 125, he summarizes his position:

> A full supply of matter (*res*) begets a full supply of words, and if the subjects themselves are of an elevated character this produces a spontaneous brilliance in the language. . . . Nature of herself, if only she has received training, given a plentiful supply of matter, will find her way without any guidance to the adornments of oratory.

This formulation, however, raises a problem. If the relationship between knowledge of things and eloquence in expression is so intimate and direct, then the distinctive qualities of the orator must come from philosophical knowledge. A complete identification between knowledge and eloquence, where the latter simply follows the former, suggests that the orator has no special function and that there is no need to cultivate oratory; all one has to do is achieve wisdom.

Consequently, Crassus is made to refine his position in a way that ironically identifies orators with philosophers but also offers grounds for separating their pursuits. The designation "orator" or "philosopher," he explains, is unimportant, so long as the goal remains command of both thought and expression. No one, of course, would prefer glib ignorance to knowledge "lacking the power of expression." But the highest achievement certainly must be that of the "orator who possesses learning. And if they allow him also to be a philosopher, that is the end of the dispute: but if they keep the two separate, they will come off second best in this, that the consummate orator possesses all the knowledge of the philosophers, but the range of the philosophers does not necessarily include eloquence" (142).

Philosophical knowledge, then, is a necessary but not sufficient cause of eloquence. Since the goal of philosophy is knowledge for its own sake, it can rest content within a self-contained arena of contemplation. The orator's work must reach outward and translate this knowledge into a publicly accessible form, and so the orator has to equip (*ornare*) knowledge of a subject in such a way that it can function effectively in the social and political arena. This task is functional, but the functionalism here proves complex; it is not simply a one-dimensional effort to fit the representation of the subject to a contingent external context, since an eloquent representation necessarily arises from the nature of the subject itself. Hence, the forms of rhetorically effective speech must derive their appeal not just from their exterior manifestations, but also from their connection with the nature of things.

As he develops his theory of *ornatus*, Crassus engages this problem by arguing that aesthetic form follows practical function.[38] The appeal of rhetorical ornament arises from a natural connection between what is necessary or useful and what is beautiful or pleasant. A rhetorical representation achieves its effect because it simultaneously blends practical utility with aesthetic pleasure.

Crassus never lays this argument out in a single, systematic, and comprehensive analysis. Instead, as is appropriate for an eloquent speaker, he advances his position through a repetitive and cumulative method that works its way across the text. Nevertheless, at 176–82, where Crassus launches his discussion of prose rhythm, we get the gist of the matter. The technicalities involved in prose rhythm, Crassus remarks, are formidable, but its practical use is not so difficult, since the technical rules do no more than describe the natural processes by which we adapt the sounds of language to meaning. "Thus the style of our oratory follows the line of thought we take and changes and turns to suit all the requirements of pleasing the ear and influencing the mind of the audience." The point is immediately generalized: "But in oratory as in most matters nature has contrived with incredible skill that the things possessing the most utility also have the greatest amount of dignity and indeed often of beauty also" (177–78). To support this claim, Crassus illustrates this union of form and function through the various orders of our experience, beginning at a cosmic level and then working his way down to rhetoric. The complex, ordered structure of the universe, he asserts, has a functional purpose, a purpose so intricate that should any part be altered the whole would collapse. At the same time, it "is so beautiful that no lovelier vision is even imaginable." This unity also displays itself in natural phenomena such as the human form and trees, and in products of human art such as ships and buildings. And, finally, it accounts for the effect of rhythmic prose: "Virtually unavoidable practical requirements produce charm of style. . . . It was failure or scantiness of breath that originated periodic sentence structure and pauses between words, but now that this has once been discovered, it is so attractive that even if a person were endowed with breath that never failed we should still not wish him to deliver an unbroken flow of words" (178–81).

The same principle holds good for metaphor, which originates, on Crassus's account, in catachresis—the necessity of borrowing a word to name something which has no proper name. But though metaphor arises from this utilitarian function, it "has been subsequently made popular by its agreeable and entertaining quality" (155). And in the case of delivery, we also discover that "the thing most useful is also in a way most becoming." Here Crassus notes that nothing is more conducive to avoiding strain and maintaining a healthy voice than frequent changes of tone. And yet nothing is more pleasant to the hearer than a voice that alters and varies (224).

In sum, Cicero presents a sophisticated conception of the relationships among form, content, and subject. As opposed to the more conventional rhetoricians, he does not divide form from content along the line of style and argument. Rather, by equating the levels of style with the modes of proof, he holds that thought and language work cooperatively as they blend within the texture of a discourse. This interaction yields a representation of the subject, and a representation achieves decorum by reference to the nature of the subject itself. Consequently, the orator must have knowledge of the subject, but must also have the capacity to make its nature apparent in discursive form. Eloquence occurs when that form appropriately illuminates the subject, and at this point, a natural harmony is produced; the aesthetic and practical aspects of representation merge in a way that elicits a unified response in the mind of the auditor.

The whole apparatus ultimately turns on the matter of response, and so it is a functionalist rhetoric. But, as opposed to its placement in Todorov's binary scheme, decorum in Cicero does not work to insulate the practical function of rhetoric from the aesthetics of form; instead, Cicero links the aesthetic and the practical, the beautiful and the useful, within the economy of the rhetorical act. His aim is to discover points of local stasis where function, form, and subject interact harmoniously. In such cases, the language of the discourse does not dissolve into the context nor display itself in splendid aesthetic isolation. The locus of decorum is that moment when the discourse becomes luminous in itself through its illumination of a subject, and it is just at that moment that discourse attains its greatest practical force.

NOTES

1. Jonathan Valin, *Days of Wrath* (New York: Avon, 1982), 11.
2. See, for example, *De officiis* 1.94–98; and *Orator* 70.
3. *Complete Prose Works of John Milton*, ed. Don M. Wolfe et al., vol. 1 (New Haven: Yale University Press, 1953), 405. For an account of propriety in Milton's thought, see J. Mueller, "The Mastery of Decorum: Politics as Poetry in Milton's Sonnets," in *Politics and Poetic Value*, ed. Robert von Halberg (Chicago: University of Chicago Press, 1987), 63–96.
4. Quoted by Marvin Mudrick, afterword to Jane Austen, *Persuasion* (New York: New American Library, 1964), 241. Mudrick provides a useful explanation of the central role of propriety in Austen's novel.
5. Timothy Engstrom, "Philosophy's Anxiety of Rhetoric: Contemporary Revisions of a Politics of Separation," *Rhetorica* 7 (1989): 209–38.
6. The phrase "pure speech" is from John Locke; the call for an "objective science" independent of opinion is Hegel's. Both quotations are taken from Engstrom, "Philosophy's Anxiety of Rhetoric."
7. The references here are to Georg Wilhelm Friedrich Hegel, *The Philosophy of History*, trans. E. S. Haldane, 11–17, cited by Engstrom, "Philosophy's Anxiety of Rhetoric," note 40.
8. Terry Eagleton, "A Small History of Rhetoric," in *Walter Benjamin; or, Towards a Revolutionary Criticism* (London: Verso, 1981), 106.
9. Concerning the formalism of modern political theory, see Ronald Beiner, *Political Judgment* (Chicago: University of Chicago Press, 1983). Concerning policy studies and their antirhetorical bias, see James F. Klumpp, "Beyond the Social Engineering Paradigm: *Public Policy Decision-Making*—Fifteen Years Later," in *Argument and Critical Practices: Proceedings of the Fifth SCA/AFA Conference on Argumentation*, ed. Joseph W. Wenzel (Annandale, VA: Speech Communication Association, 1987), 395–98.
10. Stanley Fish, "No Bias, No Merit," in *Doing What Comes Naturally: Change, Rhetoric, and the Practice of Theory in Literary and Legal Studies* (Durham, NC:

Duke University Press, 1989), 173.

11. Wesley Trimpi, *Muses of One Mind: The Literary Analysis of Experience and Its Continuity* (Princeton, NJ: Princeton University Press, 1983); E. C. White, *Kaironomia: On the Will to Invent* (Ithaca, NY: Cornell University Press, 1987); James Kinneavy, "Kairos: A Neglected Concept in Classical Rhetoric," in *Rhetoric and Praxis*, ed. Dietz Moss (Washington, DC: Catholic University of America Press, 1986).
12. Victoria Kahn, *Rhetoric, Prudence, and Skepticism in the Renaissance* (Ithaca, NY: Cornell University Press, 1985); Eugene Garver, *Machiavelli and the History of Prudence* (Madison: University of Wisconsin Press, 1987).
13. Eugene Vance, "Chaucer's Pardoner: Relics, Discourse, and Frames of Propriety," *New Literary History* 20 (1988–89) 723–45; and Mueller, *The Mastery of Decorum.*
14. A telling example of how these two foci have blocked attention to decorum comes from a comparison of Chaïm Perelman and Lucie Olbrechts-Tyteca, *The New Rhetoric: A Treatise on Argumentation*, trans. John Wilkerson and Purcell Weaver (Notre Dame, IN: University of Notre Dame Press, 1969); and G. Dubois et al., *A General Rhetoric*, trans. P. D. Durrell and E. R. Slotkin (Baltimore: Johns Hopkins University Press, 1981). The two books present highly influential new rhetorics, worked out at about the same time in the same relatively small country (Belgium). But neither takes serious notice of the interests represented in the other; the one is exclusively concerned with argument, the other with style, and, significantly, neither deals with decorum.
15. This point needs some qualification. Even as a technical element of style-theory, decorum suggested a connection between form and content. This is evident in classical literary theory, where, as D. A. Russell observes, "There is a good deal of understanding of the organic connection between form and content. This connection is indeed seen in terms of the doctrine of decorum, and of the assumption that great words suit great things, and little words little things." *Criticism in Antiquity* (Berkeley: University of California Press, 1981), 130. The rhetoricians seem less sensitive to this point, but as I will argue below, Cicero seizes on it as he develops his broad conception of decorum.
16. Paul Ricoeur, *The Rule of Metaphor: Multi-disciplinary Studies of the Creation of Meaning in Language*, trans. Robert Czerny (London: Routledge and Kegan Paul, 1978), 32.
17. Ricoeur, *Rule of Metaphor*, 11. Ricoeur here suggests that the project of resurrecting rhetoric is "hopeless."

18. See Perelman and Olbrechts-Tyteca, *The New Rhetoric*, 167–71.
19. Perelman and Olbrechts-Tyteca, *The New Rhetoric*, 398–410.
20. See, for example, Paul de Man, *Allegories of Reading: Figural Language in Rousseau, Nietzsche, Rilke, and Proust* (New Haven: Yale University Press, 1979).
21. Engstrom, "Philosophy's Anxiety of Rhetoric."
22. For example, Roland Barthes, "The Old Rhetoric: An Aide-Memoire," in *The Semiotic Challenge*, trans. Richard Howard (New York: Hill and Wang, 1988), 11–94. (The original paper appeared in the journal *Communications* in 1970.)
23. Tzvetan Todorov, "The Splendor and Misery of Rhetoric," in *Theories of the Symbol*, trans. Catherine Porter (Ithaca, NY: Cornell University Press, 1982), 61.
24. Todorov, "Splendor and Misery," 61–62.
25. Todorov, "Splendor and Misery," 62.
26. Todorov, "Splendor and Misery," 66–67.
27. Todorov, "Splendor and Misery," 68.
28. Todorov, "Splendor and Misery," 66.
29. Todorov, "Splendor and Misery," 70–81.
30. A very clear articulation of this view is found in Douglas Ehninger, "On Systems of Rhetoric," *Philosophy and Rhetoric* 1 (1968): 131–44.
31. Helen de Witt, "Quo Virtus? The Concept of Propriety in Ancient Literary Criticism," PhD dissertation, Oxford University, 1988, 181–82.
32. De Witt, "Quo Virtus?," 336.
33. Elaine Fantham, "*Orator* 69–74," *Central States Speech Journal* 35 (1984): 124.
34. The ambiguity of *res* makes interpretation of this passage somewhat difficult. I take it that it sometimes refers to the subject of a discourse, sometimes to the external facts relevant to a discourse, and sometimes to both simultaneously. But it does seem that Cicero has in mind here a fairly clear distinction between the subject and the facts and circumstances surrounding a case.
35. *De oratore* 3.212; *De officiis* 1.94–98.
36. *Orator* 69–74; and Elaine Fantham, "*Varietas* and *Satietas: De oratore* 3.96–103 and the Limits of *Ornatus*," *Rhetorica* 6 (1988): 275–90.
37. A. E. Douglas, "A Ciceronian Contribution to Rhetorical Theory," *Eranos* 60 (1957): 18–26.
38. On Cicero's functionalism, see Fantham, "*Varietas* and *Satietas*."

In Search of Ariadne's Thread: A Review of the Recent Literature on Rhetorical Theory

My assignment was to review the articles on rhetorical theory that appeared in the speech communication journals during the years 1976 and 1977. Although the editor provided a list of the relevant journals, I was left to my own devices in selecting the articles that fell under the heading of rhetorical theory. I approached this task with profound reservations, since, as we all know through bitter experience, rhetorical theory is virtually impossible to define. Thus, I was afraid that I would either have to report on everything in the journals or appear to be arbitrary.

After reading a few essays, however, my fear dissipated. I soon learned that rhetoric was, among other things, a method for reaching decisions. Furthermore, the method worked best in situations where abstract principles were in doubt, where the rigorous standards of logic were

From *Central States Speech Journal* 29 (1978): 73–91.

impractical, and where the decision led directly to some sort of selection. This suited my purposes entirely. What could be more appropriate than to define the literature of rhetorical theory according to a rhetorical method? If I could not devise a logically coherent definition of my subject, I could at least select those materials likely to engage the interest of rhetorical theorists.

Unfortunately, the solution of this first problem led directly to a second and far more serious one. I had gathered together a group of essays and referred to them as a body of literature. This act of classification brought with it certain assumptions, since a body of scholarly literature should reveal common agreements about the subjects and issues that delimit an area of inquiry. But the more I read, the more I wondered whether these essays on rhetorical theory exhibited any coherence. The literature simply did not appear to build on itself. Consequently, my original purpose had to be revised. I had intended to abstract and comment on the issues that already existed in the literature. The circumstances, however, mandated a more indirect approach, and the resulting essay is an exercise in inference. Its aim is to make a plausible conjecture about the direction of recent rhetorical theory and to suggest some potential issues that might confront us as we move in that direction.

Before turning to this task, I need to make one more point about my methodology. Two types of articles seem to dominate the recent literature. The first type may be called metarhetorical. Essays in this category are very abstract in character, since they deal with the scope, nature, and ethical burden of rhetoric as a concept. The second category consists of historical/textual studies, and these take several different forms. Most often, such essays deal with a single well-known figure in the rhetorical tradition (e.g., Plato, Augustine, Perelman), but some of them are comparative (e.g., Burke and Richards), and a few attempt to survey a period (e.g., the twelfth century).[1] In general, these two types are distinct, works in one category haying very little to do with works in the other. Historical/textual essays sometimes make introductory or concluding remarks that apply to metarhetorical concerns, but the burden of these essays is explication, and they achieve general theoretical interest only as they are accumulated and interrelated. Metarhetorical essays use the historical tradition as a source for examples, but they rarely show a sustained interest in the traditional authorities, and there are few references to the historical/textual studies.

Obviously, both types of studies are important, since a discipline cannot proceed effectively without examining its philosophical bases and its historical tradition. Yet the separation between the two approaches to theory creates serious problems for both. On one side, the metarhetorical studies are alive with items of theoretical interest, but, lacking concrete points of reference, they are often so difficult to understand that they appear vacuous. On the other side, the historical/textual essays are so wedded to the particular that it is difficult to understand their theoretical significance.

The very formulation of this problem suggests its solution, since the deficiencies of the two approaches are symmetrical. That is, the metarhetorical studies can provide a needed theoretical framework for the historical/textual studies, and the historical/textual studies can provide a concrete grounding for metarhetorical speculation. At any rate, the union of these two approaches offers a convenient strategy for reviewing the literature as a coherent whole. And in the following pages, I have attempted to isolate some of the leading tendencies in the metarhetorical literature and explicate them by reference to historical/textual studies that have appeared recently in the journals. The fit between the two categories is not always perfect; at times, I have not been able to find historical essays that respond to the issues raised in the more purely theoretical literature, and in some cases, I have had to interpret the historical essays in a rather loose fashion. Consequently, the argument may sometimes oversimplify matters, but oversimplification seemed necessary in order to preserve coherence.

Rhetoric as Epistemic

If there is any unifying thread running through the recent literature, it is a heightened interest in the relationship between rhetoric and epistemology. Moreover, this interest regularly expresses itself in terms that rearrange the conventional modern distinctions between knowledge and communication. Witness the following quotations from essays on a variety of different subjects: "At any given moment, what we know to exist in the world is a product of an evolving set of human agreements."[2] "It seems safe to conclude that there is a new rhetoric, grounded not in the quest to make truth effective, but rather in the quest to evoke truth *via* rhetoric."[3] "Rhetoric can no longer be seen simply as a means of persuasion. It becomes instead the medium in which selves grow."[4] "While rhetoric may be defined in many ways and on many levels, it is in the deepest and most fundamental sense the advocacy of realities."[5] "In many circumstances one can 'know' only through engagement in rhetorical activity."[6] The terminology changes somewhat as we move from one of these quotations to another, but the basic point is consistent. All of these authors, and others who could be cited, agree that rhetoric is a serious philosophical subject that involves not only the transmission, but also the generation, of knowledge. In other words, there appears to be an emerging consensus in support of Scott's view that rhetoric is epistemic.[7]

Furthermore, there is a growing tendency to assert that an epistemic view of rhetoric signifies a major break in the modern rhetorical tradition. One author goes so far as to identify a "postmodern" rhetoric.[8] This assertion marks our first issue: Does the epistemic view constitute such a radical departure from the recent past that we are entitled to distinguish between a modern and a postmodern approach to theory?[9] In order to deal with this issue, I propose to summarize the findings of a number of historical studies on modern rhetoric and compare them with the central tenets of the epistemic view. Specifically, we shall look at Jamieson's comparative study of Pascal and Descartes,[10] McKerrow's essay on Whately,[11] and Hostettler's analysis of Saintsbury.[12]

Jamieson draws a sharp contrast between the views of Descartes and Pascal on rhetoric. Descartes abandons rhetoric as it respectable intellectual enterprise, since he regards his geometric *methode* not only as the proper means of conducting an inquiry, but also as the most effective mode of persuasion. He, therefore, subsumes persuasion, insofar as it can be studied rationally, within the confines of demonstrative logic. Pascal assumes a less rigid stance, since he believes that rational appeals to the understanding cannot maintain absolute control over the will. He, therefore, rejects Descartes's assumption that persuasion can be reduced to demonstration and constructs a rhetoric that is "enthymematic, audience-based, psychologically oriented."[13]

Pascal, then, salvages a place for rhetoric within the system of the arts, but he certainly does grant it epistemic status. Subscribing to a psychology that separates the will from the understanding, Pascal does not allow for the active integration of cognition and affect. From his perspective, rhetoric works its effects through appeals to pleasures and emotions governed by the volitional faculty, and such appeals have no bearing on the understanding, the faculty that yields rational knowledge. Rhetoric has the power to influence decisions, but not the power to generate or advance knowledge. Pascal's recognition of the importance of rhetoric, then, does not imply an enlargement of the Cartesian conception of rationality. It is merely a concession to the rational imperfections of the soul.

Ray McKerrow's recent essay on Whately provides a second case study in modern rhetorical epistemology. In analyzing the Whately/Campbell debate concerning the merits of deduction, McKerrow notes that Whately makes a crucial distinction between investigation and argument. Investigation, Whately contends, is a matter of inductive inquiry, and its function is to ascertain the truth or probable truth of propositions. Argument, on the other hand, is deductive, and it deals with the interrelationships among propositions already known. Consequently, evidentiary knowledge falls outside the province of rhetoric and logic, the two arts of argumentation. Whately makes this point succinctly in one of his early writings: "It is not the design of *argument* to make any progress, except in effecting conviction, nor to gain new truths, but merely to *expand* and *unfold* what is, as it were, wrapt up in the truths you set out with."[14] And despite his differences with Campbell on the value of syllogistic logic, Whately's rhetorical epistemology is thoroughly consistent with eighteenth-century thought. Like Campbell and Priestley before him, Whately reduces "rhetoric to a purely managerial or supervisory science—science which assumes responsibility for communication only after the substance of the message has been derived and its general purpose and direction determined."[15]

In one sense, then, Whately simply reiterates the eighteenth-century presumption that communication does not generate knowledge. But his position on the matter is particularly telling, since he is the most practical of the modern rhetoricians. Surely, it is significant that such a practical theorist and such a skilled advocate does not allow the contact of minds in an argument to count as a possible source for new knowledge. For Whately, intersubjective agreement is not a valid ground for knowledge.

Finally, we may turn to George Saintsbury's *A History of Literary Taste in Europe*, a massive three-volume work published at the turn of the century. As Hostettler notes, the work presents a radical form of the belletristic view of rhetoric. Saintsbury holds that "rhetoric's *only* function was to be, and always should have been, literary criticism."[16] And since literary art, in Saintsbury's scheme of things, exists purely for the sake of art, rhetoric assumes a narrowly conceived aesthetic function. It has nothing to do with ethics, or social history, or even persuasion. It deals exclusively with the treatment of a subject, not with the subject itself. Thus, Saintsbury effects a complete separation between rhetoric and knowing.

This brief survey certainly does not amount to a definitive statement about the epistemological presumptions of modern rhetorical theory. There were certain eccentric figures on the modern landscape who foreshadowed the epistemic approach to the art. Vico was surely one such exception, and, following Wilkie, we might also include Marx.[17] Nevertheless, it is safe to say that the positions we have just reviewed represent the mainstream of opinion in the post-Cartesian era. Rhetoric was variously collapsed into demonstrative logic, revived as a mode of dealing with the irrational aspects of the psyche, confined within the aesthetics of style, and redeemed as a way of transmitting truths obtained from other disciplines. But it was almost never regarded as a method of inquiry or a vehicle for enlarging knowledge. The evidence, then, supports the assertion that in viewing rhetoric as epistemic, we are making a radical break from the modern tradition.

More important, perhaps, this historical analysis may help us acquire an operational definition of the epistemic view of rhetoric. We are in a better position to understand what the concept is after we have understood what it is not. To put the point in another way, the epistemic approach achieves greater clarity when it is limited by reference to well-known theories of rhetoric that fall outside its purview. At any rate, we have isolated some basic assumptions that militate against an epistemic conception of rhetoric: an unlimited faith in the power of pure reason, a willingness to separate cognitive and affective processes, a refusal to grant in intersubjectivity (i.e., audience agreement) as a criterion for knowledge, and a disinterest in the way that the contact of minds alters the shape of knowledge. It requires no great act of imagination to change these statements into their contraries and thereby derive a preliminary list of the characteristics of an epistemic rhetoric. But, at best, the list would be partial, and, at worst, it might lead us into philosophical byways that distract our attention from the central question. Negative definitions can take us only so far, and sooner or later, we have to face up to the problem of dealing with the concept on its own terms.

The problem deserves more disciplined treatment than it has received in the recent literature. Since the epistemic view is revolutionary in the context of modern thought, we lack a stable vocabulary in which to attempt to define it, and since it is also an extraordinarily complex notion, it invites attention at a multitude of different levels. Under the circumstances, scrupulous caution seems advisable. At the same time, however, the connection between rhetoric and knowing has had an exhilarating effect on rhetoricians who have suffered through years of abuse from positivists, idealists, intuitionists, and other pure thinkers who occupy the higher levels of the academic totem pole. Hence the tendency to welcome the new concept with greedy enthusiasm and to attempt to gulp it down whole.

A careful reading of the literature reveals at least four different senses in which we may construe rhetoric as epistemic. Although all four are sometimes wrapped around each other in the same essay, it seems the better part of discipline to attack them separately. Each of these four approaches is complex in itself and therefore difficult to describe in a phrase. Nevertheless, let me make this tentative distinction among them: (1) Rhetoric is epistemic because it allows us to know how particular objects and events relate to fixed, abstract principles. (2) Rhetoric is epistemic because it represents an active, social form of thinking that allows us to gain knowledge both of particulars and of principles in respect to practical matters. (3) Rhetoric is epistemic since it can serve a metalogical function that helps us to secure knowledge of the first principles of theoretical disciplines. (4) Rhetoric is epistemic since knowledge itself is a rhetorical construct.

The first of these senses represents that weakest claim that rhetoric can make to epistemic status. Scott outlines the nature of this claim in this way:

> Even those who take the position that there must be some unified hierarchy of stable standards in order to achieve decent individual and social lives will agree that such standards must be applied in specific sets of circumstances. Few will argue that in practice, at least, applications are seldom, if ever, possible in such a way that the standards are engaged without discomfort. . . . The existence of some set of circumstances in the guise of a case to be settled seems to suggest rather strongly the human participation of relating standards to particular, concrete events.[18]

In this instance, rhetoric imparts knowledge by clarifying the relationship between a problematic particular and a fixed, absolute standard of truth. Since the status of the particular is uncertain before the occurrence of the rhetorical event, we can say that the transaction creates new knowledge. Furthermore, since the relationship between the particular and the abstract standard remains logically problematic, we must conclude that the knowledge is sanctioned by an intersubjective consensus stemming from the interaction between the rhetor and his audience. And for this reason, we can call this knowledge "rhetorical." Thus, even in this weak sense of the concept, rhetoric is epistemic, because it has the capacity to locate concrete events within the ambit of stable principles.

The second sense of the epistemic view of rhetoric entails a more fluid conception of the relationship between particulars and abstract standards. Advocates of this position argue that intersubjective agreement requires an interaction between particular experiences and the general categories for judging experience. Consequently, they conceive of an autonomous form of knowledge based on social consensus in which rhetoric plays a decisive role.

This form of knowing can be called "social knowledge." As Farrell defines this term, it comprises "conceptions of symbolic relationships among problems, persons, interests, and actions, which imply (when accepted) certain notions of preferable public behavior."[19] At every point, the characteristics of social knowledge correspond closely with the function of rhetoric. Such knowledge is essentially symbolic; it must be adjusted to the interests of those involved in a decision; it is validated by intersubjective agreement, and it is active in character. This last point is clarified in terms of a simple contrast: "Whereas technical or specialized knowledge is actualized through its perceived correspondence to the external world, social knowledge is actualized through the decision and action of the audience."[20]

The active quality of social knowledge explains how it operates to integrate particular events and general principles simultaneously within the context of a rhetorical transaction. Since social knowledge is intersubjective, it does have some claim to objectivity. Yet such knowledge can never be reduced to the clear order and precision of a scientific system. The categories of social knowledge are not fixed. They are transitive, indeterminate, and potential.[21] Consequently, social knowledge only works in reference to specific problems that demand action on the part of a specific group of people. In general, the values of the group are sufficiently well established to provide a general frame of reference for attacking the problem. But there is almost always a significant margin of ambiguity about how to construe these values, about which values are relevant, and about which have priority. This ambiguity is resolved on a case-by-case basis in terms of a deliberation about some specific problem. Thus, when we conceive of rhetoric as an instrument of social knowledge, we must conclude that rhetorical discourse influences both the perception of the situation and the conception of the abstract standards that apply to it.

In her essay on Aristotle's theory of epideictic, Oravec shows how this process might work. Objecting to interpretations that render the epideictic experience as pure observation, Oravec argues that the epideictic audience is required to make two sorts of judgments. First, the audience renders an aesthetic judgment about the skill of the speaker, about his command of the techniques of art. Second, and more important for our purposes, the audience judges whether the speaker has succeeded in achieving his goal. But to make a decision on this matter, the audience must consider the plausibility of the message; it must decide whether the object under consideration really deserves praise or blame. As Oravec describes it, the decision engages the auditor in an active process that has important epistemic consequence:

> Finally, the insight created by the presentation is not only a criterion of audience judgment, it also produces understanding and comprehension in the audience. The listeners learn the significance of their experience by witnessing the application of common values to familiar objects. The praiseworthy object, if represented with accuracy, may become a standard for practical action. . . . Thus the rhetor receives common values and experiences from his audience and, by reshaping them in artistic language, returns these experiences heightened and renewed. The process of "observation" which begins with perception and functions through judgment finally ends in heightened appreciation and intellectual insight.[22]

Epideictic rhetoric, then, influences the general standards of social knowledge. On one level, the rhetor may use the particular object or person as a vehicle for establishing or attacking abstract values. In such instances, one can appreciate the force of Oravec's comment about the object becoming a standard for practical action. The object serves as a model or antimodel and thus as a synecdochal representative of an abstract virtue or vice. On a more subtle level, interaction between the object and the value may alter the auditor's conception of the value. The process is most easily explained by analogy to the interaction that occurs between the elements of a metaphor. When we encounter a metaphor, normally we are aware only of the way that the vehicle affects our understanding of the tenor. But, as Richards has demonstrated, some energy always flows back in the other direction.[23] (Thus, if someone says, "Smith is a lion," we regard the metaphor as a description of Smith. Nevertheless, our attitude toward Smith may have a subtle, often unconscious, influence on our attitude toward lions.) Likewise, even when an epideictic orator assumes stable values and concentrates on evaluating the particular object, the juxtaposition between the object and the values may alter the values themselves. For example, let us suppose that an orator delivers an extremely skillful encomium on Richard Nixon, basing his argument on Nixon's diligence. The desired reaction is to change the auditor's attitude toward Nixon. Yet, intentions notwithstanding, the speech might cause the auditors to reduce the value they attach to diligence as a standard for judging a man's character.

In sum, we have now reviewed two senses in which we may regard rhetoric as epistemic. We have found that rhetoric may make a weak claim to epistemic status because of the power of persuasive discourse to alter our perception of a specific object within a fixed scheme of general standards. Or rhetoric may make a stronger claim based on a theory of active knowledge in which objects and standards interact during the course of the rhetorical transaction.

The third approach to this concept moves us into the domain of theoretical knowledge. Rhetoric, in this sense, constitutes a method for deciding between alternative conceptions of reality. More specifically, advocates of this position view rhetoric as a kind of metalogic. It functions to secure the first premises of science and speculative philosophy by overcoming the limitations in formal systems of argument.

Scientific and logical demonstrations progress from the known to the unknown according to a fixed system of entailments. That is, they resolve problematic issues by deriving consequences from what is already known. When we examine this process carefully, we can trace the progression of proofs back to first principles that are themselves unproven and unprovable according to the rules of the discipline.[24] Consequently, logical and scientific systems are limited by the character of the assumptions that set them in motion.

For the most part, these basic assumptions are either unrecognized or unquestioned. Nevertheless, there are certain crisis situations in which rival "paradigms" interpret the material of the same discipline in different ways (i.e., present different views of reality). If both systems exhibit internal coherence, then there is no purely formal means of demonstrating the superiority of one over the other.[25] This is true because the rival theories differ in respect to first premises which cannot be demonstrated. Given these conditions, we can resolve the conflict only by resorting to a mode of argument that is more flexible than formal logic. This line of reasoning has encouraged recent authors to assert that rhetorical argumentation has a legitimate place in science.[26] It is also one of the reasons that Perelman advocates a rhetorical approach to ethical theory.[27]

Precisely how does rhetoric discharge this metalogical function? No one has yet offered a direct and detailed answer to this question, but several interesting suggestions emerge from the recent literature. Holmberg, for example, advocates a return to an original and pure form of rhetoric.[28] In this guise, rhetoric is functionally distinct from dialectic. Dialectic, Holmberg argues, seeks correction to truth and therefore assumes that there is a single, correct view of reality. Pure rhetoric, on the other hand, assumes a pluralistic view, and it attempts to balance and harmonize different conceptions of the real. This attempt, we might add, seems especially necessary when we seek to assess competing philosophical and scientific paradigms.

Grassi offers a second and quite different approach. He distinguishes between a temporal, unconnected, and imagistic form of speech, and the rational, sequential, and ordered speech of scientific logic. The former puts us in direct emotional contact with the first principles of reality. But this type of speech lacks the power to explain itself to an audience. The exclusively rational speech of science has the virtue of clarity, but in itself it cannot put us in contact with first principles. The problem, then, is to bridge the gap, and Grassi assigns this function to rhetoric.[29]

Perelman's concept of presence suggests another possible approach to our problem. On first inspection, the possibility may seem remote, since Perelman carefully avoids epistemological issues when he discusses the elements of argumentation. Moreover he asserts that his concept of presence applies only to the technical analysis of rational argumentation, and he denies that it has any connection with a theory of knowledge.[30] Nevertheless, Karon has argued persuasively that the *New Rhetoric* implies an epistemology, and that presence is a crucial part of it.[31] Her argument leads to some interesting speculations about the function of rhetoric in determining the first principles of theoretical knowledge.

For Perelman, presence is a matter of focusing the attention on certain elements in a situation to the exclusion of others. This power to direct the attention, in effect, determines what is relevant in an argumentative situation and what should receive priority. Presence, therefore, becomes "a means by which reality is constructed and consequently a vehicle for transposing a phenomenon from the realm of the contingent to the realm of the absolute."[32] More specifically, Karon maintains that presence affects knowledge through its capacity to influence our apprehension of consensus relative to a premise.[33]

In order to interpret Karon's argument, we must understand Perelman's conception of how the rhetorician obtains his premises. Since he believes that all argumentation is relative to the audience addressed, Perelman holds that the rhetor must draw his premises from points of agreement within a given audience. In constructing the discourse, however, the rhetor does not confront an actual audience, and he must, therefore, construct an audience and assume points of agreement. This construct may be very abstract. In fact, the rhetor may conceive of an audience composed of all rational men, a universal audience. At this level, we enter into the realm of selecting first principles for the interpretation of reality.

But on what basis can we construct the universal audience? How do we obtain a sense of the premises that will win its assent? The answer, Karon argues, is that the universal audience is a construct created by the speaker's notion of reason, and the source of this construct is largely dependent on presence. That is, a premise will appear acceptable to all rational men to the extent that it is present in the mind of the thinker. As the presence of an idea increases, other ideas are forced out of attention, and we become more secure in asserting the universal rationality of the idea. Hence, presence plays an indispensable role in determining what is real.

Karon adds that this analysis exposes a problem in Perelman's system. Although Perelman rejects the Cartesian dichotomy between internal and external experience, the source of reality for him appears to be an internal sense of what is externally binding. The universal audience is the source of reality, but it proves to be a radically subjective construct.[34] But one must exercise some caution at this point. In Descartes, the force and clarity of the idea in the thinker's mind represents the end point of the epistemological process. In Perelman, however, it is only the starting point. Premises derived from the conception of the universal audience must be tested against actual, particular audiences.[35] Thus, our theoretical knowledge is constantly in flux, always in a state of dialectical tension between our subjective concept of reason and the intersubjective agreements of an actual audience. It is precisely this tension that allows us to develop a rhetorical approach to the basic premises of theoretical knowledge.[36]

We come now to the final and boldest claim for the epistemic status of rhetoric. In considering this version of the concept, we no longer view rhetoric as epistemic, but rather view epistemology as rhetorical. The basic tenets of this position are similar to those advanced by Farrell, Scott, and the other advocates of the social knowledge theory. These theorists, however, claim only that rhetoric is one among the many ways of knowing. On the other hand, this final sense of the epistemic view entails the claim that knowledge itself is a rhetorical construct. I should add that this position is only incipient in the current literature. Nevertheless, several authors have at least flirted with it, and it is an idea that bears watching.

The best way to approach the rhetoric as knowledge concept is to understand that it explicitly reverses the basic terms of positivistic philosophy. The positivists, seeking to achieve mechanical objectivity, collapsed the symbolic into the empirical. The function of language was simply to present an accurate report of the events that occurred in the real world. The theory of rhetoric as knowledge, to borrow a phrase from Brummett, collapses the tunnel at the other end.[37] The empirical is subordinated to the symbolic. Or, to be a bit more accurate, reality is regarded as fundamentally symbolic, and thus language itself becomes the primary unit of empirical knowledge. Furthermore, since language is inherently valuative, all aspects of human life, even the hard sciences, are pervaded by value. Thus, Walter Weimer writes:

> This conception of rhetoric emphasizes the intrinsic valuational or ethical dimension inherent in all scientific activity. Knowing and valuing are inseparable. . . . In the past both scientists and rhetoricians accepted, seemingly as revealed truth, the idea that science and logic are value-free in contrast to properly rhetorical concerns (where values were grudgingly accepted). Methodologists of science have known otherwise for some time. Many have emphasized that the growth of knowledge and the practice of research, since they are embedded in pragmatic action, entail ethical and valuational considerations at (literally) every step. Knowing, doing, and valuing can and must be reunited. Insofar as

> all involve the argumentative function, rhetoric is the domain in which unification must occur.[38]

All in all, the complete version of this rhetoric-as-knowledge position involves two claims: (1) the symbolic and normative aspects of knowledge are prior to the objective and mechanical, and (2) the rhetorical function is the dominant aspect of the symbolic process.

The elevation of the symbolic over the literal is most forcefully developed in the works of Kenneth Burke. In his recent debate with Howell, Burke summarizes this point of view rather clearly.[39] Burke asserts that the central issue in his thought is "a total distinction between the realms of (symbolic) action and (nonsymbolic) motion." Furthermore, while "action is not reducible to motion," Burke holds that symbolic action encompasses sheer motion. In other words, the symbolic forms of drama apply not only to literature, but also to the construction of reality: "I began to see how my defining literary form in terms of 'expectations' could be extended to an empirical notion of 'reality' itself as a structure of expectations, plus the further step whereby our views of the future involve a set of (right or wrong) expectations."[40]

Burke, however, does not place rhetoric at the apex of the symbolic process. He recognizes it only as one of several dimensions of symbolic action. (In his most recent essay, he divides the symbolic into five components: poetic, rhetorical, logical, scientific, and philosophical.[41] While all five work with the same instruments on the same objects, they differ in respect to function.) Thus, Burke's thought leads to a symbolic, though not a strictly rhetorical, view of knowledge. If we are to obtain a clear statement of the epistemological autonomy of rhetoric, we must move far to the other side of the "modern" period, to the classical origins of rhetorical theory.

For some time, scholars in speech communication have recognized the relevance of the doctrine of Gorgias of Leontini to the issues of contemporary rhetorical theory. Richard Enos's essay "The Epistemology of Gorgias' Rhetoric: A Re-examination" is the latest in a series of essays devoted to this theme.[42] Enos rightly stresses the close connection between Gorgias's epistemology and his rhetoric. (In fact, the two seem inseparable.) Denying the possibility of certain and immutable knowledge,

Gorgias holds that our view of reality is based exclusively on opinion. We know what we know on the basis of encounters with actual situations as they are defined by the perceptual screen of language. The antithetical power of language creates the illusion of reality by framing our responses in terms of simple oppositions. Language provides concrete models and antimodels that allow us to make sense of the world. Furthermore, as its antithetical structure suggests, language itself operates through conflict and is therefore fundamentally persuasive in character. Consequently, the rhetor commands the whole field of epistemology:

> Since all human inquiry moves within the realm of opinion, where deception is easy, all persuasion (philosophic, "scientific," legal or other) is a result of the force of eloquence rather than of rational insight. . . . If men *knew*, there would be a great difference between deception and truth. As it is, we can only distinguish between successful and unconvincing, persuasive and fruitless arguments.[43]

Our epistemological tour of the current rhetorical literature is now complete. We have moved from the "modern" views of Descartes, Pascal, and Whately, to the "postmodern" epistemic view, and, by only a slight departure from the main road, we have ended by returning to antiquity. Surely it is significant that the thinking of Gorgias, rather than Plato or Aristotle, provided the point of entry into antiquity. Even in the absence of other evidence, this fact should alert us to the profound changes occasioned by granting rhetoric an epistemic status. The epistemic view, in any of its forms, alters the assumptive grounds of modern rhetorical theory, and it thereby reopens some basic questions about the nature of rhetorical theory. The two most prominent of these issues relate to the ethics of rhetoric and the proper scope of the art. And we must now turn our attention to these issues.

Epistemic Rhetoric and the Problem of Values

The epistemic view of rhetoric leads to a number of serious ethical problems. Since the view is implicitly relativistic, its advocates are open to the charge that they are undermining the grounds for rational decision-making. Scott is well aware of the charge, and he replies to it on two levels. First, he argues that the "objectivist" alternative has problems of its own. The evidence shows that this position encourages fanaticism, intolerance, and an abrogation of responsibility in making decisions. Second, he points out that epistemic rhetoric is intersubjective, not subjective. Since it is based on the standard of communal assent, the epistemic view encourages cooperation and saves us from solipsism. In general, then, Scott seems to accept rhetorical relativism as a fact of epistemological life, and argues that its effects are not debilitating. In fact, it encourages such desirable goals as tolerance, mutual respect, and responsibility.[44]

Nevertheless, this general defense is not acceptable to everyone. Although fanatics may often distort objective philosophy, intersubjective relativism also contains the seeds of its own corruption, since it is likely to degenerate into demagoguery. Consequently, it is not surprising that a number of scholars have attempted to qualify and purify rhetorical relativism. Some have placed specific ethical limitations on epistemic rhetoric; others have attempted to balance the intersubjective criterion against the more stable criterion of self-evident truth, and still others have sought to limit the range of intersubjectivity by acknowledging the objective force of public issues. Each of these positions deserves separate treatment.

In his essay "Rhetoric as a 'Way of Knowing': An Attenuation of the Epistemological Claims of the 'New Rhetoric'" Cherwitz makes a direct attempt to bring the epistemic view under the control of ethical guidelines.[45] Cherwitz agrees with Scott that rhetoric has an epistemic function and with Brummett that rhetoric involves the advocacy of reality. Yet he is not willing to let the mere fact of intersubjective consensus define the nature of rhetorical truth. Instead, he argues that "the speech act must . . . meet certain criteria before it can be considered as truth creative."[46] The criteria are (1) rhetoric "must be viewed as an activity of correction, wherein the clash of contradictory ideas exposes error and yields truth," (2) participants "must be afforded an equal amount of control and initiative regarding lines of influence," and (3) the rhetoric must function "as an enterprise in person-risking and person building."[47] These qualifications are extraordinarily broad, and I leave the reader to his own devices in interpreting and assessing them.

It is clear, however, that Cherwitz has done much more than "attenuate" Scott's conception of an epistemic rhetoric. He has, in fact, shifted the ground of the concept from a description of rhetorical practice to a prescription about how rhetoric ought to proceed. Scott claims that rhetoric is epistemic because rhetoric-in-action yields intersubjective knowledge. He then defends this position ethically by justifying the rationality of intersubjective agreement as a standard of truth. Cherwitz, however, defines epistemic rhetoric in terms of certain ethical standards; rhetorical acts that do not measure up to these standards are by definition epistemologically insignificant.

Obviously, Cherwitz's view is not acceptable at the descriptive level. We can cite a long list of rhetorical discourses deficient in respect to one or more of Cherwitz's criteria that have succeeded in affecting public consensus. But this slight confusion does not vitiate the main force of Cherwitz's argument. For once in the literature, we encounter a rather clear issue: Should the term "epistemic" refer solely to the effect of rhetorical discourse in promoting intersubjective agreement, or should it also refer to the quality of the discourse as judged against standards derived from social philosophy?

The two remaining positions develop a more subtle approach that balances the relative standard of intersubjective agreement against a more stable mode of knowledge. We have already glanced at one of these approaches, Scult's analysis of the universal audience, but it seems useful to review his argument again in the present context.[48] Scult maintains that Perelman seeks to achieve an epistemological middle-ground between the closed systems of formal logic and the open field of skepticism. He effects this compromise through his conception of the interaction between the universal audience and particular audiences. The speaker obtains his concept of truth through his construction of the universal audience. But he must test this subjective construct against some particular audience. Arguments, therefore, are validated by gaining the adherence of both the universal and the particular audience. Since the particular audience is not constant, since it is always shifting in composition and ideology, the rhetorician can never gain final validation for his argument. He cannot achieve absolute, unshakeable truth.

Yet his commitment to the process furthers the cause of knowledge, and the interaction between the two audiences rectifies the problem involved in dealing with either one separately. The rhetorician is saved from sophistic argument *ad populum* because his own sense of rationality guides the selection of arguments. And he is saved from pure subjectivism since he must admit his arguments to the scrutiny of an actual audience.

The final position uses the concepts of situation and issue as external criteria for limiting the range of intersubjectivity. In an essay that combines Bitzer's concept of the rhetorical situation with a relativistic epistemology, Hunsaker and Smith indicate how these constraints might work.[49] Following Bitzer, they maintain that rhetorical discourse is grounded in a situation. The situation, in turn, guides the perception and formation of issues, and the issues determine the character of the rhetorical response. This process, however, is not mechanical or deterministic, since subjective and intersubjective factors intrude at every point. Both the situation and the issues that apply to it reflect the social and personal biases of those involved in the deliberation.

Nevertheless, there are certain limits on the construction that the speaker can impose on the situation, and certain conventions that restrict his license to interpret the issues. In respect to situation, Hunsaker and Smith argue: "Just as a block of wood precludes certain possibilities, such as a bronze statue, while allowing others, so the rhetorical situation, as first actuality, precludes certain issues from arising while allowing others."[50] Thus, the objective character of the situation as an event in the external world has some influence in delimiting the rhetorical transaction. In respect to issues, Hunsaker and Smith note that they are actualized in terms of subjective perceptions, but "because cognitive and affective experiences are not completely private, but to some extent shared through common experience and communication, there exists a common core of perception. . . . It is within the realm of commonality of perception that rhetorical issues arise."[51] The perception of an issue, therefore, depends upon those relatively stable aspects of intersubjective agreement that constitute norms and traditions. In sum, the objective nature of the situation limits the possible selection of issues, and relatively fixed conventions exert a degree of control over the perception and formulation of issues.

Hunsaker and Smith's essay is a descriptive analysis of issue formation. It is not a study in the ethics of rhetoric and should not be construed as such. Nevertheless, the connection between external constraints and relativism suggests a possible approach to the ethics of rhetoric within the context of the epistemic view. If we believe that issues frame the rhetorical act, then we might carefully study the nature of issues in order to determine points of psychological and logical regularity. Of course, these regularities largely reflect socially determined norms, but it is always possible to convert the norm into the normative. In this way, we might be able to construct relatively stable points of reference for the conduct of arguments verified by intersubjective agreement.

J. Michael Sproule's essay on Whately's theory of presumption offers an interesting point of departure for speculation on this matter.[52] Sproule contends that Whately's theory of presumption is not entirely logical or legal. Rather, Whately believes that presumption also encompasses the psychological reaction of an audience to an issue. The rhetor, then, must adjust his argumentation to both an assigned and a psychological burden of proof. When these two aspects of presumption are juxtaposed, it is apparent that certain consistencies emerge in the direction of psychological response to an issue. For example, although audiences normally hold a presumption in favor of the status quo, the introduction of a novel idea may turn the presumption in the other direction. Or, again, deference to an authority may create a psychological presumption that overwhelms the logically assigned burden of proof. Thus, we have a logical norm and certain norms of psychological reaction that move in a contrary direction. If we abandon Whately's faculty psychology in favor of a broader view of rationality, we might next ask under what circumstances the psychological reaction constitutes a legitimate violation of the logical norm.

More generally, the notion of presumption may help us stabilize the concept of intersubjectivity. For example, Edward Hawkins, a contemporary and friend of Whately's, argues that there should be an initial disposition to accept "that side of an argument where the first presumption of truth appears." This rule applies, for example, in any case where an "uninterrupted tradition brings with it a reasonable *presumption* in its behalf."[53] Translated into the terms of an epistemic rhetorician, Hawkins's argument might be rendered this way: An arguer ought to respect intersubjectively certified traditions, agreements, and conventions, especially when they have survived over a long period of time. Where such agreements exist, the arguer ought to accept their truth unless he has good reason to doubt them. Stated in this way, the doctrine of presumption bears a striking resemblance to Wayne Booth's "postmodern" rhetoric of assent.[54] Both concepts reverse the terms of the skepticism implicit in modern dogma, since they hold that we should presume the truth of well-established traditions unless there is compelling evidence to the contrary. Viewed in this light, the intersubjective approach to rhetoric not only respects the norms of thought, but it can also draw from them normative standards for the conduct of argument.

The Scope of Rhetoric

The attempt to define the limits of rhetoric constitutes one of the oldest and most persistent problems in the speech communication literature. Traditionally, the issue has centered on the distinction between rhetoric and poetic, and two rather clear positions have emerged. The first argues that the two arts deal with different types of objects. Rhetoric, in this view, applies to discourses that are literal in character and persuasive in intent, whereas poetic applies to discourses that are figurative and fictional. The second position distinguishes between the two on the basis of function. The rhetorical function in language is instrumental, designed to "produce effects 'beyond' the act."[55] The poetic function, on the other hand, is consummatory, designed to exercise "symbolic action in and for itself."[56] Rhetoric and poetic, therefore, represent two complimentary dimensions in discourse. They usually coexist in the same discourse, and no clear line can be drawn between "rhetorical" literature and "poetic" literature.

During the past decade controversy over this issue abated. But the colloquy between Burke and Howell in the February 1976 issue of the *Quarterly Journal of Speech* has renewed the debate. Burke, of course, "argues in favor of the functional approach, while Howell defends the distinction between the literature of literal statement and the literature of fiction."[57]

The consensus view in recent scholarship supports Burke's side of the issue.[58] This alignment is virtually mandated by the prominence of the epistemic theory of rhetoric, since that theory requires a functional approach to the art. Nevertheless, even as the contemporary emphasis on function and process ends the rhetoric/poetic controversy, it raises new and equally pressing issues about the limits of rhetoric. When we define rhetoric functionally, we immediately encounter questions about the range of application of the rhetorical function. Does it apply to scientific as well as axiological deliberations? Does it apply to theoretical as well as practical issues? Is this function so broad that it embraces all forms of argumentative discourse?

Or should we follow the views of the ancient theorists who generally limit the function of rhetoric to practical deliberations about civic business?

In general, contemporary theorists expand the scope of rhetoric well beyond the boundaries established by the classical authorities. Thus, although Perelman restricts the application of rhetoric to the humanities and social sciences, he regards it as relevant to abstract philosophy as well as to public debate.[59] Grassi is even more emphatic about the philosophical character of rhetoric. He argues that rhetoric is not properly a "technique of exterior persuasion," but rather "the speech which is the basis of rational thought."[60] And a number of theorists, Weimer, Wander, Overington, and Finocchiaro among them, argue that rhetoric functions in an important way in scientific argument.[61] Some of them, Weimer most notably, go so far as to argue that science is fundamentally a rhetorical transaction. There is, however, one important essay that manifests sympathy for the more restricted claims of the classical tradition. In fact, Farrell begins his essay "Knowledge, Consensus, and Rhetorical Theory" with praise for Aristotle's conception of the relationship between rhetoric and "a generally accepted body of knowledge pertaining to matters of public concern."[62] He proceeds to make a sharp and rather Aristotelian distinction between active and theoretical knowledge, and he restricts rhetoric to the domain of active knowledge. Finally, he asserts that rhetoric has a definite substance:

> Having considered several distinguishing rhetorical characteristics of social knowledge, it should now be apparent that rhetoric, whatever its own attributed status is not purely a formalistic enterprise. There

> is something which this art is about. That 'something' is a kind of knowledge which is attributed, audience-dependent, potential in state, generative, and normative in implication.[63]

It appears that Farrell has not only limited the scope of rhetoric, but has also resolved the old process/substance dichotomy in favor of substance and thereby dissociated himself from those who entertain a purely functional or process view of the art. That is, having defined a subject matter for rhetoric, it follows that Farrell should delimit the art in terms of a certain class of objects. His argument, however, subtly circumvents this issue, since it turns out that the substance of rhetoric is social knowledge, and social knowledge is itself a process. In the manner of Abelard, Farrell answers the question of substance both affirmatively and negatively, and thus he can define rhetoric as functional without sacrificing the logical right to restrict its area of operation. In short, rhetoric is functional, but it only functions in cases where social knowledge is engaged.

This position, as I interpret it, involves a synthesis of the classical and the more expansive contemporary views of the scope of rhetoric. On the one hand, Farrell reaffirms the classical conception of the function of the art; rhetoric is still an active faculty that bears on practical matters of social consequence. On the other hand, he does not limit the operation of this faculty to civic business as it is conducted in law courts, political assemblies, and public ceremonials. Instead, he expands the concept of social knowledge to the point that it might apply in any situation involving the deliberations of a group. Accordingly, one can justify the extension of rhetoric beyond its classical boundaries, but only insofar as the classical function of the art applies to discourses that fall outside the realm of normal public business.

Conclusion

The most consistent feature of the recent theoretical literature is the repetition of such key terms as "epistemic function," "intersubjective truth," "active knowledge," and "social consensus." These terms are closely related, and taken together, they reveal a certain consistency in the direction of recent thought. In general, the literature moves toward a revisionist theory of the epistemological status of rhetoric that rejects the modern dichotomy between communication and knowledge as it embraces the humanist conception of rhetoric as a way of knowing. The common goal, then, is to establish an epistemic base for the study of rhetoric. But this is a difficult goal, and despite the effort expended in pursuing it, the main features of the epistemic position are still opaque. We have yet to clarify the different levels of meaning that attach themselves to the epistemic view; we do not fully understand how it bears on the traditional issues of the discipline, and even when we have formulated issues, the analysis has failed to progress beyond the most primitive stages. Thus, although it is safe to say that rhetorical theory is changing, we have only a vague notion of what the change will bring.

In some measure, this lack of clarity results from problems inherent in any attempt to redefine the presumptions of a well-established academic tradition. Nevertheless, these unavoidable problems are compounded by the most serious defect in the literature—the void in the conceptual space between the specificity of the historical/textual studies and the grand abstractions of the metarhetorical essays. The literature tells us something about the history of rhetorical theory. It tells us a great deal about how we might identify the first principles of a new theory. But there is virtual silence about the middle-level issues that form the content of a theory.[64] Thus, the literature leaves us in a state of limbo; we have a past and a future, but no present.

The problem may be set in context by means of comparison. A number of teachers of English composition also call themselves rhetoricians, and they have produced a body of literature that we can follow in such journals as *College English* and *College Composition and Communication*. This literature has its abstract moments. One can find grand speculations on a scale to satisfy the readership of the *Quarterly Journal of Speech* or *Philosophy and Rhetoric*. Nevertheless, beneath the level of metatheory, there is a rather clear assumption about the common purpose of the enterprise. Almost everyone in the discipline centers his inquiry on the problem of how to teach students to write good English prose. And this common purpose translates itself into such issues as these: How does one find arguments to support a thesis? What is the best way to organize the main components of an essay? How does word order affect the meaning of a sentence? These issues are theoretical in character, but they also have practical ramifications, and consequently they offer a tangible ground for applying the results of metarhetorical speculation.

In turning to the speech communication literature one finds no counterpart to this stability of purpose or this commitment to middle-level theory. What practical issues are affected by our metatheories? The answer clearly does not come from pedagogy, since the literature maintains strict silence about speech composition.[65] The history of public address is another possibility, and the abstract discussion of the relationship between theory and criticism continues. As a practical matter, however, the link between the two has yet to be made.[66] In fact, then, our metarhetorical speculation is autotelic. It does not have an outlet for application, and as a result, our theoretical literature stutters at the level of pure abstraction. Ironically, however, this same literature keeps insisting that rhetoric is a practical discipline, that it operates mainly in the context of concrete problems, and that it calls for decisions leading to action.

In a recent review article, Littlejohn notes that "the tremendous growth in research and theory has created an information overload making integration and synthesis very difficult."[67] The normal response to this problem is to search for a macro-theory that can serve as a magic thread leading us out of the conceptual maze into a position of theoretical clarity. Although rhetorical theorists cannot be accused of contributing to the information overload, they have joined enthusiastically the search for Ariadne's thread. The effort has given us a vague sense of direction, but it has done little to enhance our theoretical knowledge of persuasive communication. And until we have done more research and theory, it is difficult to understand how we can achieve a viable synthesis at the metatheoretical level. Perhaps there is a magic thread, but I doubt that we can find it before we have explored the labyrinth more carefully and learned much more about its conceptual twists and turns.

NOTES

1. The decline in the number of these survey articles reflects the increasing maturity of scholarship in the history of rhetoric. Such essays obviously are unnecessary

when the scholarship has advanced past the preliminary stages. Most of the recent essays of this type deal with the Middle Ages, a period for which we still lack comprehensive knowledge of the primary sources. See James Bliese, "The Study of Rhetoric in the Twelfth Century," *Quarterly Journal of Speech* 63 (December 1977): 364–83; Luke M. Reinsma, "Rhetoric in England: The Age of Aelfric, 970–1020," *Communication Monographs* 44 (November 1977): 390–403; and John H. Timmis III, "Christian Rhetoric and the Western Church Fathers," *Central States Speech Journal* 27 (Winter 1976): 280, 284.

2. Philip C. Wander, "The Rhetoric of Science," *Western Journal of Speech Communication* 40 (Fall 1976): 226.
3. Richard Cherwitz, "Rhetoric as a 'Way of Knowing': An Attenuation of the Epistemological Claims of the "New Rhetoric,'" *Southern Speech Communication Journal* 42 (Spring 1977): 219.
4. Elaine Ognibene, "Review of Wayne Booth, *Modern Dogma and the Rhetoric of Assent* and a Rhetoric of Irony," *Southern Speech Communication Journal* 42 (Fall 1976): 84.
5. Barry Brummett, "Some Implications of 'Process' on 'Intersubjectivity': Postmodern Rhetoric," *Philosophy and Rhetoric* 9 (Winter 1976): 31.
6. Walter Weimer, "Science as a Rhetorical Transaction: Toward a Nonjustificational Conception of Rhetoric," *Philosophy and Rhetoric* 10 (Winter 1977): 19, quoting an unpublished paper by Carroll C. Arnold.
7. See Robert L. Scott's essay, "On Viewing Rhetoric as Epistemic," *Central States Speech Journal* 18 (February 1967): 9–16; and its sequel, "On View Rhetoric as Epistemic: Ten Years Later," *Central States Speech Journal* 27 (Winter 1976). I use Scott's "epistemic" as central term in this essay.
8. Brummett, "Some Implications of 'Process,'" 21.
9. For the purposes of this essay, modern is defined as post-Cartesian.
10. Kathleen M. Jamieson, "Pascal vs. Descartes: A Clash over Rhetoric in the Seventeenth Century," *Communication Monographs* 43 (March 1976): 44–50.
11. Ray E. McKerrow, "Campbell and Whately on the Utility of Syllogistic Logic," *Western Journal of Speech Communication* 40 (Winter 1976): 3–13.
12. Gordon F. Hostettler, "George Saintsbury's View of Rhetoric," *Western Journal of Speech Communication* 41 (Fall 1977): 210–20.
13. Jamieson, "Pascal vs. Descartes," 50.
14. McKerrow, "Campbell and Whately," 9, quoting from an unpublished manuscript by Whately.

15. Douglas Ehninger, in the introduction to his edition of Whately's *Elements of Rhetoric* (Carbondale: Southern Illinois University Press, 1963), xxvii.
16. Hostettler, "George Saintsbury's View of Rhetoric," 220.
17. For Vico, see Vincent Bevilacqua, "Vico: 'Process' and the Nature of Rhetorical Investigation: An Epistemological Perspective," *Philosophy and Rhetoric* 7 (Summer 1974): 166–74. For Marx, see Richard Wilkie, "Karl Marx on Rhetoric," *Philosophy and Rhetoric* 9 (Fall 1976): 232–46. It should also be noted that the epistemic view has clear and strong antecedents in premodern rhetorical theory. The concept of rhetoric as a way of knowing is carried through a humanistic tradition beginning with the early Greek Sophists, continuing with Isocrates and Cicero, and extending into the thought of the Renaissance humanists. For a summary of this tradition see Nancy S. Struever, *The Language of History in the Renaissance: Rhetoric and Historical Consciousness in Florentine Humanism* (Princeton, NJ: Princeton University Press, 1970), 5–39.
18. Scott, "On Viewing Rhetoric as Epistemic," 265.
19. Thomas B. Farrell, "Knowledge, Consensus, and Rhetorical Theory," *Quarterly Journal of Speech* 62 (February 1976): 4.
20. Farrell, "Knowledge, Consensus," 4.
21. See Farrell, "Knowledge, Consensus," 9.
22. Christine Oravec, "Observation in Aristotle's Theory of Epideictic," *Philosophy and Rhetoric* 9 (Summer 1976), 171–72.
23. For an analysis of this interaction, see William J. Jordan and W. Clifton Adams, "I. A. Richard's Concept of Tenor-Vehicle Interaction," *Central States Speech Journal* 27 (Summer 1976): 136–37.
24. See Ernesto Grassi, "Rhetoric and Philosophy," *Philosophy and Rhetoric* 9 (January 1976): 200–201.
25. Cf. Edwin Black's concept of "argumentative synthesis," in *Rhetorical Criticism: A Study in Method* (New York: Macmillan, 1965), 168–76. Black argues that if two opposing syntheses are equally coherent, then style determines which one will be most persuasive, 174–75.
26. See the essays by Weimer, "Science as Rhetorical Transaction," and Wander, "The Rhetoric of Science," as well as Michael A. Overington, "The Scientific Community as Audience: Toward a Rhetorical Analysis of Science," *Philosophy and Rhetoric* 10 (Summer 1977): 143–63; and Mario Finochiaro, "Logic and Rhetoric in Lavoissier's Sealed Note: Toward a Rhetoric of Science," *Philosophy and Rhetoric* 10 (Spring 1977): 111–22.

27. Chaïm Perelman, *The New Rhetoric: A Treatise on Argumentation*, trans. John Wilkinson and Purcell Weaver (Notre Dame, IN: University of Notre Dame Press, 1969), 1–10.
28. Carl B. Holmberg, "Dialectical Rhetoric and Rhetorical Rhetoric," *Philosophy and Rhetoric* 10 (Fall 1977): 232–43.
29. Grassi, "Rhetoric and Philosophy." This is a very condensed and simplified version of Grassi's argument. His essay demands, and rewards, close reading.
30. Perelman, *The New Rhetoric*, 119. See also Louise A. Karon, "Presence in *The New Rhetoric*," *Philosophy and Rhetoric* 9 (Spring 1976): 97.
31. Karon, "Presence in *The New Rhetoric*," 97–101.
32. Karon, "Presence in *The New Rhetoric*," 97.
33. Karon, "Presence in *The New Rhetoric*," 106–10.
34. S. M. Halloran, "Tradition and Theory in Rhetoric," *Quarterly Journal of Speech* 62 (October 1976): 240, argues a similar point.
35. For a more complete version of this argument, see Allan Scult, "Perelman's Universal: One Perspective," *Central States Speech Journal* 27 (Fall 1976): 176–80.
36. One should note, however, that Perelman's system applies only to the humanities since he makes no claims about a rhetoric of science.
37. Brummett, "Some Implications of 'Process,'" 28.
38. Weimer, "Science as Rhetorical Transaction," 13.
39. Kenneth Burke, "The Party Line," *Quarterly Journal of Speech* 62 (February 1976): 62–68.
40. Burke, "The Party Line," 65. In a delightful essay that uses a Burkean method to analyze Burke, Laura Crowell clarifies the way that symbolic action establishes reality. Symbolic action allows us to discriminate and classify situations, to change them by linguistic encompassment (i.e., by naming and renaming them), to confront and control uncertainty, to bring matters to completion, and to realize and embody the whimsicality of the whole symbolic process. See Laura Crowell, "Three Sheers for Kenneth Burke," *Quarterly Journal of Speech* 63 (April 1977): 152–67.
41. Burke, "The Party Line," 66.
42. Richard Leo Enos, "The Epistemology of Gorgias Rhetoric: A Re-examination," *Southern Speech Communication Journal* 38 (Fall 1972): 27–38; and Richard A. Engnell, "Implications for Communication of the Rhetorical Epistemology of Gorgias of Leontini," *Western Speech* 37 (Summer 1973): 175–84.
43. L. Versenyi, *Socratic Humanism* (New Haven: Yale University Press, 1963), 47–48.
44. Scott, "On Viewing Rhetoric as Epistemic," 263–66.

45. See Cherwitz, "Rhetoric as a 'Way of Knowing,'" 219.
46. Cherwitz, "Rhetoric," 217.
47. Cherwitz, "Rhetoric," 217–19.
48. See Scult, "Perelman's Universal," 176–80.
49. David M. Hunsaker and Craig R. Smith, "The Nature of Issues: A Constructive Approach to Situational Rhetoric," *Western Journal of Speech Communication* 40 (Spring 1976): 144–55.
50. Hunsaker and Smith, "Nature of Issues," 146.
51. Hunsaker and Smith, "Nature of Issues," 148.
52. J. Michael Sproule, "The Psychological Burden of Proof: On the Evolutionary Development of Richard Whately's Theory of Presumption," *Communication Monographs* 43 (June 1976): 115–29.
53. Sproule, "Psychological Burden of Proof," 124.
54. Wayne Booth, *Modern Dogma and the Rhetoric of Assent* (Chicago: University of Chicago Press, 1974), esp. 87–140.
55. Burke, "The Party Line," 66.
56. Burke, "The Party Line," 66.
57. Wilbur Samuel Howell, "The Two Party Line: A Reply to Kenneth Burke," *Quarterly Journal of Speech* 62 (February 1976): 69–77.
58. For a dissenting view, however, see Hostettler, "George Saintsbury's View of Rhetoric," 220.
59. Perelman, *The New Rhetoric*, 6.
60. Grassi, "Rhetoric and Philosophy," 202.
61. See Weimer, "Science as Rhetorical Transaction"; Wander, "The Rhetoric of Science"; Overington, "The Scientific Community," 143–63; Finochiaro, "Logic and Rhetoric in Lavoissier's Sealed Note," 111–22.
62. Farrell, "Knowledge, Consensus," 1.
63. Farrell, "Knowledge, Consensus," 11.
64. In fact, only two articles in the literature I reviewed directly attacked a limited theoretical issue. See George P. Boss, "Essential Attributes of the Concept of Charisma," *Southern Speech Communication Journal* 41 (Spring 1976): 300–313; and David A. Kaufer, "Irony and Rhetorical Strategy," *Philosophy and Rhetoric* 10 (Spring 1977): 90–110. Kaufer's essay is a model of what might be accomplished by identifying and thinking through specific problems in theory.
65. I exaggerate only slightly. Of the essays that I read for this review, only one, Sproule's article on Whately, makes direct reference to pedagogy.

66. This assertion requires some qualification. A number of rhetorical critics have made good use of postmodern epistemology in specific studies. See, for example, Michael McGuire, "Mythic Rhetoric in *Mein Kampf*: A Structuralist Critique," *Quarterly Journal of Speech* 63 (February 1977): 1–13; Michael McGee, "The Fall of Wellington: A Case Study of the Relationship between Theory, Practice and Rhetoric in History," *Quarterly Journal of Speech* 63 (February 1977): 28–42; and Ernest G. Bormann, "Fetching Good Out of Evil: A Rhetorical Use of Calamity," *Quarterly Journal of Speech* 63 (April 1977): 130–39. This sort of approach, however, is relatively new and still in its formative stage.
67. Stephen W. Littlejohn, "Symbolic Interactionism as an Approach to the Study of Human Communication," *Quarterly Journal of Speech* 63 (February 1977): 84.

PART THREE

Theories of Criticism

"In Search of Ariadne's Thread" shows how Leff's understanding of the classical tradition made him sympathetic to, yet critical of, the changes occurring in the field in the 1970s. Leff's mixed response to these changes as a historian of rhetoric is interesting in its own right. More impressive, however, is how persistently he sought to work through the complexities of his response through elaborating (and continually modifying) his own "theory" of rhetorical criticism—close reading.

What Leff at times also deemed "textual analysis" and "textual criticism," close reading was cultivated across the expanse of his theoretical, historiographical, and critical work (and in the spaces where these all came together) neither as a systematic interpretative protocol nor as merely an exhortation to resist such protocols in the name of some unmediated interaction with a text. Though displaying the same fine-grained analytical style popularized by the New Critics, close reading, in Leff's hands, became the synecdoche for his broader, increasingly explicit vision of rhetoric as a living, transformative art made concrete in its local manifestations. Perhaps the earliest statements of Leff's thinking on this matter emerge in the first two essays of this section, "Interpretation and the Art of the Rhetorical Critic" and "Textual Criticism: The Legacy of G. P. Mohrmann."

"Interpretation and the Art of the Rhetorical Critic" layers its central analytic focus—the critique of a piece by Leff's contemporary Edwin Black—within a broader account of the field as captured in a collection of essays for a special issue in 1980 of the *Western Journal of Communication*. Leff sees Black's essay as bringing into focus the other essays in the volume, and as a representative anecdote of the progress and continuing problems with "theory" for the entire speech communication tradition. Building on the work of Clifford Geertz in anthropology, Leff offers an interpretive view of theory as used in sister disciplines that is also grounded in the practice of classical rhetorical education. The animating idea of criticism in "Interpretation and the Art of the Rhetorical Critic" is the capacity for the critic to stay close to the contours of the case while at the same time to rise sufficiently above it to place key features in a rhetorical context that gives them meaning and explanatory force. The critic, like the psychologist or anthropologist, must be able to enter into the rich particulars of the matter at hand while at the same time relinquishing the ambition of complete explanation.

Occasioned by Mohrmann's death, "Textual Criticism" shares a thematic symmetry with "Interpretation and the Art of the Rhetorical Critic" and can be seen as an elaboration of the earlier essay's key insights. "Textual Criticism," in addition to providing personal background on the Leff-Mohrmann collaboration, critiques and extends the program Leff and Mohrmann began. One of the most haunting images of Leff's writing, which also well captures the humanistic spirit of close reading, comes in the closing lines of "Textual Criticism" as Leff points to the distinctly human scale of Mohrmann's vision and to the need for critics to foster theories and practices that honor our ordinary capacities for judgment and perception. In stressing Mohrmann's own emphasis on "the motile, adaptive character of rhetorical discourse" as a way to "identify theoretical knowledge with a complete understanding of a material case," Leff's tribute stakes out the broader territory for what became his defense of close reading in the 1990s and anticipates the challenges this defense would face.

Together, "Interpretation and the Art of the Rhetorical Critic" and "Textual Criticism" form a programmatic statement of the rationale and collaborative background of close reading. The next two essays—"Words Most like Things: Iconicity and the Rhetorical Text" (with Andrew Sachs) and "Things Made by Words: Reflections on Textual Criticism"—exemplify the development of close reading as it came into contact with opposing forces and ideas. "Words Most like Things" is both a paradigm example of close reading (its central object being Edmund Burke's "Address to the Electors of Bristol") and one of the first essays in which Leff and Sachs respond directly to Leff's critics' major objections—namely, that close reading encourages a celebration of the rhetorical object at the expense of an awareness of a text's ideological commitments. The concept of "iconicity," developed by the linguists Geoffrey Leech and Mick Short, provides Leff and Sachs with a bridging device in the essay; he uses it to yoke together close reading's core aim of overcoming the form/content divide with an elaboration of the relevance of his approach for understanding rhetoric as a cultural formation. In striving to counter the vocal, often skeptical disciplinary response to close reading, "Things Made by Words" continues the agenda of "Words Most like Things" but with a new twist. Leff not only grants his critics' claim that close engagement with the object can deflect attention from larger ideological formations in which a particular speech participates; he stresses the possibility of a "co-operative" relationship between his local, case-based approach and the more global coordinates of his peers. Looking, as might be expected, to antiquity, Leff first locates contemporary debates over rhetorical criticism in terms of enduring tensions in rhetoric between its "intentional" and "extensional" dimensions. Then, through a brief reflection on the origins of his own approach, and a turn to the idea of controversy, he proposes if not a resolution to this tension, at the very least a way for critics to attend to broader networks of social power, while still allowing particular texts to "retain their integrity as things made by words."

In line with Leff's efforts to modify and clarify the nature of close reading, and as evidence of the lengths to which he carried his approach into fundamental questions of interpretation and history, the final essay in this section, "Hermeneutical Rhetoric" features both an original gloss on Lincoln's use of the Declaration of Independence in the Gettysburg Address and a friendly rejoinder to Steven Mailloux's notion of "rhetorical hermeneutics." For Mailloux, rhetorical hermeneutics helps to explain the historical relativity of interpretative strategies over time. In short, all interpretation becomes subsumed into the contextual features that presumably drive all rhetorical activity. Leff grants Mailloux's point but notes that his view of the hermeneutic process provides no explanation of the role of an agent in moving streams of interpretation in one direction or another. In contrast to Mailloux's view of hermeneutics as itself a kind of super-agent, Leff develops his own strand of hermeneutics in which an orator engages his or her community in a reconsideration of its past as it seeks to set a course for its political future. Whereas Mailloux inquires into the rhetorical strategies that define interpretative activity, Leff asks "how hermeneutical strategies enter into the production of political rhetoric." Though "Hermeneutical Rhetoric" came rather late in Leff's career, one can discern the germinal elements of its thinking—and, too, its debt to the heritages of classical rhetoric—in Leff's earliest attempts at criticism.

FURTHER READING

"Lincoln at Cooper Union: Neo-Classicism Revisited." *Western Journal of Communication* 65 (2001): 323–48.

Interpretation and the Art of the Rhetorical Critic

The purposes of this essay are both diagnostic and prescriptive. The diagnosis involves an attempt to locate a few common themes that recur throughout this issue. In some measure, this task is no more than a summary of ideas developed in the preceding pages, but as these ideas are isolated and connected with one another, an argumentative configuration begins to emerge. The authors represented here find evidence of health and vigor in the field, but a comparative reading of their essays indicates that the art suffers from a set of related problems. These problems are expressed in terms of confusion about the relationship between theory and practice, complaints about methods that lose contact with the object of study, and warnings about the mechanical imposition of a priori categories on rhetorical artifacts. The second purpose is to find a cure for these maladies, and Edwin Black's brief but important essay

From *Western Journal of Speech Communication* 44 (1980): 337–49.

provides the focus for this inquiry. Black's polemic against "etic criticism" summarizes earlier concerns about the state of art and throws them into conceptual relief. A critical analysis of that argument suggests implications that extend beyond the original formulation of the issue and that force a reconsideration of conventional assumptions about the role of theory in rhetorical criticism. Both diagnosis and prescription, however, depend upon some knowledge of the case history of the patient. We cannot understand the meaning of the essays collected here or the direction in which they are leading us until we read them in the context of the recent history of rhetorical criticism. And for this reason, the symposium on criticism published in this journal in 1957 offers an appropriate point of departure.

In assessing the quality of critical practice, the participants in the 1957 symposium present a uniformly pessimistic diagnosis of the situation. Almost all assert that the existing state of criticism is unhealthy and that strong correctives are necessary. Thus, Bryant proposes a reassessment of the role of style in rhetorical criticism and quickly adds that reassessment "cannot but imply enhancement, for hardly could there lie occasion at present to further depress the repute of style or to relegate style to a more distant peripheral position than it has achieved in most professional rhetorical speculations."[1] He finds that critics sometimes attend to the mechanics of stylistic analysis, "but almost always they back away from the central questions or strike them but glancing blows in the twilight."[2] Other authors extend Bryant's gloom beyond the canon of style. Baskerville complains of having to wade through "a spate of undistinguished, unimaginative 'critical studies.'"[3] Clark concludes that existing practice has yielded "a criticism that adheres too closely to its formal topoi; it is frequently stereotyped, occasionally banal."[4] Hochmuth argues that a reading of contemporary criticism would lead to the conclusion that there is virtually only one approach open to the critic. The result of this monism is unfortunate, not only because of the lack of options, but also because the standard system results in "Aristotelian rhetoric read out of the context of Aristotle," and thus encourages the "practice of seizing upon the more mechanical aspects of the lore."[5] Redding maintains that the criticism of the period moves the critic out of, rather than more deeply into, his or her own subject. Unwittingly caught up in the neopositivism of an earlier generation of literary scholars, rhetoricians preoccupy themselves with a factual, historical, and extrinsic approach to criticism. The central datum of the enterprise, the text, is shunted to the side: "Putting the matter bluntly, is not some re-examination in order when we find, upon examining twenty-five representative papers published since 1940, that about three-fourths of the space is typically devoted to historical and biographical information, with sometimes as little as one-tenth allotted to rhetorical analysis of speeches?"[6]

All told, the 1957 symposium presents an impressive catalogue of woes besetting the field of rhetorical criticism. The details of the lament, having been repeated ad nauseam during the past two decades, are now thoroughly familiar and need not detain us here. Yet the general attitude of these critics of criticism is remarkable in itself and important as a sign of later developments in the field. The frequency and strength of attacks on the status quo betoken not so much an attempt to reform the system as an urge to move outside of it entirely. This urge, moreover, expresses itself in terms of a consistent pattern. Three steps are involved: (1) The process begins with comments that deplore the existing state of criticism; for the most part, critical studies are dismissed as mechanical, unimaginative, and incomplete. (2) The deficiency in critical practice is linked with deficiencies in method; the field is in bondage to a single method, and that method obscures the critic's vision of the text by deflecting attention to the historical background and by filtering the critic's perception through a set of static categories. (3) The correlation between problems of critical method and critical practice gradually emerges as a cause/effect relationship; deficient method is the cause, deficient practice the result. Consequently, the solution to the problem appears to lie in developing new methods that provide alternatives to the tyranny of the old approach and that remedy its theoretical defects.

In the 1957 symposium, Bryant is the only contributor who departs from this pattern. While he diagnoses the situation in the same way as the other authors, he breaks ranks at the third and final stage of the process by proposing a solution that rejects more theory as a corrective to the deficiencies of existing theory. He seems, in fact, to distance himself from any systematically articulated method, preferring (by implication) to rely on the ingenuity of the critic and an absorbing concentration on the particular object of study. Thus, when Bryant defines style as the order and movement given to thought, he suggests that the analysis of style brings the critic directly in contact with the rhetorical workings of the text. Moreover, he insists that such analysis cannot depend on a "blueprint" or on a "check-list of devices." An inventory of these devices is useful, but it is merely a tool, for the essence of style is the way it functions within a particular discourse. And in confronting this issue, all a priori categories and theoretical constructs fade into the background:

> When the critic comes to grips with his subject, no Buffon or Hochmuth, no Oppenheimer or Reynolds, can prescribe for him the emphasis and proportions which the several critical categories ought to assume in his analysis. With the aid of such resources as he can muster, he must strive to see the speech for what it was and what it is. He will listen to the voice of the theorist, but he will look at the phenomena through his own eyes.[7]

The language here calls to mind Black's description of "emic criticism." And while Bryant's formulation of the approach is sketchy, it certainly constitutes a reasonable response to the problem as he and most other critics of the period conceived it. If criticism suffers from the mechanistic application of theory to particular cases, a shift in focus to the rhetorical texture of the particular work seems a potentially effective antidote.

Whatever the merits or liabilities of Bryant's position, however, it was, and still remains, a minority view. The other contributors to the 1957 symposium regard the problem not in terms of the limitations of theory, but in terms of the limitations of the theory then in vogue. Thus, they all look for a different theoretical perspective, and they all obtain it by searching through another shelf in the academic cabinet. Clark, for example, relies on literary theory as a model; Hochmuth presents a more specific and more useful model based on the works of Kenneth Burke; Redding turns to the method of content analysis developed in the social sciences; and Nilsen seeks to ground rhetorical interpretation in ethical theory."[8] These speculations anticipate the main line of development in the field for the next two decades. The outburst of revisionism in the sixties and seventies follows the sentiment and often the pattern of these earlier essays. For twenty years a substantial portion of the critical literature enacts the same ritual: anathematize traditional practice and method, sanctify a new theoretical approach (usually borrowed from another discipline), and, if possible, incarnate the newly risen faith by imposing it on some artifact. This quest for the critic's Grail manifests itself in a bewildering variety of forms—in the attempt to refine a dramatistic or sociological base for the rhetoric of movements, in the proliferation of Burkean criticism, in the call for a more scientific form of criticism, in the rise of generic studies, and in a dozen other less well developed angles of theoretical vision.[9] In more recent years, while the mortification of neo-Aristotelian sin disappears from the process, the hope for rebirth through conversion to an alien god continues, with critics variously seeking enlightenment through social-psychological, dramaturgical, phenomenological, or structuralist theory.

By the early seventies, the monism of the fifties dissolves into a kaleidoscope of theoretical patterns. Scott and Brock, writing in 1972, report the demise of the old tradition and the emergence of a new "critical pluralism." While some are dismayed by this apparent Babel of critical approaches, the majority believe that its effects are salutary. Thus Karlyn Campbell, one of the most perceptive of our critics, expresses an enthusiasm for the work of her colleagues that has virtually no precedent in this field: "The presence of many theoretical and methodological viewpoints is not a sign of chaotic instability but evidence of the health and maturity of our discipline which is becoming increasingly able to account for the many meanings of rhetorical and communicative acts." The attack on the unitary modality of the tradition indicates "returning health," as well as "maturity and vigor," and it corresponds with the rise of "much more and better rhetorical criticism."[10]

Is Campbell's optimism justified? The evidence collected in this issue gives reason both to support and to qualify her judgment. On the positive side, no author, save perhaps the one assigned to deal with the traditional approach, expresses the sense of gloom that pervades the 1957 symposium. There are caveats and complaints about current practice, but these are balanced by genuine and sustained outbursts of enthusiasm. For the most part, the authors represented here are more disposed to work within the frame of existing critical systems than to overturn their foundations.

This fact surely marks a distinction from and an improvement in the state of the art compared to what it was twenty-three years ago.

Much of the reason for this change of attitude arises from an apparent growth and internal development within a number of critical approaches. In many cases, the sheer bulk of the literature is impressive. For example, where Hochmuth could cite only one study to illustrate the application of Burkean criticism, Gronbeck lacks sufficient space to list the relevant scholarship. More important, however, as the literature expands in bulk, the various approaches integrate more sophisticated material into their conceptual apparatus, and they assume a more coherent shape. Logical subdivisions emerge; gaps are uncovered; analysis of certain kinds of artifacts achieves greater precision, and problems encountered in earlier studies provide fertile ground for later research. Evidence for these developments is spread throughout the essays, ranging from Riches and Sillars' discovery of seven different foci for research in social movements to Farrell's account of the increasing sophistication in the logic of symptom criticism. In short, contemporary critics perceive a growing weight and depth of critical literature within a number of identifiable approaches, and this perception results in a new sense of confidence about the status of rhetorical criticism as a discipline.

The state of the art has improved; there are unmistakable signs of health, vigor, and maturity, but there is also reason to temper our optimism. Some of the old maladies seem to afflict the new forms of critical inquiry. The connection between theory and practice remains unclear, and complaints about critical works that drift away from the particular object of study still persist. These issues surface in almost all of the preceding essays, and their successive appearances should be noted carefully.

Mohrmann attacks one aspect of the problem directly and bluntly, arguing that attempts at theoretical innovation often merely substitute new molds for old. The greatest fault of neo-Aristotelianism is its failure to encourage intensive analysis of texts. But new approaches sometimes embody this fault even as they reject the apparatus of the old criticism: "The earlier abuses of traditional concepts and current pretenses about them eventually coalesce." Preoccupation with disembodied categories, whatever the name and nature of the categories, deflects the critic's attention from its proper object—the particular rhetorical phenomenon under investigation. A new critical vocabulary does not necessarily guarantee fresh insight into texts.

Riches and Sillars deal with a different aspect of this problem when they maintain that a wall of separation divides theorists from practitioners of movement criticism. Critical studies rarely reflect the controversies that animate the theoretical literature, and the theorists argue about definitions and abstract concepts without paying much heed to critical practice. There is no hostility between the two camps, only mutual indifference. Thus, Riches and Sillars conclude: "At the present time, theory and practice appear to be separate. Each has little direct effect on the other."

Fisher, though he treats the matter rather briefly, manages to touch on both sides of the problem outlined above and to indicate how its aspects coalesce. The danger implicit in the generic approach, he argues, is that it can overwhelm the critic. By overwhelm, he clearly means that attention to genre theory per se may obscure the critic's perception of the concrete artifact. This form of idolatry divides into two species: the separation of theory from critical practice and the mechanical imposition of theory on the object of critical inquiry. The critic may succumb to the temptation to write theory instead of criticism and thus create principles that never touch the objects of criticism. Or the critic may succumb to the temptation to impose genre on a work and thus distort it by forcing it into a preconceived mold. Both aspects of this problem occur not only in genre criticism but in all systematic approaches to criticism, and both arise from a failure to maintain proper balance between the main elements in the process of critical inquiry. The temptations toward imbalance, Fisher argues, may be avoided if the critic assumes a stance of "informed innocence." This phrase is striking, and the idea it conveys moves us some distance toward resolving the tension between theory and practice.

Farrell presents the most detailed analysis of the problem. This emphasis reflects the nature of his topic, since any consideration of model criticism immediately raises the questions of how abstract constructs relate to concrete particulars. Yet, despite Farrell's careful and sympathetic review of the literature, his essay repeatedly testifies to the absence of clear answers to this central question. The problem haunts each of the major types of model criticism.

In symptom criticism, the movement from model to artifact to social context involves dangerous leaps of inference at every step and a corresponding temptation to leap before looking. Farrell argues that certain critics mitigate the danger by examining the artifact in great detail and by tightening the logic of critical justification (Farrell does not explain, however, how a more detailed analysis of the particular allows the critic to escape the blinders imposed by the conceptual brackets contained within the model). Yet, even when such controls are deployed, the model critic still confronts "a recurring difficulty with standards of evidence. There is, one might say, a tendency to chew more than is bitten off; some studies seem to be a model in search of an appropriate object of analysis."

The problems of didactic and thematic criticism are variations on the theme developed in the analysis of symptom criticism. Didactic models apply qualitative standards to artifacts, and subjective distortions are likely to influence the selection and conception of the model as well as the process of assessing the artifact. As a consequence, this approach often leads to a report on the state of the critic's glands rather than an analysis of a rhetorical event. Thematic criticism constructs rhetorical phenomena by gathering fragments into composite structures. By its very nature, this procedure encourages the critic to view specific artifacts as grist for his or her synthesizing mill; there is a temptation to disengage from the artifact and to concentrate on the abstract pattern. The dangers here, Farrell maintains, are serious, since "ontology does not yield comfortably to extrinsic systems." This warning concerning thematic criticism applies with equal force to all forms of the model modality. Though Farrell finds much to praise in the work of critics operating within the system, he also finds equally important signs of real or potential abuse. Thus, he leaves us dangling between the conceptual attractiveness of the approach and the perils involved in failing to harness its abstract energy to the requirements of particular cases.

Perhaps some of the reservations and complaints just summarized should be discounted. Nonetheless, they accumulate in a way that makes it difficult to deny that a problem exists. To put the matter simply, critics lack perspectives that enable them to make adequate connections between theoretical constructs and the concrete data of rhetorical experience. The rise of pluralism has broken us loose from old constraints and encouraged fresh activity in the field, but the multiplication of theories does not resolve the tension between theory and practice. Thus, one of the central problems diagnosed in the fifties still plagues us. We still complain that much of our criticism adheres too closely to formal topoi and that it leads us out of rather than more deeply into our subject. We no longer lack theories; yet we still lack secure footing in the territory that lies between the regularity of abstract patterns and the idiosyncrasies of particular rhetorical events. And this situation is especially troublesome, since the gap concerns the most fundamental step in the critical process—the act of interpretation by which the critic attempts to account for and assign meaning to the rhetorical dimensions of a given phenomenon."[11]

All these considerations lead us to Black's essay. That essay places the earlier reservations about theory into a conceptual frame of reference, and in doing so, suggests a new approach to the task of interpretation. Reacting to the problems inherent in criticism based on theoretical models, Black sharply distinguishes between such "etic" criticism and its "emic" opposite. The etic stance, he argues, not only forces phenomena into preconceived molds, but it also stultifies rhetorical theory by shutting off access to fresh insight drawn from rhetorical practice. Consequently, Black advocates an emic approach to criticism, an approach that seeks to "coax from the critical object its own essential form of disclosure." The critic must deal with the work on its own terms, must interpret the work "without conscious expectations drawn from any source outside the work." But while the emic enterprise concentrates on the particular, it is not without theoretical consequences, since it stretches toward or eventuates in general truths about human experience. Theory is the outcome of critical practice, not its starting point.

This connection between theory and practice reverses the pattern that has dominated rhetorical criticism for the past few decades.[12] It indicates a significant shift in Black's own thinking; the implied emphasis on the relationship between critic and method in *Rhetorical Criticism* now changes to an explicit emphasis on the relationship between critic and subject.[13] On a more general level, this shift implies important consequences for the field as a whole, perhaps even more important than the consequences which followed Black's definitive attack against neo-Aristotelian method.

Yet the essay is very brief; as its title indicates, it is a note rather than a fully elaborated doctrine. And even as the essay promises to free us from old dilemmas, it raises new problems of its own. In short, Black's argument represents an important advance, but its premises must be tested and extended before its full significance can be appreciated.

Let me begin by disposing of an objection likely to be raised against Black's position—that it entails a radically subjective view of the act of interpretation. Obviously, Black does assume that interpretation is subjective, but the assumption strikes me as a strength and not a weakness. Interpretation is not a scientific endeavor. Systematic principles are useful in attempting to validate interpretations, but the actual process of interpretation depends upon conjectures and insights particular to the object at hand. Thus, E. D. Hirsch argues: "The very process and psychology of understanding are not reducible to systematic structure (despite the many attempts to do so), because there is no way of compelling a right guess by means of rules and principles. Every interpretation begins and ends as a guess, and no one has ever devised a method for making intelligent guesses."[14] As Farrell notes, even when the critic works within the confines of a fully articulated model, he or she must still rely on hunches to match features of the text with the configuration of the model. In and of themselves, abstract theories and models provide no rules for their connection to a particular phenomenon, and the study of this connection moves us outside the realm of any formal system.

A subjective conception of interpretation, then, in no way weakens Black's argument. Yet, having duly noted the subjectivity of the process, one wonders why Black excludes all expectations that the critic has prior to the examination of the work. In the terms of Fisher's oxymoron, innocence and information operate simultaneously; they are suspended in tension throughout the course of the interpretive process. The critic may begin with an attempt to assume the stance of innocence, but the critic's information, the conceptual baggage unavoidably dragged into the act of observation, always intrudes and colors subjective understanding of the object at every moment of its observation. No act of will can eliminate this interaction, since it is bound up with the very nature of the interpretative act. Interpretation requires a translation from the expression in the text to the meaning assigned by the critic. Through sympathetic understanding, the critic may become "consubstantial" with the text, may merge his or her own consciousness into the text as he or she understands it. Yet this process of identification brings with it the ambiguities of substance, since the merger joins together things that remain separate. If the text as it stands is a given, so is the critic's frame of reference, and the critic cannot assimilate the text until it is filtered through his or her own conceptual apparatus. Meaning cannot be assigned to expression except by reference to something outside the original expression, and thus, to cite Hirsch again, "All interpretations at some point have recourse to categories and conceptions that are not native to the original."[15] Directly or indirectly, consciously or unconsciously, extrinsic threads weave their way into the fabric of guesswork that forms the basis of interpretation. And since the process is so subjective, so little given to control by a priori dicta, I hesitate to eliminate on a priori grounds a process of guessing that begins with theoretical principles.

Black also attempts to dismiss etic criticism by arguing that it is circular, in that its theoretical principles presuppose its critical findings, and the critic sees only what he or she is disposed to look for. I do not deny this argument, but a careful analysis of Black's essay indicates that the emic critic confronts the same problem, though in a somewhat different form. The emic critic's progress from "suspension of judgment to the rendering of judgment" involves a crucial intermediate step: "But at some moment—probably early—in his engagement with an object, the emic critic will aspire to so sympathetic an account, that the critic's audience will understand that object as, in some sense, inevitable." Thus, the critic at some point—probably early—in the interpretative process comes to form a conception of the object as a whole, a conception so strong as to appear inevitable. This conception, moreover, is something other than the actual expression in the text; otherwise, there would be no interpretation. Consequently, while still engaged in the interpretative act, the critic constructs a meaning for the object, a hypothesis or model that explains what it is. And the emic critic is now caught up in the same process that circumscribes the thought of his or her etic colleagues. Just as the etic critic, once convinced that his or her theory accounts for the rhetorical dimensions in a work, assimilates the text into the theoretical categories, so also the emic critic, once convinced of the inevitability of his or her conception of the work, forces the particular features of the work into conformity with the conceptual representation of its meaning. Since interpretation is inherently circular, this problem is unavoidable. The interpreter's explanatory hypothesis constitutes and organizes the internal evidence, and thus the evidence naturally tends to support the hypothesis.[16] The same cycle applies whether the hypothesis is abstracted from the text or brought in from an external source. The emic critic may circle closer to the ground, but like all other members of the critical flock, the flight is still circular.

Black's argument, then, requires qualification. The sharp outlines of his distinction between emic and etic criticism begin to blur, and the categorical preference for one over the other stretches the point too far. Extrinsic principles do not resolve the problem of how to interpret a subject, but subjects do not interpret themselves. The act of interpretation mediates between the experience of the critic and the forms of experience expressed in the text. To perform this act successfully, critics must vibrate what they see in the text against their own expectations and predilections. What critics are trained to look for and what they see interact in creative tension; the two elements blend and separate, progressively changing as altered conceptions of the one reshape the configuration of the other.

In theory, etically derived starting points need not overwhelm this interaction. A knowledge of rhetorical theory is an important part of the critic's experience, and the sensitive critic may vibrate an extrinsic model against the text instead of imposing it on the text. In practice, however, few critics demonstrate the required sensitivity. The temptations to lose sight of the text are enormous, and, as the essays in this issue demonstrate, rhetorical critics succumb to these temptations with alarming frequency. Worse yet, the strong etic orientation in the field encourages a thorough preoccupation with abstract theories and methods and dulls the critic's sensitivity to the problem of interpretation. Thus, we obtain a proliferation of critical methods, without any of these methods solving the problem that lies at their collective origin—the neo-Aristotelian tendency to impose mechanistic categories on texts. The emic alternative, of course, is not a panacea. It is no guarantee against distortion of the text, but at least it forces the critic to engage the text before distorting it. In any event, we have erred so long in the direction of the abstract that it now seems reasonable to encourage efforts that begin with the particular. And although Black's categorical idiom overstates the case, the tendency of his argument has much to recommend it. I would reformulate his position in these terms: our skepticism about an interpretative construct should increase as a function of the distance between the origins of the construct and the particular object of study.

If a heavy concentration on theory leads to a neglect of particular objects, then it might follow that a heavy concentration on particulars leads to a neglect of theory. This reversal of terms and relationships is the basis for another objection to the emic approach—that the approach seduces the critic away from any contact with theory and leaves him or her abandoned to work on projects of isolated and momentary interest. Black implicitly attempts to blunt this objection by arguing that the critic plays a vital role in theory construction. On the surface, this position seems to entail a conventional appeal for an inductive approach to rhetorical theory, with particular critical studies providing the basic data. Yet a close reading of his essay suggests a less conventional approach that profoundly challenges existing assumptions about the logic of inquiry in rhetorical criticism.

When interpreted as a conventional inductive approach to theory, Black's position cannot withstand analytic scrutiny. Suppose, for example, he means that each critical act should work toward generalization. In that case, a very inadequate form of induction would be obtained. The theoretical precepts derived from critical practice would have the support of only one instance, and, in terms of traditional logic, the critical enterprise would yield a mass of hasty generalizations as its legacy. In response to this problem, the matter might be approached more systematically and accumulate the results of many critical studies in order to support theoretical generalizations. But this is no solution either, since it is subject to three crucial objections. These objections, in ascending order of importance, are as follows: (1) An emphasis on systematic induction immediately relegates the critic to the basement of the rhetorical edifice. Since the critic is absorbed completely in the particular case, the task of compiling and arranging the links between particulars belongs to those officed on a higher floor where conceptual tidiness counts for more than sympathetic and compassionate understanding. (2) Whoever has the task of turning the results of critical inquiry into sound inductive generalizations is bound to experience frustration. Each case study, after all, proceeds from a radical concentration on the particular phenomenon as a unique event. This type of inquiry does not lend itself to the controls necessary for proof of regularities across cases. The stuff of rigorous induction is not made of such quivering jelly as a compassionate understanding of the "Coatesville Address" or a sense of inevitability about Lincoln's speech at the Cooper Institute. (3) If the required inductive connections were possible, the emic critic would chart the course for his or her own extinction.

As the works of the emic critic grow and multiply, so does the corpus of rhetorical theory. By extension, this process would lead to the identification of genuine regularities and the discovery of etic principles that really do hold across cases. Ultimately, emic criticism would become obsolete.

I do not believe that Black, wittingly or unwittingly, supports hasty generalization or a neopositivistic commitment to particulars as a moment in the history of a grand theoretical enterprise. He must have some more subtle concept in mind, and he gives us an important clue to the deeper meaning of his position toward the end of his essay, when he compares the emic critic to the psychoanalyst. The analogy reverberates with implications for rhetorical criticism.

Psychoanalytical interpretation is simultaneously particular and theoretical. It originates in the unique subject, since the relevant motives are discovered in the particular case, and it ends with the particular case, since its results are confirmed in relation to the unique subject. Yet the process always involves explanation, and the attempt to explain puts the analyst in contact with matters of theoretical interest. The contact with theory does not merely refer to standard collections of psychological lore or to the general knowledge the analyst acquires through training. Rather, in the context of the interpretative situation, the explanation of the specific phenomenon under investigation is itself theoretical. Whether self-generated or borrowed from external sources, principles always enter into explanations, but the forms these principles assume are inextricably bound up with the particular circumstances the analyst confronts. That is, theoretical precepts attain meaning only as they are vibrated against the particular case and are instantiated in an explanation of it. We have here a form of theory that eventuates in diagnosis, not in a hierarchical arrangement of principles nor in observations of regularities that lead to prediction. Theory functions not to generalize to or from cases, but within them.[17]

This paradigm of interpretative theory obviously has implications that extend beyond psychoanalysis. In fact, it seems relevant to any interpretative act that seeks to explain human behavior as it occurs in complex situations. Thus, in his analysis of anthropological interpretation, Clifford Geertz uses medical and psychoanalytical analogies that are strikingly similar to the ones found in Black's essay. Moreover, Geertz provides an intriguing account of how theory progresses in an emic system of interpretation:

> The major theoretical contributions do not lie in specific studies—that is true in almost any field—but they are very difficult to abstract from such studies and integrate into anything one might call "culture theory" as such. Theoretical formulations hover so low over the interpretations they govern that they don't make much sense or hold much interest apart from them. . . . One can, and this in fact is how the field progresses conceptually, take a theoretical attack developed in connection with one exercise in ethnographic interpretation and employ it in another, pushing it forward to greater precision and broader relevance.[18]

The progress of theory in an interpretative discipline, then, does not take the form of a ladder leading up to and down from high-order abstractions. Instead, such theory moves along the broken ground covered by the specific material of the discipline. The interpreter keeps his or her attention focused close to the ground, and while the explanation of what is seen often has potential implications that extend beyond the particular case, this potential is not realized in terms of a disembodied abstraction. An interpretative hypothesis moves across a discipline as a fire burns through a forest, growing, shifting, and receding in irregular patterns, gathering intensity from the matter it consumes, but having no existence apart from that matter.

Since rhetorical artifacts are complex expressions of human culture, they are clearly similar to the objects of study in anthropology and psychoanalysis. Yet, if there is an understandable reluctance to borrow a method from outside disciplines, we should remind ourselves that the approach to theory I have just outlined has strong precedent within the history of our own discipline. Though often neglected because of the contemporary preoccupation with Aristotle, there is a vital tradition in rhetoric that proceeds from the Greek Sophists and Isocrates, to Cicero and Quintilian, and from there to the rhetoricians of the Renaissance. This humanistic tradition consistently opposes attempts to sever theory from practice. It is less concerned with forms of argument and devices of style per se than with the rhetorical principles embodied in a particular case. Thus, of the three traditional components of rhetorical pedagogy—theory, practice, and imitation—theory receives the least attention. The aim of rhetorical humanism is to produce a form of practical wisdom that expresses itself in the ability to encompass particular situations. Abstract theory, therefore, is suspect, since it deflects attention from concrete situations and is insufficient as a guide to practical affairs. The humanist prefers to learn principles through experience, experience gained by practicing the art or by studying the works of other practitioners. Finally, and to sum up all the previous points, this approach concentrates on the orator rather than the art of oratory, since eloquence depends upon the orator's creative ability to respond to complex and changing situations.

This humanistic tradition, of course, concerns itself mainly with the production rather than the analysis of rhetorical discourse. Yet, in an age when the critic regularly assumes the role of an active participant in the rhetorical drama, the transition between the function of the orator and of the critic creates little strain. And thus, the general perspective of the tradition merges with the main assumptions of contemporary interpretative practice; each reinforces the other, and both recommend themselves to us with added vigor.

All told, then, Black's conception of emic and etic criticism is less useful as a distinction between a theoretical as opposed to an atheoretical approach to criticism than as a distinction between two forms of critical theory. The etic approach, which has dominated contemporary criticism, follows the model of conventional scientific and logical theories. It seeks to discover high-order abstractions that inform or govern rhetorical practice, and these abstractions enjoy a privileged status whether the system works from general precepts to particular cases or from particular cases to general precepts. Thus, etic theories eventuate in predicative generalizations or in extremely abstract models of the rhetorical transaction. Such theories provide an orderly direction for inquiry, and their proliferation has proved useful in breaking down the staid monism of earlier criticism. Yet, at worst, the etic approach preserves orderliness at the expense of the complexities of actual rhetorical phenomena, and, at best, it leaves the critic stuttering in the void between theoretical constructs and concrete artifacts, since it provides no practical means of articulating a connection between the two within the terms of its own logic.

The emic approach adopts the paradigm of interpretative theory. Its goal is explanation, and therefore the emic stance begins and ends with the particular object of study. Theoretical principles enter at the intersection between the object and the assignment of meaning to it, but such principles are so closely connected with the object of study that they are not easily isolated in abstract form. Consequently, theory does not progress in terms of a hierarchical arrangement of abstract principles. Hypotheses move laterally as they are drawn by intuition and analogy from one case to another, and since the objective is diagnosis rather than prediction, a hypothesis assumes a different form each time it is instantiated in a given case. Thus, form and matter interact and ultimately consume one another. The etic tension between theoretical constructs and particular objects resolves itself into a single unified explanation of the meaning of an object. The interpreter, generalizing within cases, discovers an abstract meaning in a concrete expression and the concrete expression of an abstract meaning.

Finally, the contrast between emic and etic perspectives on critical theory is supplemented and completed by a consideration of the different conceptions of critical method that follow from these two approaches. A method, in the most basic sense of the term, is a way into a subject, and depending on the nature of the subject and the inclinations of its students, methods vary considerably in their specificity. The etic approach tends toward a formal logic of inquiry, a set of specific and systematic ways of studying the critical object. The etic approach describes a general outlook and orientation, a way of looking at the subject, but it does not prescribe the specific steps to be followed in the conduct of inquiry—that is a matter for the trained intuition of the critic. But while this method is not formally rigorous, it need not result in undisciplined research. Emic interpretation stresses the role of the critic, and in doing so, it shifts the standards of rigor from the method of investigation to the person of the investigator. The standards imposed on emic critics are severe. They must have a thorough knowledge of hypotheses relevant to rhetorical criticism, a knowledge gained not primarily through the study of theory but through intensive analysis of specific critical studies. And they must also have a detailed, intimate, and sympathetic understanding of the subject under investigation. Thus, we obtain a method that demands rigor from the critic even as it allows him or her the freedom to adapt to the changing demands of particular situations. It is a method that leads us more deeply into our subject, and it offers a way of solving the more than twenty-year-old problem of how to merge theory and practice in rhetorical criticism.

NOTES

1. Donald C. Bryant, "Of Style," *Western Speech* 21 (1957): 103.
2. Bryant, "Of Style," 104.
3. Barnet Baskerville, "Selected Writings on the Criticism of Public Address," *Western Speech* 21 (1957): 117.
4. Ruben D. Clark, "Lessons from the Literary Critics," *Western Speech* 21 (1957): 84.
5. Marie Hochmuth, "Burkean Criticism," *Western Speech* 21 (1957): 89.
6. W. Charles Redding, "Extrinsic and Intrinsic Criticism," *Western Speech* 21 (1957): 100.
7. Bryant, "Of Style," 110.
8. Thomas R. Nilsen, "Interpretative Function of the Critic," *Western Speech* 21 (1957): 70–76. In raising the issue of interpretation in criticism, Nilsen pursued a point developed later in the essay. The two approaches, however, are considerably different, since Nilsen emphasizes the interpretation of the ethical and logical implications of rhetorical discourse.
9. For additional examples of the variety of theoretical approaches lo rhetorical criticism, see Gerry P. Mohrmann, Charles Stewart, and Donovan Ochs, eds., *Exploration in Rhetorical Criticism* (University Park: Pennsylvania State University Press, 1973).

10. Karlyn Kohrs Campbell, "The Nature of Criticism in Rhetorical and Communication Studies," *Central States Speech Journal* 30 (Spring 1979): 9–12.
11. I hesitate to use the term "interpretation" here and elsewhere in this essay, since it is ambiguous in general usage and subject to a number of differing technical definitions. Yet no other term seems adequate. By interpretation, I refer to the process of assigning meaning to a text, and in rhetorical criticism, the process applies specifically to the meaning of the rhetorical dimensions of a work. Cf. Wayne Brockreide's concept of "explanation," in "Rhetorical Criticism as Argument," *Quarterly Journal of Speech* 60 (1974): 170–71. For reasons that become clear later in this essay, however, I disagree with Brockreide's claim that explanation always depends on a concept or category system more general than the object under scrutiny.
12. There are some notable exceptions to this pattern. For example, Lawrence Rosenfield, "The Anatomy of Critical Discourse," *Speech Monographs* 35 (1968): 50–69, treats the problem of the relationship between constructs and objects with considerable sensitivity. He argues that "although both terms and observations are logically essential, they need not be expressed separately" (56). Thus, he leaves room for these two elements to interact in the critical process. Moreover, the notion of analog criticism, developed in the same essay, provides a very flexible mode of critical inquiry. Rosenfield extends his arguments with respect to the relationship between the critic and his subject in "The Experience of Criticism," *Quarterly Journal of Speech* 60 (1974): 489–96. Also significant is Karlyn Campbell's attempt to develop a form of generic criticism that adheres strictly to the rhetorical features of a particular type of discourse. Her persistent emphasis on the fusion of elements within a genre allows for the construction of low-level theoretical principles that maintain close contact with the objects of criticism. See, for example, her essay "The Rhetoric of Women's Liberation: An Oxymoron," *Quarterly Journal of Speech* 59 (1973): 74–86. The theoretical foundations of this approach are developed mote fully in Karlyn Kohrs Campbell and Kathleen Hall Jamieson, "Form and Genre in Rhetorical Criticism: An Introduction," in *Form and Genre: Shaping Rhetorical Action* (Falls Church, VA: Speech Communication Association, 1978), 18–25. One should also note Walter Fisher's argument that rhetorical criticism represents a compromise between history and theory, "Method in Rhetorical Criticism," *Southern Speech Communication Journal* 35 (1969): 101–9.
13. For Black's own comments on this shift, see the author's foreword in the reprinted

edition of his *Rhetorical Criticism: A Study in Method* (Madison: University of Wisconsin Press, 1978), ix–xv.

14. E. D. Hirsch Jr., *Validity in Interpretation* (New Haven: Yale University Press. 1976), 170; cf. Paul Ricoeur, "The Model of the Text: Meaningful Action Considered as Text," *Social Research* 38 (1971): 548–53.
15. Hirsch, *Validity in Interpretation*, 136.
16. See Hirsch, *Validity in Interpretation*, 164–69.
17. This phrase is adapted from Clifford Geertz. "Thick Description: Toward an Interpretative Theory of Culture," in *The Interpretation of Cultures* (New York: Basic Books, 1973), 26.
18. Geertz. "Thick Description," 25–26.

Textual Criticism: The Legacy of G. P. Mohrmann

At the moment of his fatal heart attack last November, Jerry Mohrmann was engaged in his normal academic business. He was writing rhetorical criticism. More specifically, he was completing a close analysis of a short but important speech text—John Calhoun's oration "On the Reception of the Abolition Petitions." This study had a specific and seemingly narrow focus, but it arose from a number of complex, general issues and incorporated many of Jerry's characteristic interests. Thus, to recall the history of this project allows us to learn much not only about the man but also about the vocation he pursued.

During the last decade of his life, Jerry was greatly concerned about achieving a better and deeper understanding of that vocation. The period was one of accelerating and often bewildering change within the discipline. It spawned revisionist movements in several directions, as

From *Quarterly Journal of Speech* 72 (1986): 377–89.

rhetorical critics attempted to alter and expand the traditional objects and methods of study.[1] In some measure, Jerry participated in this revisionist impulse. He found traditional speech criticism wanting; it was, he argued, narrowly and mechanically conceived, and thus it failed to take us "into the text of the speech and its workings."[2] In an effort to prove this point, he invoked an uncharacteristic method—he did some counting. But he expressed his point in characteristic prose:

> We used to study speeches, right? Wrong! How about Clay, Calhoun, and Webster for openers? A total of seventeen articles in national and regional journals, but no writer has seen fit to deal with the entire text of one of their speeches. Emerson? Eight articles, none on a particular speech text. Jonathan Edwards? Not one article. Acres of Diamonds? No article. The New South? One, a Hegelian analysis. Abraham Lincoln? Thirty-two articles, but only if we are generous can we say that as many as three explore the rhetoric of a given speech.[3]

For Jerry, this inattention to speech texts was a symptom of a more fundamental problem. It indicated a failure to engage the rhetorical process as it manifested itself in the actual conduct of discourse. Thus, in Jerry's words, the critic became a "circuit rider, forever circling the herd, but never getting to its center."[4]

Other critics shared this skepticism about the older approach, but most were inclined to abandon rather than to refurbish it. The prevailing mood called for new methods and attention to new forms of discourse. Jerry, however, feared that the stampede away from tradition might decenter and shatter an already fragile enterprise. It was important, therefore, to retain certain common objects and methods of study, and if some of our revisions worked within the tradition, we might achieve that goal. Moreover, in his view, revisionism too often concentrated entirely on methodological and terminological interests; this focus yielded only a cosmetic change, a substitution of new molds for old ones, and the central problem of understanding the "text and texture of messages" was obscured rather than resolved.[5] Genuine progress, he concluded, depended upon closer attention to the phenomena we studied rather than the generation of abstract methods for its study.

Having adopted this position, Jerry obviously had to do more than preach about what needed doing. He had to demonstrate the value of textual studies by providing concrete models. During the last years of his life, this task occupied much of his attention, and the critique of Calhoun represented the leading edge of the project. The work, however, proceeded at a very slow rate. Part of the reason for this was Jerry's characteristic habit of mulling things over, of writing and rewriting drafts in an effort to flesh out rather than flatten interpretative problems. But, more important, the project proved to involve unexpected complications.

The motive for textual criticism, as Jerry conceived it, is to divert attention away from theoretical constructions and to focus on the rhetorical action embodied in particular discourses. Consequently, the enterprise begins with a severely empirical orientation; the critic must attend to the elements contained within the text itself. The empirical contents of a text, however, are in no way equivalent to the symbolic action that marks a work as a rhetorical discourse. Texts simply do not yield up their own rhetorical interpretation. Critics must move from what is given in the text to something that they themselves produce—an account of the rhetorical dynamics implicit within it. At minimum, this act of interpretation requires a means to justify the identification of significant features in the text and to explain the interactions among these features. Since this process necessarily entails principles or categories "not native to the original," it requires an exercise of judgment at some level of abstraction, and it eventuates in something we might call theoretical understanding of the particular case.[6]

Paradoxically, then, the effort to displace theory with action leads from action back to theory. Of course, the new perspective alters the placement and status of theory; to paraphrase Clifford Geertz, theory functions not to generalize to or from cases but within them.[7] But, judged by the prevailing standards in our discipline, this formulation seems odd, if not unintelligible. And in the absence of already established models, the critic striving to advance from the text to a theoretical account of its particular rhetorical action confronts a number of bewildering problems. The features in the text seem to knot and unravel in an almost constant motion, and attention to the particular strains against the requirements of theoretical understanding. The difficulties involved are so complex and so intimately connected with the study of specific texts that they are virtually impossible to describe in abstract terms. Fortunately, however, Jerry's effort to explain Calhoun's "Speech on the Reception of the Abolition Petitions" offers a useful and well-documented case history. The story of his tribulations provides the best mechanism for locating the problems I have just suggested.

The project originated almost a decade ago, when Jerry and I jointly taught a course devoted to the masterpieces of oratorical literature. As we approached the unit on deliberative rhetoric, I suggested that we begin with Calhoun's speech. It probably did not merit the title of "masterpiece," but it had a number of virtues for pedagogical purposes. The speech was short, easy for students to read and comprehend, and easy for us to analyze, since, like Calhoun's oratory in general, it moved in a straightforward linear and logical direction. Although not very subtle or interesting in and of itself, the speech, I thought, might gently introduce students to the complexities they would confront in Demosthenes or Edmund Burke. Jerry listened to my argument, grunted assent, and departed carrying the text of the speech home with him.

When I arrived at the office the next morning, Jerry was already prowling the halls, his eyes twinkling with cantankerous delight. There was no phatic communication that morning—no greeting, no prefatory remarks. Instead, there was a whirling half turn toward me, the pointing of a well-exercised index finger in my direction, and the simple announcement: "Young man, you're wrong." And I was.

Beneath the progression of Calhoun's overt assertions and arguments, Jerry had uncovered a rather subtle conceptual pattern layered within the text. This pattern, occluded by the seemingly dead metaphors used in its expression, consisted in a related pair of spatial images. The first of these worked along a horizontal axis and depicted the union as a container. Its contents were parts or sections arranged in discrete compartments which occupied positions of absolute parity. The container, moreover, was less important than the divided parts it contained. The second image turned the spatial axis in a vertical direction as Calhoun constructed a theory of social hierarchy. Civilized nations, Calhoun imagined, rested upon a structure of class relations that moved from bottom to top. This vertical arrangement arose out of historical necessity, and both the material and moral progress of society required a stable stratification of the various orders within the population.

Once recognized, these two spatial orientations seemed to explain the order and movement of the text. The speech, that is, apparently pivoted from the horizontal to the vertical axis. In the first part of his argument, Calhoun invoked the horizontal image of separate but equal sections contained within the union. Congress was not a fit place to entertain petitions advocating an end to slavery, since such abolitionist rhetoric constituted an assault on the autonomous space occupied by the Southern states. Toward the middle of the speech, however, Calhoun rather abruptly shifted his orientation, announcing that he would assume "the higher ground" and defend slavery as "a positive good." It was here that he clearly invoked the vertical image of separate and unequal classes in the social order. All societies, he asserted, relegated the laboring class to the bottom of the heap. The existence of an underclass, therefore, was not grounds for passing moral judgment. The real issue depended upon the treatment accorded those who held this position, and by that standard, the South's peculiar institution proved beneficent, a point underscored by contrast to the "wage slavery" oppressing laborers in the industrial North.

This scheme of alternating spatial and argumentative directions offered an attractive and promising interpretative hypothesis, but it did not tell the whole story, since it could not account for much of the detail in the text. As Jerry returned to the text, he discovered some fascinating complications. In the first place, vertical dimensions insinuated themselves into the dominantly horizontal emphasis of the opening argument. Early in the speech, for example, Calhoun identified abolitionism as a contagion which was spreading and working its way *upward* through the fabric of Northern society. Left unchecked, it would infect those in the *highest stations* in the North, and under that circumstance, the abolitionist spirit would break across territorial boundaries as one section attempted to impose its moral predilections on another. Thus, a kind of vertical lift was conceived as a force moving to disrupt the properly static, horizontal relations among the parts of the union.

Likewise, the horizontal dimension intruded into the dominantly vertical imagery of the concluding argument. As Calhoun described the vertical symmetry of Southern society, he provided a motive for its defense against incursions from without. In the face of the impending abolitionist threat, the South must close ranks and take concerted action. It must defend every inch of its territory. In this instance, images of sectional conflict suggested a movement across space that endangered a stable, vertical structure. And once again, the intersection between spatial axes delineated a course of movement.

These observations not only complicated assessment of the external structure of the text, but they also raised general questions about the function of spatial metaphors. These questions prompted a study of the literature on the subject, and what Jerry found there confirmed what he had seen operating in Calhoun's discourse. "Spatial images," Jerry concluded, "are very far from being static entities. Certainly they may suggest a security born of stability, but at the same time, few are not freighted with ramifications nourished in a potential for movement. . . . When we talk of metaphorical space and place, we are not talking of passive constructs, we are talking instead about constructs alive with the potential for action."[8] This conclusion is interesting in its own right, but within the economy of Jerry's project, it was only a preliminary, a guideline to help direct further encounters with the text. The crucial task was to understand how the potential in such constructs became actualized.

Furthermore, since the discourse was an oration presented under the pressure of specific circumstances, interpretation could not rest content with isolated judgments about the text itself. The demands of the situation had to be entered into the equation. Thus, examining the text from yet another angle, Jerry viewed it in the context of the debates of the period and of Calhoun's place within them, noting especially his effort both to speak as the voice of his section and to play a decisive role in national politics. These historical and biographic data did more than illuminate details in the text; they were essential to an informed judgment of its general configuration. Without reference to them, no one could hope to comprehend the pattern Calhoun saw in the events he recounted; no one could explain the fragmented and tortured logic that such a skilled logician wove into the text and attempted to project onto the world. This was a logic that demanded preservation of slavery and social inequality as the only secure means of maintaining free and equal institutions. The segmented images of space and place ranging through the text must have reflected a context that promoted an analytic psychosis—a habit of mind so preoccupied with the division of parts as to preclude synthetic reflection about the whole.

In short, the history of this exercise in textual criticism reveals the formidable number of elements involved in the enterprise: the close reading and rereading of the text, the analysis of the historical and biographical circumstances that generate and frame its composition, the recognition of basic conceptions that establish the coordinates of the text, and an appreciation of the way these conceptions interact within the text and help determine its temporal movement. Unfortunately, Jerry did not complete the project. The last and best draft of his essay breaks off just as he began to integrate the elements of his analysis. Nevertheless, the work he did accomplish is sufficient to alert us to the importance of his effort to allow us to outline a program for carrying his objectives forward.

In the remainder of this paper, I want to pursue the implications in Jerry's work—to generalize, expand, and, in some respects, to reinterpret the basic assumptions that animated his critical practice. I would emphasize, however, that the whole formulation is tentative. This is necessarily true, since the approach under consideration aims toward the understanding of practice rather than the articulation of a method. The ultimate test of its value, therefore, must refer to case studies. Nevertheless, Jerry and I have used this approach for some time, and it now seems appropriate to reflect on its general features. My objective is simply to clarify some implicit principles, and in keeping with Jerry's commitment to tradition, I shall try to so do within the context of the literature in our field.

The critique of Calhoun clearly reveals the most fundamental premise in Jerry's critical program: *Oratory is an art form.* A well-constructed oration possesses a high degree of artistic integrity and density, and its proper understanding requires careful interpretative work. This position might seem to call forth a truism, but, for reasons I will soon explain, to entertain it seriously involves a significant departure from much of the existing rhetorical scholarship. Moreover, on reflection, this stance seems to entail some crucial issues. Unlike poetry and other "purer" forms of verbal art, the oration does not call attention to its own status as an art form. Oratory succeeds best when it appears to blend into the context of ordinary experience. It is a genre of discourse that effaces its own constructions. Placed at the margins of art and ordinary experience, oratorical discourse strains simultaneously toward autonomous coherence and transparent reference to the world in which it appears. The referential dimension is the more obvious, and its prominence often blinds the observer to the embedded artistic strategy that makes its referential surface appear plausible and natural. In fact, when the artistic imagination engages the public world, when the discourse cannot invoke suspension of disbelief, artistic strategy and referential content become virtually consubstantial. As a consequence, if the critic is to remain faithful to the object of study, the grounds for artistic judgment appear ambiguous and fragile.

To clarify this problem, we can again refer to Jerry's critique for concrete guidance. The critique began with the identification of two metaphoric conceptions that seemed to undergird the argument. These images, when seen in relation to other properties in the text, exerted a powerful influence on the internal, formal dimensions of the discourse. They established the conceptual space in which the discourse operated, and as the space shifted from horizontal to vertical dimensions, these conceptions also directed the temporal progression of the discourse. Thus, we can appreciate how the text developed internally through symbolically constructed relations in space and time. But, even as these symbols manifested themselves in the text, they reached outward to embrace and impart attitudes toward the things and events they symbolized. Moreover, these symbols were not fictional constructs made to be contemplated within their own self-contained horizons; they were actions on the minds of the audience bearing on its direct experience of public events. In short, Calhoun's oration was both an artistic construction and a literal representation of the public world. And, in addition, it was also an instrument designed to prompt further action in the world to which the text referred.

This teleological reading of the speech seems to afford the only adequate ground for effecting artistic rhetorical judgment. To rely exclusively either upon a formal/intrinsic or a representational/extrinsic criterion is to distort the rhetorical integrity of the discourse. Though critical analysis separates these dimensions, the fact is that they occur simultaneously and work cooperatively within the fabric of the discourse. Attention to the purpose of the discourse, however, acts as shuttle to the threads unraveled in the analytical process. It preserves the interdependence of the intrinsic and extrinsic strands, since it refers analysis back to a synthetic judgment about the discourse in its entirety.

From this perspective, the oration achieves unity as it formulates a response to circumstances and events in public consciousness and deploys its own internal resources to alter public consciousness about these circumstances and events. This rhetorical process negotiates between the symbolic action manifested by the text and the more ambiguous symbolic world based in the plurality of ordinary public experience.

Two points implied in this formulation require additional comment. First, I need to explain how and why the term "art" has shifted meaning in the course of my argument; second, I need to consider the status of rhetoric as a temporal art, a point that is crucial to but still only implicit in my argument. In fact, these two issues are very closely connected. For the sake of convenience, however, I will deal with them seriatim.

Earlier, and in keeping with conventional usage, I used the terms "art" and "artistic" to indicate formal or aesthetic properties in a text. But, just a few moments ago, in defining a standard for rhetorical judgment, I invoked notably different meanings for these terms. The art of and the artistry in oratory were identified in respect to a coordinating function, specifically the coordination between the internal and external impulses inherent in the rhetorical enterprise. The ground for unifying these impulses, moreover, was found in the end or purpose animating the particular discourse.

From this perspective, oratory assumes a rather special status as an art form, a status that allows us to appreciate Jerry's insistence on close textual analysis eventuating in generalization within cases. To put the point simply, a program of close textual analysis changes received notions about the relationship between the general and the particular, between theory and critical practice. The assessment of a rhetorical discourse must now hinge on the particulars of the case—the local circumstances that frame and motivate the work and the unique blend of formal and material elements that constitute its substance. Abstract, general principles may aid in guiding this judgment, but they do not represent the content of rhetorical theory. Theory is something that arises from an understanding of the particular, and abstract principles become important only as they are instantiated and individuated within the texture of an actual discourse. This perspective, then, stresses the motile, adaptive character of rhetorical discourse so as to identify theoretical knowledge with a complete understanding of a material case.[9]

This position may seem paradoxical—how can theoretical knowledge arise from a particular, material instance, especially when the object of study is the product of ephemeral interests and circumstances? The answer rests in the capacity that exemplars or touchstones possess for generating theoretical understanding of rhetorical action. The action in an oration is bound to the moment of its utterance, and in this sense, oratory is radically particular. Yet, a well-constructed oration can encompass particulars in a way that establishes an abiding rhetorical standard. I emphasize the phrase "rhetorical standard," since I do not mean that a speech may display noteworthy literary features or express great ideas capable of being appreciated outside the context of the discourse. Judgments made along these ideological and aesthetic lines constitute a legitimate and important aspect of the critical endeavor. But insofar they must fail to account for the rhetorical integrity of a particular discourse, they cannot render an adequate assessment of the rhetorical dimensions of that work. Thus, what I am arguing is that some discourses coordinate particulars in such a striking and compelling fashion that they command attention as models of rhetorical excellence independent of our interest in these particulars *per se*. As rhetorical artifacts, their enduring significance consists in the artistic unity they display in response to specific and transitory circumstances. The critic who achieves a thorough understanding of such a discourse preserves its integrity by remaining mindful of its status as a material embodiment of rhetorical action, and the discourse, understood in this light, can serve as a paradigm or exemplary case.

Since the exemplary case instantiates a standard of excellence, it provides access to qualitative grounds for rhetorical judgment. As Edwin Black notes, reference to such cases allows the critic "to hold certain expectations of what rhetorical discourse ought to do" and to "gain certain insights into what rhetorical discourse is capable of doing."[10] These expectations and insights provide a basis for judging a discourse as a unified and complete field of action, since the standard invoked is a paradigm case itself judged in its entirety. Moreover, I think it fair to regard such critical activity as theoretical, though not in the dominant contemporary sense, which refers to theory as a body of doctrine, an abstract set of principles organized in a self-contained and coherent structure. Instead, theory becomes linked with a kind of activity, and its meaning approximates the early Greek sense of *theoria*, which, as Wesley Trimpi explains, denotes "a viewing or observing of something as a whole in order to understand it."[11]

The recognition of the circumstantial, time-bound nature of rhetorical discourse leads to the second issue I must address—the status of oratory as a temporal art. Once more Jerry's study of Calhoun offers a convenient way to set our bearings. In Calhoun's speech, Jerry discovered that the rhetorical action moved along two basic coordinates—the temporal and the spatial. Owing to the special characteristics of the text, Jerry began with conceptions of space. In general, however, I believe that time is the more important dimension, for it holds priority in respect to both the intrinsic and extrinsic functions discharged by the oratorical art. Considered intrinsically, oratory, like the novel and other verbal forms, is a dominantly temporal art; that is, it develops in time through the progression of spoken or written words. Considered extrinsically, oratory directs itself toward what the Greeks called *kairos*—a fitting, appropriate, or timely response to a given situation. Both these dimensions of time, moreover, require careful attention if we are to develop an adequate base for textual criticism. This point becomes fully apparent when we examine the literature in our field.

Though not always recognized as such, the intersection between time and rhetoric has played a persistent and crucial role in the history of our discipline. The origin of the field traces itself back to the effort of the Cornell school to define a territory for oratorical studies. And this effort pivots on a temporal distinction between the functions of rhetoric and poetic. On this view, poetic discourse addresses a diffuse, timeless audience about matters of enduring concern. Rhetorical discourse, by contrast, addresses a well-defined, immediate audience about issues of momentary concern. Hence, rhetoric is a captive of historical time, and the critic, qua rhetorical critic, remains bound to the circumstances that define case at hand.[12]

As a rough and general principle, this distinction has considerable merit. Unfortunately, perhaps because of the anxiety to distance the fledgling rhetorical enterprise from its literary parent, the point was stretched out of all proportion, and the result was inattention to the properties of the rhetorical text per se. The oration simply became a medium for organizing historical and biographical research or a resource for illustrating the elements contained in the abstract taxonomy that passed for a theory of rhetoric. The text offered no organic resistance of its own. It was simply there, a closed but accessible space ready to be entered whenever someone wanted to find live specimens of the fauna classified in the various rhetorical bestiaries.

Even after the scholarship had drifted away from its original moorings, the transparency of the text persisted as a general assumption. Thus, in 1957, Thomas Nilsen argued that critical interpretation must work itself out through the history of ideas, since particular oratorical texts did not pose any significant interpretative problems.[13] And twelve years later, Philip Tomkins located the interpretative task in the study of audience reactions; textual analysis, he maintained, could not explain the interaction between the rhetorical structure of a message and its impact on receivers.[14] An undeclared allegiance to similar assumptions has colored most of the critical studies that have directly addressed time as a rhetorical consideration. In the early seventies, for example, Barbara Larson, Bruce Gronbeck, and Edwin Black wrote important essays on the subject, but all of them conceived time as an extrinsic influence on the production or reception of a rhetorical text without considering that it might function as a constituent of the text.[15]

This macroscopic, extrinsic approach perhaps receives its most sophisticated treatment in Thomas Farrell's essay "Knowledge in Time." Farrell clearly identifies rhetoric as a temporal phenomenon. He writes: "Whether any public position may prove well-founded, appropriate, even true can come to depend on its placement in the long run of unfolding moments."[16] Here again the sweep of historic time receives priority, but Farrell is not thinking simply of the text/context relationship. Among other things, he is concerned about the placement of a rhetorical act in relation to "an endless succession of discursive acts."[17] Consequently, rhetoric achieves a certain durability through a network of intertextual influences. This perspective, of course, still decenters the particular rhetorical text, since, as Farrell argues, "rhetorical argument generally is not determined by any single author."[18] In short, Farrell attributes conceptual solidity to rhetoric, but it is entirely diachronic, something charted across the arc of historic change.

It is possible, however, to narrow this perspective, to punctuate the flow of historic time and to conceive a notion of "unfolding moments" that applies to particular texts. For this purpose, we need only recognize that rhetorical discourses are themselves temporal phenomena. They emerge in time; they are conditioned by other discourses and by the progression of events, but they are also constructed things that occupy a span of time. And while it is true that rhetorical "argument generally is not determined by any single author," it is also true that rhetorical argument generally is constructed by a single author. Every rhetorical text is a particular construction that unfolds in time as it is written or spoken and as it is processed by a listener or reader. The rhetorical text, then, is a historical development occurring within a broader context of historical developments. However circumscribed by extrinsic events, the text retains an internal history of its own.

The oration, therefore, engages time on at least two levels. It is constrained by and refers to the order and relation of events in the world, but it also constructs a certain order and relation of elements within its own pattern of utterance. This internal pattern, the timing in the text, determines the appearance of the discourse as an intervention in historic time, but the discourse also stretches beyond its own margins to influence the appearance of the world in which it is made. The timing in the discourse mediates our perception of time in the public world. *The central task of textual criticism is to understand how rhetorical action effects this negotiation, how the construction of a symbolic event invites a reconstruction of the events to which it refers.* The complexity of this process, moreover, reveals the artistic density of well-made rhetorical texts and the reason that they demand and reward careful interpretive study.

The rhetorical significance of the ratio between time and timing is yet another matter better understood when exemplified rather than described in abstract terms. Unfortunately, the time limits for this presentation do not allow the opportunity to deal with a case study in adequate detail.

Nevertheless, even though there is the risk of oversimplification, a short illustration seems necessary to clarify the issue. For this purpose, Lincoln's "House Divided Speech" offers a useful point of reference, since Lincoln coordinates this ratio in exemplary fashion.[19]

Lincoln delivered his speech immediately after receiving the Republican nomination for the Senate in 1858. His purpose was to solidify support within his own party by preventing desertion in favor of Stephen Douglas, the Democratic incumbent. For a variety of reasons, Douglas's doctrine of popular sovereignty had attracted favorable notice among Republicans, and Lincoln set out to demonstrate that Douglas's position actually was incompatible with the tenets of the Republican Party. The order of Lincoln's argument proceeded through three carefully timed main sections. The opening section articulated the conceptual ground for the speech as a whole. Here Lincoln described the union as a house. The house was divided against itself, but it would not remain so. The currents of time and circumstance would render it all one thing or the other, all free or all slave. This image subtly worked to undercut Douglas's position, since it imparted a moral impulse to events, a directional tendency that overwhelmed such efforts at political temporizing as the doctrine of popular sovereignty. The remainder of the speech ramified the implications compacted within this image; as Lincoln filtered recent political history through its moral lens, he constructed a narrative that drove Douglas outside the ambit of Republican principle.

This symbolic ostracism moved through two uneven steps. In the second major section of the text, Lincoln narrated the leading political events of the period between 1854 and 1858. The nuanced story he told implicated Douglas in a virulent, covert conspiracy designed to promote slavery and overturn free state constitutions. In the final section, however, Douglas emerged in a rather different light. He was a "caged and toothless" lion, rendered impotent by his own temporizing, and duped into a position that encouraged the proslavery tendency.

The sequence of these two steps brilliantly illustrates the artistic and persuasive force of rhetorical timing. Given the context, Lincoln could discredit Douglas either by proving that he pretended moral neutrality in order to advance the proslavery tendency or by proving that the stance of moral neutrality unwittingly gave impetus to that tendency. Either point was sufficient to undercut Douglas, but the first obviously was the more serious charge and the more difficult to establish. Thus, as Lincoln worked to render this charge credible, he opened the ground for his less ambitious but equally effective second point. An audience induced to consider seriously whether Douglas had directed a conspiracy to force slavery into Illinois was thoroughly prepared to receive the argument that his position simply did not measure up to the standards demanded by the Republican Party.

In this way, Lincoln develops a strategy to encompass his local contest with Douglas. But we are in the presence of a rhetorical genius, and so it is not surprising that his discourse extends to broader and more profound aspects of the context. Even as he stretches the fabric of events so as to leave Douglas comfortably outside the Republican frame, Lincoln weaves these events into a new pattern. Previously confused tendencies begin to assume choate form and to progress in ethically tilted directions, and ultimately political history is reconfigured as moral narrative. This pattern unfolds as the discourse progresses, as its ideas, images, rhythms, and allusions appear, combine, and sort themselves out. This dynamic within the text induces the auditor to follow and assent to its internal movement, and as it does so, it places the auditor in contact with the vision of the world it represents. Thus, to experience the text is to be coached to experience the world as the text constructs it.[20]

In referring to the "House Divided Speech," one further problem surfaces. Some time ago I divided the basic coordinates of rhetorical action into the categories of time and space, and then shunted conceptions of space to the side, arguing that the temporal dimension had priority. Yet, in Lincoln's speech, the whole movement of the text appears to devolve from the initial spatial metaphor. That is, when Lincoln conceives the union as a house, he establishes a conceptual frame that regulates and orders the progression of elements across the text. Moreover, it is not difficult to cite other evidence that reveals the power of metaphor to frame and localize rhetorical action. In Jerry's critique of the Calhoun speech, for example, much of the rhetorical action hinges on the two basic spatial images. More generally, Michael Osborn's study of archetypes demonstrates how powerful recurrent symbols, such as light, or elevation, or the sea, can inform and control the content of a text.[21] And recently Robert Ivie has shown how clusters of unobtrusive metaphors often reveal the basic assumptions guiding certain kinds of discourse.[22] Using a method that allows critics to track metaphoric patterns to their base, Ivie has uncovered foundational conceptions that set the direction of foreign policy debates. Thus, for example, among rhetors advocating detente with the Soviet Union, some view international relations as a "game" in which cooperation yields better results than competition. Other rhetors, however, conceive the antagonism between the two superpowers as a "disease" that must be cured. Obviously, these root conceptions are important, and they seem to operate at a level beneath the temporal flow at the surface of a discourse.

At the least, this evidence mandates some revision in my original position. If a rhetorical discourse is a field of action, it is also necessary to conceive boundaries that delimit the field. Recent studies of the tropes, metaphor in particular, clearly indicate that such boundaries normally consist in images or clusters of images that subsist below the surface action of the discourse.[23] These images, then, define the conceptual space of the discourse. The textual critic must recognize these base concepts and incorporate them into the interpretative process, and for this reason, a *purely* temporal orientation seems untenable.

It is possible, however, to press this point more aggressively. The conceptual base of the discourse, its "spatial" location, may seem to hold priority over the temporal dimension, since the base concepts apparently limit and exert some control over the movement of the other elements in the discourse. In certain respects, this arrangement of priorities is reasonable, but I am skeptical about its general application to rhetorical criticism. Insofar as we regard rhetoric as a form of action, a determination of the foundations implicit in a text seems less central than an understanding of the interactions that occur across and within its phenomenal surface. The temporal dimension, the timing in the text, conveys the rhetorical action, and thus, although critics cannot discount the force of the textual substructure, their primary attention should remain focused on the unfolding surface.

This position seems consistent with the temporal movement of the critical process itself. Even those critics bent on discovering root concepts cannot proceed until they have studied the surface structure of the text with great care. A good many conceptual tokens appear along that surface, and unless judgment is prejudiced or arbitrary, none of them can be deemed fundamental without an understanding of the movement of the whole. And so the critic must start with the superstructure in order to locate the substructure. More important, the identification of root concepts does not represent the proper end of the critical process. From a purely rhetorical perspective at least, the interest in conceptual foundations is motivated by the desire to gain a better insight into what happens in the discourse itself. After all, to do nothing more than reduce the discourse to its conceptual bases is to convert a field of action into a set of static entities. The critic, therefore, must rise back to the surface of the text in order to understand how the rhetorical process breathes life into concepts and turns them into palpable incentives for action.

I must confess some uneasiness about this last argument, and as I wrote it, a vision of an old friend prowling the hallway came to mind. In this instance, I do not think he would say: "Young man, you're wrong." For one thing, I am no longer so young, and more to the point, I hope my argument actually is not "wrong." What Jerry Mohrmann probably would say is that I have not mulled things over long enough, have not looked carefully enough at the actual phenomena, and have allowed my thinking to stray too far in a single direction. In fact, the argument I have just sketched describes a rather narrow perspective, which might best be labeled as a "purely" or "radically" rhetorical approach to the text, an approach that single-mindedly concentrates on understanding rhetorical action for its own sake.

The long history of the tradition warns us about the dangers and difficulties involved in trying to purify the discipline. There are, in fact, almost as many conceptions of rhetoric as there are rhetoricians, and one person's "pure rhetoric" is another's sophism. Furthermore, the business of rhetorical criticism hardly can be reduced to a single set of motives. There are critics interested in rhetorical discourse as a way of understanding how we use metaphor and what its use tells us about our conceptual apparatus. And other critics seek to understand the base concepts in a kind of discourse so as to enter into rather than just observe the debate, to understand the rhetoric of the peace movement, for example, in order to make it a better and more effective agency for changing the political world. These motives are not only legitimate, but, to some degree, they always insinuate themselves into the most purely academic study of particular cases.

What I have attempted, therefore, is to clarify one critical perspective and not to discredit or displace other perspectives. In this process, I have identified certain basic conceptions implicit in a kind of critical practice, and I have tried to organize them and drive them toward coherence. At the end of the line, the project begins to come undone. An approach devoted to the theoretical understanding of particulars cannot suffer translation into a purely programmatic vision. Nevertheless, clarification of this vision serves an important purpose; it establishes a conscious base of operation, and in doing so, it not only makes a certain kind of critical practice more accessible, but it also alerts us to what we might not otherwise notice—the limitations necessarily involved whenever we adopt a perspective.

These limitations are not necessarily debilitating, since as Jerry Mohrmann's work demonstrates, a critical perspective need not close itself into a system rotten with its own perfection. The critic can invoke what Walter Fisher calls "informed innocence" and remain open to the particular object of study.[24] To achieve this end, however, we must pay heed to the human voice that resonates in all rhetorical discourse. In the face of the almost infinite abstractions we can use to analyze rhetorical performance in general, we need to find ways to approach our subject on a human scale. That, I believe, was Jerry Mohrmann's guiding concern and his surest connection with the tradition. For him, the study of rhetoric was satisfying only insofar as it remained attached to the integrity of a discourse unfolding within the drama of local circumstances and straining to encompass and alter the configuration of those circumstances. In its particular moments, rhetorical discourse brings us into intimate contact with the human condition, and critics who dwell in those moments participate in the long arc of a tradition that stretches from Isocrates to Jerry Mohrmann, for they too speak with a human voice.

NOTES

1. The report of the National Developmental Project on Rhetoric held in 1970 adumbrated this development. See Lloyd F. Bitzer and Edwin Black, eds., *The Prospect of Rhetoric* (Englewood Cliffs, NJ: Prentice Hall, 1971), especially the

chapter "Report of the Committee on the Advancement and Refinement of Rhetorical Criticism," 220–27. For evidence of Mohrmann's participation in this movement, see the book he coedited with Charles J. Stewart and Donovan J. Ochs, *Explorations* in *Rhetorical Criticism* (University Park: Pennsylvania State University Press, 1973).

2. G. P. Mohrmann, "Elegy in a Critical Grave-Yard," *Western Journal of Speech Communication* 44 (1980): 331–36.
3. The quotation comes from an unpublished paper, "Old Paths and New: A Fable for Critics," presented at the Speech Communication Association convention held at Washington, DC, in 1977. Mohrmann and I coauthored that paper, but those familiar with Mohrmann's style will recognize that he is the author of the passage cited in the text.
4. Mohrmann, "Elegy," 272.
5. Mohrmann, "Elegy," 273.
6. E. D. Hirsch Jr., *Validity in Interpretation* (New Haven: Yale University Press, 1976), 170.
7. Clifford Geertz, *The Interpretation of Cultures* (New York: Basic Books, 1973), 26.
8. The quotation is from page 5 of the unfinished manuscript of the Calhoun study. It bears the title "Place and Space: Calhoun's Fatal Security." I want to thank Marilyn Mohrmann for allowing me access to this manuscript as well as some of Jerry's other papers.
9. This position has some affinity with Michael Calvin McGee's argument in "A Materialist Conception of Rhetoric," in *Explorations in Rhetoric: Studies in Honor of Douglas Ehninger*, ed. Ray E. McKerrow (Glenville, IL: Scott, Foresman, 1982), 23–48, esp. 28–31. Also Barry Brummett, "Rhetorical Theory as Heuristic and Moral: A Pedagogical Justification," *Communication Education* 33 (1984): 97–105.
10. Edwin Black, *Rhetorical Criticism: A Study in Method* (New York: Macmillan, 1965), 67.
11. Wesley Trimpi, *Muses of One Mind: The Literary Analysis of Experience and Its Continuity* (Princeton, NJ: Princeton University Press. 1981), xiii.
12. This position receives its classic formulation in Herbert Wichelns's 1925 essay, "The Literary Criticism of Oratory." The essay is reprinted in *Methods of Rhetorical Criticism*, ed. Robert L. Scott and Bernard L. Brock (New York: Harper and Row, 1972), 27–60. Also see G. P. Mohrmann and Michael C. Leff, "Lincoln at Cooper Union: A Rationale for Neo-classical Criticism," *Quarterly Journal of Speech* 60 (1974): 460.

13. Thomas R. Nilsen, "Interpretative Function of the Critic," *Western Journal of Speech Communication* 21 (1976): 70–76.
14. Phillip K. Tompkins, "The Rhetorical Criticism of Non-oratorical Works," *Quarterly Journal of Speech* 55 (1969): 438–39.
15. Barbara A. Larson, "The Election Eve Address of Edmund Muskie: A Case Study of Televised Public Address," *Central States Speech Journal* 23 (1972): 78–85; Bruce E. Gronbeck, "Rhetorical Timing in Public Communication," *Central States Speech Journal* 25 (1974): 84–94; and Edwin Black, "Electing Time," *Quarterly Journal of Speech* 59 (1973): 125–29. A broader conception of time, such as I am attempting to explain, may stand near the origin of artistic rhetoric in the fifth century BC. See John Poulakos, "The Place of Time in Gorgias," paper, Speech Communication Annual Convention, Louisville, KY, 1982.
16. Thomas B. Farrell, "Knowledge in Time: Toward an Extension of Rhetorical Form," in *Advances in Argumentation Theory and Research*, ed. J. Robert Cox and Charles Arthur Willard (Carbondale: Southern Illinois University Press, 1982), 123.
17. Farrell, "Knowledge in Time," 128.
18. Farrell, "Knowledge in Time," 124.
19. For a much more detailed development of the argument that follows, see my paper "Rhetorical Timing in Lincoln's 'House Divided' Speech," in *The Van Zelst Lecture in Communication* (Evanston, IL: Northwestern University, 1983).
20. My language here, as well as the whole drift of the argument, clearly borrows from Kenneth Burke. See, for example, *A Rhetoric of Motives* (Berkeley: University of California Press, 1969), 58.
21. Michael Osborn, "Archetypal Metaphor in Rhetoric: The Light-Dark Family," *Quarterly Journal of Speech* 53 (1967): 15–26; and "The Evolution of the Archetypal Sea in Rhetoric and Poetic," *Quarterly Journal of Speech* 63 (1977): 347–63.
22. Robert L. Ivie, "Metaphor and the Rhetorical Invention of Cold War 'Idealists,'" paper presented at the Speech Communication Association convention, Denver, CO, November 1985.
23. In addition to the sources cited above, see George Lakoff and Mark Johnson, *Metaphors We Live By* (Chicago: University of Chicago Press, 1980).
24. Walter R. Fisher, "Genre: Concepts and Applications in Rhetorical Criticism," *Western Journal of Speech Communication* 44 (1980): 299.

Words Most like Things: Iconicity and the Rhetorical Text

Thirty-five years ago, in his classic essay "The Study of Speeches," Wayland Maxfield Parrish argued that critics ought to isolate and carefully evaluate the "content" of a speech. This "often difficult task" required separating "*what* was said from *how* it was said," a matter best done "by making a summary or précis of the speaker's thought which avoids the wording of the original."[1] Holding consistently to this dualism between wording and content, Parrish regarded style as "another" aspect of persuasion, something to be set off from the rest of the critical apparatus. The major elements of style—vivacity or "setting a thing before the eyes," metaphor, example, analogy, and narratives—were not matters of substance but of manner, and their function was to overcome indifference and distraction so as to hold the attention of the audience.

With Andrew Sachs, from *Western Journal of Speech Communication* 54 (Summer 1990): 252–73.

Occasionally, the critic encountered "passages of sustained nobility and beauty," but these momentary highlights were not essential to the art; where they occurred they lifted "oratory into the realm of poetry," and they moved us through their "intrinsic aptness and beauty" in a way that was quite distinct from the "ideas and sentiments that inspired them."[2]

Parrish asserted these points with casual confidence, and he had good reason to do so. His categories and priorities fitted squarely within the prevailing orthodoxy: argument and style were distinct processes; argument represented the substance of rhetorical discourse; style was something added to this substance. Under the circumstances, of course, style did not attract much serious attention, and in 1957, Donald Bryant complained that there could hardly "lie occasion . . . to further depress the repute of style or to further relegate style to a more distant peripheral position than it has achieved in most professional rhetorical speculations." While critics sometimes invoked the more mechanical aspects of stylistic analysis, Bryant found that they almost always backed away from "the central questions" or struck "them but glancing blows in the twilight."[3]

Obviously, things have changed. Elements that Parrish left at the periphery now are working their way toward the center of attention. Thus, for example, Walter Fisher has subsumed his quest for a rhetoric of good reasons within the framework of narrative;[4] Robert Ivie has asserted with casual confidence that, so far from being a mere ornament, metaphor rests at the base of the inventional process;[5] and Michael Osborn has suggested that depiction—the setting of something before our eyes—is the "soul of eloquence,"[6] a "master-term of modern rhetoric."[7] Osborn, moreover, recognizes that his suggestion turns the old paradigm on its head. To promote depiction as master term is to challenge "rhetoric's own depiction as a study primarily of rational calculations. . . . This approach shifts the emphasis in rhetorical studies from that advanced state of awareness in which speakers devise complex arguments and proofs to defend well-considered positions."[8] Instead, the more primitive force of image-generation controls things—not only absorbing much of the function of argumentation but also forming the base from which argument proceeds.[9]

All told, we are reaching the point where the manner of expression, the generation and use of symbols, has become the substance of our study, and argument appears as a supplement, as a surface maneuver added on to more basic modes of articulating a worldview. This change in perspective is revolutionary, but the revolution is rather tidy and symmetrical. One generation dissolves metaphor within argumentative structures; the next reduces argument to a metaphorical base. One generation regards narrative as a supplement to analytical reason; the next frames inference within a narrative paradigm—and so on through the rhetorical lexicon. The opposition between form and content remains intact; only the valences attached to the terms have changed.

When viewed as the two sides of this form/content dialectic, the older preoccupation with invention and the more recent preoccupation with style prove to have an important common characteristic. Both deflect attention from the complex, variegated texture of specific rhetorical products and focus upon abstract, essentialized conceptions of the rhetorical process. That is, both have a strong tendency toward reductionism.

In respect to neo-Aristotelian rhetoric, this tendency led to an unexpected and disastrous contradiction built into the whole project. On the one hand, the neo-Aristotelians committed themselves to a radical particularism: the defining characteristic of rhetorical discourse was its responsiveness to specific circumstances, and the rhetorical perspective was "patently single," devoted to communication with a particular audience.[10] On the other hand, when they engaged particular works, the neo-Aristotelians filtered those works through their bias in favor of argumentative content, and since argument was conceived ultimately as an abstract, logical process, they were driven along a reductive trajectory which eventuated in an effort "to 'uncover' the essential (logical) structure of an argument—to *reduce* the manifest rhetorical appearance to its underlying (real) form."[11] The result was to reconstitute texts in an abstract language alien to their own particular constructions. As Conley has put the point, these invention-oriented approaches abridged "speeches to their 'arguments' or 'strategies,' stating the speech, in effect, in ways not stated by the speech itself, throwing out everything but 'motive' and 'message content.'"[12]

From its first stirrings, the attack against neo-Aristotelianism recognized that the program encouraged mechanical abstractions and thus moved critics away from rather "than more deeply into" their subject.[13]

Nevertheless, in general, the problem was not conceived as an internal contradiction that blocked critics from exercising their proper interpretative function. Instead, the revisionists stressed more encompassing problems that sanctioned a total shift in theoretical perspective or a redefinition of the proper object of study.[14] Consequently, efforts to escape neo-Aristotelianism often redirected attention from the single text toward larger discursive formations. The first of these efforts, the "history of ideas" approach sponsored by Ernest Wrage and his students, conceived public address as part of the broader movement of ideas across time. Viewed as popular and practical instruments for disseminating ideas, particular oratorical texts did not present the density needed for interpretive work.[15] Thus, the rhetorical critic either did not have an important interpretive function, or that function emerged only through the abstraction and aggregation of ideas from many texts.[16] Wrage's commitment to "ideational content" was not shared by proponents of the "social movements" approach, but obviously this approach also sought to conceive the material of criticism in terms of aggregates rather than single products.[17] Likewise, Edwin Black coupled his attack against the excessive rationalism of neo-Aristotelianism with an "alternative frame of reference" that located generic clusters of rhetorical discourse. And Black concluded that "critics can probably do their work better by seeing and disclosing the elements common to many discourses rather than the singularities of a few."[18]

Black accurately predicted the later course of scholarship, and the old interest in speakers and their isolated performances continued to recede. In 1971, Becker argued that rhetoricians needed to redefine their conception of "message" by understanding that the communicative process operated within a complex mosaic, and within this mosaic, "single message encounters" were an inadequate source for generating useful observations.[19] Restating the point more bluntly, Brockriede concluded that individual speech texts were "not an appropriate unit of analysis."[20] Moreover, two of the leading developments in the seventies and early eighties—the extension of genre theory and the growing interest in ideology—also reflected the trend toward using larger discursive formations as the base for critical inquiry.

In short, the revival of style occurred not only after the demise of the "rational world paradigm," but at a point when critical attention had drifted away from particular discourses and toward such complex intertextual phenomena as social movements, genres, and ideologies. It is no wonder, then, that interest in style did not center on rhetorical texts but extended toward more general conceptions of the symbolic process—as in Fisher's interest in narrativity as ground for a philosophy of communication, or in Osborn's concern for depiction as a recurrent form, or in Ivie's effort to uncover a finite set of metaphorical structures informing a large number of related discourses.[21] Given the scope and the ambitions of these projects, a tendency toward formal reductionism was almost inevitable.

Reductionism is not necessarily an evil; in fact, it seems implicit in certain kinds of theoretical reasoning, and in the present case, it has established a number of competing perspectives for encountering something that the old rhetoric totally neglected—the long-term cultural and ideological force of symbolic formations. Thus, one outcome of current trends has been a better understanding of rhetoric as a symbolic process. Nevertheless, the tendency to reduce the surface content of particular discourses to formal structures also entails certain dangers. Attention to basic forms occludes the situated character of rhetorical discourse and its function as a practical mode of encompassing concrete social and political issues. And when not grounded within particulars, efforts at rhetorical interpretation rigidify along the axis of the form/content dichotomy, since interpretation finds its end in abstract regularities rather than in the complex interplay among representational content, discursive form, and the context of situation.

The persistence of the form/content dichotomy, then, has stifled attempts to generate grounded interpretations of rhetorical discourse. The older, neo-Aristotelian paradigm locates an appropriate ground for interpretation, but encumbered by a rigidly logical conception of content, it cannot account for the symbolic action displayed within the texts it attempts to study. The newer paradigms take us more deeply into the symbolic process, but they deflect attention from the particular texts which ground its manifestations. Between these two approaches, there exists a kind of textual criticism that views the rhetorical work, not as a mirror of reality, but as a field of action unified into a functional and locally stable product. An understanding of the integrity of this kind of product requires careful interpretive work, since although it generally lacks either the formal density of poetic discourse or the ideational density of philosophical discourse, it creates a complex structure of meaning by imbricating the formal and ideational dimensions of language. A rhetorical discourse, then, becomes a verbal construction that blends form and content into a concrete whole—a whole that assigns meaning to a region of shared public experience and solicits an audience to embrace the meaning it constructs.

This critical stance, sometimes called "close reading," has appeared only recently in our literature.[22] Within the last decade, we have witnessed an increasing number of studies devoted to a single text[23] and several efforts to justify a more grounded approach to critical practice.[24] The whole development is still in its formative stages, but at least some common features are beginning to emerge. On this view, rhetorical criticism finds its end in interpretative understanding; such understanding locates itself in the full complexity of a particular transaction rather than in the discovery of abstract regularities or disembodied theoretical principles. While the critic must frame the discourse within its context, the focus of attention centers on the text itself and the rhetorical features embedded within it. These features combine to produce what Stephen Lucas calls a "textual context,"[25] an unfolding sequence of arguments, ideas, images, and figures which interact through the text and gradually build a structure of meaning. Rhetorical meaning, of course, is not autotelic; it is designed to reach outward to the world beyond the text and to guide the audience's understanding of and behavior within that world. Thus, in Thomas Benson's words, the critic inquires "into the states of thought and feeling an audience is invited to experience."[26] The critical stance, then, retains an audience perspective, but as opposed to neo-Aristotelianism, this perspective does not entail measurement of actual responses. Instead, the critical process seeks to explain how the rhetorical performance invites certain kinds of response. Working from the evidence within the text, the critic proceeds to make inferences about what the work is designed to do, how it is designed to do it, and how well that design functions to structure and transmit meanings within the realm of public experience.

By rejecting the neo-Aristotelian commitment to objective "content" and by contextualizing interest in symbolic processes, "close reading" disarms the tension between form and content and thus opens the way toward a more fluid understanding of rhetorical action. Nevertheless, rhetorical action is a complex business that occurs at several levels simultaneously. If it surfaces most clearly in specific discursive products, it also operates more broadly within the cultural and ideological formations that embed these products. A single-minded concentration on particulars, therefore, may tend to promote its own kind of formalism—readings that isolate the text and constrain interpretation within the orbit of the text's own constructions. Thus, the critic may succumb to a "local formalism" that seals the text from judgment about its long-range moral and political consequences. Robert Hariman has specified this problem: as critics become absorbed by the internal movement of the text, they may—perhaps unwittingly—bracket rhetorical time within the stable space of the text. Thus spatialized, the text can become an aesthetic object that loses contact with real historical time. In this way, our formal satisfaction with a rhetorical structure may obstruct our perception of larger problems in the social order. Hariman notes that while close reading assumes that "the audience will transfer the consciouness [*sic*] created (through temporal definition) within the text of the speech into the world outside the text," there also exists a corresponding "inducement to substitute the satisfactions of the text for the labor of working in the world it supposedly describes."[27]

In principle, since the critic must ground the rhetorical text in a context, it seems possible to sustain a balance between the intrinsic and extrinsic dimension of the critical process. In practice, however, the effort needed to fathom the intrinsic workings of the text often sponsors an appreciative response and encourages the critic to accept the negotiations effected by it as something more than the construction of a partial and momentary closure. Given the direction of reading, there is a temptation to collapse the context into the text and to lose sight of any larger ideological horizon—temptation which is especially strong when dealing, as close readers often do, with exemplary rhetorical works. Consequently, if close reading promises to dissolve the form/content dichotomy, it also threatens to alienate intrinsic and extrinsic approaches to rhetorical discourse.

But these two sets of oppositions do not have the same status. The form/content dichotomy imposes a rigidity which affects both of its two poles and consistently blocks efforts at grounded interpretation. In the case of extrinsic and intrinsic readings, we have something closer to a productive tension about the proper grounding for readings. Neither approach precludes the other, and it is not necessary to assume that the critical apparatus appropriate to one is inappropriate to the other. To the contrary, the close reading of specific texts often provides both data and methods for comprehending larger discursive formations, and shifting interpretations of cultural and ideological scenes open space for new readings of texts. The difference between the two approaches is mainly a matter of tendency and seems an inevitable and desirable feature of a discipline that, as Wichelns observed, studies discourses that hover in the margins between literature and politics.[28] If, because of differences imposed by training and temperament, the same people are unlikely to practice both kinds of reading, those who adopt different orientations are at least in a position to engage in dialogue.

In the remainder of this paper, we hope to contribute to this dialogue. Our objective is to further clarify an aspect of close reading and indicate its relevance for rhetoric as a cultural and ideological formation. As we have already noted, one of the assumptions of close reading is that meaning in a rhetorical work results from an interaction between discursive form and representational content. This interaction is specified in a phenomenon that contemporary linguists call "iconicity." After briefly explaining this concept, we will attempt to illustrate it through close analysis of passages selected from Edmund Burke's "Speech to the Electors of Bristol." And finally, using this analysis as a tentative base, we will speculate about the way such an approach to meaning might be extended to broader contexts.

Iconicity

An icon, according to semiotic theory, is a sign that has a nonarbitrary relation to what it represents. As opposed to a symbol, an icon is a representational mark (signifier) bearing an actual resemblance to whatever it signifies—as, for example, "a portrait signifies the person of whom it is a portrait not by convention only but by resemblance."[29] A system of representation (a code), therefore, "is iconic to the extent that it imitates, in its signals or textual forms, the meanings that they represent."[30]

It is an accepted principle of contemporary linguistics that languages are symbolic codes. Except for a few onomatopoetic words, the signifiers of language are noniconic; the relationship between words and meanings is arbitrary, the product of conventions adopted by users of a linguistic code. The form of the signifier does not imitate what it signifies, and so form bears only an arbitrary relationship to meaning.

Yet, as recent studies in the pragmatics of language indicate, this position requires modification when we deal with meaning above the level of individual words. While word meanings are conventional and arbitrary, we encounter a rather different situation when words are combined in phrases, sentences, paragraphs, and discourses. At these higher levels, "Iconicity takes a 'quantum leap,' the syntactic relations between words characteristically imitating relations between the objects and events which those words signify."[31] In short, above the level of the word, discursive form often enacts representational content.

To illustrate this principle, we can refer to a simple example used by Lakoff and Johnson. To say that someone is "very, very, very tall" conveys a different meaning than if we merely say: "He is very tall." In this case, iteration lengthens the sentence and changes its meaning even though no new semantic content is added. The change of meaning occurs because the form of the longer sentence iconically represents the person described. This imitative relationship occurs generally and ordinarily because of our expectation that "more of form is more of content"[32]—that is, the bigger the linguistic container, the greater the matter it must contain. (This observation has special significance for oratorical prose, since one of its dominant "stylistic" features, the heavy use of repetition, now seems to function not only as an aesthetic embellishment, or an aid to memory, but as a way of adding "content" to the discourse, and thus it assumes an argumentative function.)[33]

Leech and Short[34] identify three other, and somewhat more complex, types of iconicity: (1) chronological in which textual time imitates real time (the unfolding order of events in a text follows from and maps itself onto our temporal experience in the real world); (2) psychological in which syntactic order imitates psychological experience (the configuration of language in a text embodies states of mind and feeling that occur in real-world experience); (3) juxtapositional in which placement of elements in a text imitates our general conception of psychological or locative relatedness (words that are grouped close together in sentences suggest connections and relations attached to other levels of experience). This typology is not exhaustive, for, as Leech and Short observe, "The possibilities of form enacting meaning are virtually unlimited." In this respect, iconicity has "a power much like metaphor: it rests on the intuitive recognition of similarities between one field of reference (the form of language) and another."[35] Thus, as in the case of metaphor, the functional uses of iconicity outstrip our capacity to describe them in theoretical terms.

Iconicity, then, is a principle more readily apprehended through an interpretative rather than a formal approach to discourse. Perhaps it is for this reason that, while the principle implicitly appears throughout the rhetorical tradition, it operates most notably in the work that places the greatest stress on critical interpretation—Longinus's *On the Sublime*. Longinus, of course, never explicitly names or discusses this principle, but he certainly understood its power, and he put this understanding to use throughout the treatise. And by briefly considering his critical practice, we can gain insight into how iconicity applies to the traditional objects of rhetorical criticism.

Relatively early in the treatise, as he explains how the proper combination of details may yield sublimity, Longinus cites a passage from Homer—a simile describing a great storm at sea:

> He rushed upon them, as a wave storm driven,
> Boisterous beneath black clouds, on a swift ship
> Will burst, and all is hidden in the foam;
> Meanwhile the wind tears thundering at the mast.
> And all hands tremble, pale and sore afraid,
> As they are carried from under death.

In analyzing this passage, Longinus explains how its words are configured to depict and embody the experience it describes: Homer does not localize the danger, but "draws a picture of men avoiding destruction many times, at every wave." (That is, the wavelike structure of the syntax imitates what it represents.) More profoundly, the words are joined in a way that virtually hands the experience of terror over to the reader: prepositions are unnaturally joined in the phrase "from under death"; the line is "tortured into conformity with the impending disaster, and by the compactness of his language, he brilliantly represents the calamity and almost stamps upon the words the very shape of the peril."[36] Moreover, such effects are by no means limited to poetry; Longinus notes their presence in *On the Crown*, when Demosthenes describes how the Athenians reacted to news of the fall of Elatea.[37]

When Longinus turns to the figures, the iconicity principle becomes a key to his explanation of their force. For example, citing passages from Demosthenes's *First Philippic*, Longinus argues that rhetorical questions can amplify and extend content that would be thin when stated simply. Thus, this formal device can alter the meaning of a passage by adding bulk to it and rendering it "more convincing."[38] (Here Longinus displays an intuitive grasp of Lakoff and Johnson's principle that "more of form is more of content.") Again, in treating the use of several figures at once, Longinus explains how Demosthenes's combined use of asyndeton, repetition, and vivid representation yields an iconic representation of a physical assault. The uninterrupted succession of short, repetitive clauses beats on the consciousness of the hearers as though they were actual blows, and the speaker "achieves the same result as the assailant." The audience is startled, made to experience what the speaker says as though responding to the event rather than a mere verbal description.[39]

For present purposes, the most important section of *On the Sublime* concerns hyperbaton, the figure that encompasses deviations from the normal sequence of words or ideas. Longinus believes that this figure "is, as it were, the true stamp of living passion." When people undergo strong passions, he explains, they become disoriented, and their speech proceeds erratically, violating the normal patterns and sequences. "The best writers imitate this aspect of real life by means of hyperbata." Again, Demosthenes is the exemplar. He uses the figure not only to impart actuality and spontaneity to his discourse, but to lead the audience through an emotional development that seems to assume an extradiscursive reality. Through his prolonged hyperbata, he leaves ideas suspended, "piles up extraneous matter" in the midst of sentences, and reaches a point where he seems to have lost control of his speech. As they follow this orderly disorder, the auditors become panicked "lest his whole argument collapse as his realistic vehemence compels them to experience that danger with him; then, unexpectedly and after a long interval, he comes to the long-awaited conclusion at the end and the right moment."[40]

Much more could be said about the concept of iconicity and its prefigurations in the rhetorical tradition. Our present purpose, however, is not to explore all the ramifications of the concept nor to trace its history. And we think that we have said enough to establish the following points: (1) Iconicity is a regularly occurring phenomenon of language use that reveals a cooperative interaction between form and meaning. (2) This interaction raises great doubt about any approach to rhetorical criticism that implicitly or explicitly sponsors a form/content dichotomy. (3) The concept of iconicity promises to have important applications in the interpretation of rhetorical discourse. We now want to give further support to this last point by illustrating the use of iconicity.

Words the Most Like Things: Edmund Burke's Iconic Rhetoric

In his "Speech at Bristol, Previous to the Election," Edmund Burke faced charges that he had neglected his constituents and voted against their sentiments on a number of crucial issues. Burke, however, did not respond by denying or excusing his actions. Instead, he spoke to endorse his own conception of the relationship between the representative and his constituents and to reaffirm his stance on the issues. In the introduction, he announced this attitude and conveyed it most strikingly in this sentence:

> The part I have acted has been in open day, and to hold out to a conduct, which stands in that clear and steady light for all its good and all its evil, to hold out to that conduct the paltry winking tapers of excuses and promises, I will never do it.[41]

The sentence is a powerful example of physical representation through language. Much of its power, of course, results from metaphorical depiction. The contrasting images of "open day" with its "clear and steady light" and the "paltry winking tapers" give visual presence to Burke's thematic opposition between judgments based upon "the nature of things" and judgments based upon the "humors of men." The light of open day is clear, natural, stable, and expansive. The light of paltry winking tapers is obscure, unnatural, unstable, and confined. These metaphors are nearly perfect visual representations of the theme. But there is something more at work here, for the syntax also has an iconic value.

Although relatively easy to comprehend, the sentence is quite long and rather convoluted. If we recast the sentence in a more usual word order, it might read: "The part I have acted, for all its good and all its evil, has been in open day, and I will never hold out to a conduct which stands in that clear and steady light the paltry winking tapers of excuses and promises." This paraphrase, structured through two independent clauses of relatively equal length, offers less resistance to our comprehension, and in doing so, it changes our understanding of the text. Not only does the paraphrase lose the dramatic suspense of the original, but it also alters the progression of semantic values: our rewritten version moves from an image of stability (open day) to an image of instability (winking tapers).

Burke, however, by inverting the normal order through hyperbaton, frames the sentence between two points of semantic and syntactic stability (that is, "the part I have played has been in open day" at the beginning, and "I will never do it" at the end). In between these poles, he places two rather long clauses that introduce elements of instability and invite the auditor to recognize and experience the perspective he rejects. At the syntactic level, these two dependent clauses cause the sentence to waver as they suspend meaning and violate the norms of ordinary syntax (the infinitives coming before the main verb). Burke controls this "disorder" and thus provides a degree of coherence through repetition and parallelism ("to hold out to a conduct" . . ."to hold out to that conduct"), but the auditor must still remain somewhat disoriented until the meaning is resolved in the final clause. Moreover, this syntactic development exactly parallels the semantic progression in the sentence: the syntax itself seems to flicker with irresolute complications just as Burke presents the key image of unstable judgment—the "winking tapers of excuses and promises." And then the final clause suddenly and decisively ends all irresolution. Everything stabilizes and becomes clear as Burke makes a crisp, unqualified assertion in the first person—"I will never do it." In short, the form of the sentence directs the auditor's response in a way that powerfully influences its meaning.

One other aspect of this sentence deserves notice. While it begins and ends at points of stability, the extreme clauses are not quite parallel in syntax or rhetorical force. The first clause completes an independent meaning in ten words cast in the passive, while the last clause resolves the meaning suspended in the preceding dependent clauses and does so in five words arranged in the active voice. Thus, if, in one sense, the sentence circles back to its origin, there is also a sense in which it moves forward—shifting from the scene of past action to the person of the actor as he speaks in present time and commits himself to future conduct ("I will never do it"). The circle becomes a wheel, gathering forward momentum as it turns on itself.

This kind of enactment, based upon the imbrication of form and meaning, recurs throughout the speech, and in our view, governs the structure of the whole. On its surface, the speech is divided into five discrete sections. The introduction presents Burke's general theory of representation, which requires independent, stable judgment on the part of the representative, and hence a substantial degree of distance between the representative and his constituents. Or to put the point negatively, Burke argues that if representatives adhere too closely to popular opinion, their judgment becomes unstable, narrow, and servile, and hence incapable of serving the genuine interests of the people they represent. The other four sections then address the specific charges leveled against Burke—that he neglected his constituents (this point being connected closely with his position regarding the American war), that he voted against their interests in matters pertaining to the regulation of Irish trade, that he acted against their expressed will in supporting a bill for debt reform, and that he offended public opinion by endorsing measures designed to liberalize restrictions on Roman Catholics. The linear progression through these points follows the order of a well-behaved debater's brief. Yet a careful reading of the speech reveals a more subtle and organic form embedded within it.

Burke structures each separate section so that it turns back to his original argument about the character and judgment of the representative.

In respect to each issue, Burke shows that he exercised exemplary judgment and that the policies he opposed were flawed, because they were too much immersed in immediate circumstances and too closely connected with momentary whims of popular sentiment. Thus, Burke simultaneously justifies his positions through argument and presents a series of narratives that display his character. The narratives work repetitively to demonstrate how the speaker, in a variety of different circumstances, concretely enacted the kind of proper judgment he had described at the outset of the speech. As this organic pattern develops, its elements feed off one another: the arguments justify Burke's actions in particular situations; these justifications cumulatively build an impression of stable character, and, in turn, as the orator establishes and vindicates his character, his character lends weight to the arguments. Moreover, since his character embodies the principles enunciated abstractly in the introduction, the whole development repetitively circles back to its point of origin. The text constructs a formal network of relationships that embody its meaning. The form iconically represents Burke's meaning.[42]

In analyzing the sentence from Burke's introduction, we noted a circular movement as the sentence progressed syntactically from stability through instability back to stability. We have just noted a similar kind of progression within the speech as a whole; in each of its sections, the movement from principle through material circumstances resolved itself in the same principles which Burke established as his starting point. Moreover, there seems another interesting analogy between the microcosm of the sentence and the macrocosm of the discourse. Though the pattern of the sentence was circular, the circle exhibited directional movement—an advance from a passive description of the scene to an active assertion by the speaker. Within the speech as a whole, we can also detect a pattern of forward motion—one that involves the two major topics of deliberative rhetoric—the expedient and the honorable. Both topics are intertwined throughout the speech, but the balance between them changes as the speech proceeds. In the first two "narratives," the emphasis falls on the expedient; Burke stresses the way that the policies he opposed were self-defeating; because they were shortsighted, they worked against the nature of things and brought practical disaster to those who endorsed them. In the third narrative, however, the topic of the honorable emerges more clearly. Beauchamp's debt reform bill recommends itself equally as a practical solution to a problem and as a moral reform intended to eliminate injustices suffered by debtors. In the final narrative, considerations of honor achieve priority. Opposition to religious toleration is condemned less because it is unwise (though Burke argues that it is) than because it is inhumane. Those who support anti-Catholic codes do not simply harm themselves; they sponsor tyranny and cruelty. As Burke narrates his role in the debate about this issue, he displays a moral energy that has no parallel in the earlier sections of the speech. No longer operating on the basis of cool reason alone, Burke acts with zeal, warmth, and vigor, calling forth "every faculty" in his possession to defend a just reform against popular discontent and insurrection, and the section ends with a strong statement of moral principle. Thus, as the text unfolds, Burke transforms himself into a moral agent speaking on a still controversial issue and drawing from this issue abiding principles of moral and political conduct.

The progression we have just outlined is subtle and complex, and a full explication is beyond the limits of this paper. Nevertheless, analysis of a few representative passages can reveal some of its dimensions, and as we examine these passages, we can complete our discussion of iconic form in the speech. Having already dealt with its manifestation at the sentence level and at the level of the discourse as a whole, we now turn to units of intermediate length, and it is at this level that Burke's artistry manifests itself most clearly.

Our first passage appears relatively early in the speech, in the section where Burke deals with Irish trade policy. Having argued that his view of the matter followed from "old, standing, invariable principle" (295), he proceeds to narrate what happened when the parliamentary majority, reflecting momentary, popular attitudes on the matter, adopted a different course:

> [1] The British Parliament, in a former session frightened into a limited concession by the menaces of Ireland, frightened out of it by the menaces of England, was now frightened back again, and made a universal surrender of all that had been thought the peculiar, reserved, incommunicable rights of England—the exclusive commerce of America, of Africa, of the West Indies—all the enumerations of the Acts of

> Navigation—all the manufactures, iron, glass, even the last pledge of jealousy and pride, the interest hid in the secret of our hearts, the inveterate prejudice molded into the constitution of our frame, even the sacred fleece itself, all went together. [2] No reserve; no exception; no debate; no discussion. [3] A sudden light broke in upon us all. [4] It broke in, not through well-contrived and well-disposed windows, but through flaws and breaches; through the yawning chasms of our ruin. [5] We were taught wisdom by humiliation. (296)

The opening sentence is extraordinarily long and divides into two main units marked off by a dash. The first unit achieves iconicity through parallel dependent clauses placed in medial position. The sentence wavers syntactically in the same way that Parliament vacillated. That is, in the gap between the subject and the main verb, the auditor is left suspended while clauses describing the machinations of Parliament shift in one direction and then the other. Then after Parliament is frightened back to its original irresolute course, we discover the result: "universal surrender." The second main unit specifies the magnitude of this surrender, and here iconicity is achieved through a "left-branching" construction—that is, through incomplete clauses placed at the beginning of the unit. Deploying the "more of form is more of content" principle, Burke separates and enumerates each item surrendered, piling them atop one another in a succession of short clauses. The last item is the most important, and thus the form of sentence expands as Burke approaches it—the phrases become longer and three separate clauses amplify its significance. And just as the "sacred fleece" (i.e., the woolen trade) completes the pile, the whole structure suddenly collapses. This great long sentence ends with three simple words: "all went together." Sentence 2 (no reserve; no exception; no debate; no discussion) reinforces the impression of an abrupt and total clash as its four exceedingly short, negative clauses reverberate in the ears of the audience.

The rapid, staccato movement conveyed through sentence 2 continues in sentence 3, a very short sentence that rushes immediately to attention. Yet it also arrests attention, for, changing the whole line of development, this sentence introduces a new theme—the moral of the story. Having already experienced the frenzy of vacillation and the ensuing downfall, the auditor, now iconically placed amid the rubble of a collapsed structure, is prepared for sudden enlightenment, just as the English nation was at the time of the event, when a "sudden light broke in upon us all." Sentence 4 ramifies this image, connecting it with the latent iconic structure built and leveled in the syntax of the preceding sentences. The moral is simple: irrational temporizing yields enlightenment, but only after disaster and through "breaches" and "flaws" which the "well-disposed windows" of stable judgment could have prevented. Nevertheless, lest the auditor miss his point, Burke restates it in more direct language: "We were taught wisdom by humiliation." But even in this seemingly literal formulation, an iconic suggestion still persists in the last word, since to suffer humiliation is to be brought low.

A critic interested in condensing the speech to an outline undoubtedly could paraphrase this passage in propositional form. For certain purposes, this exercise might prove useful, but it would be a mistake to believe that this formal reduction specified the "content" of the passage. Nor would the mistake consist simply in the failure to incorporate the inventional force of the metaphors it contains. As our analysis reveals, the form and content of the passage do not operate at different levels; both merge within a pattern of meaning, and the meaning results from the interaction of all the elements—the themes, the images, the syntax, and perhaps other things as well.[43] The meaning is an experiential gestalt—something, as McGee might say, that makes its actual presence felt and commands our attention.[44]

Before turning from this passage, we need to add one more comment about its meaning that is important within the larger context of the discourse. At this point. Burke fixes his attention on the topic of expediency. Unstable, narrow political judgment proves futile and harmful, but the harm is self-inflicted and largely material. As the speech progresses, the same rhetorical configurations reappear, but they assume new meanings as Burke broadens the range of his critique: political temporizing becomes a moral as well as a practical danger.

In the last and longest major section of the speech. Burke presents a history of anti-Catholic sentiment which culminates in the enactment of a statute in 1699—the statute he had sought to reform. Burke considers how and for what reasons this law was "fabricated," and he explains that at the time there existed a party in the nation opposed to King William and the "system of the Revolution":

> [1] The party I speak of (like some among us who would disparage the best friends of their country) resolved to make the king either violate his principles of toleration, or incur the odium of protecting Papists. [2] They therefore brought in this bill, and made it purposely wicked and absurd, that it might be rejected. [3] The then Court party, discovering their game, turned the tables on them, and returned the bill to them stuffed with still greater absurdities, that its loss might lie upon its original authors. [4] They finding their own ball thrown back to them, kicked it hack again to their adversaries; and thus this act, loaded with the double injustice of two parties, *neither of whom intended to pass* what they hoped the other would be persuaded to reject, went through the Legislature, contrary to the real wish of all parts of it, and of all the parties that composed it. [5] In this manner, these insolent and profligate factions, as if they were playing with balls and counters, made a sport of the fortunes and liberties of their fellow-creatures. [6] Other acts of persecution have been acts of malice. [7] This was a subversion of justice from wantonness and petulance. [8] Look into the history of Bishop Burnet. [9] He is a witness without exception. (301)

Thematically, the image of the legislative process as "sport" dominates the passage. This metaphor depicts the parties as passing the bill/ball back and forth, so absorbed in the game that they fail to comprehend the real consequences of their actions. (We are reminded of children amusing themselves by torturing a helpless animal—an image that Burke invokes more explicitly at the end of the section.)[45] Once again, however, the syntax of the passage foregrounds the metaphor and complicates and enriches its meaning.

Syntactically, the paragraph repeats the familiar progression from stability through instability back to a stable base. In this instance, the instability is conveyed not only by sentence structure but by increasingly vague referents to the agents in the scenario.[46] Thus, the first sentence, though quite long, is straightforward and immediately intelligible. Burke clearly identifies the agent to whom he is referring ("the party I speak of"); the parenthetical remark fixes the reference as it assigns an attitude based in contemporary politics, and this agent then consciously devises a strategy—makes a seemingly rational calculation based in the immediate political circumstances. In sentence 2, this calculation results in an action, and the adverb "purposely" stresses the connection between act and motive. At the same time, however. Burke hints that we are witnessing a game where motive and action do not correspond on the surface. The first party has made the bill "wicked" not out of a desire to be wicked, but to outmaneuver the other party in a political contest. The much longer third sentence takes us into the game, and as we become involved in it, the agents become more difficult to distinguish and lose control of their actions. The sentence begins with a clearly delineated subject—"the then Court party"—but through the rest of sentence 3 and the first clause of sentence 4 the word "party" and all other descriptors of the actors disappear. Actions become more indefinite as "this party" and "that party" give way to a succession of "th" pronouns: "their . . . them . . . them . . . they . . . them." While the phonetic repetition lends structural coherence to these clauses, it becomes difficult to determine who is doing what to whom. The game seems to take control of the players, and Burke's syntax iconically represents the resulting confusion.

The third and fourth sentences contain other devices that create an impression of instability and loss of agency. In the former, the sentence shifts in the middle as the Court party "turned the tables on them, and returned their bill to them stuffed with still greater absurdities." The first of these clauses contains a notable use of alliteration. The two "th" and the two "t" words tick and lisp off the tongue evenly, and they level out the clause. The cadence is consistent with the uniform, smooth surface of a table. But what is smooth is also slippery, and if the clause has a syntactic and phonetic integrity, it also suggests further movement—an anticipation that the table will turn yet again. In the next clause, the word "return" amplifies this suggestion, and we learn that the Court party reacts precisely as the other party did—it "stuffs" more absurdities into the bill hoping that it would embarrass the original authors.

The fourth sentence fulfills earlier anticipations: the bill, already having been passed to and fro twice, now becomes a ball, which is thrown in one direction and kicked in the other, and the balanced opposition of the first two clauses of the sentence imitates the movement of the ball. At this point, however, the pattern changes. The vague pronouns of the earlier clauses made it somewhat difficult to understand who was acting, it was still clear that human agents did the throwing and kicking. In the third clause, the ball, which before was a bill, now becomes—significantly enough—an act, and this act not only serves as the subject of the clause but takes on a life of its own. Burke stresses the independent status of the act by inserting two clauses between the subject and main verb—clauses which explain that the act was loaded with injustices the parties had used for strategic purposes in the game but did not intend to pass into law. Yet the act has such momentum that, contrary to the wishes of all "parts" and "parties," it went through the legislature. The fifth sentence summarizes the whole development, using the metaphor of "balls and counters" to mirror the action just described, and invoking the word "sport" to emphasize the legislators' callous indifference to "the fortunes and liberties of their fellow-creatures."

As in the earlier passage we studied, this paragraph moves through a temporal/causal sequence: unstable political action leads ineluctably to disaster—to a situation where events control the actors. And also as in the earlier passage, the sequence ends with a judgment. This judgment takes us well out of confusion, and the recovery of stability is heavily marked by Burke's syntax. The paragraph ends with four short, clear sentences of the same approximate length. Moreover, if we examine these sentences with care, we can note the artistry involved in maintaining their status as short, independent units. Sentences 6 and 7 express adversative ideas that seem to invite connection into a single sentence through the conjunction "but." The separation of sentences 8 and 9 is even more striking. A more fluid and "natural" way of presenting Burke's point could be achieved through a single sentence, such as "Bishop Burnet's history confirms this account without exception." In both instances, however, Burke resists more fluid constructions, and he divides the sentences into a balanced series of four simple, discrete units. The resulting clipped style achieves maximum simplicity in the expression of each point, while the whole achieves solidity through the progression of evenly balanced short sentences. Each point stands in stable isolation while blending into a larger structure. The syntax here contrasts sharply with the convoluted sentences that describe the capricious, unstable judgment of the legislators, and it is from this stable base that Burke renders his own judgment. This pattern is hardly a coincidence. For Burke, syntax serves as the substrate of judgment.

In one important respect, as we have already noted, this passage does depart from the one we examined earlier. The later passage strongly emphasizes the moral dimensions of the issue. The legislators of 1699, like all others who impede enlightened religious tolerance, do not simply act unwisely; their blindness causes the enactment and perpetuation of tyrannical laws—laws that violate basic principles of liberty and humanity. This addition is important, since it gives the speech a sense of progressive development. The other main themes—Burke's character, the soundness of his policies, and the wisdom of his theory of political representation—circle organically through the text, gaining strength through their repetitive interconnection in Burke's arguments, images, and syntactic constructions. But as the expedient gives way to the honorable, the text exhibits a forward impulse. And Burke can rest his case by tying all its elements into a plea for justice:

> When we were sent into a place of authority, you that sent us had yourselves only one commission to give. You could give none to wrong or oppress, or even suffer any kind of oppression and wrong, on any grounds whatsoever; not on political, as in the affairs of America; not on commercial, as in those of Ireland; not in civil, as in laws for debt; not in religious, as in the statutes against Protestant and Catholic dissenters. The diversified but connected fabric of universal justice is well cramped and bolted together in all its parts; and, depend upon it, I never have employed, and I never shall employ, any engine of power which may come into my hands to wrench it asunder. All shall stand if I can help it, and all shall stand connected. (309)

Here Burke's prose iconically represents stability, but not at all in the same way that it is represented in his clipped style. As the speech advances to the moral plane, its expression must not simply identify parts but must connect the whole, and Burke responds accordingly: the elegant symmetry and balance of his syntax iconically reproduces the well-cramped and bolted fabric of universal justice.

Conclusion

Our analysis of the Bristol speech, though incomplete, is sufficient to demonstrate that Burke's style is not separable from the "content" of the discourse. Form and meaning are imbricated at every level—the sentence, the paragraph, and the discourse as a whole, and all the elements of Burke's rhetoric interact cooperatively to produce a structure of meaning. This meaning, of course, is ideological, and while the ideology of the speech participates in a context of larger discursive formations and material conditions, it is also something represented within the tissue of connectives that the text constructs. In this speech, a political ideology evolves within the meaning of the text, and hence an ideological reading would require careful attention to the modes of articulation indigenous to the text.

Nevertheless, if we accept conventional wisdom, what is true for Edmund Burke hardly seems a secure base for generalization. Burke is almost universally acknowledged as sui generis among English-language orators because of his capacity to turn political discourse into literary art. Thus, while Burke's oratory commands admiration, it is regarded as so atypical as to have little relevance to the normal practice of public address.

This attitude, however, rests upon the assumption that literary and practical discourse are different in kind—an assumption which is no longer accepted universally and has come under increasingly sharp attack from a number of different directions.[47] As we have already suggested, the iconicity principle is itself evidence of the continuity between ordinary usage and literary language. The imitative representation of meaning through form is a resource used in all linguistic practices. Literary discourse "makes a special exploitation" of this resource, developing it to a higher degree and using it more systematically than other forms of discourse,[48] but iconicity operates in even the most mundane texts. This point is nicely illustrated by the British critical linguists, who have rejected the dualism of form and meaning and have explained how syntax "can code a world view without any conscious choice on the part of the writer or speaker."[49] Thus, critical interpretation reveals subtly embedded ideological structures in such ordinary texts as newspaper articles and bureaucratic memoranda.[50]

If we abandon the form/content dichotomy in public address, Burke's status changes, and his oratory takes on renewed significance for critics. The literary excellence of his discourse seems to differ from more normal practice in degree rather than in kind. We can regard his oratory not as transcending the genre but as perfecting its resources. Since form is no longer abstracted (or subtracted) from meaning, the aesthetic dimension of his work now appears intimately connected with its political function. Thus, Burke offers a paradigm of rhetorical excellence—a touchstone which concretely embodies the potential of the art and exploits resources common to the art in an exemplary fashion. We do not mean, of course, that critics should mechanically and literally apply Burkean standards to other discourses. As Edwin Black explains, touchstones are "not models for copying," but referents which can inform our expectations of "what rhetorical discourse ought to do" and of what it is "capable of doing."[51] To use Burke as a touchstone, then, is not to confine the critic to eighteenth-century sensibilities, but to sensitize the critic to potentialities realized only through their enactment in discourse. Viewed in this light, Burke's example shows us something that abstract theory disguises—the power of discourse to blend form and meaning into local unities that "textualize" the public world and invite audiences to experience that world as the text represents it.

NOTES

1. Wayland Maxfield Parrish, "The Study of Speeches," in *American Speeches* (New York: Longmans, 1954), 14.
2. Parrish, "The Study of Speeches," 17–18.
3. Donald Bryant, "Of Style," *Western Speech* 21 (1957): 103–4.
4. Fisher first announced his position in "Narration as a Human Communication Paradigm: The Case of Public Moral Argument," *Communication Monographs* 51 (1984): 1–22. He elaborates on his conception of narrative in *Human Communication as Narration: Toward a Philosophy of Reason, Value, and Action* (Columbia: University of South Carolina Press, 1987). Also see his recent paper, "Clarifying the Narrative Paradigm," *Communication Monographs* 56 (1989): 55–58.
5. Robert Ivie, "Metaphor and the Rhetorical Invention of the Cold War 'Idealists,'" *Communication Monographs* 54 (1987): 168.

6. Michael Osborn, "Rhetorical Depiction," in *Form, Genre, and the Study of Political Discourse*, ed. Herbert W. Simons and Aram A. Aghazarian (Columbia: University of South Carolina Press, 1986), 79.
7. Osborn, "Rhetorical Depiction," 80.
8. Osborn, "Rhetorical Depiction," 97.
9. Osborn, "Rhetorical Depiction," 82, 99–100.
10. Herbert Wichelns, "The Literary Criticism of Oratory," in *The Rhetorical Idiom: Essays in Rhetoric, Oratory, Language, and Drama*, ed. Donald C. Bryant (Ithaca, NY: Cornell University Press, 1958), 35.
11. J. Robert Cox and Charles Arthur Willard, "Introduction: The Field of Argumentation," in *Advances in Argumentation Theory and Research*, ed. J. Robert Cox and Charles Arthur Willard (Carbondale: Southern Illinois University Press, 1982), xxi.
12. Thomas Conley, "The Linnaean Blues: Thoughts on the Genre Approach," in Simons and Aghazarian, *Form, Genre*, 73.
13. W. Charles Redding, "Extrinsic and Intrinsic Criticism," *Western Speech* 21 (1957): 100.
14. For differing accounts of this development, see J. Michael Sproule, "The New Managerial Rhetoric and the Old Criticism," *Quarterly Journal of Speech* 74 (1988): 474–81; and Dilip Gaonkar, "Epilogue: The Oratorical Text; The Enigma of Arrival," in *Texts in Context: Critical Dialogues on Significant Episodes in American Political Rhetoric*, ed. Michael C. Leff and Fred Kauffeld (Davis, CA: Hermagoras Press, 1989), esp. 256–64.
15. See Ernest J. Wrage, "Public Address: A Study in Social and Intellectual History," *Quarterly Journal of Speech* 33 (1947): 451–57.
16. Barnet Baskerville, "The Critical Method in Speech," *Central States Speech Journal* 4 (1953): 1–5; and Thomas Nilsen, "Interpretative Function of the Critic," *Western Speech* 21 (1957): 70–76. Gaonkar, "Epilogue," 260–62, provides a commentary on the "history of ideas" approach.
17. See, for example, Leland Griffin, "The Rhetoric of Historical Movements," *Quarterly Journal of Speech* 38 (1952): 184–88; and "The Rhetorical Structure of the 'New Left' Movement: Part I," *Quarterly Journal of Speech* 50 (1964): 113–35. The latter essay moves decisively out of the orbit of the "history of ideas" approach and adopts a dramatistic perspective.
18. Edwin Black, *Rhetorical Criticism: A Study in Method* (New York: Macmillan, 1965), 177.

19. Samuel Becker, "Rhetorical Studies for the Modern World," in *The Prospect of Rhetoric: Report of the National Developmental Project*, ed. Lloyd F. Bitzer and Edwin Black (Englewood Cliffs, NJ: Prentice Hall, 1971) 31.
20. Wayne Brockriede, "Trends in the Study of Rhetoric: Toward a Blending of Science and Rhetoric," in Bitzer and Black, *Prospect of Rhetoric*, 125–26.
21. In his most recent statement about narrative, "Clarifying the Narrative Paradigm," Fisher explains that his primary concern is not rhetorical criticism but a philosophy of communication. In "Rhetorical Depiction," Osborn's interest in depiction as a "recurring form" (80) indicates an emphasis that is more theoretical than critical, a point which becomes explicit at the end of the essay (97–100; in his last sentence, he uses the word "theory" to describe the content of the essay). It is interesting to compare this essay with the critical study, "'I've Been to the Mountaintop': The Critic as Participant," that Osborn presents in Leff and Kauffeld, *Texts in Context*, 149–66. Ivie is directly and fundamentally concerned with criticism, and no one can doubt the significance of his work in uncovering basic motives informing larger discursive formations; see, in addition to "Metaphor and the Rhetorical Invention of the Cold War 'Idealists,'" "Images of Savagery in American Justifications for War," *Communication Monographs* 47 (1980): 279–94; and "Metaphor and Motive in the Johnson Administration's Vietnam War Rhetoric," in Leff and Kauffeld, *Texts in Context*, 121–41. Nevertheless, the explanatory power gained by concentrating solely on base metaphors also brings with it a strong tendency toward reductionism. For comment on this point, see Michael C. Leff, "Textual Criticism: The Legacy of G. P. Mohrmann," *Quarterly Journal of Speech* 72 (1986): 386–87; Gaonkar, "Epilogue," 273–75; and Barry Brummett, "Some Burkean Roads Not Taken: A Response to Ivie," in Leff and Kauffeld, *Texts in Context*, 143–48.
22. See Martin J. Medhurst, "Public Address and Significant Scholarship: Four Challenges to the Rhetorical Renaissance," in Leff and Kauffeld, *Texts in Context*, esp. 35–37; and Gaonkar, "Epilogue," 255–75.
23. Of the six case studies contained in *Texts in Context*, five are devoted to single texts: Stephen H. Browne, "Burke's *Speech on Conciliation*: The Pragmatic Basis of Rhetorical Judgment," 55–80; Karlyn Kohrs Campbell, "*La Pucelle D'Orleans* Becomes an American Girl: Anna Dickinson's 'Jeanne D'Arc,'" 91–112; Michael Osborn, "'I've Been to the Mountaintop': The Critic as Participant," 149–66; J. Robert Cox, "The Fulfillment of Time: King's 'I Have a Dream' Speech," 181–204; and Celeste Michelle Condit, "Nixon's 'Fund': Time as Ideological Resource

in the 'Checkers' Speech," 219–42. *Communication Reports* 1 (1988) presents a symposium on Lincoln's Second Inaugural, with four essays devoted to the interpretation of that speech: James Arnt Aune, "Lincoln and the American Sublime," 14–19; Ronald H. Carpenter, "In Not-So-Trivial Pursuit of Rhetorical Wedges: An Historical Approach to Lincoln's Second Inaugural Address," 20–25; Michael C. Leff, "Dimensions of Temporality in Lincoln's Second Inaugural," 26–31; and Martha Solomon, "'With Firmness in the Right': The Creation of Moral Hegemony in Lincoln's Second Inaugural," 32–37. Among the other recent efforts at "close reading," we would note Stephen E. Lucas, "Justifying America: The Declaration of Independence as a Rhetorical Document," in *American Rhetorical Context and Criticism*, ed. Thomas W. Benson (Carbondale: Southern Illinois University Press, 1990); David Henry, "The Rhetorical Dynamics of Mario Cuomo's 1984 Keynote Address: Situation, Speaker, Metaphor," *Southern Speech Communication Journal* 53 (1988): 105–20; Stephen H. Browne, "Edmund Burke's *Letter to a Noble Lord*: A Textual Study in Political Philosophy and Rhetorical Action," *Communication Monographs* 55 (1988): 215–29; G. P. Mohrmann, "Place and Space: Calhoun's Fatal Security," *Western Journal of Speech Communication* 51 (1987): 143–58; Bruce Gronbeck, "Ronald Reagan's Enactment of the Presidency in His 1981 Inaugural Address," in Simons and Aghazarian, *Form, Genre*, 226–45; Joseph W. Wenzel, "The Rhetorical View of Argumentation: Exploring a Paradigm," *Argumentation* 1 (1987): 73–88; Michael C. Leff, "Rhetorical Timing in Lincoln's 'House Divided' Speech," in *The Van Zelst Lecture in Communication* (Evanston, IL: Northwestern University, 1983); and Karlyn Kohrs Campbell, "Stanton's 'The Solitude of Self': A Rationale for Feminism," *Quarterly Journal of Speech* 66 (1980): 304–12. Also notable are such applications of this approach to documentary film and television as Thomas Rosteck, "Irony, Argument, and Television Documentary: *See It Now* versus Senator McCarthy," *Quarterly Journal of Speech* 75 (1989): 277–98; Martin J. Medhurst and Thomas Benson, "*The City*: The Rhetoric of Rhythm," *Communication Monographs* 48 (1981): 54–72; and Thomas W. Benson, "The Rhetorical Structure of Frederick Wiseman's *High School*," *Communication Monographs* 47 (1980): 233–61.

24. Conley, "The Linnaean Blues"; Leff, "Textual Criticism," and "The Habitation of Rhetoric," in *Argument and Critical Practices: Proceedings of the Fifth SCA/AFA Conference on Argumentation*, ed. Joseph W. Wenzel (Annandale, VA: Speech Communication Association, 1987), 1–8; Robert L. Scott, "Against Rhetorical Theory: Tripping to Serendip," in Leff and Kauffeld, *Texts in Context*, 1–10;

Stephen E. Lucas, "The Renaissance of American Public Address: Text and Context in Rhetorical Criticism," *Quarterly Journal of Speech* 74 (1988): 241–60; and Edwin Black, "A Note on Theory and Practice in Rhetorical Criticism," *Western Journal of Speech Communication* 44 (1980): 331–36.

25. Lucas, "Renaissance of American Public Address," 249.
26. Benson, "Frederick Wiseman's *High School*," 235.
27. Robert Hariman, "Time and the Reconstitution of Gradualism in King's Address: A Response to Cox," in Leff and Kauffeld, *Texts in Context*, 213.
28. Wichelns, "Literary Criticism of Oratory," 41.
29. Jonathan Culler, *Structuralist Poetics: Structuralism, Linguistics and the Study of Literature* (Ithaca, NY: Cornell University Press, 1975), 16.
30. Geoffrey N. Leech and Michael H. Short, *Style in Fiction: A Linguistic Introduction to English Fictional Prose* (London: Longman, 1981), 233.
31. Leech and Short, *Style in Fiction*, 234.
32. George Lakoff and Mark Johnson, *Metaphors We Live By* (Chicago: University of Chicago Press, 1980), 127–28.
33. This point was understood by Daniel Webster. See his letter to John Brazer, November 10, 1828, *The Papers of Daniel Webster: Correspondence*, vol. 2, *1825–1829*, ed. Charles Wiltse (Hanover, NH: University Press of New England, 1976), 378–80.
34. Leech and Short, *Style in Fiction*, 233–43.
35. Leech and Short, *Style in Fiction*, 242.
36. Longinus, *On the Sublime*, 10. This quotation is from the translation by G. M. A. Grube (Indianapolis: Bobbs-Merrill, 1957). All citations refer to this translation, and we cite the traditional section numbers rather than pages.
37. *On the Sublime*.
38. *On the Sublime*, 18.
39. *On the Sublime*, 20.
40. *On the Sublime*, 22.
41. Edmund Burke, "Speech of Mr. Burke at Bristol, Previous to the Election, Delivered September 6, 1780," in *Select British Eloquence*, ed. Chauncey A. Goodrich (Indianapolis: Bobbs-Merrill, 1963), 293. All future references to the speech are to this edition and are indicated in the text.
42. For a more detailed analysis of the structure of the speech, see Stephen H. Browne and Michael C. Leff, "Political Judgment and Rhetorical Argument: Edmund Burke's *Paradigm*," in *Argument and Social Practice: Proceedings of the*

Fourth SCA/AFA Conference on Argumentation, ed. J. R. Cox, M. Sillars, and G. Walker (Annandale, VA: Speech Communication Association, 1985), 200–208.

43. At the least, the patterns of rhythm and assonance in this passage also deserve careful attention.
44. Michael Calvin McGee, "A Materialist's Conception of Rhetoric," in *Explorations in Rhetoric: Studies in Honor of Douglas Ehninger*, ed. Ray McKerrow (Glenview, IL: Scott Foresman, 1982), 23–48.
45. "We are all a sort of children that must be soothed and managed. I think I am not austere or formal in my nature. I would bear—I would even myself play in any innocent buffooneries to divert them [the people]; but I will never act the tyrant for their amusement. If they will mix malice in their sports, I shall never consent to throw them any living, sentient creature whatsoever: no, not so much as a kitling, to torment" (310).
46. Here we are referring to an aspect of the rhetoric of the text that linguists call "cohesion." See Leech and Short, *Style in Fiction*, 243–54.
47. In our discipline, both Fisher's conception of narrative and Osborn's theory of depiction cast doubt on the traditional disjunction. Also see Richard B. Gregg, "Criticism of Symbolic Inducement: A Critical-Theoretical Connection," *Speech Communication in the Twentieth Century*, ed. Thomas W. Benson (Carbondale: Southern Illinois University Press, 1985), 43–49. For a brief review of the issue in linguistics, see Leech and Short, *Style in Fiction*, 10–40, and for literary criticism, see the introduction by Jane Tompkins in *Reader-Response Criticism: From Formalism to Post-structuralism* (Baltimore: Johns Hopkins University Press, 1980), ix–xxvi.
48. Leech and Short, *Style in Fiction*, 234, 254.
49. Roger Fowler and Gunther Kress, "Critical Linguistics," in *Language and Control*, ed. Roger Fowler, Bob Hodge, Gunther Kress, and Tony Trew (London: Routledge and Kegan Paul, 1979), 185; and also see 185–96.
50. Bob Hodge, Gunther Kress, and Garreth Jones, "The Ideology of Middle Management," 81–93; and Tony Trew, "'What the Papers Say': Linguistic Variation and Ideological Difference," in Fowler et al., *Language and Control*, 117–56.
51. Black, *Rhetorical Criticism*, 67.

Things Made by Words: Reflections on Textual Criticism

This essay is in part an effort to influence the continuing debate about textual criticism and critical rhetoric and in part an exercise in self-criticism. Since I am a principal in the debate, I cannot pretend to assume a neutral or disinterested position, but my present concern is not polemic, or at least not explicitly polemic. Instead, following and extending a point made by Dilip Gaonkar,[1] I want to frame the debate in terms that differ from the prevailing conception and in fact differ from the way I have thought about it in the past. Gaonkar argues—quite rightly, I believe—that unlike earlier disputes in the field which concentrate on method, the conflict between critical rhetoric and textual criticism centers on the object of study (that is, on the conception of rhetorical practice). On reflection, I have discovered—much to my own surprise—that this distinction is theoretically motivated, and that my work

From *Quarterly Journal of Speech* 78 (1992): 223–31.

does not simply promote a direct encounter with rhetorical texts, but that it involves something very like a "theory" of rhetorical reading. From this perspective, not only does the difference between textual criticism and critical rhetoric emerge in clearer relief, but certain modifications in my approach to reading seem necessary.

Critical rhetoric and textual criticism present fundamentally opposed views of rhetorical practice, and the differences appear in a great number of manifestations. At bottom, however, I believe that this opposition reflects a basic and persistent distinction embedded in the classical tradition, which recognizes two different foci for rhetorical persuasion. Rhetoric, on this account, is persuasive in two senses, since it has both an intentional and an extensional dimension.[2] The intentional dimension has to do with the purpose of the rhetor as he or she composes a discourse designed to persuade an audience. The extensional dimension has to do with persuasive effect, the actual impact of discourse on an audience. In *De inventione*, Cicero succinctly expresses this commonplace when he defines rhetoric both in terms of its duty (*officium*) and its end (*finis*). The duty is to "speak in a manner suited to persuade," whereas the end is to "persuade by speech."[3] And this separation allows the rhetorician to distinguish between what is done by an orator and what happens to an audience. The first consideration, of course, stresses the artistic integrity of a discourse; the second stresses its social impact.

Broadly speaking, this distinction seems to apply to the two contemporary approaches to practice. Textual criticism (or "close reading") centers on the effort to interpret the intentional dynamics of a text. Ideological criticism (or "critical rhetoric") studies the extensional, social, and political force of discursive practice. This traditional terminology, however, does not mesh precisely with contemporary developments, and it remains useful only if we recognize important differences that exist between current interests and the older frame of reference. Thus, in the case of "textual criticism," as the focus shifts from composition (which is primary in the classical tradition) to criticism, the initial locus of interest becomes the finished text rather than the person who intends to make one. This change obviously complicates the status of intention, since the ratio between intention and production, though still crucial, emerges from interpretative work rather than direct consciousness. In the case of "critical rhetoric," the departure from the tradition is much more dramatic. The discourse/audience ratio no longer centers on a single point of contact, since the effect of rhetoric is charted through the accumulation of discursive practices, and these practices establish a network of social control that constrains the production as well as the reception of texts. In fact, the traditional conception of "text" becomes problematic within this frame.

In spite of these qualifications, however, the contrasting general direction of inquiry developed in the two approaches seems strikingly similar to the intentional/extensional distinction located in the old rhetoric. This point might encourage us to view textual criticism and critical rhetoric as connected through a tension inherent within the study of rhetorical practice, since the modes of producing discourse and the effects of discourse seem necessary but not entirely commensurable aspects of persuasion. Moreover, the revival of this dormant tension suggests some general points of commonality between the two projects. It is significant, I believe, that both find a common, albeit negative, origin in their resistance to "modernist" rhetoric[4] and thus both deny received notions about the relationships between knowledge and opinion, theory and practice, and form and content. Textual criticism is directly and heavily indebted to premodern sources, most notably to the Isocratean and Ciceronian texts that attempt to hold form and content in solution and give pride of place to concrete practice over abstract theory. Critical rhetoric, of course, is decisively postmodern, but its advocates acknowledge classical antecedents in Isocrates and the older Sophists, and some of its crucial tenets fit comfortably with both the older tradition and its more recent incarnation. Celeste Condit rather clearly indicates these lines of similarity in this explication of McGee's position:

> For McGee an ideological study *cannot* separate form and content. It is precisely the thrust of McGee's theoretical program to deny that we can or should study abstract "ideas" that are not embodied in particular historical movements and therefore in particular "forms" (which he calls usages). An ideograph, like "liberty," is *not* an idea (a content disembodied from any form); it is precisely a particular constellation of usages, identifiable solely by the specific forms it takes in past history and the

> present historical moment. The apparent simplicity of ideographs disguises a complex "dispositional" structure. The meaning of "liberty" is every bit as complex as a sentence from Longinus. It is simply that the disposition of an ideograph is to be found by reaching out to other parts of a text or to other texts, rather than by treating a phrase or a text as self-contained.[5]

Condit's remarks, in fact, suggest both the crucial points of convergence and divergence between the two approaches. Both seek to ground themselves in practice and to explain rhetoric in terms of the way it actually manifests itself in practice. They differ, however, in their conception of the level at which this practice achieves integrity. As a textual critic, I regard ideographs as fragments that appear in texts, the text being a whole construction and the fundamental unit of the rhetorical art. As a critical rhetorician, McGee views the ideograph itself as a kind of text, a fundamental unit of social/rhetorical construction, and what I call a text (e.g., Lincoln's "Second Inaugural") is a fragment. That is, a particular speech is part of a larger ideological formation, and the whole "text" emerges only at the collective level constituted by the system of ideographs. To return to my earlier terminology, the difference here is between an intentional approach that works from a finished product toward the processes that constitute it and an extensional approach that breaks down these products in order to apprehend their participation in much broader social/political processes. These two orientations do not admit the same conception of text, and as critics accept one or the other, they not only turn their readings in different directions, but they arrive at different conceptions of what it is that they are reading.

Viewed from this angle, the two positions appear as nearly polar opposites, and both take on a distinctively radical tincture. This radical quality is also, I believe, a result of common origins. Both projects arise out of an impulse to reform rhetorical criticism by clearing away the taxonomic, historical, and biographical clutter that encumbered the old paradigm and by shifting attention to genuinely rhetorical phenomena. Having moved out of the modernist frame, both projects regard practice and not theory as the focal point for rhetorical inquiry, and so the problem is to locate the radical of practice. But at this point things take an ironic turn. As McGee might say, no one has seen rhetorical practice strut into her office. Rhetorical practice is not a simple, tangible, and objectively present phenomenon, but something that must be identified through conceptual effort. Thus, in order to displace theory so as to concentrate on practice, one has to theorize—at least implicitly—about the domain of practice.

Consequently, the distance between these two conceptions of practice follows from different theoretical impulses. Concerned about establishing the autonomy of rhetoric and influenced by critical social theory, McGee expands the domain of practice until it becomes "a globally pervasive constitutive agency."[6] Concerned about the status of rhetoric as a verbal art and influenced by the classical tradition, I narrow the focus by concentrating on what I regard as the "primitives" of rhetorical art—exemplary oratorical texts. The specific elements that inform these positions reflect differing currents now at work in the academic world and accidental differences of temperament and training. Nevertheless, I do not believe that the emergence of the schism is an accident. Once rhetoricians focus upon practice, the tension between intentional art and extensional power enters almost inevitably, even if unconsciously, into the conceptual arena. What we have now, therefore, is a contemporary embodiment of a persistent problem rooted in Western thought about rhetorical practice.

One way to deal with this problem is to attempt to disarm it by merging the two opposing orientations. Given the apparently radical and symmetrical contrast between the two, this option almost automatically suggests itself. Moreover, existing critical practice routinely works within this middle ground as critics move between ideological issues and specific features of texts. Yet this negotiation is often awkward, and the conceptual grounds for effecting it remain very murky. And if our disciplinary history teaches us nothing else, it surely proves that conceptual confusion on this matter can have disastrous practical consequences.

No flaw in the neo-Aristotelian program was as telling as its failure to acknowledge the tensions between the intentional structure of texts and their extrinsic effects. Implicitly following the existing literary model, the neo-Aristotelians accepted the oration as the basic unit of study in rhetorical criticism and regarded the oration as an artistic product. Yet at the same time, anxious to break free from the domain of literary criticism, they evaluated oratory according to the standard of extrinsic effect. This unrecognized inconsistency between the conception of the object and the standard of judgment forced critics to stagger aimlessly between texts and contexts without learning much about either.

The current generation of critics is less inclined to entrap itself in this bald contradiction, but our literature still does not offer a secure basis for achieving equilibrium between the intentional and extensional dimensions of practice, and the persistence of this issue, in varying forms, might suggest that it is very difficult to give equal weight to both simultaneously. A hasty synthesis is liable to occlude the issues involved here and produce apparently reasonable but less than fully considered compromises. Consequently, I think there are good theoretical and practical reasons to acknowledge the poles represented by textual criticism and critical rhetoric and to give some critics the space needed to work within and through this opposition.

Thus, while others quite reasonably advocate synthesis, I would prefer to hold the two orientations in a dialectical relationship. This dialectical interaction, as I imagine it, is not designed to merge the two positions nor to subsume one within the other. Instead, the opposition would be sustained as a friendly but serious competition which might produce leveraged adjustments within the economy of either project. Since both projects gravitate toward extremes, they have a tendency to purify themselves to the point that they lose contact with the grounded complexity of practice. Irritations arising from the other side of the pole should help prevent either side from becoming rotten with its own perfection.

I am not in a position to know whether this dialectic would prove useful for critical rhetoric, but I am reasonably certain that it can help refine my own efforts in thinking about textual criticism. Critical rhetoric reminds adherents of close reading that questions of power and social circumstance always enter into the texts they study. In my own case, I certainly did not intend to ignore these matters but to locate them appropriately within a conception of rhetoric as a practical art. Nevertheless, in the effort "to construct a rhetoric at least as full as that of Cicero,"[7] I am afraid that I have adopted a narrow and probably anachronistic view of power. In general terms, the problem is this: In my version of textual criticism, the text becomes stabilized as a field of rhetorical action through a calculus that subsumes its extensional thrust within its intentional dynamics. This allows for a synthetic judgment about particular cases, but it also tends to fix the particular text outside the larger field of intertextual developments. The narrowing of focus, I believe, has some heuristic and pedagogical advantages, but it tends to deflect attention from the scenes of controversy out of which these texts arise and for which they are made. Thus, the project is incomplete on its own terms, since it does not accommodate issues of power and social circumstance that decisively influence the focal object of study. The issue, then, is whether I can adjust my position to better encompass these social and political matters—not in terms of the way that McKerrow and McGee conceive power (since that would be to capitulate altogether), but on some basis that seems reasonable for current critical purposes. Before I can address this question, however, I need to present a clearer explanation of the origin and nature of the problem, and this entails some autobiographical reflection.

Most critics of my generation were motivated by a desire either to rescue or displace the classical tradition. I adopted the first of these alternatives; and, in pursuing this course, the most pressing problem was to refurbish traditional criticism by giving it some interpretative density. The neo-Aristotelian approach had treated classical lore as a collection of taxonomic modules, and "criticism" became an exercise in dissecting texts into so many bits that fitted within this static system. The result was to obstruct judgment of the whole and render interpretative work almost impossible. Moreover, the problem was assumed (I now think wrongly) to stem from Aristotle's effort to produce a theoretically coherent account of rhetoric.[8] Since "theory" (on the then prevailing modernist view) consisted in locating and organizing general regularities, it was an inappropriate vehicle for generating grounded interpretations of rhetorical texts. The composition of a text represented a synthetic response to a particular situation, and so it followed that abstract structure of "theory" was inadequate to engage the concrete requirements of rhetorical practice.

These considerations encouraged attention to Cicero, who offered a different account of the relationship between theory and practice. For Cicero the faculty of the orator had absolute priority over the theory of rhetoric. Since theory was general and the orator's task was particular and gauged against constantly shifting circumstances, the theory of rhetoric could have no more than a thin and equivocal status. The real issue, therefore, was the development of the oratorical faculty, the flexible capacity possessed by an individual to engage situations as they arose. Rhetorical precepts had some value in nurturing this faculty, but knowledge of them was never an end in itself, and the faculty gained more from other sources, such as broad knowledge, experience, and the study of models. The use of models, of paradigms of eloquence, proved more useful than abstract precepts because a paradigm embodied the organic integrity of eloquence as it displayed itself in response to concrete issues and circumstances, and thus the paradigms could show what the precepts could not tell.

Since oratory was not regulated by abstract rules but by the changing demands of practice, only one principle could apply to the art universally, and that was decorum or appropriateness—the flexible standard that measured the quality of a discourse against the context of the situation; and decorum became the master term in Ciceronian rhetoric. As explicated in the *Orator*, decorum exercised a complex function, coordinating both the internal structure of a discourse and its extrinsic accommodation to the occasion. Internally, decorum governed the relationships among all the elements within a discourse, rounding them out into a coherent pattern. Extrinsically, decorum worked to adjust the discourse as a whole so that it could offer a fitting and effective response within a specific context. Decorum, then, regulated both form and content even as it mediated between the formal and functional dimensions of a discourse.[9]

This conception cuts across the bias of the modern form/content dichotomy which has plagued criticism in our field since its inception. Form or style is no longer alienated from content or argument. Instead, the two blend together within the unfolding development of a discourse, a development that simultaneously holds the discourse together and holds it out as a way of influencing the world in which it appears. Form, then, plays a decisive role in rhetorical discourse, but only as it promotes the function of the discourse, as it acts to produce an effect on auditors and to do some work in the social world. A somewhat similar concern manifests itself in Kenneth Burke's effort to coordinate the intrinsic and extrinsic aspects of rhetoric, and it appears in his definition of form as "an arousing and fulfilling of desires. A work has form in so far as one part of it leads to another, to be gratified by the sequence."[10] Here the form of a work extends toward the auditor's response, and the critic's task is to discover how a work is constructed in order produce a response. Or, as Tom Benson nicely puts the point, the critic "inquires into the states of thought and feeling an audience is invited to experience."[11]

In short, by taking a Ciceronian turn and then by turning Cicero to critical purposes, we achieve something that might be called formal/functional criticism. This approach is committed to understanding discourses in their full complexity, comprehending them both as linguistic constructions and as efforts to exercise influence, and it operates through paradigm cases rather than abstract principles. The critic occupies the position Cicero assigned to the orator, and equipped with general knowledge, including a practical command of the percepts of the art, he or she studies paradigm texts. Over time, the critic develops a repertoire of such texts and a heightened sensitivity to the possibilities of rhetorical practice gained from the study of situated practice. In this way, the critic attempts to cultivate the capacity, the practical judgment, necessary to interpret and assess any new case that comes to hand, and judgment moves laterally across cases, thus fixing attention on embodied rhetorical performance rather than on abstract forms. Within this project, the lore of classical rhetoric becomes something more than a guide to the naming of parts; it becomes available for doing interpretative work, since metaphors and enthymemes, prose rhythms and topics, hyperboles and examples take on a life within the metabolism of a discourse.

This whole operation depends upon restricting rhetorical action to one level—its manifestation in a particular text. But, as McGee and others constantly remind us, rhetorical action is a complex business that occurs simultaneously at many levels, some of them extending far beyond the artistic representations located in a single case. Thus, if this project disarms the dichotomy between form and function, it may also unwittingly sponsor another version of formalism—a local formalism that isolates the text from larger discursive formations and restricts interpretation within the orbit of the text's own construction. Hence, the project lies open to the charge that it "aestheticizes" practical discourse and discounts the ratio between rhetoric and social action—a complaint registered by virtually everyone who has commented on this matter.[12]

A minimal response to this problem requires attention to the interplay between texts, and this involves something more than just increasing the number of texts studied. Condit, I believe, mistakes the complexity of the issue when she argues that "theoretically close readers of multiple texts would end up doing the same things done by readers of a single text, only more of it."[13] Within the economy of my project, the problem is that readers would do the same thing—namely read each of the multiple texts one at a time, since the text itself defines the horizon of critical attention. Nothing pushes the critic across intertextual space in the effort to locate and assess the movement of rhetorical strategies and themes. The extensional dimension of power is not wholly neglected, since each discourse must be treated as a functional intervention in a local context. Nevertheless, the conception of power is limited to the dynamics of the particular case and refracted through intentional constructions found within the text. It seems that, in putting the critic into the slot Cicero gives to the orator, I have overextended the Ciceronian view of power as a personal attribute and failed to appreciate the way that ongoing social and intertextual developments influence rhetorical practice. Thus, I believe John Campbell is correct when he argues that my "concern to preserve and celebrate the uniqueness of the text and protect it from the distortions of reductionism limits . . . attention to history to the immediate context of a single event."[14]

Is it possible, then, to sustain this concern for the unique integrity of the oratorical text and to remain sensitive to the social and historical dimensions of rhetorical practice? Perhaps it is not—at least not in the long term, and my textual psychosis ought to be incorporated within some larger frame of reference. Nevertheless, while still working within the premises of the original system, I believe that the approach can be adjusted and rendered more sensitive to intertextual developments. This adjustment absolutely demands attention to a unit beyond the single text, but once established, the larger unit tends to absorb the unique features of any particular work. Thus, as critics in our discipline have become more concerned about intertextual issues, their attention has shifted away from the single transaction. Genre studies, for example, seek to identify the stylistic and argumentative features common to a body of texts, and this focus "reduces the significance of any single speech."[15] Particulars assume importance only as "paradigms" that represent the generic norm or as deviations from this norm. Likewise, movement studies stress systematic regularities, grouping discursive practices into phases and assimilating single texts into the composite structure of the movement itself. Neither approach seems compatible with the intense concentration on particulars required by my theory of reading.

The study of controversy seems to offer a more promising alternative, since a controversy is not a discursive formation but a sustained activity consisting of particular instances of oppositional discourse. As matters now stand, these instances are not central to the study of controversy, since the prevailing method is thoroughly analytical. Once a controversy is identified, the critic abstracts recurring issues from the relevant texts and defines the controversy in terms of these issues.[16] But it is possible to conceive controversy in a different way and to stress its fully embodied manifestations rather than its persistent themes. From this perspective, critics can focus upon synthetic moments, selecting certain texts as "representative anecdotes." Such texts (e.g., Booker T. Washington's "Atlanta Exposition Address" paired with W. E. B. DuBois's "Of Mr. Booker T. Washington and Others") function as paradigms not because they represent what is typical, but because they offer "substantial representations" of opposing positions. In other words, the texts do not represent the controversy through schematic reduction but through synecdoche, each text as a whole standing for one of the positions in the debate, and the ensemble of paradigm texts constituting an embodied representation of the entire controversy. At this point, the controversy is open to close reading, since the critic can deal with these texts in their full complexity and treat them as substantive wholes.[17] A thorough understanding of the intentional construction of the paradigm cases, then, links the critic's effort to differing visions of the social world as they are embodied in the controversy. The texts become connected within an intertextual network and with the issues of power and situated interest that inform the whole development, but they retain their integrity as things made by words.

In short, controversy, when approached through "representative anecdotes," offers an appropriate frame for expanding textual criticism into an intertextual arena. This frame preserves the unique and complex integrity of the particular text while it prevents the critic from closing interpretation within the orbit of any single perspective. The presence of opposing texts constantly calls attention to other perspectives and other ways of achieving closure. Viewed in this light, the text is not an autonomous container of meaning, nor is it a failed paradigm of truth. Instead, we can see it as a positioned response set within a constellation of other positioned responses.

What I have just presented is a bare sketch that requires more detailed explanation and further development through case studies. Even when fully articulated, however, this approach would leave important problems unanswered, since students of argumentation would continue to study the issues involved in controversies, generic critics would persist in their effort to understand the common characteristics of types of discourse, movement critics would still investigate complex aggregates of symbolic behavior, and critics generally would remain concerned about the extrinsic effects of persuasive discourse. These are matters that textual criticism is not intended to engage directly, and it does not seek to displace or even compete with these critical interests. On the contrary, it exists in a cooperative relationship with all critical practices that deal in interpretative understanding and evaluation. Textual criticism sustains a narrower focus than other types of criticism, but it does so in order to concentrate on the fundamental operations of rhetorical language. If the focus becomes too narrow, the theory of reading loses contact not only with other critical endeavors but with the social world where practice occurs. On the other hand, if its focus is extended too broadly, it loses the discipline required to engage texts with precision and to comprehend the fundamentals of practice. If it achieves the proper balance, textual criticism can offer a theoretically sound and practically useful base for the one activity shared in common by all other interpretative projects—the rhetorical reading of texts.

NOTES

1. Dilip Gaonkar, "Object and Method in Rhetorical Criticism: From Wichelns to Leff and McGee," *Western Journal of Speech Communication* 54 (1990): 290–316.

2. I was alerted to this point by reading an unpublished manuscript by George Kennedy.
3. *De inventione* 1.6.
4. My referent for "modernist" rhetoric is an approach based in conventional social scientific notions of theory. This position in probably best articulated by Roderick Hart. See his essays "Theory-Building and Rhetorical Criticism: An Informal Statement of Opinion," *Central States Speech Journal* 27 (1976): 70–77; and "Contemporary Scholarship in Public Address: A Research Editorial," *Western Journal of Speech Communication* 50 (1986): 283–95.
5. Celeste Condit, "Rhetorical Criticism and Audience: The Extremes of Leff and McGee," *Western Journal of Speech Communication* 54 (1990): 332.
6. Gaonkar, "Object and Method," 290.
7. Condit, "Rhetorical Criticism and Audience," 342. Condit's essay implies that I do not measure up very well against this standard. I admit it, but it is a high standard, and I continue to struggle toward it. The Ciceronian tincture in my critical approach is noted by Gaonkar, "Object and Method," 311–12, and is elaborated below in this paper.
8. Recent uses of Aristotle's *Rhetoric* indicate a different interpretation of the text and a markedly different attitude toward theory than is apparent in "neo-Aristotelianism." Farrell, for example, holds that the function of theory is to inform practice and argues that Aristotle offers a way to ground theory in practice. See Thomas B. Farrell, "Practicing the Arts of Rhetoric: Tradition and Invention," *Philosophy and Rhetoric* 24 (1991): 183–212; and "Inventing Rhetorical Culture: Some Issues of Theory and Practice," *Rhetoric Society Quarterly* 21 (1991): 17–25. Likewise, Michael Hyde and Craig Smith, "Rethinking 'The Public': The Role of Emotion in Being with Others," *Quarterly Journal of Speech* 77 (1991): 446–66, reread Aristotle's theory of the emotions so as to provide a less modular and more fluid way to apprehend the theory/practice relationship. These efforts at practical theory come very close to the interest in a theory of rhetorical reading; in fact, it is difficult, perhaps impossible, to draw a dear line of demarcation between them, and both are far closer to each other than either is to the conception of theory sponsored by Hart. The important point is that criticism cannot divorce itself from theory, and much of the recent "theory bashing" in our field results from the failure to distinguish the modernist version of theory from other possibilities.
9. For a more fully elaborated account of decorum and related matters, see my papers "The Habitation of Rhetoric," in *Argument and Critical Practices:*

Proceedings of the Fifth SCA/AFA Conference on Argumentation, ed. Joseph W. Wenzel (Annandale, VA: Speech Communication Association, 1987), 1–8; and "Decorum and Rhetorical Interpretation: The Latin Humanistic Tradition and Contemporary Critical Theory," *Vichiana* 3rd series, 1 (1990): 107–26.

10. Kenneth Burke, *Counter-statement*, 2nd ed. (Los Altos, CA: Hermes, 1954), 124.
11. Tom Benson, "The Rhetorical Structure of Frederick Wiseman's *High School*," *Communication Monographs* 47 (1980): 235.
12. Robert Cox, "On 'Interpreting' Public Discourse in Post-modernity," *Western Journal of Speech Communication* 54 (1990): 326–27; John Angus Campbell, "Between the Fragment and the Icon: Prospect for a Rhetorical House of the Middle Way," *Western Journal of Speech Communication* 54 (1990): 362–63; Gaonkar, "Object and Method," 313–14; and Condit, "Rhetorical Criticism and Audience." Robert Hariman, "Time and the Reconstitution of Gradualism in King's Address: A Response to Cox," in *Texts in Context: Critical Dialogues on Significant Episodes in American Political Rhetoric*, ed. Michael C. Leff and Fred Kauffeld (Davis, CA: Hermagoras, 1989), 210–13, also offers some perceptive comment on this issue.
13. Condit, "Rhetorical Criticism and Audience," 331. One sentence later, however, Condit asserts that the unique feature of my approach is its attention to "the *dispositio* of the single text."
14. Campbell, "Between the Fragment and the Icon," 366.
15. Karlyn Kohrs Campbell and Kathleen Jamieson, *Deeds Done in Words: Presidential Rhetoric and the Genres of Governance* (Chicago: University of Chicago Press, 1990), 9. Interestingly, however, Karlyn Campbell's *Man Cannot Speak for Her*, vol. 1, *A Critical History of Early Feminist Rhetoric* (New York: Praeger, 1989), while it also deals with a genre, devotes much more attention to single speech texts; in some cases, such as her critique of Stanton's "Solitude of Self," Campbell presents detailed and nuanced readings that are models of textual criticism. Following the model she presents in this close reading and genre would appear more compatible.
16. David Zarefsky, *Lincoln, Douglas and Slavery in the Crucible of Public Debate* (Chicago: University of Chicago Press, 1990), clearly illustrates this method.
17. The key terms I use here—"representative anecdote," "substantial representation," and "metonymy"—are, of course, borrowed from Kenneth Burke. Concerning substantial representation and its relation to metonymy, see the essay by Kenneth Burke, "Four Master Tropes," in *A Grammar of Motives* (Berkeley: University of

California Press, 1969), 503–18; and my essay, "Burke's Ciceronianism," in *The Legacy of Kenneth Burke*, ed. Herbert W. Simons and Trevor Melia (Madison: University of Wisconsin Press, 1989), 115–27. I am indebted to Bill Balthrop, who suggested to me that the "representative anecdote" might serve as a way of dealing with the kinds of problems outlined in this paper. I am also indebted to Tom Goodnight for encouraging and guiding my interest in controversy. Goodnight's keynote address at the 1991 Alta Conference, "Controversy," was very useful to me in preparing this paper.

Hermeneutical Rhetoric

"Hermeneutical rhetoric" is the counterpart of Steven Mailloux's "rhetorical hermeneutics." In an article bearing that title and more extensively in his book *Rhetorical Power,* Mailloux offers an "anti-theory theory" of interpretation that situates literary hermeneutics within the context of rhetorical exchange.[1] Traditional literary theory, Mailloux argues, relies upon a general conception of interpretation as the basis for justifying particular interpretative acts. Such "theory" takes two forms—"textual realism," where meaning is found in the text, and "readerly idealism," where meaning is made through intersubjective agreements among a community of interpreters. As theories, these positions are diametrically opposed, but, Mailloux maintains, both are theoretical precisely because they share the assumption that standards of interpretation must refer to a

From Rhetoric and Hermeneutics in Our Time: A Reader, ed. Walter Jost and Michael Hyde (New Haven: Yale University Press, 1997), 196–214.

general ground that exists outside the context of a particular interpretative act; in one case, the text itself acts as a constraint on meaning, and in the other case, shared conventions constrain and shape meanings—but both alike seek to justify interpretations through something extrinsic to the specific context in which the interpretative work occurs. And, Mailloux contends, both fail to meet their own standards; they suffer "'radical embarrassments" because they cannot offer theoretically coherent accounts of how interpretation works in practice.[2] Moreover, Mailloux denies that the problems of idealism and realism can be solved either by combining the two or by displacing both in favor of some other theory. The problem is theory itself and the answer is to stop doing it. In its place, Mailloux advocates a form of "interpretative neo-pragmatism" that views interpretation as a grounded rhetorical process:

> Such a hermeneutics views shared interpretative strategies not as the creative origin of texts but rather as historical sets of topics, arguments, tropes, ideologies, and so forth which determine how texts are established as meaningful through rhetorical exchange. Such communities are actually synonymous with the conditions in which acts of persuasion about texts take place. Concepts such as "interpretative strategies" and "argumentative fields" are, we might say, simply descriptive tools for referring to the unformalizable context of interpretative work, work that always involves rhetorical action, attempts to convince others of the truth of explications and explanations.[3]

In other words, contexts always enter into interpretation, and because contexts are theoretically indeterminate, they cannot be formalized and subjected to standards extrinsic to the ground of a particular rhetorical exchange. Interpretative theory is only a species of rhetorical politics, and rather than attempting to resolve interpretative controversies by rising above them, hermeneutics ought to ground itself within rhetorical histories; it ought to provide thick descriptions of interpretative practices that are mindful of the shifting political positions of those who engage in them.[4]

As this brief summary indicates, Mailloux's rhetorical hermeneutics not only alters conventional notions about the theory-practice relation, but it also blurs distinctions between the political and the literary. Nevertheless, his position clearly and self-consciously emerges from within a specific disciplinary context. His argument begins with debates about theory and meaning in literary studies, and, although he extends his interests into the domain of politics, his focal point remains the problem of interpretation per se, and his dominant referent is literary texts. The adjective-noun relation in rhetorical hermeneutics indicates this emphasis. Mailloux, that is, works through rhetoric to generate a more sophisticated conception of the hermeneutic enterprise. Because of my own disciplinary interests, I would like to reverse this orientation so that the stress falls on rhetoric. Hence, I wish to reverse the position of the adjective and the noun and propose a hermeneutical rhetoric. The focal interest here centers on rhetorical practice as manifested in texts that directly and overtly engage political circumstances. And this change in focal object also suggests a different motive—a shift from how rhetoric constrains understanding of texts to how interpretative processes become inventional resources in texts that purport to address extraverbal reality. To put the point simply: where Mailloux asks how rhetorical strategies enter into hermeneutic activity, I ask how hermeneutical strategies enter into the production of political rhetoric.

This antithesis is too simple and tidy to serve as anything other than a provisional distinction between disciplinary perspectives. In critical practice, the two orientations are not easily separated, and whoever begins with one almost inevitably becomes entangled with the other. Mailloux's book illustrates this fluidity as it moves from a consideration of theoretical texts to literary texts to texts generated in Senate hearings, and at every phase of this movement, simple distinctions between production and interpretation give way to an analysis that reveals how the two processes blend in the communicative context. Likewise, my interest in the production of political discourse must necessarily proceed through an interpretative process grounded within a disciplinary community. The hermeneutic strategies of the rhetor are not just there to be plucked out of a text; to locate and assess them, I must engage in interpretative work and offer explanations and arguments rhetorically appropriate to the community of rhetorical critics. Thus, a complex interaction between hermeneutic inquiry and rhetorical exchange operates in both disciplinary contexts, whatever the differences between the two in their initial orientations. Or, from a broader perspective, we might say that all interpretative work involves participation in a rhetorical exchange, and every rhetorical exchange involves some interpretative work.

These considerations might tempt us to close the circle at either point indifferently and to regard rhetorical hermeneutics and hermeneutical rhetoric as two ways of saying the same thing. But I believe that this would be a serious mistake, for it would disregard one of Mailloux's fundamental premises. Holding that practice has priority over theory—indeed that theory is a form of practice—Mailloux's argument proceeds through "rhetorical histories," and it is anchored in the disciplinary history of literary studies. Rhetorical criticism (in speech communication) and literary hermeneutics (in literary disciplines) have had significantly different histories, and scholars in the two domains typically engage in significantly different practices. Even if these distinctions are arbitrary and counterproductive (although I don't think they always are), they remain a practical fact that cannot be ignored. Consequently, we would distort Mailloux's project if we simply transposed its results into rhetorical criticism. Instead, we need to develop a hermeneutic (in Hans-Georg Gadamer's sense of the term) that recognizes the "otherness" of disciplinary interests while it opens space for fusing these differences into new perspectives. This effort requires recognition of points of resistance as well as affinity; it is for this reason that I propose to make hermeneutical rhetoric a counterpart rather than a species or a genus of rhetorical hermeneutics.

Invention, Interpretation, and Imitation in the Rhetorical Tradition

Hermeneutical rhetoric entails a realignment of the relation between interpretation and production in the rhetorical tradition, as that relation is now generally conceived. At present, the dominant view is that classical rhetoric must be sharply distinguished from contemporary criticism because of the productive/performative emphasis of the one, and the hermeneutic/interpretative emphasis of the other. The earliest version of this distinction, so far as I know, appeared fifteen years ago in Jane Tompkins's influential essay "The Reader in History: The Changing Shape of Literary Response."[5] Tompkins notes a number of similarities between classical literary criticism formed on the rhetorical model and contemporary reader-response theory. But she also identifies a crucial difference: contemporary critics, she observes, take "meaning to be the object of critical investigation," whereas classical critics are concerned with language as power and not as signification. Hence, their purpose in studying texts is not to understand the texts' meaning but to identify techniques useful for future rhetorical production. In the classical approach, the goal of criticism is to enhance the reader's inventional skills as writer or speaker rather than to treat the text as a privileged locus of meaning.[6]

More recently Dilip Gaonkar has adopted a similar perspective as the basis for constructing a disciplinary history of rhetorical criticism. For Gaonkar, classical rhetoric deals with production and looks forward to the making of a text. By contrast, contemporary rhetoric, as it has followed in the wake of the "interpretative turn," has adopted a hermeneutic goal and seeks to interpret texts that have already been made. The two orientations, he argues, are distinct, and the productionist vocabulary of classical rhetoric therefore offers a thin and inherently flawed basis for contemporary rhetorical criticism. Yet after conducting a detailed reading of the literature, Gaonkar concludes that practicing critics still rely heavily, though often unconsciously, on the assumptions and techniques embedded in the classical model of production. The use of this model, he notes with regret, has persisted despite the overt renunciation of neo-Aristotelianism; the resulting tension between unrecognized presuppositions and professed interpretative objectives has had a debilitating effect on the critical work in the discipline.[7] The distinctions drawn by Tompkins and Gaonkar have the merit of clarity, and up to a point they are plausible and useful. Classical rhetoric and the criticism associated with it surely place emphasis on reading as a resource for future production rather than as an exercise in assigning meaning. Moreover, the technical apparatus of classical rhetoric is intended mainly as a guide to rhetorical performance and production, and its application to critical interpretation does raise problems that often have been neglected. And Gaonkar rightly emphasizes the persistence and magnitude of these problems in the disciplinary history of modern rhetorical criticism.

Nevertheless, if these paired distinctions between periods and focal interests indicate plausible differences of tendency, they are misleading when considered as global and essential oppositions. Production and interpretation, as we have learned from Mailloux, cannot be isolated from each other, and just as contemporary interpretative theories emerge through rhetorical production, so also the productive emphasis in classical rhetoric has its hermeneutic moments. Unfortunately, modern rhetorical critics, who have concentrated almost exclusively on the technical lore of classical rhetoric, have failed to appreciate the way interpretation and production interact in the full program of traditional rhetorical education. And Gaonkar, because he begins with a strong and unqualified binary opposition between production and interpretation, assumes that the problems in applying classical rhetoric to interpretative work stem from the productive essence of that rhetoric. He does not consider that these difficulties might result from the way modern scholars interpret the tradition, and thus he falls victim to the disease of conceptual rigidity he intends to cure.

The appropriation of classical rhetoric by modern critics was not the result of unmediated contact with the essence of the tradition. It occurred within an academic milieu that favored—almost demanded—foundationalist conceptions of theory and method.[8] Modern critics left the impress of their prejudices and needs on the tradition, selecting and interpreting its elements to conform with their interest in abstract theory and objective methodology. Not surprisingly, then, they isolated the preceptive lore as almost the sole focus of attention and treated the precepts as theoretical principles capable of objective, somewhat mechanical application to texts. Other aspects of classical rhetorical education—its extensive program of reading, for example, or its compositional exercises and its rather antitheoretical stress on pragmatic judgment—were largely ignored. The result was a critical program that had little interpretative energy. The fault here, however, was less a consequence of the original model than of the way the model had been reconstructed. Moreover, the efforts to reform rhetorical criticism have typically proceeded through efforts to displace rather than reinterpret the older tradition.

Yet, Gaonkar's binary analysis notwithstanding, the contemporary hermeneutic turn invites such reinterpretation. By denying that texts have fixed, objective meanings, the new hermeneutics opens space for the concepts of probability, social exchange, and situated interests to become matters of serious concern. And, as we have noted in Mailloux's work, these concepts undermine the assumption that interpretation and production are distinct activities. Underscoring these points of affinity between rhetoric and hermeneutics, Gadamer argues that "the grasping of the meaning of the text takes on something of the character of an independent productive act, one that resembles more the art of the orator than the process of listening. Thus it is easy to understand why the theoretical tools of the art of interpretation (hermeneutics) have been to a large extent borrowed from rhetoric."[9] Gadamer, however, has never elaborated this relation between traditional rhetoric and hermeneutics, and I suspect that the reason is indicated in this passage. He emphasizes the productive (rhetorical) aspect of interpreting a written text, but because he seems to regard rhetoric as an oral art (defined by the speaker-hearer relationship), the idea of a hermeneutic component in rhetoric may be foreign to him. If, however, we take a broader view and consider how a program of reading and criticism entered into rhetorical education, we might perceive how hermeneutic processes of understanding through application can enter into the primarily productive economy of the rhetorical system.

In classical rhetoric, the doctrine of *imitatio* provided the most obvious intersection between the reading of texts and the production of persuasive arguments. Although this doctrine held a prominent place in traditional rhetoric, modern scholars have only begun to give it serious attention, and it is sometimes badly misunderstood because of the aversion to "imitation" that we have inherited from Romantic thought. *Imitatio* is not the mere repetition or mechanistic reproduction of something found in an existing text. It is a complex process that allows historical texts to serve as equipment for future rhetorical production. Classical literary criticism, drawn into the orbit of rhetorical functionalism, largely served as a vehicle for developing productive skills through *imitatio*, and Tompkins notes that this orientation militated against reading literary texts as free-standing units, but she underestimates the role that interpretation played within this rhetorical approach to literature.

The function of rhetorical education, at least in its more liberal versions, was to impart the practical judgment and linguistic resources needed to adapt to changing circumstances. Eloquence demanded the capacity to make the appropriate response to concrete situations, and hence propriety (*prepon* or *decorum*) in rhetoric, like prudence in ethics, could not be reduced to theoretical rules. Rules were general, but rhetorical cases were particular and could not be resolved simply by theoretical knowledge. Consequently, the perceptive lore of rhetoric did not constitute a theory or method in the modern sense of these terms. Instead, the body of precepts served as an armamentarium of possible strategies, whose potential could be realized only as they were used in actual rhetorical production. Thus, a knowledge of rhetoric limited to abstract principles would yield what Quintilian called a "dumb science."[10] The goal of the system was not to generate theory but to assist in developing a faculty for judging when to use a strategy and how to embody it appropriately in a particular case.

Given the limitations of theoretical instruction, *imitatio* played a vital role in rhetorical education, for it could show what the rules could not tell. In the first phase of this process, the reader would learn to identity strategies and forms as actually embodied in a historical text and to judge their significance relative to the construction of the text as a whole and its situated rhetorical purposes. In the second phase, such strategies and forms would be reembodied in a new composition addressed to a different situation. Throughout both phases, invention and interpretation interact with each other. Significant features of the historical text must not only be recognized but be applied to an understanding of how they function in the rhetorical metabolism of that text—something that implies an inventive act on the part of the reader—and then, as reader becomes writer, interpretative judgment must be used to determine whether, when, and how these strategies can be appropriated for new uses. And within this practice, the interplay between understanding and production creates an organic connection between the historical text and the new composition; the old text leaves its impression on the rhetor's product, but the rhetor's productive act has left its interpretative impression on the original. In her astute analysis of classical *imitatio*, Rita

Copeland summarizes this complex development when she observes that "the relationship between model and copy, like that of lineage, is predicated on the act of invention; the model, or ancestor, discovers and posits the ground for future invention. Such an evolutionary pattern is enabled or sustained by the very interpretative community which it creates. Hence, to justify the imitative enterprise, the copy produces, not conspicuous likeness of the original, but rather what is understood and revalued in the original."[11]

As Copeland's remarks suggest, *imitatio* can become something much more than a technical classroom exercise. In practice, of course, it is sometimes used for limited and technical stylistic purposes, but it can also function as an important resource for developing extended arguments. Or again, through a process similar to Kenneth Burke's "casuistic stretching," imitation of the structure and language of an old text may help introduce radically new ideas. Even more broadly, historical texts may serve as political and moral as well as artistic paradigms—paradigms that embed themselves deeply into the rhetorical performance and help constitute the persona of the rhetor.

At all these levels, but especially in cases that involve a strong political and ethical tendency, *imitatio* functions as a hermeneutical rhetoric that circulates influence between past and present. As the embodied utterances of the past are interpreted for current application, their ideas and modes of articulation are reembodied, and old voices are recovered for use in new circumstances. Hermeneutic rhetoric, then, is at once a mechanism for technical production and a vehicle for achieving what J. Robert Cox calls the invention of usable traditions.[12]

This capacity for stable innovation—for building community through tradition without becoming mired in a staid traditionalism—marks the most significant feature of hermeneutic rhetoric as constructive counterpart to rhetorical hermeneutics. In formulating a rhetorical hermeneutics, Mailloux strips hermeneutics of a foundational basis by situating it in rhetorical practice. This conception leaves him open to the charge of pernicious relativism, and Mailloux attempts to blunt this charge by arguing that acknowledgment of the contingency of rhetorical politics "is not to avoid taking a position. Taking a position, making an interpretation, cannot be avoided. Moreover, such historical contingency does not disable interpretative argument, because it is the only ground it can have. We are always arguing at particular moments in specific places, to certain audiences. Our beliefs and commitments are no less real because they are historical, and the same holds for our interpretations."[13]

This endorsement of positioned argument in place of argument fixed against a standard outside historical circumstance fits comfortably within the rhetorical tradition. Yet when focused upon interpretation, this position has greater power for diagnostic and descriptive purposes than for invention. Rhetorical hermeneutics can provide thick descriptions of how interpretative practices change at different times and in different rhetorical communities, but it offers no account of how members of a community can invent new interpretative strategies while remaining within that community. In other words, Mailloux teaches us how we enter into rhetorical situations, but his program does not consider how we can alter them. Taking a stand within a contingent situation seems to reflect either the existing communal structures of argument and belief or an idiosyncratic, wholly subjective reaction against those standards. Hermeneutical rhetoric, however, focuses upon interpretation as a source of invention and suggests how traditions can be altered without destroying their identity. It offers a view of community as a locus of deliberating subjects who change themselves and one another by renewing and revaluing moments in their history.

This sketch of hermeneutical rhetoric has proceeded along abstract, theoretical lines, but I have argued that the concept cuts across the bias of theory and practice and manifests itself through concrete application. Consequently, it is best explained by reference to particulars; in the remainder of this chapter, I would like to illustrate the concept through a case study—specifically, Abraham Lincoln's use of the Declaration of Independence as a ground and vehicle for dealing with issues of his own time. I have selected this case because I believe it offers a clear instance of hermeneutical rhetoric and because the texts in question have already received detailed and expert study from many interpreters.[14] I have little new to say about Lincoln's use of the Declaration, but I hope to indicate how some of the existing interpretations can be synthesized and supplemented through the concept of hermeneutical rhetoric.

A Case Study in Hermeneutical Rhetoric

Lincoln's most famous reference to the Declaration appears in the opening sentence of the Gettysburg Address: "Four score and seven years ago our fathers brought forth on this continent, a new nation, conceived in Liberty, and dedicated to the proposition that all men are created equal."[15] These words are so familiar, so comfortably imprinted in memory, that we normally do not pause to consider how Lincoln, without naming the Declaration, positions himself in relation to it. A moment's reflection, however, reveals that the relation is both complex and controversial. When Lincoln says that the nation was brought forth "four score and seven years ago," he confidently asserts something that is not a simple historical fact. It is equally possible to date the origin of the nation at other times and in respect to other documents, such as the Articles of Confederation or the Constitution. Thus, Lincoln selects a particular text to represent the origins of the American people, to locate their most fundamental principles, and to frame his own rhetorical effort.

Lincoln's sentence also recalls the language of the Declaration's second paragraph, which begins: "We hold these truths to be self-evident: That all men are created equal; that they are endowed by their Creator with certain unalienable rights; that among these are life, liberty, and the pursuit of happiness." Again Lincoln is selecting, using some of the key terms from the original while omitting others. More important, he not only places the phrase "all men are created equal" in an emphatic position, he alters its epistemological status. While Jefferson holds the principle to be a self-evident truth, Lincoln regards it as a proposition to which the nation is dedicated. As several commentators have explained, this difference is significant, and I shall return to it later. For my present purposes, however, it is enough to note that the Gettysburg Address does not open with an elegantly neutral reference to the Declaration but with a carefully selected and nuanced view of how the document should be understood.

Once we recognize these rhetorical complications, it should come as no surprise that interpreters of the Gettysburg Address have reached very different conclusions about how Lincoln stands in relation to the Founding Fathers. Edwin Black, for example, holds that the speech expresses "a profound conservatism. The first sentence having announced the historical founding of a destiny, the speech serves the perpetuation of that original purpose." It is concerned with "the conservation of a political idea and with the republic that instantiates it."[16] Other readers, including a number of conservatives, reach the opposite conclusion. For them, the traditional language and the appeal to traditional authority disguise a radical purpose—"a startling new interpretation of that principle of the founders which declared that 'all men are created equal.'"[17] Distorting the teachings of the fathers for his own immediate political purposes, Lincoln, according to M. E. Bradford, constructs an "imaginary history" and then uses it as an instrument to transform the Union into a "unitary structure."[18] Still other readers find in the speech a complex blend of traditional and innovative elements. Thus, for Garry Wills, the Gettysburg Address is a revolutionary text, forever altering the self-perception of Americans as a people. But Wills argues that Lincoln effects this revolution through a rhetoric of correction rather than radical subversion. By reinterpreting the Declaration, Lincoln discovers a way to "correct the Constitution itself without overthrowing it."[19] For Glen Thorow, the Address sustains a complex, lively interaction between past principles and current interests, and "in apparently repeating the principles of the Declaration of Independence, Lincoln subtly changes their meaning."[20] Lincoln, Thorow maintains, does not simply invoke the authority of the fathers; he interprets "their advice in light of their deeds for the present time."[21]

This third position, especially as Thorow articulates it, represents Lincoln as engaging in something very similar to the kind of hermeneutical rhetoric I have described earlier. From this perspective, past and present—interpretation of an old text and rhetorical invention for current purposes—work together simultaneously. Having established the Declaration as a point of reference (in fact, as the originary point of reference for the nation), Lincoln is constrained by that document, but he can also open space to reinterpret it and redefine the nation. Thus, the rhetorical power of the Gettysburg Address, in some large measure, results from the circulation of influence between Lincoln's words and the words of the original he both copies and reinvents. Thorow and Wills both offer useful readings of the speech in terms of this interaction.

Thorow's is precise and comprehensive in noting how Lincoln's text follows and departs from the Declaration, but he does not connect the text with its antecedents in Lincoln's antislavery rhetoric of the 1850s—a matter of real importance in understanding the "new birth of freedom" Lincoln announces at Gettysburg. Wills offers a detailed account of this connection, but his reading of the Address is less sensitive to its internal structure and to the hermeneutic energy it develops. In what follows, I hope to combine the virtues of both approaches and offer a more fully realized description of the intersection between rhetoric and hermeneutics in Lincoln's discourse. For this purpose, I need to begin with Lincoln's use of the Declaration in the period preceding his election to the presidency.

On August 17, 1858, shortly before his first debate with Stephen Douglas, Lincoln delivered a campaign speech in Lewistown, Illinois. Included in it was one of his most impassioned appeals to the Declaration of Independence. In that document, Lincoln said, the "Fathers of the Republic" revealed nothing less than their majestic interpretation of the economy of the universe. This was their lofty, wise, and noble understanding of the justice of the Creator to his creatures.

> Yes, gentlemen, to all His creatures, to the whole great family of man . . . they erected a beacon to guide their children and their children's children, and the countless myriads who should inhabit the earth in other ages. . . . While pretending no indifference to earthly honors, I do claim to be actuated in this contest by some thing higher than an anxiety for office. I charge you to drop *every* paltry and insignificant thought for any man's success. It is nothing; I am nothing; Judge Douglas is nothing. But do not destroy that immortal emblem of Humanity—the Declaration of American Independence.[22]

This passage comes from a campaign speech, and its language is inflated, the sentiments hyperbolic. Nevertheless, it is difficult to deny their sincerity, for Lincoln repeats them so often and, in his more reflective moments, grounds them in an economical and precise logic. Three years before his senatorial campaign, in a letter to his friend Joshua Speed, Lincoln had written:

> Our progress in degeneracy appears to me to be pretty rapid. As a nation, we began by declaring that "all men are created equal." We now practically read it "all men are created equal, except negroes." When the Know-Nothings get control, it will read "all men are created equal, except negroes, and foreigners, and catholics." When it comes to this I should prefer emigrating to some country—to Russia, for instance, where despotism can be taken pure, and without the base alloy of hypocrisy.[23]

For Lincoln, then, the Declaration was not just a historical document, but "a living creed."[24] Its principle of equality, as he understood it, was the universal, eternal, and essential bedrock of American democracy, or of any other self-governing polity. Any exception to or limitation on this principle subverted liberty, because it sanctioned the exercise of tyrannical control by one individual or group over another. The proposition that "all men are created equal," therefore, constituted the basis for political morality, and unless the public accepted and acted in accordance with this proposition, free government would inevitably erode and degenerate into tyranny.

This conception of the Declaration and the centrality of equal political rights did not emerge through philosophical contemplation. It was generated in and through the political controversies of the 1850s, when slavery emerged as the dominant issue nationally, and in the state of Illinois, where opinion was sharply divided. If, as Richard Hofstadter has said, the Declaration "was the primary article of Lincoln's creed,"[25] that creed was itself developed within the crucible of political debate. Thus, Lincoln's immediate political purposes shaped his views of the Declaration and offered "political ammunition" for him as a controversialist.[26] Merging interpretation and invention, Lincoln used the Declaration as a rhetorical instrument to build a political constituency for himself and to discredit his opponents, the most notable of whom was Douglas.

In countering Douglas's program of popular sovereignty, which attempted to drain the moral charge from the slavery issue, Lincoln repeatedly cited the plain language of the Declaration; slavery was not consistent with the moral truth that all men are created equal, and those who believed in the Declaration could not assume an ethically neutral position concerning slavery. Thus, Douglas's misguided effort to diffuse this issue did not offer a middle course. Instead, Lincoln argued, it was a radical deviation from the wisdom of the founders and a threat to the most fundamental principle of a free government; Douglas was attempting to "blow out the moral lights around us."

The plain language of the Declaration, however, was open to more than one interpretation, and Douglas responded with a vigorous counterattack based upon well-known historical evidence. When the Declaration was enacted, slavery was legal in all thirteen colonies, and many of the signers of the Declaration, including Jefferson himself, owned slaves. Consequently, unless the founders were the worst sort of hypocrites (and thus not worthy of credence), they could not have meant to include blacks in the phrase "all men are created equal." In the debate at Galesburg, Douglas charged that Lincoln's "Chicago doctrine"—his claim that the "negro and the white are made equal by the Declaration of Independence and by Divine Providence—is a monstrous heresy. The signers of the Declaration of Independence never dreamed of the negro when they were writing that document. They referred to white men, to men of European birth and European descent, when they declared the equality of all men." For Douglas, "This government was made by our fathers on the white basis. It was made by white men for the benefit of white men forever, and was intended to be administered by white men for all time to come." Thus, it was Lincoln who had distorted the sentiments of the founders and who, by assuming that he was "a wiser man than those who framed the government," threatened to subvert the edifice they had constructed.[27] Douglas's argument rests upon assumptions that are unacceptable to a twentieth-century reader, but at the time and in the context of its utterance the argument carried substantial weight. Lincoln could not credibly claim the authority of the founders and of the Declaration without fashioning an effective reply. Moreover, the strictly historical parts of Douglas's argument were undeniable—the Declaration was written and promulgated by men who lived in a society that sanctioned slavery, and many of them were slave owners. Consequently, Lincoln needed to discover an interpretative perspective that de-emphasized inferences based on the literal historical record and that stressed ethical principles relevant to the issues of his own day. His answer to this problem was a hermeneutic tour de force that first appeared in a speech he delivered in June 1857 and that he repeated verbatim in the final debate at Alton. After accusing Douglas of "doing violence to the plain unmistakable language of the Declaration," Lincoln commented:

> I think the authors of that notable instrument intended to include all men, but they did not intend to declare all men equal in all respects. They did not mean to say that all were equal in color, size, intellect, moral developments, or social capacity. They defined with tolerable distinctness in what respects they did consider all men created equal—equal in "certain inalienable rights, among which are life, liberty, and the pursuit of happiness." This they said, and this they meant. They did not mean to assert the obvious untruth that all were then actually enjoying equality, nor yet, that they were about to confer it immediately upon them. In fact, they had no power to confer such a boon. They meant simply to declare the right, so that the enforcement of it might follow as fast as circumstances should permit. They meant to set up a standard maxim for free society, which should be familiar to all, and revered by all; constantly looked to, constantly labored for, even though never perfectly attained, constantly approximated, and thereby constantly spreading and deepening its influence, and augmenting the happiness and value of life to all people of all colors everywhere.[28]

In this remarkable passage, we witness hermeneutical rhetoric at work, as Lincoln constructs a vehicle for connecting the past utterance with its present application so that meaning and use interact. The principle of equality is not a statement of fact, but a maxim—a truth that we ought to use in measuring and directing our actions. This truth is eternal and universal, but we may never realize it, and we can never understand it except as it applies to circumstances that no one, not even the wise men who formulated the principle, could foresee. It is an ideal that we must constantly pursue although we cannot know where it will lead us. We do not grasp this truth in detached isolation, but we enact it through our political and ethical judgments, deepening and spreading its meaning, altering its precise content, through time and circumstance. The principle that all men are created equal is a legacy from our fathers but not a legacy that comes in the form of a fixed and finite property that can be measured, catalogued, and stored. Rather, we have been bequeathed a principle we can understand only through use. The founders, then, have left us a maxim that establishes a universal standard for a free society—a minimal principle of human respect and dignity—but it is a maxim that we renew and revalue in our constant effort to sustain the legacy of a free society under the pressure of constantly changing circumstances. The meaning of the maxim is not fixed at the moment of its utterance but develops in and through the nation's history.

Lincoln's argument was not an abstract exercise in hermeneutics per se. It was a positioned response framed within a heated political controversy and designed to do partisan work. Nevertheless, his partisan position reflected and embraced a general conception of history and the proper interpretation of historical texts. As David Zarefsky argues, Lincoln regarded history not as a documentary record but as a dynamic force "projected forward into the future from motives uncovered through a reflective reading of the past."[29] This perspective allowed Lincoln to effect a dissociation between "empirical description and ideal principle, between the Declaration as fact and as norm.'"[30] And when he argued that the phrase "all men are created equal" was a moral norm, he suggested that its verification must "come over time in the life of the country."[31] In the Gettysburg Address, the principle specifically assumes this meaning as the moral norm becomes a proposition.

As I noted earlier, the opening sentence of the Gettysburg Address both echoes and alters the language of the Declaration. In the Declaration, the principle that "all men are created equal" is held as a self-evident truth. In Lincoln's version, it is a proposition to which the nation is dedicated. A self-evident truth requires no proof; it is verified as it is uttered. A proposition, however, "may be true or false and must be proven one or the other."[32] But there is a paradox here, for Lincoln had frequently and emphatically maintained that equality in political rights was the most fundamental principle of the nation. How, then, could it be proven true? What proof could be adduced to verify the most basic and essential premise of a system?

The second sentence of the Address answers this problem by framing the issue in national history: "Now we are engaged in a great civil war, testing whether that nation, or any other nation so conceived and so dedicated, can long endure." What is to be proved, then, is not the truth of the proposition per se—the question is not Are all men created equal? Rather, the question is whether the proposition can be verified in human history—Can a nation dedicated to it endure?

In raising this question, Lincoln implicitly calls attention to the historical distance between the Founding Fathers and his own generation. They founded the nation on the basis of a self-evident truth, but as the terrible fact of the Civil War demonstrates, repeated assertion of that truth is not enough to bind and sustain the nation through time. The principle that "all men are created equal" remains essential to the identity of the American people—it is the genetic link connecting later generations to the fathers. But if later generations are to act on this principle appropriately, they must reinterpret it and make it relevant to their own circumstances. The progeny, then, stand in a complex, equivocal relationship to the fathers. They are both identified with and other than the fathers. Speaking eighty-seven years after the birth of the nation, Lincoln acknowledges his patrimony, but he cannot simply restate the principles of the founders. If he is to preserve these principles, he must change them—or, more precisely, he must change the way the public mind conceives and applies them. What was fitting and proper for one time and purpose must change to meet the demands of other times and purposes.

The structure of the Gettysburg Address, I believe, explicates and enacts this complex, equivocal relationship between generations by creative equivocation of the verb *dedicate*. That verb appears six times in this short speech and, as Edwin Black has shown, its meaning shifts significantly at different points in the text. The most dramatic shift—and the one Black stresses—occurs between the second paragraph and the third, "where the dedication of the cemetery is transformed into the dedication of the audience."[33] In the second paragraph, Lincoln speaks of the literal purpose of the occasion, which is to "dedicate" (to hallow or consecrate) a final resting place for the dead. In the third, however, he speaks to a larger and more appropriate purpose, which is for the living to rededicate themselves (commit or devote themselves) to the unfinished work the dead have "so nobly advanced." But there is yet another sense of this term that appears in the text. In the opening sentence, Lincoln says that the founders dedicated the nation to the proposition of political equality. In this sense, *dedicate* means to set apart or designate something for a special purpose. The fathers, that is, dedicated the nation by setting it apart and giving it a special mission through recognition of the principle of equality. Their progeny, on the other hand, must rededicate the nation by committing themselves to that principle and applying it to the work ahead—the work of proving the moral truth of that principle through their actions.

In the unfolding rhetorical economy of the speech, the shifting senses of *dedicate* establish a complex relationship between the living and the dead that applies not only to the audience and the fallen soldiers but also to the audience and the founders of their nation. At its point of origin, the nation was set apart and given a special mission by the founders, and this mission was to prove the proposition that "all men are created equal." The nation is now engaged in a civil war testing whether a nation set apart in this way can endure; more immediately, those who "have come together" at Gettysburg are engaged in consecrating a cemetery for the men who gave their lives for that nation, and it is "altogether fitting and proper" that they do so.

To this point, Lincoln's text proceeds in a straightforward direction, progressively moving from past to present, progressively narrowing the focus to the immediate occasion, and finally affirming the propriety of its conventional purpose. But then comes a peripety, "But in a larger sense, we cannot consecrate—we cannot hallow—this ground." The occasion demands something more than a memorialization of the dead. It requires that the living commit themselves to the purpose to which the dead were devoted. Thus, the living most appropriately honor the dead not by consecrating their graves but by projecting their spirit into the future and dedicating themselves to the still unfinished work. Thus, at the present moment and in the present occasion, Lincoln defines and then redefines the purpose of both his speech and his audience, turning from a piety that sets the dead apart in consecrated ground to one that reaffirms their example through action. It is in just this sense that Lincoln calls for the nation to rededicate itself to the principles of the fathers. Rather than hallowing or consecrating these principles, the nation must dedicate itself to them. Rather than repeating and conserving the words of the fathers, the living must imitate them, giving them new meaning in the effort to prove the proposition that sets the nation apart and gives it an identity and mission. It is for the living to realize a "new birth of freedom" and to ensure that "government of the people, by the people, for the people shall not perish from the earth."

In sum, the Gettysburg Address follows and extends the rhetorical trajectory of Lincoln's earlier antislavery speeches. In the debates of the 1850s, Lincoln had sought to justify a specific and controversial attitude toward slavery through his interpretation of the Declaration of Independence. The same strategy appears in the Gettysburg Address, but it is directed toward a more general end. The focus shifts from justification of an attitude about a specific issue to justification of a perspective about how attitudes ought to evolve in a free society. The conception of history implicit in the earlier discourses manifests itself explicitly in the structure of the Gettysburg Address, and it is coupled with metaphors that disclose a conception of the nation as a living organism. Structurally and metaphorically, the Address establishes a generational relationship between Lincoln and the Founding Fathers in which the fathers offer models for rhetorical and political imitation. That is, the fathers provide the genetic basis for national identity, but their words cannot simply be copied nor their actions repeated; their legacy can be preserved only through renewal and revaluation as historical circumstances demand. In all of Lincoln's discourse, the Declaration stands as the model of models, representing the moment of national origin and the source of the nation's most fundamental principle. The course of history and the tendency of present events are charted against the standard established in the Declaration. That standard, however, is not fixed in time or conceptual space. It is a maxim or proposition that guides and tests conduct without controlling it, and thus the authority of the Declaration merges with contemporary sensibilities, while, at the same time, these sensibilities enter into the understanding of the authority of the Declaration. This circulation of influence between past and present allows Lincoln to change tradition without destroying it, and it illustrates what I have called a hermeneutical rhetoric.

NOTES

1. Steven Mailloux, "Rhetorical Hermeneutics," in *Interpreting Law and Literature: A Hermeneutic Reader*, ed. Sanford Levinson and Steven Mailloux (Evanston, IL: Northwestern University Press, 1988), 345–62; and Mailloux, *Rhetorical Power* (Ithaca, NY: Cornell University Press, 1989).
2. Mailloux, *Rhetorical Power*, 4–14.
3. Mailloux, *Rhetorical Power*, 15.
4. Mailloux, *Rhetorical Power*, 16–18.
5. Jane Tompkins, "The Reader in History: The Changing Shape of Literary Response," in *Reader Response Criticism: From Formalism to Post-structuralism*, ed. Jane P. Tompkins (Baltimore: Johns Hopkins University Press, 1980), 201–32.
6. Tompkins, "The Reader in History," 202–6.
7. Dilip Gaonkar, "The Idea of Rhetoric in the Rhetoric of Science," *Southern Communication Journal* 58 (1993): 258–95.
8. For a detailed account of how these forces influenced critical theory, see William L. Nothstine, Carole Blair, and Gary A. Copeland, "Professionalization and the Eclipse of Critical Invention," in *Critical Questions: Inventions, Creativity, and the Criticism of Discourse and the Media*, ed. William L. Nothstine, Carole Blair, and Gary A. Copeland (New York: St. Martin's Press, 1994), 15–70.
9. Hans-Georg Gadamer, "On the Scope and Function of Hermeneutical Reflection," trans. G. B. Hess and R. E. Palmer, in *Philosophical Hermeneutics*, ed. David E. Linge (Berkeley: University of California Press, 1976), 24. See also Gadamer, "Rhetoric, Hermeneutics, and Ideology-Critique," in *Rhetoric and Hermeneutics in Our Time: A Reader*, ed. Walter Jost and Michael Hyde (New Haven: Yale University Press, 1997), 313–34.
10. Quintilian, *Institutio Oratoria*, trans. H. E. Butler (Cambridge, MA: Harvard University Press, 1931), 5.10.119.
11. Rita Copeland, Rhetoric, Hermeneutics, and Translation in the Middle Ages: Academic Traditions and Vernacular Texts (Cambridge: Cambridge University Press, 1991), 27.
12. J. Robert Cox, "Cultural Memory and Public Moral Argument," in *The Van Zelst Lecture in Communication* (Evanston, IL: School of Speech, Northwestern University, 1987).
13. Mailloux, *Rhetorical Power*, 180–81.
14. Among the works dealing with this topic, I have been most influenced by Glen E. Thorow, *Abraham Lincoln and American Political Religion* (Albany: State

University of New York Press, 1976); David Zarefsky, *Lincoln, Douglas, and Slavery in the Crucible of Debate* (Chicago: University of Chicago Press, 1990); and Gary Wills, *Lincoln at Gettysburg: The Words That Remade America* (New York: Simon and Schuster, 1992). In writing about Lincoln's discourse of the late 1850s, I rely heavily on Zarefsky. My reading of the Gettysburg Address is greatly indebted to Thorow, and my thought about the connection between the earlier speeches and the Gettysburg Address depends in great part upon Wills.

15. I quote from the text in Abraham Lincoln, *Speeches and Writings*, ed. Don Fehrenbacher, 2 vols. (New York: Library of America, 1989), 2:536. All subsequent references to the Gettysburg Address are to this edition.
16. Edwin Black, "Gettysburg and Silence," in *Readings in Rhetorical Criticism*, ed. Carl R. Burgchardt (State College, PA: Strata, 1995), 557–58.
17. Nellie D. Kendall, ed., *Willmoore Kendall Contra Mundum* (Arlington, TX: Arlington House, 1971), 69; quoted in Wills, *Lincoln at Gettysburg*, 39.
18. M. E. Bradford, "Against Lincoln: An Address at Gettysburg. Commentary on 'Lincoln and the Economics of the American Dream,'" in *The Historian's Lincoln: Pseudohistory, Psychohistory, and History*, ed. Gabor S. Boritt (Urbana: University of Illinois Press, 1988), 111. Also see Bradford, "The Gnosticism of Lincoln's Political Rhetoric," *Modern Age* 23 (1979): 10–24.
19. Wills, *Lincoln at Gettysburg*, 147.
20. Thorow, *Abraham Lincoln*, 65.
21. Thorow, "Abraham Lincoln and American Political Religion," in Boritt, *The Historian's Lincoln*, 142.
22. Abraham Lincoln, "Speech at Lewistown, Illinois," August 17, 1858, in *The Collected Works of Abraham Lincoln*, ed. Roy P. Basler, vol. 2 (New Brunswick, NJ: Rutgers University Press, 1953), 546.
23. Abraham Lincoln, letter to Joshua F. Speed, August 24, 1855, in *Speeches and Writings*, 1:363.
24. Zarefsky, *Lincoln, Douglas, and Slavery*, 149.
25. Richard Hofstadter, "Abraham Lincoln and the Self-Made Myth," in *The American Political Tradition and the Men Who Made It* (New York: Vintage, 1973), 130.
26. Hofstadter, "Abraham Lincoln," 130.
27. Stephen Douglas, "Opening Speech in the Galesburg Debate," October 7, 1858, in *Created Equal? The Complete Lincoln-Douglas Debates of 1858*, ed. Paul M.

Angle (Chicago: University of Chicago Press, 1958), 294. Douglas had made similar remarks in the Jonesboro debate; see 201.

28. Abraham Lincoln, "Speech on the Dred Scott Decision," Springfield, Illinois, June 27, 1857, in *Speeches and Writings*, 1:398.
29. Zarefsky, *Lincoln, Douglas, and Slavery*, 164.
30. Zarefsky, *Lincoln, Douglas, and Slavery*, 152.
31. Zarefsky, *Lincoln, Douglas, and Slavery*, 153.
32. Thorow, *Abraham Lincoln*, 72. This paragraph and the next follow Thorow, 72–78.
33. Black, "Gettysburg and Silence," 555.

PART FOUR

The Practice of Rhetorical Criticism

The first two essays in this section—"Lincoln at Cooper Union: A Rhetorical Analysis of the Text" and "Lincoln at Cooper Union: A Rationale for Neo-Classical Criticism"—have earned a place in the literature of rhetorical criticism as milestones of inventional practice. In the generation immediately following their publication in the early 1970s, the Cooper Union essays, each written with G. P. Mohrmann, challenged rhetorical critics of diverse theoretic tendencies to reconsider the potential resources of a rich heritage that the neo-Aristotelian program had at best only hinted at and, at worst, had discredited and distorted rather than deployed. The essays exemplify, too, the temporal unfolding over Leff's career of the architectonic themes on display in the first part of this volume.

However, the key to understanding these essays in the context of his intellectual biography is to grasp Leff's shrewdness in choosing not to encase each and every element of his program against attack but to accentuate the suppleness and adaptability of his perspective to circumstance and counterargument. In the previous part, one sees this suppleness on display in all of the essays but most notably in the metatheoretic style of "Things Made by Words." As Leff found room to accommodate the objections to his work, and to see these objections as opportunities for further invention and adaptation, he also found the space necessary to deepen and diversify his approach. Testaments to this capacity can be found in "Instrumental and Constitutive Rhetoric in Martin Luther King Jr.'s 'Letter From Birmingham Jail'" (with Ebony A. Utley) and "Lincoln among the Nineteenth Century Orators," two quite different exemplifications of close reading that display Leff's restless spirit of improvisation even within the stabilizing ambience of a tradition he himself sought to reinvent.

Though it was published after "Lincoln among the Nineteenth Century Orators," "Instrumental and Constitutive Rhetoric in Martin Luther King Jr.'s 'Letter from Birmingham Jail'" comes first in our arrangement for the clarity with which it embodies the close reading project in its original form. Through its examination of how King constructed a character for himself that turned his literal status as outside agitator into that of a spokesman for the highest values of both black and "moderate" white communities in Birmingham, the essay explores the unity of substance and form in a single situated rhetorical product. Through its attention to numerous surface elements of the text, the essay shows how King's ethos was not just "instrumental" in that it was ready to hand for use, or simply *used*, but "substantive" in that out of the words appropriate to the man, his audiences, and occasion, King constituted a distinctive character. Leff shows how this "constitutional" sense of character then becomes a kind of charter for future negotiation between King and his white moderate audience, and King's followers, who, "overhearing" his letter, are beckoned to embody this same character in their protest. "Lincoln among the Nineteenth Century Orators" exemplifies, as clearly as the King essay, Leff's aim of moving across the surface elements of a text and examining its invitation for encompassing an occasion. The essay is unique in that it also shows Leff extrapolating close reading beyond the immediate text and its context by examining how an argument can expand over different contexts by different speakers. In showing how Henry Grady, Frederick Douglass, and Jane Addams address a common theme and how their texts can be analyzed each in its situated particularity across the later nineteenth century, Leff demonstrates the capacity of close reading to travel across time, fulfilling part of the promise made in "Things Made by Words."

FURTHER READING

"Ad Hominem Argument in the Bush/Kerry Presidential Debates." In *Proceedings of the 6th Conference of the International Society for the Study of Argumentation*, ed. F. H. van Eemeren, J. Anthony Blair, Charles Arthur Willard, and Bart Garssen. (SicSat: Amsterdam, 2008), 859–66.

"Agency Performance, and Interpretation in Thucydides' Account of the Mitylene

Debate." In *Theory, Text, Context: Issues in Greek Rhetoric and Oratory*, ed. Christopher Johnstone (Albany: State University of New York Press, 1996), 97–106.

"Dialogic Figures and Dialectical Argument in Lincoln's Rhetoric," with Jean Goodwin. *Rhetoric and Public Affairs* 3 (2000): 59–69.

"Dimensions of Temporality in Lincoln's Second Inaugural." *Communication Reports* 1 (1988): 26–31.

"Grover Cleveland and the Non-Rhetorical Presidency." In *Before the Rhetorical Presidency*, ed. Martin J. Medhurst (College Station: Texas A&M Press, 2008), 289–306.

"The Polemicist as Artist: W. E. B. DuBois 'Of Mr. Booker T. Washington and Others,'" with Robert Terrill. In *Argumentation and Values: Proceedings of the 9th AFA/SCA Conference on Argumentation*, ed. Sally Jackson (Annandale, VA: SCA, 1995), 230–36.

"Rhetoric and Dialectic in Martin Luther King's 'Letter from Birmingham Jail.'" In *Anyone Who Has a View: Theoretical Contributions to the Study of Argumentation*, ed. F. H. van Eemeren, J. Anthony Blair, Charles A. Willard, and A. Francisca Snoeck Henkemans. (Dordrecht: Kluwer, 2003), 255–268.

"The Rhetoric of War and Remembrance: An Analysis of President Bill Clinton's D-Day Discourses," with Mary Kahl. *Qualitative Research in Communication* 7 (2006): 15–22.

"Rhetorical Timing in Lincoln's 'House Divided' Speech." The Van Zelst Lecture in Communication, Northwestern School of Speech, Evanston, IL, 1984.

"Time and the True Light in Lucretia Coffin Mott's Discourse on Woman," with Meg Zulick. *Rhetoric Society Quarterly* 25 (1995): 20–31.

Lincoln at Cooper Union: A Rhetorical Analysis of the Text

When Abraham Lincoln spoke at the Cooper Union on the evening of February 27, 1860, his audience responded enthusiastically, and the speech has continued to elicit praise throughout the intervening years. Biographers, historians, and literary scholars agree that it was "one of his most significant speeches,"[1] one that illustrated "his abilities as a reasoner,"[2] and one to which posterity has ascribed his "subsequent nomination and election to the presidency."[3] Ironically, however, this model of "logical analysis and construction"[4] has failed to generate a critical response in kind. Most of what has been written treats of the background, and, too often, the man as myth has intruded; caught up in the drama of the performance, writers find no bit of information too trivial to report, whether it be the price of tickets or the fit of Lincoln's

With G. P. Mohrmann, from *Quarterly Journal of Speech* 60 (1974): 346–58.

new shoes.[5] Such details can deepen our appreciation of the event, but they do not illuminate the speech as a speech.

Unhappily, little light is shed by those who do comment on the speech text. Nicolay and Hay assert, for example, that Lincoln's conclusions "were irresistibly convincing,"[6] but their sole piece of supporting evidence is a four-hundred-word excerpt. And if they happen to be "firmly in the hero-worshipping tradition,"[7] those of sterner stuff fare no better. Basler makes the curious claim that the rhetorical "high-water mark" occurs toward the end of the first section;[8] Nevins mistakenly argues that the speech "fell into two halves";[9] reputable scholars equate summary and quotation with explication;[10] and it is generally accepted that Lincoln demonstrated a conciliatory attitude toward the South.[11]

Certainly all is not dross in previous studies, but wherever one turns in the literature, no satisfying account of the speech is to be found.[12] We are convinced that a systematic rhetorical analysis can help rectify the situation, and what follows is our attempt to accomplish such an analysis. In that attempt, we center on the text of the speech, but our purpose demands some preliminary remarks about the rhetorical context.

Although it was not until after the speech that Lincoln frankly admitted his presidential aspirations, saying, "The taste *is* in my mouth a little,"[13] he had been savoring the possibility for months. The preceding November, he had written that the next canvas would find him laboring "faithfully in the ranks" unless "the judgment of the party shall assign me a different position,"[14] but even as he wrote, Lincoln was grasping for a different assignment, "busy using the knife on his rivals . . . and doing all he could to enhance his reputation as an outstanding Republican leader."[15] Small wonder that he decided early to "make a political speech of it" in New York.[16] Here was the opportunity to make himself more available to Republicans in the East. The appearance alone would make for greater recognition, but political availability required more; Lincoln had to be an acceptable Republican, and he had to be an attractive alternative to the Democratic candidate.

William A. Seward and Stephen A. Douglas were the presumptive nominees, and they, patently, were Lincoln's antagonists. Moreover, their views on slavery created an intertwining threat that menaced his conception of the party and his personal ambitions. When Seward spoke about a "higher law" and an "irrepressible conflict," he strained Lincoln's sense of moral and political conservatism; these pronouncements smacked too much of radicalism.[17] Douglas, meanwhile, exacerbated the situation with his doctrine of popular sovereignty. Lincoln feared that this siren song would cause wholesale apostasy in Republican ranks, an eventuality all the more likely if the party nominee was tinctured with radicalism. He knew, however, that a middle ground existed, and he long had occupied it with his insistence that slavery should be protected but not extended. Consequently, when Lincoln addressed the eastern Republicans, both principle and expediency permitted, even dictated, that he speak for party and for self and that he maintain party and self in a position between those taken by Seward and Douglas.

That he took such a course is revealed by an examination of the speech text, but all the external evidence shows a man running hard, if humbly, for political office, and while Lincoln spoke for his party, he spoke first for his own nomination. In fact, the Cooper Union Address is best characterized as a campaign oration, a speech designed to win nomination for the speaker. This identification of genre is basic to our analysis, and the nature of the genre is suggested by Rosenthal's distinction between nonpersonal and personal persuasion;[18] in the former, the speaker attempts to influence audience attitudes about a particular issue, and ethos is important insofar as it lends credence to the substance of the argument. In the latter the process is reversed. The focal point is the speaker, and the message becomes a vehicle for enhancing ethos. Campaign orations, on this basis, tend to be examples of personal persuasion, for while "the ostensible purpose of a given speech may be to gain acceptance of a particular policy . . . the actual purpose is to gain votes for the candidate."[19] In other words, the ultimate goal of the campaign orator is to promote himself as a candidate. Both policies and character are in question, but the treatment of issues is subsidiary to the purpose of creating a general identification between the speaker and the audience. The objective, then, in a campaign oration is ingratiation.

With genre and purpose in mind, we can approach the speech through familiar topics. Addressing himself first to the people of New York, then to the South, and finally to the Republican Party, Lincoln divides his speech into three sections, and this pattern of organization invites seriatim analysis of the major dispositional units. Furthermore, argument and style immediately loom as important elements, since they disclose essential characteristics in and significant interrelationships among the main units of the discourse. Consequently, our critique will follow Lincoln's pattern of organization and will have special reference to matters of argument and style. This approach, however, is not without its hazards. The convenience of tracing the natural sequence of the argument may foster fragmentary analysis and obscure the dominant rhetorical motive. Yet to be mindful of the genre is to find a corrective. The central concern is ingratiation, and recognition of this purpose unifies the elements of analysis by giving them a more precise focus; awareness of the ultimate goal becomes shuttle to the threads of structure, argument, and style.

In the address, Lincoln deals exclusively with slavery, and although this inflammatory issue might seem a shaky bridge to ingratiation, the choice is a fitting response to the rhetorical problem. What better point of departure than the paramount issue of the day, the issue with which he was most closely identified, and the issue that had spawned the Republican Party?[20] And Lincoln starts with the very motivation that had driven men to Ripon only a few years before, the question of slavery in the territories. Capitalizing on these initial associations, he counters the emotionalism inherent in the topic by assuming a severely rational posture and enunciating a moderate but firm set of principles. The approach distinguishes him from his chief rivals and solicits an intensified association from eastern Republicans. These objectives govern the matter and manner of the opening argument, and this argument lays a foundation for subsequent developments in the speech. In the opening section and throughout, Lincoln associates himself and Republicans with the founding fathers and constitutional principle, and he dissociates rival candidates and factions from those fathers and that principle.

Acknowledging his "fellow citizens of New York," Lincoln begins by adopting a "text for this discourse."[21] The text is a statement in which Stephen A. Douglas had asserted, "Our fathers, when they framed the government under which we live, understood this question just as well and even better than we do now." Defining terms in catechistic sequence, Lincoln maintains that "the frame of government under which we live" consists of the Constitution and the "twelve subsequently framed amendments" and that "our fathers" are "the 'thirty-nine' who signed the original instrument." He then asks, what is the question "those fathers understood 'just as well and even better, than we do now'?" The answer "is this: Does the proper division of local from Federal authority, or anything else in the Constitution, forbid our Federal Government to control as to slavery in our Federal Territories?" The question joins the issue because it is a matter upon which Senator Douglas holds the affirmative, and the Republicans the negative."

That Douglas should play the foil is most fitting. National newspaper coverage of the 1858 senatorial campaign had linked the two men together, and the debates were to be published in March.[22] Moreover, Lincoln had continued the argument during 1859, worrying whether the Republican Party would "maintain it's [*sic*] identity, or be broken up to form the tail of Douglas' new kite."[23] Nevertheless, Lincoln knew that Douglas was vulnerable. The Freeport Doctrine had convinced many in the North that the man was only too "willing to subordinate moral considerations to political expediency."[24] Douglas, then, was an established rival, one whom Lincoln perceived as a threat to party unity, and one whose strategic position was open to attack from principle.

On a tactical level, the "text" quoted from Douglas affords Lincoln an ideal starting point. The allusion to the fathers is a symbolic reference with the potential for universal respect, and Douglas's implicit attack upon the principles that had generated the Republican Party creates an antithesis binding speaker and audience together in opposition to a common enemy. This antithesis is a channel for ingratiation; Lincoln makes Republicanism the voice of rational analysis, and the precise terms of Douglas's assertion form the premises of logical inquiry. Moving into the inquiry, Lincoln pursues a vigorous ad hominem attack.[25] He accepts Douglas's logic and then turns it against him.

The argument of the first section develops out of a single hypothetical proposition: if the better understanding evinced by our fathers shows that they believed nothing forbade federal control of slavery in the territories, then such regulatory power is inherent in the governmental frame. Lincoln affirms the antecedent with an elaborate chain of inductive evidence. Instances in the induction consist of actions by the fathers before and after they signed the Constitution because the question "seems not to have been directly before the convention."[26] From the Northwest Ordinance of 1784 to the Missouri Compromise of 1820, Lincoln enumerates seven statutes regulating slavery in the territories, and he accounts for votes by twenty-three of the fathers.[27] Twenty-one voted in favor of such regulation. Since these men were bound by "official responsibility and their corporal oaths" to uphold the Constitution, the implication of their affirmative votes is beyond question. To conclude that the twenty-one would have condoned federal regulation if they thought it unconstitutional would be to accuse these fathers of "gross political impropriety and willful perjury," and "as actions speak louder than words, so actions under such responsibility speak still louder."

Emphasizing deeds and "adhering rigidly to the text," Lincoln cannot offer in evidence "whatever understanding may have been manifested by any person" other than the thirty-nine, nor can he cite the sixteen who left no voting records. But the latter include the likes of Franklin, Hamilton, and Morris, and he believes that this group "would probably have acted just as the twenty three did." In any event, "a clear majority of the whole" understood that nothing "forbade the Federal Government to control slavery in the Federal Territories," and with the remaining fathers probably agreeing, there can be little doubt about "the understanding of our fathers who framed the original Constitution; and the text affirms that they understood the question 'better than we.'"

Lincoln now uses this understanding to discredit arguments based on the Fifth and Tenth Amendments; he says it is "a little presumptuous" to suggest that the fathers embraced one principle when writing the Constitution and another when writing the amendments. And does not this suggestion "become impudently absurd when coupled with the other affirmation, from the same mouth, that those who did the two things alleged to be inconsistent, understood whether they really were inconsistent better than we—better than he who affirms that they are inconsistent?" The touch of sarcasm reveals a more aggressive attitude, but it is justified by the inductive process; Douglas's own criterion forces the conclusion that he doesn't comprehend the understanding of the fathers. Lincoln will become even more combative before he brings the first section to a close, but some comments on style are merited, and they will lead us into his conclusion.

The style of this section is entirely consistent with Lincoln's severely rational approach. The audience probably did not expect the "rhetorical fireworks of a Western stump-speaker,"[28] but Lincoln is most circumspect. There are none of the "many excuses" that made him a Uriah Heep to some of his opponents,[29] and he avoids all display, indulging neither in anecdotes nor figurative language. The syntax is complex at times, but the complexity is that of legal rather than literary prose, as is evidenced in the following sentence: "It, therefore, would be unsafe to set down even the two who voted against the prohibition as having done so because, in their understanding, any proper division of local from Federal authority, or anything in the Constitution, forbade the Federal Government to control as to slavery in Federal territory."

The preceding quotation, with its echo of the text, points to a noteworthy stylistic element: repetition. Lincoln includes fifteen extended citations of the issue and an equal number from the "text," repetitions that accentuate the single line of argument. He adds to the emphasis by stressing certain key words and phrases. For example, there are over thirty uses of the root "understand," usually in the participial "understanding," and Lincoln alludes to the "fathers" more than thirty-five times. None of these repetitions is blatant or forced because he weaves them into the fabric of the inductive process. Furthermore, the repetitions concomitantly reinforce and control the emotional association with the fathers and their understanding of the Constitution. This point is crucial to an appreciation of Lincoln's rhetorical method. Both the direction of the argument and the symbols expressing it are fiercely emotional; yet all is enmeshed in an incisive logical and linguistic structure, and while the tone remains rationalistic and legalistic, it also creates a subtle emotive nexus between the Republican audience and the founding fathers.

As noted above, style and argument shift in the concluding paragraphs, after Lincoln already has established his logical credentials. The argument becomes bolder, and the style alters appropriately. When developing the induction, Lincoln refers to the framers of the Constitution as the "thirty-nine," but they become "our fathers" again in the conclusion of the long first section of the speech. And there periods become more polished and sophisticated:

> If any man at this day sincerely believes that a proper division of local from Federal authority, or any part of the Constitution, forbids the Federal Government to control as to slavery in the Federal Territories, he is right to say so, and to enforce his position by all truthful evidence and fair argument which he can. But he has no right to mislead others, who have less access to history, and less leisure to study it, into the false belief that "our fathers who framed the government under which we live" were of the same opinion—thus substituting falsehood and deception for truthful evidence and fair argument.

This passage completes the negative phase of Lincoln's argumentation. Both matter and manner drive a rational wedge between the speaker and his rivals. Clearly, Lincoln suggests that Douglas may be guilty of deliberate "falsehood and deception," and just as clearly, his own position represents "truthful evidence and fair argument." Lincoln, one of those with "access to history" and some "leisure to study it," attempts to set the record straight. Another direct slash at Douglas, the very source of the text and issue. At the same time, Lincoln indirectly differentiates himself from Seward and his radical posture. Lincoln's position is more to the right, closer to the demands of objective inquiry, closer also to the demands of political availability, and it is important to remark that he achieves this dissociation without recourse to divisive rhetoric. The foray against the man and his position is patent, but it is completely inferential.

Although less obtrusive than the refutation, an equally important constructive movement exists within this part of the oration. Not only does Lincoln distinguish himself from his opponents, he nurtures Republican unity because he makes himself and party the vessels for transmitting the faith of the fathers. Avoiding self-references, he presents himself as the voice of Republicanism, and he caps this appeal with words both to and from the party:

> But enough! Let all who believe that "our fathers who framed the government under which we live understood this question just as well, and even better, than we do now," speak as they spoke, and act as they acted upon it. This is all Republicans ask—all Republicans desire—in relation to slavery. As those fathers marked it, so let it be again marked,

> as an evil not to be extended, but to be tolerated and protected only because of and so far as its actual presence among us makes that toleration and protection a necessity. Let all the guarantees those fathers gave it be not grudgingly, but fully and fairly, maintained. For this Republicans contend, and with this, so far as I know or believe, they will be content.

At this point in the speech, Lincoln has associated himself and his audience with the spirit, the principles, and the actions of the founding fathers, and in doing so, he has taken the first steps toward ingratiation.

Comprising nearly half the speech, this initial section is so clearly logical that it regularly is cited as a demonstration of Lincoln's powers as a reasoner, but to say no more is to grossly underestimate his achievement. The next section, too, is remarkable for its logical development, and all that follows in the speech is anticipated and controlled by the attack upon Douglas. Failure to appreciate this unity has confounded commentators, and their confusion is strikingly illustrated in the generally accepted conclusion that Lincoln follows his attack with remarks "conciliatory toward the South."[30]

The second section does begin with an ostensible change in audience: "And now, if they would listen,—as I suppose they will not,—I would address a few words to the Southern people." But we learn more about the beholders than the object when we are told that the next twenty-six paragraphs are filled with "words of kindly admonition and protest,"[31] words of "sweet reasonableness to allay Southern fears."[32] Presuming that he will not be heard, Lincoln notes that "our party gets no votes" in the South, and he flatly asserts later that "the Southern people will not so much as listen to us." These are not idle reservations. They represent the realistic assessment of an astute politician who knows that the coming election will be won or lost in the North; it is hardly plausible that this man would detract from his ultimate purpose by directing nearly 40 percent of his speech to an unavailable audience.

In truth, the audience does not change. Lincoln merely casts the second section of the speech in the form of a prosopopoeia, a figure he had rehearsed five months earlier in Cincinnati.[33] The device suits his purposes admirably. It enables him to create a mock debate between

Republicans and the South, a debate in which he becomes spokesman for the party. In this role, Lincoln can strengthen the identification between himself and the available Republican audience. He is careful to extend the refutation of Douglas into the second section and thus carry over the lines of association and disassociation begun earlier in the discourse. If Lincoln leaves Douglas with little ground on which to stand, he performs the same argumentative service for the South, and the debate he manufactures is far from being conciliatory.

The prosopopoeia develops into another ad hominem argument. This time, however, the presentation is complicated by the need to deal with the collective contentions of a collective opposition. To provide control, Lincoln again begins by stressing reason, saying to the South, "I consider that in the general qualities of reason and justice you are not inferior to any other people." Yet, in the specific case, rational discourse is stymied because the Southerners never refer to Republicans except "to denounce us as reptiles, or, at the best, as no better than outlaws." Such responses are unjust to both sides. The proper course would be to "bring forward your charges and specifications, and then be patient long enough to hear us deny or justify." Obviously, the South is unwilling and unable to follow this procedure, and becoming persona for both Republicanism and reason, Lincoln reconstructs the charges and specifications; these include sectionalism, radicalism, agitation of the slavery question, and slave insurrections.

The putative debate begins: "You say we are sectional. We deny it. That makes an issue; and the burden of proof is upon you." The crux of the matter is whether Republicans repel the South with "some wrong principle." Republican principle, however, is based in the beliefs and actions of the fathers, and Lincoln challenges the South to respond to this fact. "Do you accept the challenge? No! Then you really believe that the principle which 'our fathers who framed the government under which we live' thought so clearly right as to adopt it, and indorse it again and again, upon their official oaths, is in fact so clearly wrong as to demand your condemnation without a moment's consideration." Closing and reinforcing this line of reasoning, Lincoln refers to the preeminent father: "Some of you delight to flaunt in our faces the warning . . . given by Washington in his Farewell Address," but if he were to speak for himself, "Would he cast the blame of that sectionalism upon us, who sustain his policy, or upon you, who repudiate it? We respect that warning of Washington, and we commend it to you, together with his example pointing to the right application of it."[34] Thus, the South claims to be the injured party, but analysis of the charge proves that the wounds are self-inflicted.

Lincoln uses the same refutational method for each of the other issues; first defining the charge with a series of rhetorical questions, he then turns the argument against the adversary. The South proclaims itself the bastion of conservatism and denounces Republican radicalism, but "what is conservatism? Is it not adherence to the old and tried, against the new and untried? We stick to, contend for, the identical old policy . . . which was adopted by 'our fathers who framed the government under which we live'; while you with one accord reject, and scout, and spit upon that old policy, and insist upon substituting something new." The South alleges that Republicans have made the slavery issue more prominent. True, the issue is more prominent, but this situation arose because the South "discarded the old policy of the fathers." Finally, Southerners complain that Republicans foment insurrection among the slaves, but they can adduce no evidence to support this allegation, cannot "implicate a single Republican" and ignore that "Republican doctrines and declarations are accompanied with a continual protest against any interference whatever" with the institution in the slave states. Indeed, were it not for the loud and misleading protestations of Southern politicians, the slaves would hardly know that the Republican Party existed. Worse yet, the South refuses to acknowledge a simple truth contained in Republican doctrine, a truth articulated "many years ago" when Jefferson indicated that the cause of slave insurrections was slavery itself. Like Jefferson, Republicans would not interfere with slavery where it exists, but Republicans do insist, as the fathers did, that the federal government "has the power of restraining the extension of the institution—the power to insure that a slave insurrection shall never occur on any American soil which is now free."

Finishing his treatment of specific charges, Lincoln builds to a more forceful and aggressive tone, just as he did at the end of the first section. His arrangement of responses to Southern allegations is itself climatic, the issue of insurrections being both last and most critical. Always volatile, this issue had become extremely explosive in the wake of the Harper's Ferry raid and the trial of John Brown, and Lincoln understandably chooses this matter as the instrument for his most extensive defense of party and principle. He is not content, however, to assume a merely defensive posture; the entire pattern of his argumentation reveals a movement from reply to attack that gathers momentum as the discourse proceeds. Thus, having disposed of the insurrection controversy, Lincoln assails the very character of the Southern position, and he concludes this section with an examination of threats emanating from the South.

The South hopes to "break up the Republican organization." That failing, "You will break up the Union rather than submit to a denial of your constitutional rights." This is a course of "rule or ruin"; the union will be destroyed unless people are permitted to take slaves into the federal territories. But no such right exists in the Constitution, and Southern threats are fruitless. Neither the Constitution nor the Republican Party is so malleable as to bend at the touch of Southern fancy. Not even the Dred Scott decision offers a refuge. That verdict was made "in a divided court, by a bare majority of the judges, and they not quite agreeing with one another in the reasons for making it." The decision rests upon "the opinion that 'the right of property in a slave is distinctly and expressly affirmed in the Constitution,'" but careful analysis shows that this right is not even implied. Surely it is reasonable to expect the Court to retract "the mistaken statement" when apprised of its error. Furthermore, the verdict runs contrary to the judgment of the fathers, those who decided the same question long ago "without division among themselves when making the decision," without division "about the meaning of it after it was made," and without "basing it upon any mistaken statement of facts." Having thus contrasted the babel of the Court with the unity of the fathers and their lineal descendants, Lincoln builds to a striking analogy:

> Under these circumstances, do you really feel yourselves justified to break up this government unless such a court decision as yours is shall be at once submitted to as a conclusive and final rule of political action? But you will not abide the election of a Republican president! In that supposed event, you say, you will destroy the Union; and then, you say, the crime of having destroyed it will be upon us! That is cool.

> A highwayman holds a pistol to my ear, and mutters through his teeth, "Stand and deliver, or I shall kill you, and then you will be a murderer!"

Adding that the highwayman's threat can "scarcely be distinguished in principle" from "the threat of destruction to the Union," Lincoln completes his ad hominem assault against the Southern position, and the prosopopoeia ends.

The parallels and interrelationships between the first and the second sections of the speech are evident. Some shifts in invention and style between the two sections are occasioned by the change of antagonist, but it is more significant that Lincoln elects to argue against adversaries in both and that he uses the same fundamental argument to dispatch them all. In both sections, he strives to become spokesman for the party by demonstrating that he is a man of reason and that this characteristic melds himself and party with the principles of the founding fathers. In addition, the same characteristic distinguishes him from other candidates. Finally, each section is based on a severely rational framework and builds to a terminal climax that unifies and heightens logical and emotional dimensions.

Merging style and argument within and between parts of the discourse, Lincoln unquestionably remains in touch with his immediate audience, and he unquestionably has his eye on ingratiation. In the first movement, he separates himself and party from Douglas and Seward; in the second, he favorably contrasts the position of the party with that of its most vociferous opponent.[35] But one further step remains. To this juncture, the identification of speaker, party, and principle has been closely tied to a series of negative definitions. A positive gesture seems necessary, and in the final section of the speech, Lincoln fuses his audience together through more directly constructive appeals.

He begins by saying he will address "a few words now to Republicans," and though he puts aside both text and issue, his remarks evolve naturally from what has proceeded. Once more reason is the point of departure. Having, in the highwayman metaphor, implied a contrast between cool reason and hot passion, Lincoln urges Republicans to "do nothing through passion and ill temper" that might cause discord within the nation, and, as he draws out the ultimate implications of the Southern position, antithesis becomes the dominant mode of argument and style. The section centers on a contrast between the Republicans and the South (between "we" and "they"); it extends and amplifies the distinction between word and deed that is present throughout the speech; and the argument is couched in and reinforced by antithetical syntax.

Recognizing Southern intransigence, Lincoln still wants his party to "calmly consider their demands" and reach conclusions based on all "they say and do." Pursuing the inquiry, he asks, "Will they be satisfied if the Territories be unconditionally surrendered to them? We know they will not." And "Will it satisfy them if, in the future, we have nothing to do with invasions and insurrections? We know it will not." It will not because past abstention has not exempted "us from the charge and the denunciation." To satisfy them, "We must not only leave them alone, but we must somehow convince them that we do let them alone." Experience shows that this is no easy task because Republican policy and actions have been misconstrued consistently. The only recourse seems to be "this and only this: cease to call slavery wrong, and join them in calling it right. And this must be done thoroughly—done in acts as well as words. Silence will not be tolerated—we must place ourselves avowedly with them." Republicans must suppress all "declarations that slavery is wrong," must return "fugitive slaves with greedy pleasure," and must pull down all free state constitutions "before they will cease to believe that all their troubles proceed from us."

Most Southerners, Lincoln admits, would not put the argument in this extreme form. Most would simply claim that they want to be left alone, but "we do let them alone." Consequently, it is apparent that "they will continue to accuse us of doing, until we cease saying." Given the nature of their arguments and the character of their actions, the Southerners cannot stop short of the demand that all Republicans desist from speaking and acting out of conviction. Those who hold that "slavery is morally right and socially elevating" must necessarily call for its recognition "as a legal right and a social blessing." Stripped of its veneer and examined in the cold light of reason, the Southern position reveals the disagreement governing the entire conflict; it also underscores the principle from which Republicans cannot retreat. Lincoln expresses both points in a final antithesis that reduces the issue of slavery to a matter of right and wrong, to a matter of moral conviction:

> Their thinking it right and our thinking it wrong is the precise fact upon which depends the whole controversy. Thinking it right, as they do, they are not to blame for desiring its full recognition as being right; but thinking it wrong, as we do, can we yield to them? Can *we* cast our votes with their view, and against our own? In view of our moral, social, and political responsibilities, can we do this?

Providing no answers because they are only too obvious, Lincoln moves on to merge self and party with the fathers, and Washington is the exemplar.

Style changes appropriately as Lincoln makes his final call for unity. Antithetical elements appear in the penultimate paragraph, but the opposed clauses are subordinated within the long, periodic flow of the final sentence, a flow that builds emotionally to a union with Washington's words and deeds. Lincoln repeats that slavery can be left alone where it exists, but he insists that there can be no temporizing when it comes to the extension of slavery:

> If our sense of duty forbids this, then let us stand by our duty fearlessly and effectively. Let us be diverted by none of those sophistical contrivances wherewith we are so industriously plied, and belabored—contrivances such as groping for some middle ground between the right and the wrong: vain as the search for a man who should be neither a living man nor a dead man: such as a policy of "don't care" on a question about which all true men do care; such as Union appeals beseeching true Union men to yield to Disunionists, reversing the divine rule, and calling, not the sinners, but the righteous to repentance: such as invocations to Washington, imploring men to unsay what Washington said and undo what Washington did.
>
> Neither let us be slandered from our duty by false accusations against us, nor frightened from it by menaces of destruction to the government, nor of dungeons to ourselves. Let us have faith that right makes might, and in that faith let us to the end dare to do our duty as we understand it.

This short third section, constituting less than 15 percent of the text, is a fitting climax to Lincoln's efforts. Rational principle develops into moral conviction, and the resulting emotional intensity emerges from and synthesizes all that has gone before. Yet the intensity is controlled. Speaker and audience are resolute and principled, but at the same time, they are poised and logical. Others may indulge in "false accusations" and "menaces of destruction," but Lincoln and Republicans will have faith in right and in their understanding.

With this closing suggestion of antithetical behavior, Lincoln harks back to what he has said, and with it, he completes his exercise in ingratiation. Douglas is a pitiful example of one who argues misguided principle in maladroit fashion, and Seward's notion of an irrepressible conflict is at odds with the true spirit of the Republican Party, a party whose words and deeds follow from what the framers of the government said and did. Neither opponent measures up to the new and higher self-conception that the speaker has created for his audience. Furthermore, Lincoln has, by this very performance, demonstrated that he is the one who will best represent party and principle. Starting with reason and principle, he has shunted aside opposition, differentiated between Republicans and the South, and pushed on to unite the party in the faith that will "let us to the end dare to do our duty as we understand it."

The very wording of the concluding paragraphs reflects the organic quality of Lincoln's quest for unity. "Understand" echoes the "text"; Washington is a synecdochic reminder of the fathers; and the antithetical language recalls dissociations that are fundamental. In examining the discourse, we have attempted to explicate this internal coherence by tracing the sequence of arguments and images as they appear in the text, by dealing with the speech on its own terms. We are satisfied that the analysis has produced a reading that is more accurate than those previously available, a reading that goes farther toward explaining why the Cooper Union Address was one of Lincoln's most significant speeches.

Our interpretation is at odds, of course, with the conventional wisdom concerning his attitude toward the South. Where others have found him conciliatory, we argue that his position on slavery was calculated to win the nomination, not to propitiate an unavailable audience. That he had made "many similar declarations, and had never recanted any of them"[36] unquestionably contributed to the triumph of availability that was to be his, but his position ultimately pointed to an ideological conflict between North and South. Some Southerners took solace from Lincoln's assurances that slavery would be left alone where it existed, but extremists perceived him as the personification of Black Republicanism, even as the source of the irrepressible conflict doctrine.[37] The latter perceptions were distorted. So are ours, if we blink the realities of political rhetoric, and whatever else the speech might have been, it was certainly an oration designed to meet the immediate problems of a political campaign.

This perspective emphasizes that alternatives sometimes really do exclude and that rhetoric may nurture exclusion. Such a perspective may be uncomfortable for those who want to cast Lincoln as the Great Conciliator, but we are convinced that an accurate reading of the Cooper Union Address demands a frank recognition of the immediate rhetorical motives. Despite the mythology, the man was human, perhaps gloriously so, and it does him no disservice to accept this speech as evidence of his political skill, as evidence that "he was an astute and dextrous operator of the political machine."[38] Nor does this acceptance detract from the speech as literature and as logical exposition. The political artistry and the rhetorical artistry are functions of each other, and an appreciation of this coalescence can only enhance our understanding of the Cooper Union Address. And viewing the speech as a whole, we are quite content to close with a slightly altered evaluation from another context: "The speech is—to put it as crudely as possible—an immortal masterpiece."[39]

NOTES

1. J. G. Randall, *Lincoln the President*, vol. 1 (New York: Dodd, Mead, 1945), 135.
2. Howard Mumford Jones and Ernest E. Leisy, eds., *Major American Writers* (New York: Harcourt, Brace, 1945), 681.
3. Benjamin Barondess, *Three Lincoln Masterpieces* (Charleston: Education Foundation of West Virginia, 1954), 3.
4. R. Franklin Smith, "A Night at Cooper Union," *Central States Speech Journal* 13 (Autumn 1962): 272.
5. The most influential account of this sort is Carl Sandburg, *The Prairie Years*, vol. 2 (New York: Harcourt, Brace, 1927), 200–216, but the most complete is Andrew A. Freeman, *Abraham Lincoln Goes to New York* (New York: Coward-McCann, 1960).

6. John G. Nicolay and John Hay, *Abraham Lincoln: A History*, vol. 2 (New York: Century, 1917), 219–20.
7. Richard Hofstadter, *The American Political Tradition* (New York: Alfred A. Knopf, 1948), 364.
8. Roy P. Basler, ed., *Abraham Lincoln: His Speeches and Writings* (Cleveland: World, 1946), 32.
9. Allan Nevins, *The Emergence of Lincoln*, vol. 2 (New York: Charles Scribner's Sons, 1950), 186.
10. Randall, *Lincoln the President*, 136–37; Basler, *Abraham Lincoln*, 32–33; Nevins, *The Emergence of Lincoln*, 186–87; Reinhard H. Luthin, *The Real Abraham Lincoln* (Englewood Cliffs, NJ: Prentice-Hall, 1960), 210.
11. Randall, *Lincoln the President*, 136; Barondess, *Three Lincoln Masterpieces*, 18; Nicolay and Hay, *Complete Works*, 220, Nevins, *The Emergence of Lincoln*, 186; Luthin, *The Real Abraham Lincoln*, 243–44.
12. Freeman treats of the text briefly, *Lincoln Goes to New York*, 84–88, and although Barondess ranges from preparation to audience reaction, *Three Lincoln Masterpieces*, 3–30, Hofstadter's observation applies, *The American Political Tradition*, 364. Earl W. Wiley discusses the address in *Four Speeches by Lincoln* (Columbus: Ohio State University Press, 1927), 15–27, but he limits analysis to the first section of the speech, a limitation also applied in his "Abraham Lincoln: His Emergence as the Voice of the People," in *A History and Criticism of American Public Address*, ed. William N. Brigance, vol. 2 (New York: McGraw-Hill, 1943), 859–77. In the same volume, the speech is the basis for comments on delivery Mildred Freburg Berry, "Abraham Lincoln: His Development in the Skills of the Platform," 828–58.
13. Letter to Lyman Trumbull, April 29, 1860, *The Collected Works of Abraham Lincoln*, ed. Roy P. Basler, 8 vols. (New Brunswick, NJ: Rutgers University Press, 1955), 4:45.
14. Letter to William E. Frazer, November 1, 1859, *Collected Works*, 3:491.
15. Richard N. Current, *The Lincoln Nobody Knows* (New York: McGraw-Hill, 1958), 199. For an indication of Lincoln's activities see *Collected Works*, 3:384–521.
16. Letter to James A. Briggs, November 13, 1859, in *Collected Works*, 3:494.
17. See Letter to Salmon P. Chase, June 9, 1859, *Collected Works*, 3:384; Letter to Nathan Sargent. June 23, 1859, *Collected Works*, 3:387–88; Letter to Richard M. Corwine, April 6, 1860, *Collected Works*, 4:36.
18. Paul I. Rosenthal, "The Concept of Ethos and the Structure of Persuasion,"

Speech Monographs 33 (June 1966): 114–26.

19. Rosenthal, "Concept of Ethos," 120.
20. In 1854, "Northern whigs persuaded that their old party was moribund, Democrats weary of planting dominance, and free-soilers eager to exclude slavery from the territories began to draw together to resist the advance of the planting power"; Charles A. Beard and Mary R. Beard, *The Rise of American Civilization*, vol. 2 (New York: Macmillan, 1937), 22. Cf. Don E. Fehrenbacher, "Lincoln and the Formation of the Republican Party," in *Prelude to Greatness* (Stanford, CA: Stanford University Press, 1962), 19–47.
21. We follow the text in *Complete Works*, ed. John G. Nicolay and John Hay, vol. 5 (New York: Francis D. Tandy, 1905), 293–328; we include no footnotes because aside from unimportant exceptions, citations are sequential. This text is more conservative in typography than that edited and published as a campaign document by Charles C. Nott and Cephas Brainerd. The latter appears in *Collected Works*, 3:522–50; 1860, 1. Substantive variations in extant are minuscule, and this consistency deserves comment. Lincoln ignored suggested alterations in the original (Sandburg, *The Prairie Years*, 210, 215–16); he proofread the newspaper copy (Freeman, *Lincoln Goes to New York*, 92–93); pamphlet copies were available by the first of April (*Collected Works*, 4:38–39); and Lincoln adamantly resisted editorial changes by Nott (*Collected Works*, 4:58–59). This evidence emphasizes the care with which he constructed the speech, but it also suggests that he anticipated a wider audience from the outset. Publication practices and his own experience told Lincoln that he would reach many who would not hear him speak.
22. General interest in the debates is underlined by the favorable editorial notice appearing in the *Brooklyn Daily Times*, August 26, 1858, an editorial written by one Walt Whitman; Walt Whitman, *I Sit and Look Out*, ed. Emory Holloway and Vernolian Schwartz (New York: Columbia University Press, 1932), 96. For letters referring to publication of the debates, see *Collected Works*, 3:341, 343, 372–74, 515, 516.
23. Letter to Lyman Trumbull, December 11, 1858, *Collected Works*, 3:345.
24. Harry J. Carman and Harold C. Syrett, *A History of the American People* (New York: Alfred A. Knopf, 1952), 588. Cf. Fehrenbacher, "The Famous 'Freeport Question,'" in *Prelude to Greatness*, 121–42.
25. Logicians often define *ad hominem* as a fallacy resulting from an attack upon the character of a man rather than the quality of argument. In this essay, however, we

use the term as Schopenhauer does in distinguishing between *ad hominem* and *ad rem* as the two basic modes of refutation. He differentiates in this manner: "We may show either that the proposition is not in accordance with the nature of things, *i.e.*, with absolute, objective truth [*ad rem*]; or that it is inconsistent with other statements or admissions of our opponent, *i.e.*, with truth as it appears to him [*ad hominem*]"; Arthur Schopenhauer, "The Art of Controversy," in *The Will to Live: Selected Writings of Arthur Schopenhauer*, ed. Richard Taylor (New York: Anchor Books, 1962), 341. See Henry W. Johnstone Jr., "Philosophy and *Argumentum ad Hominem*," *Journal of Philosophy* 49 (July 1952): 489–98.

26. Lincoln undoubtedly knew that James Wilson, Patrick Henry, and Edmund Randolph had discussed the topic (see *Collected Works*, 3:526–27 n. 9), but he is accurate in asserting that the subject did not come "directly" before the convention.
27. Washington's vote was his signature, as president, on the act of 1789 which enforced the ordinance of 1787.
28. Nicolay and Hay, *Abraham Lincoln: A History*, 220.
29. See Hofstadter, *The American Political Tradition*, 94; *Collected Works*, 3:396.
30. Randall, *Lincoln the President*, 136.
31. Nicolay and Hay, *Abraham Lincoln: A History*, 220.
32. Nevins, *The Emergence of Lincoln*, 186.
33. *Collected Works*, 3:438–54. Speaking at Cincinnati, September 17, 1859, Lincoln directs so much of his speech across the river "to the Kentuckians" (440) that one listener complained aloud, "Speak to Ohio men, and not to Kentuckians" (445). Interestingly, Nevins appreciates the *prosopopoeia* in this speech, noting that Lincoln was "ostensibly speaking to Kentuckians," *The Emergence of Lincoln*, 56.
34. The varied interpretations of Washington's warning and their longevity are illustrated in debates, early in 1850, over the purchase of the Farewell Address manuscript for the Library of Congress. Much of the debate is reproduced in William Dawson Johnston, *History of the Library of Congress*, vol. 1 (Washington: Government Printing Office, 1904), 326–40.
35. The second movement continues the implicit attack upon Seward, and all texts indicate a mimicking of Douglas's "gur-reat pur-rinciple." Buchanan also is a victim here, for he had championed popular sovereignty in his "Third Annual Message," December 19, 1859, *The Works of James Buchanan*, ed. John Bassett More, vol. 10 (New York: Antiquarian Press, 1960), 342. Lincoln's efforts were not lost on a *New York Evening Post* reporter who wrote that "the speaker

places the Republican party on the very ground occupied by the framers of our constitution and the fathers or our Republic" and that "in this great controversy the Republicans are the real conservative party." His report was reprinted in the *Chicago Tribune*, March 1, 1860, 1.

36. Abraham Lincoln, "First Inaugural Address," in *Collected Works*, 4:263.
37. Michael Davis, *The Image of Lincoln in the South* (Knoxville: University of Tennessee Press, 1971), 7–40; traces southern views from nomination through inauguration. See Dwight L. Dumond, ed., *Southern Editorials on Secession* (Gloucester, MA: Peter-Smith, 1964), 103–5, 112–15, 159–62.
38. David Donald, *Lincoln Reconsidered* (New York: Alfred A. Knopf, 1956), 65.
39. The original is Randall Jarrell's comment on a poem, Robert Frost's "Provide Provide," in *Poetry and the Age* (New York: Vintage Knopf, 1953), 41.

Lincoln at Cooper Union: A Rationale for Neo-Classical Criticism

The last issue of this journal included our critique of Lincoln's Cooper Union Address, and we assume that the neo-classical origins of the analysis were apparent, even though methodological concerns were slighted. A more elaborate statement on methodology appeared in an earlier version, but the editors cautioned that the single article did not offer sufficient scope for both an explication of the rationale and its application. Accepting their advice, we deleted most of the theoretical material, but having offered the critique, we want to explore further its theoretical bases.

Our approach is neo-classical. That is, it is rooted in the rhetorical theory of antiquity. This is the same source that produced neo-Aristotelianism, "the dominant mode of rhetorical criticism of the present century in the United States."[1] Our critique shares most of the presuppositions

With G. P. Mohrmann, from *Quarterly Journal of Speech* 60 (1974): 459–67.

that inform this traditional mode, but there is one essential difference. Treating "rhetorical discourses as discrete communications in specific contexts,"[2] neo-Aristotelianism is preoccupied with the particular. This orientation implies a rejection of formal criteria and almost forces the critic to rely on the criterion of empirical effect. On the other hand, we treat Lincoln's speech within the framework of the classical conception of oratorical genres. As opposed to the nominalism implicit in neo-Aristotelianism, genre theory permits an abstract conception of audience and of rhetorical situations. It, therefore, enables the critic to seek formal ends for critical judgment.

Our purpose, here, is to explore the potential of genre theory as a corrective to some defects in the neo-Aristotelian mode. We shall begin with reference to the development of neo-Aristotelianism, comment on its rejection of generic distinctions, and note the limitations that this rejection imposes. We shall then suggest that the conception of genre can help invigorate critical inquiry based on classical models. We would emphasize, however, the provisional nature of our formulation; we do not consider it to be definitive, and we recognize that our version of neo-classicism has its own limitations.

Neo-Aristotelian Criticism

Although the neo-Aristotelian position is most fully delineated when one moves from "The Literary Criticism of Oratory"[3] to *A History and Criticism of American Public Address*[4] to *Speech*,[5] Wichelns remains the commanding presence. His essay "set the pattern and determined the direction"[6] of this approach, and the direction in which he moved took "certain Aristotelian conceptions as safe points of departure."[7] The most crucial of these was the centrality of audience. Of course, Aristotle and other classical theorists do not spell out a critical system, but "they do imply one. If a literary work may be said to have three references—to the universe, to the writer, and to the audience—Greek rhetorical theory, like the Renaissance criticism which descends from it, thinks the audience-reference by far the most important."[8] Seeking to revive the dormant rhetorical perspective, Wichelns makes this same reference the basis for the rhetorical analysis of oratory. The importance of this principle can scarcely be exaggerated; without it, modern speech criticism would not have been possible. Nevertheless, Wichelns's determination to separate rhetoric from literature leads to a restricted conception of audience.

As the very title of his essay suggests, he thinks it important to distinguish between literary and rhetorical activity. The literary artist, he asserts, "is free to fulfill" (56) his own law because literature is concerned "with permanent values" (57). The rhetor, however, is "perpetually in bondage to the occasion and the audience" (56). Consequently, criticism of oratory must regard "a speech as a communication to a specific audience" and must be "concerned with effect" (54). Permanence and universality are reserved for the literary critic because "the result can only be confusion" when a speaker is "made to address a universal audience" (57). Rhetorical criticism, then, finds its raison d'être in the specifics of the particular situation, and it is in these terms that the critic must interpret the function of "personality," "proof," "arrangement," "delivery," or any other of Wichelns's topics (56–57), all of which originate in classical theory.

If Wichelns succeeds in establishing rhetorical criticism as an independent activity, his program also obscures formalistic aspects of the classical inheritance. Despite his many borrowings from Aristotle, Wichelns says nothing about oratorical genres. This is hardly accidental, for genre theory is notoriously abstract; it rejects time and place as bases for classification and groups historical situations into general categories. As a result, it raises questions about "the relation of the class and the individuals composing it, the one and the many, the nature of universals."[9] Such questions cannot be a part of Wichelns's program because they smack of literary judgment. It is only in literature that one hears "the voice of the human spirit addressing itself to men of all ages and times" (57), a voice transcending particular situations.

Neo-Aristotelians attempt to modify and escape this particularism. For example, one reads that the consummate critic "appraises the entire event by assigning it comparative rank in the total enterprise of speaking"[10] and that a speech may be criticized "as a finished product having certain rhetorical features which conform agreeably to fixed principles or rules."[11] One reads also of touchstones. But to assign comparative rank or to note agreeable conformity to fixed principles demands some notion of permanence, and such standards simply are not available in a system oriented completely to the specific situation. Here, the appropriate standard is that of immediate effect, and this single criterion makes it difficult, if not impossible, to develop intrinsic artistic standards. The system supplies no logical mechanism for connecting apparently disparate events.

Since Aristotle speaks of oratorical genres, this would seem a likely source for neo-Aristotelian formalism, but neo-Aristotelians, caught up in Wichelns's severe nominalism, cannot exploit this possibility. They may refer to genres, but the distinctions do not become instrumental; limiting or dividing analyses, they do not control them.[12] Ironically, neo-Aristotelians slight the genres even as they embrace the taxonomic categories to which the genres gave purpose, with the result that critics tend to classify "certain grosser properties cast under the heads of the traditional modes and canons," to produce "a mechanical accounting or summing up of how well the speech fits an *a priori* mold."[13] Any critical system will exhibit certain a priori features, but it appears that the mold of traditional criticism has become mechanically taxonomic. Stripped of generic distinctions, the neo-classical taxonomy does not encourage interaction between the critical apparatus and the broader purposes of rhetorical discourse, and the critic glances off the relationship that has been accepted as the very excuse for his being—the relationship between speaker and audience. Seeking refuge, critics turn to biography or history, but neither is an adequate resolution. That the adducing of historical details offers no escape is reinforced if we turn to an essay representing "the neo-Aristotelian tradition at its best,"[14] Marie Hochmuth Nichols's "Lincoln's First Inaugural."[15]

The most noteworthy feature of this essay is its accumulation of historical detail. Avoiding generalization, Nichols invites the reader to participate in the ambiance of the situation by recounting the particulars that surround it. Disregard the reprinted text of the address, and two-thirds of the article is devoted to a "scrupulous documentation"[16] of the events immediately preceding and following the speech. Such documentation can be an important ancilla, but the final test is whether the critic uses the accumulated detail in ways that add to an understanding and appreciation of the rhetorical transaction. Nichols faces this responsibility in the final third of her essay, but she is unable to overcome the inherent limitations of Wichelns's program.

Adhering to his tenets, she evaluates the speech "as a speech, a medium distinct from other media, and with methods peculiarly its own" (88). The special topics appropriate to this task are "Lincoln's selection of materials, his arrangement, his style, and his manner" (90). What is to unify these lines of inquiry? It is the speaker's purpose. But Nichols warns against the casual assumption that "Lincoln's purpose is easily discernable in the occasion itself" (89), and she implicitly rejects generic considerations when she turns away from the fact that "this was an inaugural ceremony, with a ritual fairly well established" (89). Genre is beside the point because Lincoln's purposes arise from the experiences "of the nation between his election as President and the day of his inauguration" (89). These experiences focus on party, nation, and man, and they lead to this conclusion: "Clearly, he intended to take the occasion of the inauguration to declare the position of the Republican party in regard to the South, to announce his considered judgment in regard to the practical questions raised by the movement of secession, and, in all, to give what assurance he could of his personal integrity" (90).

Compared to the specificity of the earlier historical documentation, the analysis following this statement of purpose is vague. For the most part, the critique is a summary. Including numerous quotations from the text and comparisons with earlier drafts, it certainly reproduces the flow of Lincoln's argument. Yet it leaves the reader to his own devices in attempting to fathom the forms and topics of argument, the nature of evidence, the interaction among parts of the discourse, and the character of appeals to the audience. Summary simply does not explain how Lincoln "became the affectionate father, the benevolent and hopeful counselor" (95). Moreover, the analysis of style does not probe deeply into the text itself; commentary becomes rigorous and specific only in terms of an external reference in relation to the wording of earlier drafts. It is interesting to view the style through a consideration of the language Lincoln did not use, but a closer examination of that which he did use is needed to support the claim that his style produced "an image of great-heartedness, great humility and great faith" (99).

To avoid misunderstanding, we want to underline that our purpose here is not to belittle this important essay. We merely want to emphasize that the critique exhibits a complete commitment to the unique context of the discourse. This commitment, in turn, produces an analysis that concentrates on external circumstances rather than on the internal development of the speech. The resulting limitations become strikingly apparent when Nichols attempts a general evaluation of the discourse.

Her position is unmistakably clear; the Inaugural Address is a rhetorical masterpiece. But what is the basis for this judgment? It cannot be found in either literary value or cultural force; these criteria are explicitly reserved for literary critics and historians (88). Thus, everything comes down to effect, to the question of whether the discourse did what it was supposed to do. And this particular speech was supposed to enunciate party policy, allay the fears of the secessionists, and establish the orator's personal integrity. The reaction of the South, therefore, becomes the salient index. Yet, by this standard, the speech was the most abject of failures. It did not mollify the secessionists. In fact, Nichols argues convincingly that, after examining the Inaugural, "the South saw little hope from Lincoln" (85). But she flees the inexorable conclusion. Ignoring immediate effect, she contends that "any fair-minded critic, removed from the passions of the times, must find himself much more in agreement with those observers of the day who believed the Inaugural met the 'requirements of good rhetoric'" (95). This will not do. It is patently inconsistent to focus exclusively on the unique and specific situation and then to ask that final evaluation be "removed from the passions of the times."

The problem we have just outlined seems insoluble within the terms of the neo-Aristotelian tradition. Certainly there is but cold comfort in Parrish's observation that "not failure, but low aim, is crime" in speechmaking (100).[17] That only papers over the gap that necessarily yawns between a philosophical dedication to the particular and a desire for a more permanent frame of reference. Parrish correctly recognizes a need for abstract standards, but he does not offer an ultimate grounding for the formalism he proposes. That grounding, we believe, exists in the theory of genres. To explain our position we must return to the ancients.

Genre Theory

As opposed to Wichelns, the dominant position in ancient rhetoric is not that situations are unique and particular, but that they fall into general categories, into "types" or "kinds." The influence of Aristotle is decisive. He describes the three familiar genres of deliberative, forensic, and epideictic, maintaining that "rhetoric falls into three divisions [*gene*], determined by the three classes of listeners to speeches."[18] Since it is the listener who "determines the speech's end and object,"[19] the audience is the central element in the system. Consequently, Aristotle paves the way for general acceptance of the proposition that "the important aspect of the speech situation is the speaker-audience relationship."[20] At the same time, however, Aristotle marks and emphasizes the similarities among certain kinds of audiences and certain speaking situations; his entire theory ultimately responds to an abstract classification of oratorical requirements.

Later classical rhetoricians thoroughly endorse this theory of genre, and we find Cicero, Quintilian, and other writers consistently treating inventional theory in terms of the three types of speaking. More importantly, the genres give meaning to the whole of the complex taxonomy in classical rhetoric. The five *officia* and their elaborate substructures are significant only insofar as they assist the speaker in achieving his goal. That goal, of course, is conditioned by the nature of the audience; the speaker, however, locates his audience with reference to the genre in which he must function. Without the genres, classical rhetorical theory loses contact with the audience, and the elaborate taxonomy becomes meaningless, a system bereft of any rhetorical purpose. For this reason, we believe that any critical program based on classical models must give serious consideration to genre theory.

The immediate advantage of generic criticism is that it permits the creation of intrinsic standards for rhetorical discourse without losing sight of the audience. Predicated upon the "expectations of the audience and the demands of the situation,"[21] the concept of genre assumes that certain types of situations provoke similar needs and expectations among audiences. Identifying and categorizing these situations are basic to inquiry, and the critic must uncover patterns of need and expectation that bind audiences together, even though they may be far removed in time and place. An adequate description of a genre, then, produces a general index of audience demands; it, therefore, locates the abstract rhetorical problems confronting the speaker and points to intrinsic standards for judging a particular kind of discourse.

To illustrate, we can expand upon the generic underpinning of our approach to the Cooper Union Address. This is a campaign speech, an oratorical form well known to American audiences and easily distinguished from other types of public address. Nevertheless, this type does not fall within the tripartite Aristotelian division. The anomaly becomes evident when we consider the campaign speech in relation to audience and purpose, the basic components of the Aristotelian distinction. One who listens to a campaign speech is a judge of a future event, and he is urged to do something (i.e., to vote for a particular candidate). This corresponds to the function of the audience in deliberative oratory. The object of judgment, however, is not a policy, as it is in deliberative speaking, but a person, as it is in epideictic. Ends also are blurred; the deliberative orator examines the "expediency or the harmfulness of a proposed course of action"; and the epideictic orator must "praise or attack a man" in order to prove "him worthy of honor or the reverse."[22] Now, the end of campaign oratory is to make the candidate appear worthy and honorable. Nevertheless it makes no sense to argue that the campaign oration is a form of epideictic, since the speaker's goal is to effect a decision, and listeners are asked to judge, not merely to sit as spectators. Evidently, no one of the traditional genres is entirely satisfactory, and it follows that intelligent application of the neo-classical approach entails the description of a separate genre for campaign oratory.

In this instance, the problem in the traditional system appears to be an omission rather than an inherent defect, and we found it relatively easy to define the genre and remain consistent with Aristotelian principles. Finding Rosenthal's analysis of ethos suggestive, we approached the campaign oration as an instance of "personal persuasion," as discourse in which the central concern is the audience's attitude toward the candidate.[23] Given this condition, the campaign orator's first responsibility is, by definition, to promote himself as an individual. Both policies and character are in question, but policy is subsidiary to the purpose of creating an identification of thought and feeling between speaker and audience—a demand inherent in the situation. The ultimate objective is ingratiation. Translating all this into neo-classical terminology, we could describe the genre of campaign oratory as speaking in which listeners act as judges of a future event, an election: the end is to effect a judgment of the candidate, a judgment based on character and upon the treatment of issues.

This consideration of generic requirements helped to focus our analysis of the Cooper Union Address. In this case our description of the genre followed Aristotle rather closely. Other situations may demand more radical adjustments of the traditional system. Surely it is unreasonable to expect the tripartite division of antiquity to encompass all subsequent forms of public address. Genres are like institutions.[24] They exhibit a degree of stability over time, but they also grow, change, and decay in response to the conditions of society. Hence they "should not be viewed as static forms but as evolving phenomena."[25] The critic must retain the flexibility needed to adjust to changing circumstances. He must remember that generic distinctions should not force every item into a preconceived category; instead, their proper function is to uncover genuine points of similarity and difference among forms of discourse.

The discovery of these similarities and differences results in the establishment of generic constraints, and the use of these constraints appears to solve the most troublesome problem in neo-Aristotelian criticism—the antithetical tension between the commitment to a particular situation and the need for formal standards of evaluation. Theoretically, the dissipating of this tension can make neo-classicism again available to the rhetorical critic. We intended that our critique of the Cooper Union Address specify some of the potential. The critique itself must stand as the sole witness to our success or failure, but the genesis deserves comment because it helps explain the rationale and points up both strengths and limitations.

The Uses of Neo-Classicism

The position we have taken in this essay and elsewhere clearly is at one with Black's call for "an alternative to neo-Aristotelianism,"[26] and the literature indicates that the search has been profitable. Nevertheless, it seemed that the common acceptance had become "any alternative to neo-Aristotelianism," and if neo-classicism had become mechanical, arbitrary rejection seemed a shortsighted reaction. To forsake traditional theory completely appeared a dubious course, and an examination of the original sources convinced us that a return to generic distinctions was the key to another useful alternative. And to a large extent genre theory anticipates the contention that the neo-classical taxonomy commits the critic to a static set of categories and deflects the true purpose of criticism. It specifically anchors a discourse in the context of other discourses and the demands of the audience, and it blunts the charge that the neo-classical orientation forces the critic to overlook "the effects of audience, situation and other contemporary discourses on the speaker's behavior."[27]

The system retains schematic features, but that seems an advantage rather than a disadvantage. If criticism is not totally whimsical and subjective, some schema must control the analysis. The critic may concentrate on archetypal metaphors, dramatistic elements, analogues from anthropology and mythology, but there must be standards for sifting and sorting the materials. In this light, the neoclassical taxonomy is but one of many schemata available, and it has the particularly appealing feature of attempting to deal with the entire rhetorical transaction on its own terms. Recently, the most important and instructive analyses have had a nontraditional bias, but many tend to isolate and emphasize a single element or concept. A complete neo-classical approach, however, centers directly on the rhetorical process and divides it into a simple but comprehensive set of constituents. Out of context, the categories can be domineering, but any other schema can become equally oppressive, and genre theory helps prevent a neo-classical tyranny. Keeping the taxonomy within proper bounds, it centers attention where it ought to be, on the speaker-audience relationship, and the system produced seems an excellent filter for the analysis for a particular speech. Examining the Cooper Union Address, for example, we did not feel prisoner to a crabbed and stultifying orthodoxy, nor find ourselves trapped in tangential concerns. We found, instead, that the system forced us to come to grips with the speech as a speech, and we found that it forced us to make choices.[28]

Whether we made the proper ones is not as important as the fact that we were not enclosed within arbitrary and debilitating confines.

The system, of course, does have confines. Genre theory presumes types, and a critic ordinarily will use the type to explore the single example. Comparisons are possible, or criticism might center on a series from one genre, but the character of neo-classicism is most appropriate to the analysis of a single speech. If the system cannot address "picketing, sloganeering, chanting, singing, marching, gesturing," and similar communicative phenomena,[29] this limitation does no more than describe the scope of neoclassicism. A more serious problem attends the charge that the neo-classic critic suffers from a rationalistic bias.[30]

From the generic perspective, this bias is an institutional one. Rhetorical genres are grounded in established practices, and genre theory must assume the existence of stable conventions that govern public communication. Capitalizing upon this area of public agreement, genre theory can present a coherent and therefore "rational" account of rhetorical argument. This is advantageous under normal circumstances, but it is quite another matter when circumstances are not normal, in times of rapid change. Here is the most significant limitation to the critical program we are advocating.

This program necessarily works best in situations where the range of disagreement is limited, where there is a broad consensus about what can be argued and how it should be argued. Thus, even an observer as sympathetic as Booth must acknowledge that "the Aristotelian tradition is suited best to analyzing the cogency of . . . rhetoric, from the point of view of someone who is at least in some sense on the inside."[31] Our proposal, then, deals with an insider's rhetoric. Yet everyone is aware of the outsider's, "the rhetoric of 'conversion,' of transformation—the rhetoric with the effect whether designed or not, of overturning personal ties and changing total allegiances."[32] This radical rhetoric may explicitly attack the stable conventions and institutions of a society; furthermore, it is likely to appear in a form that challenges the established norms of discourse, for attempts to subvert the establishment almost always involve an attempt to subvert its language.

In such situations, genre theory falters. Based on the presumption of stability, the system has no mechanism for explaining idiosyncratic and dramatic changes in ideology or style. The critic may adjust over time, but long-term flexibility is beside the point when one seeks to explain radical rhetoric in situ. Worse yet, adherence to a conventional typology can make the critic a captive of the institutional system that nascent rhetorical forms seek to destroy. The resultant analysis will condemn advocates of change because their rhetoric does not conform to conventional expectations, and the nature of that rhetoric may well go misunderstood. Nevertheless, even this limitation may prove to be of some value, if properly appreciated.

A time of rapid and drastic change is one, above all others, that may require stable points of reference. Surely it is hazardous always to evaluate new kinds of discourse in terms of the old, but there is no reason why old genres cannot be touchstones for understanding new developments. In other words, rhetorical criticism might "act on the premise that the study of historical change could greatly profit from a clearer view than we now have of what is changing."[33] We have yet to devise a critical rationale adequate to account for sudden shifts of ideology.

Conclusion

In concluding, we can do little more than repeat what we already have said. We simply propose the addition of genre theory as a means of introducing formalism into neo-classical criticism. Squarely within the tradition, this theory does not ask that critics abandon the centrality of the audience. In fact, genre theory acts as a corrective precisely because it allows for a broader conception of audience than is permitted in neo-Aristotelian criticism. If critics can identify situations that create generally similar audience demands, then they can abstract principles that will apply to a wide variety of discourses. Although these principles rest on audience analysis, the audience is conceived in generic terms, and the generalizations produced may offer formal grounds for evaluating speeches of a particular kind. These standards lack the more purely formal characteristics of certain literary genres, but they provide a point of entry into a discourse and focus the critical reaction.

Much remains to be done, of course. Our analysis of the campaign genre remains limited and tentative. To focus the neo-classical taxonomy, we established an a priori definition of the end for campaign oratory, and we were then able to construct very broad standards for rhetorical evaluation in a particular instance. Additional instances have to be accumulated before the genre can be described properly and more specific generic constraints developed. More generally, we have not examined genre theory in detail, nor have we attempted a systematic classification of modern rhetorical genres.

Fortunately, the evidence indicates a probing in those directions.[34] Much of the effort has been piecemeal, but this, after all, may prove the most satisfactory route. Modern rhetorical critics usually start with a settled theoretical position and then make an application, but in writing the two essays, we found ourselves attacking the problem from the opposite perspective. The experience was instructive, and perhaps it can be generalized. The progress of rhetorical criticism may depend more on the ability of critics to induce principles from actual critiques than on a concern with abstract issues.

NOTES

1. Edwin Black, *Rhetorical Criticism* (New York: Macmillan, 1965), 27.
2. Black, *Rhetorical Criticism*, 35.
3. Herbert A. Wichelns, "The Literary Criticism of Oratory," in *Methods of Rhetorical Criticism*, ed. Robert L. Scott and Bernard L. Brock (New York: Harper and Row, 1972), 27–60. Further references to the essay will be to this source.
4. William Norwood Brigance, ed., *A History and Criticism of American Public Address*, vols. 1 and 2 (New York: McGraw-Hill, 1943); and Marie Kathryn Hochmuth, ed., *A History and Criticism of American Public Address*, vol. 3 (New York: McGraw-Hill, 1955).
5. Lester Thonssen and A. Craig Baird, *Speech Criticism* (New York: Ronald Press, 1948).
6. Donald C. Bryant, ed., *The Rhetorical Idiom* (Ithaca, NY: Cornell University Press, 1958), 5.
7. Thonssen and Baird, *Speech Criticism*, 15.
8. D. A. Russell, "Rhetoric and Criticism," *Greece and Rome* 2nd series, 14 (October 1967): 141–42.

9. Rene Wellek and Austin Warren, *Theory of Literature* (New York: Harcourt, Brace and World, 1956), 237.
10. Thonssen and Baird, *Speech Criticism*, 18.
11. Thonssen and Baird, *Speech Criticism*, 457.
12. Even a casual reading in *A History and Criticism of American Public Address* reveals that genres are not examined systematically.
13. Douglas Ehninger, "Rhetoric and the Critic," *Western Speech* 29 (Fall 1965): 230.
14. Scott and Brock, *Methods of Rhetorical Criticism*, 21.
15. Marie Hochmuth Nichols, "Lincoln's First Inaugural," in Scott and Brock, *Methods of Rhetorical Criticism*, 60–100. Further references to this essay will be to this source.
16. Black, *Rhetorical Criticism*, 41.
17. Wayland Maxfield Parrish, "The Study of Speeches," in *American Speeches*, ed. Wayland Maxfield Parrish and Marie K. Hochmuth (New York: David McKay, 1954), 12. See Black, *Rhetorical Criticism*, 61–75.
18. *Rhetoric*, trans. W. Rhys Roberts, 1.3.1358a, 36. For comment on a general formalism in Attic oratory see R. C. Jebb, *The Attic Orators*, vol. 1 (New York: Russell and Russell, 1962), xcii–civ.
19. *Rhetoric*, 1.3.1358b, 1.
20. Thonssen and Baird, *Speech Criticism*, 15.
21. Kathleen M. Hall Jamieson, "Generic Constraints and the Rhetorical Situation," *Philosophy and Rhetoric* 6 (Summer 1973): 163.
22. *Rhetoric*, 1.3.1358b, 22–28.
23. Paul I. Rosenthal, "The Concept of Ethos and the Structure of Persuasion," *Speech Monographs* 33 (June 1966): 114–26.
24. Wellek and Warren, *Theory of Literature*, 226.
25. Jamieson, "Generic Constraints," 168.
26. Black, *Rhetorical Criticism*, 132.
27. Joe A. Munshaw, "The Structures of History: Dividing Phenomena for Rhetorical Understanding," *Central States Speech Journal* 24 (Spring 1973): 30.
28. In our critique, we deliberately suppressed details of the analysis. For example, we slighted intricacies in the argument of the first section because the reporting would have been tedious for the reader and would have made the speech appear more formalistic than it really is. We slighted other matters as well. Except by implication, we did not explore Lincoln's use of the rhetorical question or the "our fathers" refrain. We could have extended the latter into each segment of

the putative debate with the South, and we might have considered its echoic religious values for an audience all too familiar with the Lord's Prayer. We do not mean to imply that these facets of the speech would not be available to a critic of a different persuasion. We do insist, however, that genre and taxonomy brought them to our attention. That we did not report them indicates choices we made rather than any shortcoming in the approach.

29. Lloyd F. Bitzer and Edwin Black, eds., *The Prospect of Rhetoric* (Englewood Cliffs, NJ: Prentice-Hall, 1971), 225.
30. See Black, *Rhetorical Criticism*, 91–131; and Karlyn K. Campbell, "The Ontological Foundations of Rhetorical Theory," *Philosophy and Rhetoric* (Spring 1970): 97–108.
31. Wayne C. Booth, "The Scope of Rhetoric Today: A Polemical Excursion," in Bitzer and Black, *The Prospect of Rhetoric*, 97.
32. Booth, "Scope of Rhetoric Today," 102.
33. Paul Hernadi, *Beyond Genre* (Ithaca, NY: Cornell University Press, 1972), 8.
34. See Black, *Rhetorical Criticism*, 132–77; Forbes I. Hill. "Conventional Wisdom—Traditional Form: The President's Message of November 3, 1969," *Quarterly Journal of Speech* 58 (December 1972): 373–86; B. L. Ware and Wil A. Linkugel, "They Spoke in Defense of Themselves: On the Generic Criticism of Apologia," *Quarterly Journal of Speech* 59 (October 1973), 273–83; and Jamieson "Generic Constraints." The last two articles include references to a number of related discussions.

Instrumental and Constitutive Rhetoric in Martin Luther King Jr.'s "Letter from Birmingham Jail"

Almost thirty years ago, in an essay devoted to the *Autobiography of Malcolm X*, Thomas Benson commented that rhetoric is, among other things, a way of constituting the self within a scene composed of "exigencies, constraints, others and the self," and it is also a resource for "exercising control over self, others, and by extension the scene."[1] Thus, Benson assigns rhetoric a dual function. It is simultaneously generative and instrumental, since it helps to constitute the identity of self, other, and scene, while it also pulls these identities within the orbit of situated interests. Moreover, once this duality is acknowledged, it virtually forces the critic to expand and complicate the conventional interest in "ethical proof," since the persona of the rhetor emerges not just as an instrument of persuasion but also as something constituted within the rhetorical medium.

With Ebony A. Utley, from *Rhetoric and Public Affairs* 7 (2004): 37–52.

Viewed from our current vantage point, Benson's observations seem prescient. He anticipates a set of pivotal issues associated with recent interest in constitutive rhetoric and with the emergence of "interpretive" or "conceptual" criticism.[2] He also locates a subject—Malcolm X in particular and African American protest rhetoric in general—where these problems arise with special clarity and urgency. In Malcolm's texts, we encounter a persona that, as Benson says, sometimes takes on the aspect of "a magnificent anti-hero, an existentialist saint, or a mythic witness to America's oppressive racism," but that also sometimes seems to display the qualities of a hustler, an opportunist, or a cynical manipulator of words and audiences.[3] Thus, a tension between the constitutive and instrumental function surfaces almost immediately when examining Malcolm's rhetoric, and although it is generally less obtrusive in other African American rhetors during the civil rights revolution of the 1960s, it is still a prominent feature of their discourse—and for good reason. Their efforts to overcome a system that repressed and demeaned them required rhetorical instruments sufficient not only to serve immediate political ends but also to constitute a new conception of themselves and their people.

In this essay, we concentrate upon Martin Luther King's "Letter from Birmingham Jail" and argue that it displays a subtle and complex interrelationship between construction of self and instrumental appeals through character. On our reading of the text, the letter harmonizes aspects of its author's persona by blending and balancing the representation of the self in relation to what Benson calls "the exigencies, constraints, and others" connected with the scene. King's effort to move through a tangle of events and ideas toward a decorous sense of order contrasts notably with the confrontational rhetoric of Malcolm X,[4] but we hope to demonstrate that in constructing an effective persona, King shares the burden and opportunity of crossing between instrumental and constitutive concerns. Before turning to the text of the letter, however, we need to consider the context in which it appeared and some of the circumstances of its composition.

The Background

Early in 1963, the Southern Christian Leadership Conference (SCLC) targeted Birmingham, Alabama, for a nonviolent direct action campaign designed to force the city to modify or eliminate its segregation laws. For a variety of reasons, the campaign was delayed until April 3, and when it did begin, it encountered serious problems. Only a handful of protestors proved willing to subject themselves to arrest, and so the effort to force concessions by filling the city's jails was failing. Moreover, white moderates, and even some blacks, thought the campaign ill timed, since the newly elected city government had been given no opportunity to deal with the segregation issue. Worse yet, the city's attorneys obtained a federal injunction forbidding King and other SCLC leaders from sponsoring, encouraging, or participating in a demonstration unless they obtained a permit from the city. In effect, this meant that SCLC either had to abandon the campaign or violate federal court orders.

King decided that it was necessary to violate the injunction and that he himself would lead a march and submit to arrest. This "faith act," he hoped, would invigorate the campaign, and on April 12, 1963 (Good Friday, a day chosen for its symbolic importance), King headed a protest demonstration through the streets of Birmingham and was arrested. Refusing to post bail until April 19, he remained in jail for eight days.[5]

On the morning of the thirteenth, the day after King was imprisoned, the *Birmingham News* printed a short open letter signed by eight local clergymen. The clergy criticized the direct action campaign as an untimely and unwise effort "led in part by outsiders" and urged the black residents of Birmingham to obey the law, withdraw support from the demonstrations, and resolve their grievances through the courts and the negotiation process.[6] King's "Letter from Birmingham Jail" was a direct response to the clergymen's statement.

The history of the letter's composition is a matter of some interest. According to the conventional story, King began writing his response on the margins of the newspaper that published the clergymen's letter, then on odd scraps of paper provided by a sympathetic prison guard, and finally on a legal tablet provided by King's attorney. While King was engaged in composition, his visitors carried the marginalia, scraps, and pages to

SCLC headquarters, where a secretary typed the individual bits until the text was completed.

There is no reason to doubt the truth of this story as far as it goes, but it does not seem to be the whole story. Although the letter is dated April 16, no version of it circulated in public until after the first week of May, and internal evidence rather clearly indicates that the published version of the work could not have been completed until after April 19. Thus, at least some parts of the letter likely were composed and/or revised after King left prison.[7] The tone and content of the document, however, create the impression that the author wrote it from within a prison cell, and as we will note later, this impression greatly contributes to King's self-representation and to the persuasive impact of the letter as a whole.

King's Letter: The Rhetoric of the Text

With this background in mind, we can to turn to the text itself and to the construction and representation of agency within it. This interpretative inquiry has an affinity with the neo-classical concern for the rhetor's ethos, but in the neo-classical approach, the tendency is to designate character as a mode of proof, to locate instances where it is invoked, and to isolate it as a discrete element in the persuasive process. In the interpretative frame, the agency of the rhetor refers not just to the use of character appeals but also to the way that rhetors place themselves within a network of communicative relationships. At minimum, the explication of this process demands attention to (1) the rhetor's construction of self, (2) the rhetor's construction of the audience (what Edwin Black calls the "second persona"),[8] and (3) the enactment within the text of the relationship between rhetor and audience. In what follows, we will try to explain how King's letter works along all three of these lines and to indicate how they converge to create and represent an identity for King both as writer and as social/political actor.

One of the most prominent features of the text is its extensive use of direct address. Whereas the clergymen's letter is addressed to no one in particular, King begins with the salutation, "My Dear Fellow Clergyman," and the first paragraph continues in this vein as King's "I" speaks in response to the "you" who composed the earlier letter. The dialogic relationship is underscored in the final sentence of the paragraph: "But since I feel that you are men of genuine good will and your criticisms are sincerely set forth, I would like to answer your statement in what I hope will be patient and reasonable terms."[9] This pattern is sustained through the body of the letter as King organizes its content into a seriatim response to claims attributed to the eight clergymen. The following schema indicates this structure:

A. Introduction
B. Refutation
   1. That King is an outsider
   2. That King and his supporters should negotiate rather than demonstrate
   3. That the demonstrations are ill timed
      (First confession: King's disappointment with white moderates)
   4. That nonviolent direct action precipitates violence
   5. That racial problems will resolve themselves over time
   6. That King and his supporters are extremists
      (Second confession: King's disappointment with white clergy)
   7. That the Birmingham police deserve praise
C. Conclusion

Save for the fifth point on the list, King introduces every one of his refutations with the use of the second-person pronoun, and most often he fashions a direct response in the first person. (For example, discussion of the second claim begins: "You deplore the demonstrations that are presently taking place in Birmingham. But I am sorry that your statement did not express a similar concern for the conditions that brought the demonstrations into being" [85].) At times, King enhances this interpretive sensibility by means of rhetorical questions. (For example, "You may well ask, 'Why direct action? Why sit-ins, marches, etc? Isn't negotiation a better path?' You are exactly right in your call for negotiation" [86].) In short, King exploits the form of the letter to localize, personalize, and dramatize the issues in the civil rights debate.

Although King's letter literally and directly addressed the eight Birmingham clergymen, it was never delivered to them, nor were they, in fact, his intended audience. The clergymen functioned rhetorically as a synecdoche, as a representation of the larger audience King wanted to reach, and his decision to respond to their statement and his manner of doing so were both strategic. The success of the Birmingham campaign, and of SCLC efforts in general, depended heavily on support from white moderates—Americans already inclined to oppose racial segregation in principle and to feel uncomfortable about the discrepancy between their basic values and the discriminatory policies then practiced in the South, but who were also fearful about direct action campaigns and the threat they posed to public order. When the eight clergymen published their statement, they offered King an opportunity to embody this target audience (and hence to use it as a rhetorical construct) without appearing to manufacture an artificial situation. Equally important, as Richard Fulkerson has noted, the invocation of specific individuals as an ostensible audience allowed King to cultivate a personal tone and to project his personality in ways that would have been impossible in a document addressed to no one in particular.[10] The letter, then, effectively used an actual event to construct a personalized version of both writer and audience through a double synecdoche. Just as the eight clergy stood for white moderates, so also did King stand for the SCLC and the African Americans engaged in nonviolent direct action campaigns.

While the letter's external structure proceeds in a point-by-point linear order, the rhetoric of the text also develops recurrent themes—repeated ideas, images, and arguments that work through the linear sequence of refutational arguments. These themes represent King as an agent of change who embodies the basic values of his white moderate audience and who acts with restraint and respect even as he attempts to reform glaring injustices. This development, an example of what Kenneth Burke calls repetitive form,[11] allows King to disagree with his audience while still remaining consubstantial with it. His dissent thereby seems to arise from within the *habitus* of his interlocutors.

From the opening salutation, King repeatedly emphasizes his status as a Christian minister and his unwavering commitment to the church. This point achieves its most notable articulation in the course of King's "second confession," where he expresses disappointment with white clergymen who "remain silent behind the anesthetizing security of stained-glass windows," and with white churches that stand on the sideline and preach an otherworldly religion. This is strong criticism, but King explains that it comes from a person firmly embedded in the Christian tradition: "In deep disappointment, I have wept over the laxity of the church. Be assured that my tears have been tears of love. . . . Yes, I love the church; I love her sacred walls. How could I do otherwise? I am in the rather unique position of being, the son, the grandson, and great-grandson of preachers" (97). Here King's figuration overlaps at three levels of embodiment: Christianity is made physical through representation of the church as a walled, physical space; King, coming from a lineage domiciled within those walls, assumes an identity connected with that Christian space, and from this inside position his disappointment with the church can manifest itself only as tears of love. All this figurative work presents King as someone who has the appropriate credentials to criticize the church from within and to recall it to its own ideals.

More generally, King embodies his solidarity with mainstream American values through the use of appeals to authority. The text is peppered with references to venerated figures from American history, Judeo-Christian lore, and the Western intellectual tradition. These include Paul, Socrates, Reinhold Niebuhr, Thomas Aquinas, Martin Buber, Paul Tillich, Jesus, Amos, Martin Luther, John Bunyan, Abraham Lincoln, Thomas Jefferson, and T. S. Eliot, and King invokes these references to vindicate and explain his own actions. For example, in response to the charge that he is "an outsider," King cites scriptural precedent for his activity: "Beyond this, I am in Birmingham because injustice is here. Just as the eighth-century prophets left their little villages and their 'thus saith the Lord' far beyond the boundaries of their hometowns; and just as the apostle Paul left his little village of Tarsus and carried the gospel of Jesus Christ to practically every hamlet and city of the Graeco-Roman world, I too am compelled to carry the gospel of freedom beyond my particular hometown" (84–85).

King is obviously concerned to dispel the perception that he is an outsider in Birmingham and a radical who adheres to positions that fall outside the orbit of respectable American opinion. The appeals to authority counter this image at two levels. First, by citing icons of accepted belief and faith, King associates himself with figures who command unquestioned respect from his target audience, and this helps to establish commonality with it. Second, the words and deeds of these respected individuals, insofar as they appear to be the same as or similar to King's words and deeds, become exemplars that sanction King's position and open space for it within the conceptual horizons of his audience. If Amos, Paul, Socrates, and even Jesus behaved as agitators, then it follows that agitation to expose and overcome injustice is no threat to the common tradition, but is instead something needed to renew and sustain its integrity.

King not only constructs his persona through strategies of embodiment, but he also uses the text to enact the kind of agency that he wants to have associated with himself and his movement. By enactment, we are referring not just to what the text says, but to what it does, and throughout the letter, King's verbal action as writer and advocate presents a complex but consistent representation of his character. The manner of his argument and his style of arguing combine to depict the man as energetic, active, committed to principles, and committed to act in accordance with those principles but to do so in a poised, balanced, reasonable, and restrained manner. The dominant image is one of restrained energy, and this image is well calculated to diffuse the accusation that King is a dangerous radical who lacks prudent judgment and acts without due regard for practical consequence.

Throughout the sequence of refutations, the text enacts balanced judgment through what Fulkerson calls a "dual pattern."[12] King responds to the allegations against him first on an immediate practical level and then on the level of principle, and as this pattern unfolds, the reader witnesses King exercising the kind of judgment most appropriate to deliberation—judgment that simultaneously encompasses particulars and principles and that engages questions of both expediency and honor. The first of King's refutations provides a clear illustration of this strategy. In responding to the charge that he is an "outsider," King begins by explaining that the Birmingham affiliate of the SCLC asked for his assistance, and so he is "here, along with several members of my staff, because we were invited here." But this is not the end of the matter, since beyond such particular concerns there is also a moral imperative that leads King to confront injustice just as the Hebrew prophets and the apostle Paul did. And, to place the issue on an even broader ground, King recognizes "the interrelatedness of all countries and states. . . . Injustice anywhere is a threat to justice everywhere. We are caught in an inescapable network of mutuality, tied in a single garment of destiny. Whatever affects one directly affects all directly" (85). Thus, whether judgment rests on the concrete particulars of the case or on sweeping ethical principle, King should not be regarded as an outsider; his presence in Birmingham is both appropriate and right.

The second, third, and fourth refutational sections also employ this double structure, but it is in the sixth section, where King addresses the charge of extremism, that the technique achieves its most powerful articulation. He begins his response by expressing surprise that anyone would label him as an extremist, since in actuality he stands "in the middle of two opposing forces in the Negro community." On one side, there are those who simply acquiesce to injustice and do nothing, and on the other, there are the black nationalists who react to injustice with hatred and bitterness and come "perilously close to advocating violence." Between these extremes of complacency and angry despair, King offers the "more excellent way" of nonviolent protest, and he acknowledges disappointment that this position would be regarded as extremist. King, however, has a second thought on the matter, and he "gradually gained a bit of satisfaction from being considered an extremist. Was not Jesus an extremist in love—'"Love your enemies, bless them that curse you, pray for them that despitefully use you."' This appeal to authority continues through a long list of heroic figures (including Amos, Paul, Martin Luther, John Bunyan, Abraham Lincoln, and Thomas Jefferson) who are also linked to famous quotations expressing extreme ideas. And King concludes that the question is not whether "we will be extremists" but whether we be extremists for love and justice or extremists for hate and injustice (92–94).

As other commentators have noted, this passage distinguishes between extremism understood as placement along a spectrum of existing positions and extremism understood in terms of intensity of conviction.[13] By the first standard, King is not an extremist but rather a dialectically tempered moderate, since his position comes between and constructively synthesizes the antithetical forces of apathy and violence. By the second standard, however, King is an extremist since he is passionately committed in principle to act against and eradicate injustice, and as King's historical witnesses demonstrate, extremism of this type supports the fundamental values of the society. This passage, then, combines restrained practical judgment with a passionate determination to overcome injustice, and the passion, however strongly it is expressed, still moves along constructive lines, since faith, justice, and love channel its energy.

Another notable feature of this passage is King's restraint in choosing the words he uses to address his critics. When labeled as an extremist, King reacts not with an expression of anger or indignity but disappointment. This sort of verbal control recurs throughout the letter. Thus, in the two sections that digress from the sequence of refutations, King makes his most critical comments about the inaction of the white community, but he studiously avoids the language of accusation. Instead, he "confesses" his disappointment with them. This restraint not only characterizes King's choice of words, but also, and more powerfully, it is enacted in the structure of some of his sentences.

In one of the most memorable parts of the text, King offers a carefully modulated response to the charge that the demonstrations are untimely. African Americans, he reminds his readers, already have had to wait for 340 years for their rights, and it is no wonder that they are growing impatient. "Perhaps it easy for those who have never felt the stinging darts of segregation to say, 'Wait'":

> But when you have seen vicious mobs lynch your mothers and fathers at will and drown your sisters and brothers at whim; when you have seen hate-filled policemen curse, kick, brutalize, and even kill your black brothers and sisters with impunity; when you see the vast majority of your twenty million Negro brothers smothering in an airtight cage of poverty in the midst of an affluent society; when you suddenly find your tongue twisted and your speech stammering as you seek to explain to your six-year-old daughter why she can't go to the public amusement park that has just been advertised on television, and see tears welling up in little eyes when she is told that Funtown is closed to colored children, and see the depressing clouds of inferiority begin to form in

> her little mental sky, and see her begin to distort her little personality by unconsciously developing bitterness toward white people; when you have to concoct an answer for a five-year-old son asking in agonizing pathos: "Daddy, why do white people treat colored people so mean?"; when you take a cross-country trip and find it necessary to sleep night after night in the uncomfortable corners of your automobile because no motel will accept you; when you are humiliated day in and day out by nagging signs reading "white" and "colored"; when your first name becomes "nigger" and your middle name becomes "boy" (however old you are) and your last name becomes "John," and when your wife and mother are never given the respected title "Mrs.," when you are harried by day and haunted by night by the fact that you are a Negro, living constantly at tiptoe stance never quite knowing what to expect next, and plagued with inner fears and outer resentments; when you are forever fighting a degenerating sense of nobodiness; then you will understand why we find it difficult to wait. (88–89)

The most obviously remarkable feature of this sentence is its length–331 words—which makes it by far the longest sentence in the text and probably one of the longest sentences in contemporary English prose. But the syntax of the sentence also deserves attention. Because it is structured in left-branching or periodic form, the syntactic complexity of the sentence develops through the accretion of dependent clauses that occur before the main clause. This arrangement suspends the completion of the sentence as a meaningful unit until the end, and so, to understand the sentence, the reader must wait until the final twelve words provide closure. Moreover, since the dependent clauses narrate a series of injuries, insults, and outrages, the whole development iconically represents the plight of the African American.[14] The white readers, who have never directly suffered from the "stinging darts of segregation," must wait while this long list of grievances continues to assault their sensibilities, and so they vicariously experience the frustration of the African American. The sentence enacts and transmits that experience in a way that no propositional argument could accomplish.

Given the length of the sentence, the tension that mounts through it, and the vivacity with which it represents the effects of injustice, we might expect it to end on a strong note of outrage and anger, perhaps even with an accusation against those who ask King and his people to wait. Instead, however, the climax comes in the form of an understated address to the white audience: "Then you will understand why we find it difficult to wait." The understatement may work to heighten the emotional impact of the sentence, but it is also a striking enactment of King's restraint, and it is difficult to imagine a more appropriate textual representation of King's pledge to proceed in reasonable and patient terms.

Toward the end of the letter, when he questions the clergyman's praise of the police, King uses this same verbal technique for building and containing emotional energy:

> I don't believe that you would have so warmly commended the police force if you had seen its angry violent dogs literally biting six unarmed Negroes. I don't believe you would so quickly commend the policemen if you would observe their ugly inhuman treatment of Negroes here in the city jail; if you would watch them push and curse old Negro women and young Negro girls; if you would see them slap and kick old Negro men and young boys; if you will observe them, as they did on two occasions, refuse to give us food because we want to sing our grace together. I'm sorry that I can't join you in your praise for the police department. (98–99)

The loose or right-branching construction of the long sentence does not suspend meaning as does the periodic sentence King uses earlier, and partially for this reason, this passage does not have quite the same dramatic impact. Nevertheless, the pattern of energy and restraint is equally apparent. The long sentence accumulates grievances through its many clauses, and the short sentence that follows offers a controlled, understated response addressed directly to the ostensible audience.

To sum up, in the "Letter from Birmingham Jail" King attempts to reach his target audience by dispelling the perception that he is a radical given to intemperate action and committed to views that fall outside the mainstream of American society. The text consistently works to represent King in a different light, and it does so not just by direct statement, but also by demonstrating balanced, temperate forms of judgment as it engages key issues and by the enactment of restrained energy in the very structure of the prose. At the end of the letter, King articulates this theme in two nicely balanced sentences that sum up the position he occupies throughout the text:

> If I have said anything in this letter that is an overstatement of the truth and is indicative of unreasonable impatience, I beg you to forgive me. If I have said anything in this letter that is an understatement of the truth and is indicative of my having a patience that makes me patient with anything less than brotherhood, I beg God to forgive me. (100)

Persona and Audience in King's Letter

Readers of the "Letter from Birmingham Jail" often testify to its powerfully evocative effect. For many Americans, the letter produced an immediate, unified response that restructured and reframed their perception of a complex situation, and E. Culpepper has offered a plausible account for this response. King, he maintains, gathered together an ambiguous set of cultural experiences and expectations and transformed them "into the controlling metaphor for interpreting non-violent civil disobedience." Writing from the confinement in a prison, King could exercise a prophetic voice that recalled his people to their better selves and that resonated "with the Judeo-Christian struggle against human bondage."[15]

King's actual imprisonment in Birmingham Jail is a necessary condition for the metaphor to work, but the image of a man writing in a cramped, isolated prison cell is in large part constructed by the text itself. And it was not enough simply for King to construct a prisoner's voice, since not all prisoners are prophets. King also faced the more difficult task of embedding himself within a culture that segregated people of his race. The prophetic voice does not come from the outside; it must arise from within the people whom it criticizes. It must incarnate what is highest and best in the culture of that people and summon them to act on standards the prophet embodies and the audience shares.[16] The prophet is a member of the tribe, and so, to be a prophet among the Hebrews, one must be a Hebrew. And what is required to be a prophet among white Americans? That is a role King neither inherits by birth nor gains through any other easy access. He must argue himself into it, and the letter is wonderfully designed to achieve just this purpose. It constructs King as an agent who grounds his identity in the religious, intellectual, and political values of the American tribe, and it enacts a form of agency that sustains connection between author and reader even in the presence of disagreement. King emerges from the letter not just as someone who can argue with a white audience on its own terms and but as an agent who can elevate that audience by forcing it to acknowledge its sins of omission and by demanding consistency between its actions and its highest values.

To this point, our reading of the text has followed the writer-audience ratio that King explicitly marks and emphasizes. But while the white moderate surely is the ostensible target audience, King must have known that the text would also circulate among African American readers. These readers would have a rhetorical status similar to that of white audiences who heard or read the discourse of Malcolm X and other militant black rhetors. As Reike and Golden have noted, while these militant rhetors speak directly and specifically to a black audience, they are also quite aware of white "eavesdroppers" who are listening even though they are not addressed, and it seems clear that their discourse is intended to have an impact on the whites who overhear what is said.[17] By analogy, we might think of the black readers of King's letter as "eavesdroppers" who implicitly receive directions about forming a new self-conception and adopting a persona that can render more effective agents in American society.[18]

Viewed from this angle, the letter constructs a model for African Americans to adopt and enact. In the opening paragraph, King represents himself in a way that reveals key features of that model. The salutation, "My Dear Fellow Clergyman," sets King on equal footing with the white men he is addressing, and in the sentence that follows, we learn that although King is confined in jail, he is an important and busy man who generally does not have time to answer criticism. In this instance, however, since he thinks the eight clerics are sincere men of goodwill, he elects to respond to them and to do so in patient and reasonable terms. Thus, even though confined physically, King remains an active agent who exercises choice about when and how to respond to others.

King's immediate situation—his imprisonment—corresponds to the imagery he uses later in the text to characterize the general condition of African Americans. He depicts them as "smothering in an airtight cage of poverty," as forced to sleep "in the uncomfortable corners" of their automobiles, as threatened by the "quicksand of racial injustice," and as prone to fall into the "dark dungeons of complacency." Yet, like King himself, African Americans are beginning to break through these restraints. They are experiencing a new militancy, and they carry "gospel of freedom," create constructive tension, stride toward freedom, move with "a cosmic energy" toward racial justice, and rise out of the "dark dungeons" to the "hills of creative protest."

By contrast, the white moderates are inert and immobile even though they face no restraints imposed from the outside. They have become, in King's words, stumbling blocks to freedom, dams blocking social progress, silent witnesses of injustice, anesthetized behind stained-glass windows, and paralyzed by the chains of conformity. White moderates, then, are passive, while the once-passive blacks are becoming agents of change. No longer willing to accept stolid indifference, they demand their rights as American citizens and insist that sincere people of good faith lend them their support. But morally and practically, they are best advised to make these demands in the spirit of King's example. In breaking out of restraints imposed upon them, they should accept a measure of self-restraint. Although white moderates often fail to exercise proper judgment, they can be called to their better selves through actions that force injustice to their attention and through discourse that addresses them in patient and reasonable terms.

For black readers, then, King's letter offers an invitation to adopt a rather specific conception of themselves as they struggle to attain equal rights, and King's placement of himself within the African American community appears in quite a different light than it does when the text is read from the perspective of a white moderate audience. For the white reader, King's assertion that he "stands between" the "'donothingism' of the complacent" and "hatred and despair of the black nationalist" (93) appears as a strategy designed to blunt the accusation that he is an intemperate radical, and it thus functions to help unify the writer and the audience. On the other hand, for the black "eavesdroppers," this placement suggests points of differentiation as well as identity; King's position represents an option that some may accept as the "more excellent way" and others may reject. The black audience, in effect, is instructed about how to distinguish the attitudes of its members and invited make a positive choice in favor of one of the alternatives. This approach offers a marked contrast to Malcolm's rhetoric where the black community is treated as a unified whole defined negatively and by extrinsic circumstance:

> I'm not here to argue or discuss anything that we differ about, because it's time for us to submerge our differences and realize that it is best for us to see that we have the same problem, a common problem, a problem that will make you catch hell whether you're a Baptist, a Methodist, or a Muslim, or a Nationalist. Whether you're educated or illiterate . . . you're going to catch the same hell from the same man. He just happens to be a white man.[19]

In sum, "Letter from Birmingham Jail" constructs the persona of an author who is critical of his white audience but not alienated from it. He shares its Christian and democratic values, recognizes its concern about practical matters, but he also calls upon that audience to acknowledge and act in accordance with its own principles. By insinuating himself within the lifeworld of his auditors, King can deploy his ethos instrumentally as a means of allaying fears about the immediate scene of social protest, but he can also establish a model of restrained energy that encourages the white audience to reaffirm its basic values as it reconsiders its view of African Americans. At the same time, the text constructs a persona that black readers can use as a model for becoming effective actors on the American scene. Like King, they can view themselves as agents who need not and will not suffer the indifference of white moderates, who can break free of external restraints without losing self-restraint, and who can work from within American society to make fundamental changes in the way they conceive themselves and are conceived by others. Thus at several levels and in respect to different audiences, King's text functions both as an instrument that uses constructions of self to alter attitudes and as a medium for constituting self within a scene composed of "exigencies, constraints, others, and self."

NOTES

1. Thomas Benson, "Rhetoric and Autobiography: The Case of Malcolm X," *Quarterly Journal of Speech* 60 (1974): 1.
2. The terms "interpretive" and "conceptual" are used by James Jasinski to describe what he calls the most important development in rhetorical criticism during the past two decades. This approach, already suggested in Benson's essay, concentrates on providing "thick descriptions" of particular cases rather than the construction or verification of abstract theoretical principles. See "The Status of Theory and Method in Rhetorical Criticism," *Western Journal of Communication* (2001): 249–70; and also the entry entitled "Criticism in Contemporary Rhetorical Studies," in *Sourcebook on Rhetoric: Key Concepts in Contemporary Rhetorical Studies*, ed. James Jasinski (Thousand Oaks, CA: Sage, 2001), 124–44.
3. Benson, "Rhetoric and Autobiography," 6.
4. On the indecorous nature of Malcolm's rhetoric, see Robert E. Terrill, "Protest, Prophecy, and Prudence in the Rhetoric of Malcolm X," *Rhetoric and Public Affairs* 4 (2001): 34. Terrill's reading of Malcolm's the "Ballot or the Bullet" provides an interesting counterpoint to our interpretation of King's letter presented in this paper.
5. Detailed accounts of these events are provided in Taylor Branch, *Parting the Waters: America in the King Years, 1954–63* (New York: Simon and Schuster, 1988), 673–802; and David Garrow, *Bearing the Cross: Martin Luther King, Jr., and the Southern Christian Leadership Conference* (New York: Vintage, 1986), 231–64.
6. The text of this letter is reprinted in S. Jonathan Bass, *Blessed Are the Peacemakers: Martin Luther King, Jr., Eight White Religious Leaders, and the "Letter from Birmingham Jail"* (Baton Rouge: Louisiana State University, 2001), 235–36.
7. Concerning the composition and circulation of the letter, see Bass, *Blessed Are the Peacemakers*, 110–62; E. Culpepper Clark, "An American Dilemma in King's 'Letter from Birmingham Jail,'" in *Martin Luther King and the Sermonic Power of Discourse*, ed. C. C. Calloway-Thomas and J. L. Lucaites (Tuscaloosa: University of Alabama Press, 1993), 34–49; and Martha Watson, "The Issue Is Justice: Martin Luther King Jr.'s Response to the Birmingham Clergy," *Rhetoric and Public Affairs* 7 (2004): 1–22.
8. Edwin Black, "The Second Persona," *Quarterly Journal of Speech* 56 (1970): 109–19.
9. All references to the letter are from Martin Luther King Jr., *I Have a Dream: Speeches and Writings That Changed the World*, ed. J. M. Washington (San

Francisco: Harper, 1986), 83–100. Specific page references to this edition are indicated parenthetically in the text of the paper.

10. Richard P. Fulkerson, "The Public Letter as Rhetorical Form: Structure, Logic, and Style in King's 'Letter from Birmingham Jail,'" *Quarterly Journal of Speech* 65 (1979): 124. Fulkerson's essay, in our judgment, remains the most systematic guide to the rhetoric of the letter, and we have relied upon it throughout our reading of the text.
11. Kenneth Burke, *Counter-statement* (Los Altos, CA: Hermes, 1931), 125.
12. Fulkerson, "Public Letter," 127.
13. See Fulkerson, "Public Letter," 128.
14. On the structure and rhetorical impact of the sentence, see Mia Klein, "The Other Beauty of Martin Luther King's 'Letter from Birmingham Jail,'" *College Composition and Communication* 32 (1981): 30–37.
15. Clark,"An American Dilemma," 48–49.
16. On the immanent role of prophetic discourse, see Michael Walzer, *Interpretation and Social Criticism* (Cambridge, MA: Harvard University Press, 1987), 64–94. James Darsey, *The Prophetic Tradition and Radical Rhetoric in America* (New York: New York University Press, 1997), 111, puts the point somewhat differently when he says that the prophet is "simultaneously insider and outsider." But Darsey's point is fundamentally the same as Walzer's—the prophet must be inside the culture but must have achieved sufficient conceptual distance from existing practices to be able to note and criticize discrepancies between those practices and the ideals of the culture. On "rhetorical distance," see Michael Osborn, "Rhetorical Distance in 'Letter from Birmingham Jail,'" *Rhetoric and Public Affairs* 7 (2004): 23–35.
17. James L. Golden and Richard D. Rieke, *The Rhetoric of Black Americans* (Columbus: Charles E. Merrill, 1971), 18–19.
18. There is no doubt that King regarded a positive change in black self-esteem as a vital and necessary part of the movement. In other speeches and writings of this period, he maintains that nonviolent direct action precipitated psychological change—it contributed to "something revolutionary" that was occurring in the "mind, heart, and soul of Negroes all over America." *Why We Can't Wait* (New York: Harper and Row, 1964), 64. Nonviolent direct action, he maintained, challenged stereotypes about blacks, often unconsciously accepted by blacks themselves, that they were inferior and unable to act independently because it

gave them a means for peaceful action directed toward their own liberation and for connecting local communities into a national network (67).

19. Malcolm X, "Ballot or the Bullet," in *Malcolm X Speaks: Selected Speeches and Statements*, ed. George Breitman (New York: Merit, 1965), 23.

Lincoln among the Nineteenth-Century Orators

I have two purposes in writing this paper. The first and primary objective follows a conventional agenda in historical and critical studies: it is to contribute something to our understanding of Lincoln's influence on late nineteenth-century American oratory. That influence is so broad and so obvious that it would seem to command attention, but, so far as I know, no one has yet studied the matter in any detail.[1] This paper, then, attempts to help fill a gap in the historical scholarship.

Given the existing climate of academic opinion, however, this conventional objective is neither self-explanatory nor self-justifying. Traditional studies of the influence of one speaker upon others may now seem hopelessly obsolete, since they rest upon dubious assumptions about the role of agency and textuality in the rhetorical process. Mindful of this

From *Rhetoric and Political Culture in Nineteenth-Century America*, ed. Thomas W. Benson (East Lansing: Michigan State University Press, 1997), 131–56.

problem, I have adopted a second, broader, and more theoretical purpose, and that is to indicate how an interpretative approach grounded in speakers and their texts may yield interesting results. The success of this effort, of course, depends upon the criticism that follows, but the theoretical issues involved are complex and often treated in a rather imprecise fashion. Consequently, I want to make some general remarks about the scope of the paper and the issues it raises about agency, textuality, and the politics of interpretation.

The tendency to displace the conventional view of agent and text reflects a broader change in the conception of rhetoric itself. It is now generally agreed that rhetoric is not a property of certain kinds of texts but a process that inheres in all discursive practices and that influences social consciousness at every level of its manifestation. This stress on process encourages a corresponding de-emphasis on specific agents and the textual products that record their utterances. If rhetoric is a global, unbounded process manifested in general cultural and social practices, then attention to the particular mistakes a fragment for the phenomenon itself. It follows that a critical program anchored in speakers and speeches reflects a defective and archaic rhetorical consciousness. For modernists, such as Wayne Brockriede, Samuel Becker, and Rod Hart, the individual product is not an appropriate unit of analysis since it blocks perception of the theoretical coherence needed to apprehend rhetoric per se.[2] For postmodernists, such as Michael McGee, Ray McKerrow, Jim Klumpp, and Thomas Hollihan, the product model sustains an ideological blindness since it blocks perception of practices that become coherent only at the level of aggregate social and cultural performance.[3]

Theoretically, I find it difficult to dispute the status of rhetoric as a global process. I do not know of any abstract principle that would distinguish some discourses as rhetorical and others as nonrhetorical. Yet there also are some practical considerations that might encourage a restrained approach to the business of criticism. We may acknowledge, for example, that an article in *Human Communication Research* is as much a rhetorical artifact as a campaign oration. Nevertheless, this global conception should not blind us to the fact that we are dealing with very different kinds of rhetoric. The differences are obvious, and among other things, they result from the generically different conditions attached to the production of these discourses. Competent campaign orators understand, though not always at an entirely conscious level, that special resources and constraints enter into the work at hand. And so do behavioral scientists, and that is one reason their rhetoric is so far distanced from ordinary public language. Moreover, writers and speakers, even those who operate within the boundaries of orthodox science, master a genre not simply by learning abstract rules but also through the assimilation of past utterances within the genre—that is, through the interpretation and application of models or paradigms for certain kinds of discourse.[4] We choose words in order to produce an utterance suitable to a context, and the propriety of the utterance depends upon our understanding of past utterances that fall within our generic conception of the context. Thus the accumulated practices in a certain domain determine important features of the rhetoric used within it, and unless we bracket the conditions associated with the production of discourse, the view that discourse is rhetorical expresses a theoretical truism that has limited practical value for the critic. Global conceptions of rhetoric cannot adequately account for the differing kinds of rhetoric that appear and develop in the social world.

The status of rhetorical production, however, has become a problematic issue. One of the achievements of postmodernism is to challenge the conventional assumption that authors are autonomous, seemingly isolated, agents who produce discrete texts. Instead, attention shifts to the complex network of production that superintends and shapes individual efforts and places both authors and texts within a broader ideological landscape. In a very strong version of this position, such as McKerrow's "critical rhetoric," production and performance have no status except in the work of the critic.[5] "Texts" become fragments of ideological consciousness, and their meaning remains veiled until the critic assembles the fragments and textualizes the hidden architecture that informs the whole development. On this view, the specific features of any local product are insignificant except insofar as they represent signs or symptoms of the larger discursive formations that determine an author's subjectivity. What we have traditionally accepted as texts have no integrity and should not be approached as discrete utterances.

This radical displacement of texts depends upon the assumption that agents and their rhetorical actions are captive within a totalizing structure.

All local production is inert since it is drawn into the orbit of forces that it cannot alter, and hence the critic, who stands distant from the fragmentation at the surface, occupies a privileged position, since only the critic can comprehend the structure that governs the epiphenomenon of grounded utterance.

This perspective yields an extraordinarily exalted view of the critic, but it comes at the price of oversimplifying the complexity of rhetorical performance. We are asked to believe that the sense of completion, which we experience as readers and writers of texts, has no bearing on the construction of social consciousness. It is as though no circulation exists between demarcated objects and a monolithic ideological structure. Ordinary rhetors become passive receptacles, since the marks of their subjectivity and their strategic maneuvers are submerged within a larger, fixed pattern, and there is no space to rearticulate elements of that pattern into new formations. In its extreme form, then, the doctrine of fragmentation regards social and cultural constraints on production as a monolith that controls all phases of production.

Yet even if we have cause to doubt the exaggerated claims of some variants of postmodernism, the general point about constraints on production still has real force. At the least, we need to modify the received notion that rhetors are purely strategic agents employing neutral instruments to adjust people to ideas and ideas to people. This conception ignores the placement of the agent—the socially conditioned subjectivity of anyone who enters the discursive arena. Rhetors are not only producers of discourse; they are also rhetorical products. And, as Mikhail Bakhtin has explained it, the productive process involves a complicated interaction:

> The unique speech experience of each individual is shaped and developed in continuous and constant interaction with others' individual utterances. The experience can be characterized as the process of *assimilation*—more or less creative—of others' words (and not the words of a language). Our speech, that is, all our utterances . . . is filled with others' words, varying degrees of otherness or of "our-own-ness," varying degrees of awareness and detachment. These words of others carry with them their own expression, their own evaluative tone, which we assimilate, rework, and re-accentuate.[6]

Approached from this perspective, attention to the text as a complete utterance should not block perception of larger discursive developments. Instead, it should offer a way to understand the text as an assimilative social product—as something constructed through a process that submits to and reappropriates the authority of the other. The text is at once a point of local closure, an event in the ongoing development of a genre of utterance, and a productive moment in the unending process of interpreting and reinterpreting the social world.

With these general comments as background, I can now turn to the specific project at hand and define its objectives more clearly. In my earlier statement of purpose, I described my interest as an effort to understand Lincoln's influence on late nineteenth-century oratory. I used the word "oratory" rather than "rhetoric" advisedly. Though what I have to say may have some bearing on the general rhetorical ambiance of the period, my concern centers on a particular genre of discursive practice, and the question I am asking is this: How did late nineteenth-century orators use Lincoln?

The "use" of Lincoln appears in at least three related but distinguishable forms. First, orators invoke Lincoln's name—or terms, ideas, and images closely linked to his name—for some immediate strategic purpose. This is the routine and normally uninteresting use of an icon for instrumental purposes. Second, orators may imitate or reappropriate Lincoln's textual practices in producing their own texts. At the simplest level, this involves use of Lincoln's words or phrases, but there is also a more complex process of imitating broader features of Lincoln's rhetoric through the appropriation of his stylistic or argumentative patterns. (In this respect, we might note how Lincoln used Webster's texts for just this purpose, reworking Webster's themes within his own discourse.) At a still higher level, orators might seek to capture the essence of Lincoln's rhetoric—to reembody his rhetorical persona and the tone and spirit of his utterances. In principle, this sort of appropriation might be limited to a general but still technical exercise in composition. In practice, however, such broader imitation is associated with a third use of Lincoln—Lincoln as a moral and political paradigm. In this case, Lincoln emerges as a model for the conception and representation of the orator's own subjectivity, or through synecdoche, of some group with whom the orator identifies.

The more technical and specific of these usages—particularly those that fall into the first category—are easily isolated from the texts in which they appear, and they can be gathered together into abstract patterns that tell us something about the strategic uses of the Lincoln "ideograph."[7] But the other usages become apparent only as they are apprehended within the orator's own pattern of utterance, since they function to structure the utterance as a whole. At this level, Lincoln inhabits the text; the orator appropriates the ideograph within the metabolism of his or her own rhetorical creation, in a process that entails both a submission to Lincoln's authority and a reinterpretation and reembodiment of that authority. Lincoln's rhetorical and ethical persona is thus recalculated through its different textual manifestations.

My interest in Lincoln's influence, then, has to do with a complex process of assimilation and adaptation, and it cannot depend upon "statistical representations" that enumerate and isolate references or bits of texts. My objective is to learn something about how Lincoln enters into the practice of oratorical rhetoric, when practice is viewed as a complete utterance or a fully realized performance within the genre. Consequently, my unit of analysis is the "representative anecdote," and I have selected three late nineteenth-century texts that call for careful interpretation as discursive wholes. In one sense, this orientation encourages a literary or perhaps even "formalistic" approach, but by considering a number of texts in relation to one another, I believe that we can learn something about the broader social and political issues that enter into textual practices. As we shall soon discover, the appropriation of Lincoln proves to be a complex business in which rhetorical strategies merge with ideological concerns and social myths. Consider, for example, Lincoln's status as an object of strategic use or emulation. In part, that status resulted from the texts he had produced, and late nineteenth-century orators were familiar with those texts and often referred to or invoked them. But Lincoln also had become a mythic figure, and the myth functioned as a kind of text—one that was rather diffuse and ambiguous but undoubtedly powerful, both in shaping the rhetor's attitude toward Lincoln and in structuring the use of his authority as symbolic capital. In other words, Lincoln emerged as a complex, composite figure who could be interpreted and invoked in many different ways. There were, of course, limits to the range of this activity, but they were broad, and depending on the circumstances and the interests of the orator, Lincoln could be incarnated in strikingly different guises. Thus, he became a common resource for rhetorical invention, but a pliable resource that could be constructed and adapted to fit a variety of political purposes and ideological agendas. Specific textual practices, then, should tell us something about how a key symbol of national identity could be interpreted, reinterpreted, and assimilated into the changing social and cultural milieu.

I have selected three texts for this analysis: Henry Grady's "The New South" (1886), Frederick Douglass's "Speech at the Freedman's Memorial to Lincoln" (1876), and Jane Addams's "A Modern Lear" (1894).[8] These texts are the products of influential orators, all of whom became heroic figures in their own right. Obviously, however, the three occupied very different positions in the political and social world of late nineteenth-century America. As a consequence, I believe that they offer "representative anecdotes" for differing interpretations and appropriations of Lincoln.

The New South: Lincoln as Heroic Capitalist

Delivered on December 22, 1886, before the New England Society of New York, Grady's "New South" was a classic case of rhetorical accommodation in difficult circumstances. Grady, the editor of the *Atlanta Constitution*, was the first southerner ever to address the Society, and his mission was to allay sectional tensions and encourage northern migration to and investment in the South. Memory of the Civil War still remained a fresh and potent element in the consciousness of both sections, and real hazards attended any effort to plead for conciliation and unity. Moreover, Grady's task was complicated by the two speakers who preceded him on the podium. Both Dewitt Talmage and General Sherman rekindled partisan memories of the war, and to finish this display of rhetorical insensitivity, the orchestra in the balcony struck up "Marching Through Georgia" at the conclusion of Sherman's speech.[9]

Grady's response to the situation was tactically brilliant. Turning the apparent liability of his position as a Georgian into a positive advantage, Grady won an extraordinarily enthusiastic response from his audience, and in the ensuing weeks, the speech attracted much attention from the northern press, almost all of it fulsome in praise of the speaker. The southern reaction, with a few notable exceptions, was also favorable. Grady emerged as an instant national celebrity, the symbol of a new, "progressive" southerner, who commanded respect in the North and who advanced high-minded, conciliatory principles. When he died only three years later, at the age of thirty-nine, he became the object of a heroic cult. In Atlanta, the citizens erected a monument to him, bearing an inscription that praised him as a man who "was literally loving the nation into peace." A memorial volume, edited by Joel Chandler Harris, solidified and extended Grady's reputation as a heroic agent of national conciliation and goodwill.

Small wonder, then, that the "New South" became canonized as a masterpiece of eloquence. For generations, students declaimed parts of it as an exercise in elocution and citizenship; it appeared in almost all anthologies of American public address, and critics cited the speech as an example of rhetoric that rose above partisan sentiment to express a message of "justice, honesty, freedom, fairness, faith, courtesy, courage."[10]

Recent critics present a far less benign interpretation of the speech. Careful historical research, conducted by Cully Clark, Harold Davis, and others, demonstrates that Grady did not represent the South as a whole.[11] In fact, he was a spokesman for the local and special interests of the Atlanta business community and vastly (but effectively) oversimplified matters by converting its desires into a representation of the actually existing consciousness of the entire region. Moreover, for a contemporary reader, the veneer of Grady's nonpartisan, inclusive rhetoric seems transparent. Although he elevates national over sectional interests, his vision of the national interest is narrowed by an Anglo-Saxon bias. Cavaliers and Puritans happily blend into a dichromatic portrait of America that excludes all other colors and textures. The treatment of the race issue is, by current standards, totally unacceptable and almost obscene; in the "New South," as in other of Grady's speeches, his rhetoric excuses an overt policy of social discrimination and disguises a covert and brutal policy of political repression. More broadly, Grady articulates a narrow version of the capitalistic ethic that has little appeal for contemporary academics.

All told, "The New South" is an ideal target for the ax of political correctness—paradigm case of false ideology canonized as fair-minded statesmanship. Nevertheless, however we evaluate the ethical and political doctrine of the speech, it would be a mistake to dismiss it—and not just because of Grady's dexterity in responding to the immediate occasion. The speech had remarkable staying power, sustaining a favorable, if not heroic, image of the orator for several generations. That this after-dinner speech could accomplish so much for so long must surely tell us something about the rhetorical climate of the late nineteenth and early twentieth centuries and something about the way oratory could appropriate and infiltrate the ideological system.

In his careful and expert analysis of "The New South," Robert Iltis identifies Grady's key strategy as a "compensatory transformation"[12]—an effort, in Ernest Bormann's phrase, to fetch good out of evil[13] by transforming the war from a tragic conflict where one side wins and the other loses into a vehicle for redemption and rebirth for both parties. The rebirth theme echoes sentiments powerfully articulated by Lincoln in the Gettysburg Address, but Grady does not align his theme directly with Lincoln. He invokes Lincoln's symbolic authority in more subtle ways as he advances his own variant of this strategy.

The speech opens with a quotation attributed to Benjamin Hill, a fellow southerner: "There was a South of slavery and secession—that South is dead. There is a South of union and Freedom—that South, thank God, is living, breathing, growing every hour."[14] This image of a reborn South recurs throughout later parts of the speech, but Grady does not develop it immediately. He announces the quotation as his text for the evening, and then in keeping with the occasion, he tells some humorous stories and asks for a fair hearing.

Grady almost imperceptibly glides from this lighthearted introductory material into the body of the speech. In order to preserve "a sort of historical equilibrium," Grady notes that the Cavalier was as much present as the Puritan in the early development of the nation. But Puritan and Cavalier were merged in the storm of the "first Revolution," their blood shed in common to secure the Republic. The narrative is then pushed forward to its climactic moment:

> From the union of these colonist Puritans and Cavaliers, from the straightening of their purposes and the crossing of their blood, slow

> perfecting through a century, came he who stands as the first typical American, the first who comprehended within himself all the strength and gentleness, all the majesty and grace of this Republic—Abraham Lincoln.

Lincoln's name, withheld until the dramatic conclusion of the sentence, becomes a synecdoche for the nation, and by invoking the Union hero for this purpose, Grady surely ingratiates himself with his northern audience. But there is more:

> He was the sum of Puritan and Cavalier, for in his ardent nature were fused the virtues of both, and in the depths of his great soul the faults of both were lost. He was greater than Puritan, greater than Cavalier, in that he was American and that in his homely form were first gathered the vast and thrilling forces of his ideal government—charging it with such tremendous meaning and so elevating it above human suffering that martyrdom, though infamously aimed, came as a fitting crown to a life consecrated from the cradle to human liberty.

Lincoln now becomes a Christ-figure in political form—the incarnation of perfected civic virtue, whose passion redeems liberty and opens the possibility of a reborn and reunited nation.

This invocation of Lincoln is somewhat problematic. Some southerners could not stomach Grady's idealization of the president. Francis W. Dawson, editor of the *Charleston News and Courier*, asserted that no thoughtful southerner would recognize "Lincoln as an ideal type. . . . He was never a typical American, unless such an American must necessarily be coarse while kindly, awkward while amiable, and weak in act while strong in word." The negative terms in this passage (awkward, coarse, weak in action) do not fit the image of the Cavalier, and Dawson suggested that Lincoln's real affinity was with "a type of new class who are rising to prominence in part of the "New South.""[15] Dawson, who was no friend of Grady's, had his own ax to grind, but his comments seem close to the mark. As Harold Davis has argued, it is easy to discern Lincoln's Puritan lineaments, but very difficult to cast him in the Cavalier mold.[16] A bit of perspective, then, might suggest that Grady was not yielding before

Lincoln's political sanctity so much as he was using it to perfect the image of the progressive southern capitalist.

Nevertheless, within the internal development of the speech, Grady deploys the Lincoln symbol with great economy and skill. At one stroke, he makes a gracious gesture to his audience, associates Lincoln's person with the main theme of the speech, and opens space to address this theme, first articulated by Lincoln, in his own distinctively postbellum, southern voice. Grady, for a variety of obvious reasons, cannot wrap himself in Lincoln's text, and that is precisely why he discovers (or manufactures) Hill's quotation as his text for the evening. What Grady can do, however, is to "textualize" Lincoln, to represent the historical figure as a symbol authorizing a progressive, southern version of the meaning of the war and its aftermath. So, by using Lincoln without using Lincoln's words, Grady remains planted in his section even as his rhetoric stretches across the sectional divide.

After the narrative that ends with Lincoln's apotheosis, Grady proceeds to a second narrative—this one telling the story of the reborn South. He begins by depicting the Confederate soldier as he returns home after the war. The scene is one of utter desolation: "He finds his house in ruins, his farm devastated, his slaves free, his barns empty, his trade destroyed, his money worthless, his social system, feudal in its magnificence, swept away." But our southerner is a plucky lad. Faced with this disaster, he does not whine for a moment. He rolls up his sleeves and goes to work. The result is that restoration occurs in record time. The South has "planted" schoolhouses, "sowed" towns, "put business above politics," challenged the spinners in Massachusetts and the iron makers in Pennsylvania, lowered interest rates, obliterated the Mason-Dixon Line, achieved perfect harmony in every household, established thrift in country and city, fallen in love with work, let economy take root and spread, and produced con artists equal to the shrewdest down-easter from Vermont. No, our southern lad did not curse the Yankee; he was reborn as a Georgia Yankee.

This is a remarkable story—the South as Horatio Alger, the entire region yearning to become clones of Honest Abe, swallowing his values in a single gulp and striving to emulate, in economic terms, his rise from a log cabin to the White House. Starting with nothing, the South pulls itself up by its bootstraps by appropriating the virtues Lincoln had incarnated—thrift, industry, courage, self-reliance, family values, and ingenuity.

The cause of this miraculous transformation was the war, whose outcome was inevitable:

> When Lincoln signed the Emancipation Proclamation, your victory was assured; for he then committed you to the cause of human liberty, against which the arms of man cannot prevail; while those of our statesmen who trusted to make slavery the cornerstone of the Confederacy doomed us to defeat as far as they could, committing us to a cause that reason could not defend or the sword maintain in the sight of advancing civilization.

Echoing a theme embedded in the "Second Inaugural," Grady views the event as part of a divine plan: "The omniscient God held the balance of battle in his Almighty hand," and "human slavery was swept forever from American soil." The meaning of the war, however, is not to be found in the military outcome, but on its transformative power—in the recognition of progress that it forced upon southern consciousness. "The South," Grady explains, "found her jewel in the toad's head of defeat. The shackles that held her in narrow limitations fell forever when the shackles of the negro slave were broken."

The old South was feudal and anticapitalist; it spurned industrial development, concentrated wealth at the center, and resisted change because of its attachment to the archaic institution of slavery. The whole system collapsed with the demise of slavery, and once liberated from the peculiar institution, the social order, as though through an automatic reaction, achieved fluidity and changed to meet the demands of progress: "The New South presents a perfect democracy . . . less splendid on the surface but stronger at the core—a hundred farms for every plantation, fifty homes for every palace, and a diversified industry that meets the complex needs of this complex age."

Grady's tale of rebirth is told in dominantly economic terms, and in a spirit that captures only part of Lincoln's rhetorical vision. Although Lincoln hovers silently in the background as a symbol of the self-made man, the moral resonance of his "new birth of freedom" is lost altogether.

Grady acknowledges that slavery was wrong, but for him, the matter is settled. The war brought an end to slavery, and the issue of racial equality no longer troubles him. Nor should it detain his northern audience: "To liberty and enfranchisement is as far as law can carry the negro. The rest must be left to conscience and common sense. It should be left to those among whom his lot is cast." To a contemporary reader, these words ring hollow, but Grady knew his audience. By 1886, the capitalists of the Republican Party had abandoned the goals of Reconstruction. They were tired of the race issue, and given a reasonable pretext, they were more than willing to turn a blind eye toward it and get on with the business of economic development.

One of the defining developments of Gilded Age America was the transformation of the Republican Party. What was once a party of reform dedicated to the principle of equality had become the party of conservative business interests dedicated to the preservation of industrial capitalism. Grady's Lincoln fits perfectly within the new scheme of things. As a southern Democrat, Grady gains much through his identification with Lincoln, but the Lincoln he identifies is a product of a rhetorical art that highlights certain themes and commonplaces and hides others. In the end, this process of selection and composition yields a new and revised Lincoln. Removed from view are Lincoln's sense of the tragic rhythms of history, the imperfections that mark human institutions, and the struggle needed to adjust to changing circumstances.[17] Even more notably absent is the promise of equality inscribed in our founding document and against which Lincoln would measure the moral progress of the nation. Instead, we are presented with a "perfect democracy," modeled after a perfected incarnation of Anglo-Saxon virtue. In Grady's speech, the South is reborn in Lincoln's image, but it is an image transformed and gilded by the idiom of a later generation.[18]

Douglass's Memorial: Lincoln as Self-Made White Man

Through a joint resolution, Congress had set aside April 14, 1876, as a national holiday. On that date, the anniversary of Lincoln's death and the freeing of the slaves in the District of Columbia, America's black citizens dedicated a monument to Lincoln's memory. A gala celebration marked the event; a march through the White House grounds was followed by an elaborate unveiling ceremony. Among those in attendance were members of Congress, the justices of the Supreme Court, and the president of the United States.[19] The task of delivering the main speech was assigned to Frederick Douglass. In 1876, Douglass was not only America's most prominent black citizen, but also a stalwart in the Republican Party and a figure who commanded national respect. His rise to that position is, as Henry Wilson has said, "an epic which finds few to equal it in the realms of either romance or reality."[20] It is also a testament to the power of oratory as an engine of personal advancement in nineteenth-century America.

Born into slavery, Douglass somehow learned to read, and while still a boy, obtained a copy of Caleb Bingham's *Columbian Orator*. He studied the book assiduously, declaiming passages from the speeches it contained whenever he found the time and opportunity. The book deeply marked his political consciousness and offered him a vocation. After his escape from slavery, Douglass realized that vocation by enlisting as a speaker for the Garrisonian wing of the abolitionist movement—perhaps the most truly and purely radical group in American history. He rapidly emerged as a brilliant orator and the preeminent black abolitionist, and gradually his politics shifted closer to the center of the spectrum.[21]

After the war, Douglass, like most other black Americans, became a Republican loyalist, but his prominence marked him as an especially important resource for the party, and he functioned as an almost official liaison between the white leadership of the party and the black community. During the election of 1872, he had used his considerable influence to help prevent black defections from Grant, and he was selected as a Republican elector from New York. In 1876, Douglass, despite earlier disappointments, still looked forward to an important office under a Republican administration, and that hope was realized the next year when Hayes appointed him marshal for the District of Columbia.

Meanwhile, Douglass remained in demand as a speaker and earned a considerable income from his performances. No longer an agitator, Douglass often lectured on themes of general interest, and while his style sometimes showed flashes of his radical and biting irony, the tone had shifted in a direction consistent with the role of a respectable citizen and senior statesman. His message fell well within the range of mainstream values. As Waldo Martin has described it, Douglass's thought entailed a distinctive but hardly radical blend of humanism, bourgeois capitalism, and Protestant morality.[22] The most popular of his lectures, "Self Made Men," endorsed the standard set of virtues—self-reliance, independence, hard work, and courage. Douglass, of course, included black men in his list of the self-made, but his orientation was distinctively American, and for him, "Lincoln was the King of American self-made men."[23]

Douglass still remained an anomaly and an outsider. A black leader, no matter how eloquent or loyal, could not penetrate deeply into the corridors of national power or the inner circles of the Republican Party. Nevertheless, for black Americans and for some of the more liberal whites, Douglass was a heroic figure—a self-made man in the fullest sense of the term; he was to black America what Lincoln was to white America. Thus, it was altogether fitting and proper that Douglass should be invited to speak at the ceremony commemorating the Great Emancipator.

Douglass was honored and flattered to undertake the assignment, but he had misgivings about the monument itself. It depicted Lincoln standing erect, holding the Emancipation Proclamation, while a black man knelt before him his shackles broken. Douglass thought that the freed slave ought to have been presented in "a more manly attitude."[24] And Douglass made the needed correction in his address, where he assumed the "more manly attitude." In this remarkable epideictic display, the orator rose to meet Lincoln squarely in the eye he measured the Emancipator from within his own perspective as an emancipated black, a perspective made possible by the very fact of the memorial ceremony. To achieve this end, Douglass had to define the situation to suit his purposes. He needed to establish his primary objective not as a praise of Lincoln, but an act of memorialization accomplished by black citizens.

The speech has a clearly marked prooemium that extends for almost four pages in the printed text. Here the orator, consistent with the norms of the genre, considers the nature and significance of the epideictic situation. In keeping with the solemnity of the event and the standards of nineteenth-century oratorical prose, Douglass's language is elevated and rather florid, and the syntax sustains a formal, balanced dignity. But within this mannered and conventional format, Douglass develops an incisive and creative commentary on the key terms that might define his effort, and he proceeds to weight and align these terms in a manner that specifies the burden he assumes as a speaker.

The opening sentence is curious: "Friends and Fellow Citizens: I warmly congratulate you upon the highly interesting object which has caused you to assemble in such number and spirit as you have today." It is strange, I think, for a speaker to begin by congratulating the audience, but even stranger is the confusion about the reason for this congratulation. What does Douglass mean by "the object that has caused you to assemble?" Since he is positioned next to the monument, we might think that he is referring to the physical "object." But that hardly makes sense—one might congratulate the sculptor for his work, but certainly not the audience that comes to view it. On the other hand, "object" may refer to the, "objective" or "purpose" that motivates the audience to gather. That makes more sense, but the word "object" seems a rather odd choice as a replacement for a word such as "purpose" that would make his point more clearly. Perhaps, however, the ambiguity is intentional. The physical presence of the object before the audience is palpable and might dominate its attention. Douglass may be deflecting attention from that object and what it represents in order to focus upon the less tangible purpose that informs the event.

In the next sentence, he introduces another key term: "This occasion is, in some respects, remarkable." Reference to the occasion is obviously appropriate, but why is it remarkable only "in some respects"? Douglass does not explain his qualification. Other key terms appear at the beginning of the third paragraph: "We stand to-day at the national center to perform something like a national act." Here Douglass moves toward a consideration of purpose, and the purpose is to perform an act. Again there is a strange and unexplained qualifier—it is not quite a "national" act but something like one.

To this point, and indeed through the next page of the text, we have heard nothing about Lincoln. What we have is an apparently jumbled reflection about what is or should be the significance of the event. The audience is congratulated for being present. Its presence, however, is not significant because of the object that stands before it nor because of the still unmentioned man it memorializes. Instead the focus shifts toward the occasion and the act which provides the motive for the occasion. But these crucial terms are left without definition, and they are qualified in a peculiar and unexplained fashion.

It is not until the fifth paragraph that Douglass specifies the purpose of the act: "In a word we are here to express, as best we may, by appropriate forms and ceremonies, the vast, high, and preeminent services rendered by Abraham Lincoln to ourselves, to our race, to our country and the whole world." The purpose of the occasion, and hence its true significance, is to express gratitude to Lincoln. Yet Douglass still defers comment about Lincoln, and in the next two paragraphs, which end the prooemium, he stresses the significance of the act per se; in other words, the act of expression is divided from and given priority over the object of the act.

Gratitude, Douglass explains, is a high and noble sentiment, and eloquent expression of it constitutes an important aspect of the life of the polity. And the present event assumes historic

> proportions precisely because it is the first time that black citizens have joined in this high worship, and march in this time-honored custom. . . . It is the first time, in this form and manner, we have sought to honor an American great man. . . . commend that fact to notice. . . . Let those who despise us, not less than those who respect us, know it and that now and here, in the spirit of liberty, loyalty and gratitude, we unite in this act of reverent homage.

Finally, we can understand why the occasion is remarkable "in some respects." This is not one among the many normal epideictic ceremonies that periodically renew the nation's commitment to its heroes. Rather, it is a special event marking change and growth in the polity—it is a liminal moment, which enrolls black America into a sacred ritual. It is appropriate, therefore, to concentrate on the "here and now" aspects of the ceremony—on the performance of eloquently expressed gratitude that Douglass enacts as he speaks.

In the body of the speech, Lincoln comes into full view, but he is viewed from a distinctively black perspective, and that perspective forces Douglass to make a concession to the "truth":

> Abraham Lincoln was not, in the fullest sense of the word, either our man or our model. In his interests, in his associations, in his habits of thought, and in his prejudices, he was a white man. He was preeminently the white man's President, entirely devoted to the welfare of white men.

In his well-exercised ironic voice, Douglass has revealed the paradox central to his own rhetorical mission. This paradox explains the complex metadiscourse of the introduction, which separates the act from the object, and we now know why the act is only "somehow" national. The black orator is asked to praise someone who is not consubstantial with him, who is not, "in fullest sense," his man or his model. He must perform the rite of citizenship by honoring someone who did not fully recognize blacks as citizens.

This paradox prevents Douglass from relying entirely upon the normal conventions of the genre. He must do some groundbreaking rhetorical work and construct a discourse appropriate to the unique requirements of an unprecedented situation. Consequently, his task involves articulating a black perspective that can allow him to express gratitude to a preeminent American who was preeminently the white man's president.

The perspective that Douglass constructs depends upon an enlarged view of Lincoln as an agent constrained by historical circumstances. In one sense, circumstances were moving in a progressive direction as the "nature of things" conspired to eliminate slavery. Lincoln stood at the head of that movement, was swept up by it, and though he "loved Caesar less than Rome" and the union more than "our freedom," it was under his rule that blacks were raised from slavery to "liberty and manhood." Obviously, however, if judged in terms of this forward thrust of history, Lincoln deserved no gratitude; he was merely an instrument of fate and necessity—his own agency at best had no effect and at worst dragged futilely against the tide of progress.

Douglass, however, understood that history does not flow in a single, unimpeded direction. If there were forward-moving forces at Lincoln's back, there were also serious obstacles and counterforces that he had to face. Lincoln was necessarily constrained, both as a man and as a president, by these negative forces. A just assessment of him, therefore, required a general view of his character and action within the swirl of circumstances that engulfed him.

Even during the war, Douglass asserts, blacks were able to achieve this enlarged perspective. They retained faith in Lincoln, although that faith was often "taxed and strained to the uttermost." "We were able to take a comprehensive view of Abraham Lincoln, and to make reasonable allowance for the circumstances of his position." He was not judged by "stray utterances," or "isolated facts torn from their connection," or by "partial and imperfect glimpses," but by

> a broad survey, in the light of the stern logic of great events, and in view of that "divinity which shapes our ends, rough hew them how we will." We came to the conclusion that the hour and man of redemption had somehow met in Abraham Lincoln.

This view of Lincoln, attributed to the contemporary observer of his actions and words, is anchored in faith and still portrays the man in a rather passive position. As Douglass shifts to the present, he can assume an even broader perspective, since the passage of time allows for a better-reasoned and more comprehensive judgment. "Looking back" to Lincoln's time and situation, Douglass now acknowledges that only a white man's president could have emancipated the slave. Lincoln's mission was to save the country from disunion and to free it "from the sin of slavery." He could not have achieved the second goal unless he gave priority to the first. An abolitionist position at the start of the war would have doomed the union and left the Confederate slave system intact. The work had to be done by someone who hated slavery but who placed the union ahead of abolition, and once emancipation became politically feasible, Lincoln seized the opportunity and moved ahead as quickly as prudence allowed. These reflections lead to a balanced judgment: "Viewed from the genuine abolition ground, Mr. Lincoln seemed tardy, cold, dull, and indifferent; but measuring him by the sentiment of the country, a sentiment, he was bound as a statesman to consult, he was swift, zealous, radical, and determined."

Thus, Douglass has articulated an enlarged view of his subject. Blacks can express gratitude to Lincoln for doing what was possible under the circumstances; he was not their man in the full sense, but he was well fitted to serve as the instrument of their liberation. Through the exercise of mature judgment, black citizens can assess Lincoln for what he was; they can honor him without losing their identity; as befits the citizens of a republic, they can appreciate a president "entirely devoted to the white man" without sacrificing their own integrity.

Having cleared the ground for a more conventional assessment of Lincoln, Douglass inquires into the reason for Lincoln's greatness of character. Predictably enough, that reason consists in Lincoln's status as a self-made man: "Born and reared among the lowly; a stranger to wealth and luxury; compelled from tender youth to sturdy manhood to grapple single-handed with the flintiest hardships of life, he grew strong in the manly and heroic qualities to which he was called by the votes of his countrymen." Faced with the crisis of secession, Lincoln's patrician predecessor, James Buchanan, had flinched and denied to the government "the right of self-preservation—a right that belongs to the meanest insect." Lincoln, the plebeian, responded with a strength born of common sense and hardened "in the school of adversity." He did not hesitate or falter, but remained clear, calm, and brave in adhering to his duty. His self-made character, then, was suited to the heroic task of preserving the union and freedom.

Douglass, of course, was conscious of his own status as self-made hero—indeed, it was an image that he had cultivated for himself. Anything he said about self-made men had at least some self-referential force, and the connection between Douglass's praise of Lincoln and Douglass's own person must have been obvious. But I believe that the rhetoric of the speech involved another, rather more subtle aspect of this connection. The rhetorical action that reconstructed the "King of American self-made men" also worked to construct a powerful persona for the rhetor. Douglass defined his rhetorical problem as one that required opening new ground in the effort to locate a voice for a black expression of gratitude. As he engaged this problem, Douglass took the measure of his subject in a spirit of independent but balanced and mature judgment, and in the process, he enacted a model of responsible citizenship based upon an enlarged perspective. Moreover, the model was one of Douglass's own making; he had constructed himself through the heroic achievement of a self-made rhetoric. He had paid homage to Lincoln without either bowing before the white man's president or refusing to acknowledge gratitude to the man and his achievements.

After a brief and rather conventional passage concerning Lincoln's martyrdom, Douglass concludes with a peroration compressed into a single paragraph. This short section so effectively rounds out the speech that I need to quote it in its entirety:

> Fellow-citizens, I end as I began with congratulations. We have done a good work for our race to-day. In doing honor to the memory of our friend and liberator we have been doing his best honor to ourselves and to those who come after us. We have been attaching to ourselves a name imperishable and immortal; we have also been defending ourselves from a blighting scandal. When now it shall be said that the colored man is soulless, that he has no appreciation of benefits or benefactors; when the foul reproach of ingratitude is hurled at us, and it is attempted to scourge us beyond the range of human brotherhood, we may calmly point to the monument we have erected to the memory of Abraham Lincoln.

Significantly, Douglass turns our attention back to the occasion and the event. In effect, he now congratulates himself for a job well done. His speech has accomplished its goal, and by finding a rhetoric to express gratitude to Lincoln, Douglass has initiated the black citizen into a national rite. Dedicated through these words, the monument stands as testimony to a new and more equal attachment between Lincoln and the black American citizen.

Jane Addams and Lincoln as Prudential Hero

In her autobiography, *Twenty Years at Hull House*, Jane Addams reflected about an event that had occurred during the turbulent summer of 1894, when the Pullman strike had turned antagonisms between labor and capital into overt violence and Chicago seemed on the verge of chaos. She wrote:

> I walked the wearisome way from Hull-House to Lincoln Park—for no cars were running regularly at that moment of sympathetic strike—in order to look at and gain magnanimous counsel, if I might, from the marvelous St. Gaudens statue which had but recently been placed at the entrance of the park. Some of Lincoln's immortal words were cut into stone at his feet, and never did a distracted town more sorely need the healing of "with charity toward all" than did Chicago at that moment.[25]

Inspired by this silent consultation, Addams composed a speech, first delivered at the Chicago Women's Club in August 1894, designed to apply Lincoln's sensibilities to the industrial crisis of her time.[26]

But if Lincoln inspired the speech, its structure came from another source. As its title—"A Modern Lear"—suggests, the speech was based upon an analogy between the Pullman strike and Shakespeare's tragedy. That strike, Addams argued, represented a crisis in industrial relations analogous to the crisis in family relations that unfolded in *King Lear*.

> Historically considered, the relation of Lear to his children was archaic and barbaric, holding in it merely the beginnings of a family life, since developed. We may in later years learn to look back upon the industrial relationships in which we are now placed as quite as incomprehensible and selfish, quite as barbaric and undeveloped, as was the family relationship between Lear and his daughters.

In the fully developed analogy, Pullman is to his workers as Lear is to Cordelia. All of the parties in both tragedies are culpable, for all of them act out of narrow self-interest and fail to acknowledge the higher claims of the family bond or social justice. Yet, for Addams, the father figures must assume the greater share of blame. Both Lear and Pullman do not recognize changing circumstances and refuse to accept, in the one case, the growth of a child to maturity, and in the other, the maturation of the workers' movement. Just as Lear cannot understand his daughter's need to assert independence, so Pullman turns a deaf ear to his employees when, as the demands of an industrial age require, they attempt to speak in a collective voice. The indulgent parent and the indulgent employer both respond with anger to what they can only interpret as ingratitude, and their inability to adjust to change becomes the mainspring of the tragedy.

As the speech proceeds, Addams develops an unobtrusive and paradoxical comparison between Pullman and Lincoln. In some respects, Pullman is just like Lincoln. He is a man of moral integrity who advocates and practices the virtues Lincoln had embodied—individualism, self-reliance, thrift, and hard work. These were virtues Pullman has learned in his youth—in the age of Lincoln—and moved by the spirit of philanthropy, Pullman had built a model city in order to instill the same virtues in his workers. Yet, in adhering to the letter of the tradition, Pullman has killed its spirit. Isolated by his individualism and philanthropic self-righteousness, Pullman loses contact with his workers and overlooks the changing circumstances that affect their lives. He neglects the cardinal principle of a social ethic—that values must be adjusted as the society evolves:

> The virtues of one generation are not sufficient for the next. . . . Of the virtues received from our fathers we can afford to lose none. . . . But to preserve those is not enough. A task is laid out upon each generation to enlarge their application, to ennoble their conception, and above all, to apply and adapt them to the peculiar problems presented to it for solution.

Pullman, like Lear, failed to respond to social reality as he enacted the role of a self-indulgent parent, and in this respect, unlike Lincoln, he tried to rule for and not with the people: "Modern philanthropists need to remind themselves of the old definition of greatness: that it consists in the possession of the largest share of common human qualities and experiences, not in the acquirements of peculiarities and excessive virtues. Popular opinion calls him the greatest of Americans who gathered together the largest amount of American experience" and who strove to retain and represent the common people's "thoughts and feelings."

This oblique reference to Lincoln marks his first appearance in the text, and his name does not appear until the conclusion. Nevertheless, Lincoln's presence seems to pervade the text and to establish a basis for Addams's attitude toward the Pullman strike. Ironically, on her view, the moral distance between Lincoln and George Pullman consists precisely in Pullman's adherence to Lincoln's own explicit values. Inflexibly rooting his thought in the past, Pullman subverts tradition, since he treats it as a static code rather than as something that must be recovered and renewed in an interaction between past and present. The mere repetition of Lincoln's words or the unmodified reenactment of his values subverts tradition because those words and values must come to life within the flux of changing circumstances. Implicitly, then, Addams establishes a dialogical relationship with Lincoln, and her rhetorical effort is to reach beyond a literal understanding of his words in order to comprehend the living spirit they represent. This attitude allows her to appropriate Lincoln's voice even as she addresses problems he could not have conceived, and in the process, she can revise some of his values. For Addams, Lincoln's authority is not something to be reproduced, but to be imitated and emulated in new forms.

As she draws to her conclusion, Addams becomes more explicit about the connection between Lincoln's authority and social ethics. Lincoln emerges as the model for a social ethic based upon consent—an ethic that Pullman violated because his model city was run without the consent of "the men who were living in it." By contrast:

> The man who insists upon consent, who moves with the people, is bound to consult the feasible right as well as the absolute right. He is often obliged to attain only Mr. Lincoln's "best possible," and often have the sickening scene of compromising his best convictions. He has to move along with those whom he rules toward a goal that neither he nor they see very dearly till they come to it. He has to discover what the people really want, and then provide "the channels in which the growing moral force of their lives shall flow." What he does attain, however, is not the result of his individual striving, as a solitary mountain climber beyond the sight of the valley multitude, but it is underpinned and upheld by the sentiments and aspirations of many others. Progress has been slower perpendicularly, but incomparably greater because lateral.

A good many things might be said about this passage, for it implies a rather interesting theory of leadership in a democratic society and perhaps even an ethic for democratic political rhetoric. For present purposes, however, I want to focus more narrowly upon the way that passage coherently rounds out Addams's rhetorical performance—to stress the symmetry between her interpretation of Lincoln's authority as a political leader and her appropriation of that authority for her own rhetorical purposes. That authority, for Addams, arises from Lincoln's capacity to restrain his own views of the absolute right and to work within the limitations of the feasible right as he adjusts to the diversity of popular opinion. His leadership, then, is situated within historical circumstance and remains fluid. Likewise, Addams invokes Lincoln not as a fixed referent for establishing social and political values, but as a model of prudential deliberation—his is a voice that must be modulated as it is applied to differing circumstances. Her speech is at one and the same time an interpretation and an application of Lincoln's political and ethical principles, and these principles remain true to their source precisely because they are modified to meet a new situation.

Conclusion

Grady, Douglass, and Addams interpret and invoke Lincoln's authority in strikingly different ways. When taken together, their texts suggest something about the fluidity of Lincoln's influence in late nineteenth-century oratory and about the range of rhetorical and ideological purposes to which it could be accommodated. Nevertheless, one common concern does seem to emerge in all three cases—a concern that reflects the effort to deal with continuity and change in post–Civil War America. All of our rhetors are sensitive to the problem of placing new circumstances within a historical context, and all three use Lincoln as a benchmark for charting the present in relation to the past.

Grady's "The New South" presents Lincoln as fixed point of reference dividing the nation's history into two distinct compartments. The antebellum phase of this history culminates with Lincoln's emergence as an ideal American who represents a blend of "Cavalier" and "Puritan" strands in the national character. The Civil War and Lincoln's martyrdom become the tragic redemption needed to destroy slavery in the South and remove the one obstacle to national unity. In the postbellum phase of this history, Grady tells us of a South reborn in the spirit of capitalism and reorganized into a "perfect democracy." In this sweeping metanarrative, history moves inexorably toward the goal of Anglo-Saxon perfection, and Lincoln becomes a static, uncomplicated symbol of *its* realization. Grady explicitly stresses Lincoln's role as the Great Emancipator and savior of the union, and implicitly he draws upon Lincoln's image as a self-made man. These commonplaces associated with Lincoln become Grady's vehicle for generating a rhetoric of sectional harmony and for deflecting attention from the race problem; Lincoln, in short, functions as a symbol for reconciliation between North and South in the spirit of capitalistic enterprise.

Douglass presents a more complex attitude toward Lincoln and his place in history. For Douglass, the Civil War and emancipation mark a starting point and not a culmination, and Douglass cannot accept the myth of Lincoln as the Great Emancipator. Intent upon achieving the assimilation of African Americans through self-assertion,[27] Douglass confronts a double burden when he memorializes Lincoln. He must express gratitude while he also preserves his own distinctive and independent position as an African American. To meet this burden, Douglass develops a complex, self-reflexive view of history that positions both Lincoln and Douglass himself with an evolving and changing historical perspective. Adopting a broad perspective, Douglass acknowledges that, in the passage of time, his assessment of the man must change. As an abolitionist before and during the war, Douglass had found Lincoln tardy and reticent, but from his current, antebellum position, he recognizes that Lincoln's commitments and priorities were necessary in order to make emancipation possible. This reflective stance allows Douglass to celebrate Lincoln as a symbol of white American history, but leaves space for him to articulate an African American view of that history. The speech becomes a vehicle for placing the African American citizen within the history of polity, since as the speaker positions himself in relation to his subject, he becomes an active agent in shaping and reconfiguring that history. Thus, it aptly serves the purpose of assimilation through self-assertion.

Despite the many differences between Grady and Douglass, the two shared a commitment to the individualistic values of nineteenth-century capitalism, and both celebrated Lincoln as a self-made man who embodied those values. For Jane Addams, however, the tradition of individualism needed modification to meet the new conditions of an industrialized nation. Unlike her more radical contemporaries, however, Addams did not seek to uproot those values and break entirely from tradition. Instead, she sought a means to accommodate older values so that they could enter into a more cooperative and socially sensitive ethic. In "A Modern Lear," Addams uses Lincoln's authority as a bridge between traditional principles and a new social consciousness. Setting aside some of Lincoln's explicit views on ethical and economic issues, she stresses his pragmatism and his commitment to government by consent of the people. Thus, on her interpretation, Lincoln stands as a model of flexible, democratic leadership; his great virtue is his commitment to the "feasible right"—his willingness to bend principles to meet circumstances and attune them to public sentiment. Addams, then, renders Lincoln as the embodiment of a mobile, dynamic tradition, and in this hermeneutic key, his words are to be understood and applied in keeping with the ongoing history of the society.

If this summary indicates that each of our rhetors connects past and present through Lincoln, it also highlights the fundamental differences in their conceptions of history, politics, and ethics. Lincoln is not simply an influence on these orators; he is constructed by them, in part to serve their immediate rhetorical purposes, but also to help them account for and justify their own place in history. In an important sense, then, my study has not discovered much about Lincoln's "influence" in the ordinary sense of the term, since it has led to a consideration of how Lincoln was "used" by people engaged in their own rhetorical business. This use proves complex, since it blends historical understanding and rhetorical performance into a single process. This process, of course, is influenced by prevailing ideologies, and it operates within a common fund of lore about Lincoln. But the lore is not inert, and ideologies do not absolutely dictate how it is applied. Lincoln, in fact, exerts an influence that reflects the way he is constructed, and this construction occurs continuously and variously in the discourse of the period. By isolating specific passages about Lincoln from many texts and recombining them into ideological formations, we may learn something about the spoken and unspoken assumptions that constituted the temper of the time. But if we are to understand how that temper was developed, ordered, and reordered, we need to look at whole utterances and attempt to fathom the complexity of the interpretative and productive processes that enter into the rhetorical act.

NOTES

1. Merrill Peterson's book *Lincoln in American Memory* (New York: Oxford University Press, 1994) offers a detailed and expert account of Lincoln's place in American thought. Peterson's study draws much from oratory and related genres and provides a useful frame for inquiry into Lincoln's influence on oratorical practice. Especially notable is Peterson's identification of five main themes that emerged in the memorialization of Lincoln: "Lincoln as Savior of the Union, Great Emancipator, Man of the People, the First American, and the Self-made Man." These themes, Peterson argues, are "the building blocks of the Lincoln image" (27). The research for this paper, and most of its composition, was completed before publication of Peterson's book, but in what follows, the themes he identifies appear quite clearly. In contrast to Peterson, my interest centers on how Lincoln was interpreted and used in rhetorical production rather than on an understanding of Lincoln's place in American political and social history.
2. Wayne Brockriede, "Trends in the Study of Rhetoric: Toward a Blending of Criticism and Science," in *The Prospect of Rhetoric*, ed. Lloyd Bitzer and Edwin Black (Englewood Cliffs, NJ: Prentice Hall, 1971), 123–39; Samuel Becker, "Rhetorical Studies for the Contemporary World," in Bitzer and Black, *The Prospect of Rhetoric*, 21–43; Roderick Hart, "Contemporary Scholarship in Public Address: A Research Editorial," *Western Journal of Speech Communication* 50 (1986): 283–95; and "Theory-Building and Rhetorical Criticism: An Informal Statement of Opinion," *Central States Speech Journal* 27 (1976): 70–77.
3. Michael McGee, "Text, Context, and the Fragmentation of Contemporary Culture," *Western Journal of Speech Communication* 54 (1990): 274–89; Raymie McKerrow, "Critical Rhetoric: Theory and Praxis," *Communication Monographs* 56 (1989): 91–111; James Klumpp and Thomas Hollihan, "Rhetorical Criticism as Moral Action," *Quarterly Journal of Speech* 74 (1989): 84–96.
4. On this point, see M. M. Bakhtin, "The Problem of Speech Genres," in *Speech Genres and Other Late Essays*, trans. Vern W. McGee (Austin: University of Texas Press, 1986), 78–91.

5. McKerrow, "Critical Rhetoric."
6. Bakhtin, "The Problem of Speech Genres," 89.
7. Michael McGee, "The 'Ideograph': A Link between Rhetoric and Ideology," *Quarterly Journal of Speech* 66 (1980): 1–16. As McGee conceives the "ideograph" it is a condensation symbol which triggers powerful ideological and affective responses within a given culture. His ideographs are abstract terms such as "justice," "equality," and "rule of law," and I am here expanding McGee's notion to include a person, such as Lincoln, who commands great respect and authority and becomes connected intimately with certain ideologies.
8. For Grady's speech, I use the text printed in Ronald Reid, ed., *American Rhetorical Discourse*, 2nd ed. (Prospect Heights, IL: Waveland Press, 1995), 551–59; For Addams's speech, I use the text in Graham R. Taylor, ed., *Satellite Cities* (New York: Appleton, 1915), 68–88. For Douglass's speech, I use the text printed in Douglass's autobiography, *The Life and Times of Frederick Douglass* (New York: Macmillan, 1962), 481–93.
9. The circumstances surrounding this speech are reported in Raymond B. Nixon, *Henry W. Grady: Spokesman of the New South* (New York: Alfred A. Knopf, 1943), 243–44.
10. Charles F. Lindsey, "Henry Woodfin Grady, Orator," *Quarterly Journal of Speech* 6 (1920): 33.
11. Harold Davis, *Henry Grady's New South* (Tuscaloosa: University of Alabama Press, 1990); and E. Culpepper Clark, "Henry Grady's New South: A Rebuttal from Charleston," *Southern Communication Journal* 41 (1976): 346–58.
12. Robert Iltis, "Textual Dynamics of the 'New South,'" *Communication Studies* 43 (1992): 29–41.
13. Ernest Bormann, "Fetching Good out of Evil: A Rhetorical Use of Calamity," *Quarterly Journal of Speech* 63 (1977): 130–39.
14. The status of this quotation from Hill is not dear. There is no record of a speech by him at Tammany Hall in 1866. Hill did address the Young Men's Democratic Union in New York City two years later, and Raymond Nixon (*Henry W. Grady*, 245) reports that this speech contains sentiments close to those expressed in the quotation Grady attributes to Hill, but nowhere does the exact wording appear in the printed version of Hill's speech. In other words, Grady's text is, at least in some part, something that Grady manufactured himself.
15. The quotations from Dawson are taken from Clark, "Henry Grady's New South," 352.

16. Davis, *Henry Grady's New South*, 178.
17. Compare the image of Lincoln that emerges in Grady's speech to the one that appears in, for example, Garry Wills, *Lincoln at Gettysburg: Words That Remade America* (New York: Simon and Schuster, 1992).
18. Lincoln appears prominently in the peroration of the speech. As he concludes, Grady appropriates Lincoln's language, and from his position as a southerner, Grady says that he speaks from "consecrated" ground—ground "hallowed" by the blood shed by both northern and southern soldiers. The words "hallowed" and "consecrated" obviously echo the Gettysburg Address and help in the effort to appeal for sectional unity. The images and strategies at work in the concluding paragraphs of the speech are interesting and complex, but they do not add much of consequence to my interpretation of the speech, and they already have been treated in detail by Iltis, "Textual Dynamics," 37–39. Grady also conjures the ghost of Lincoln as he makes a last plea for northern tolerance: "Will she [New England] make the vision of a restored and happy people, which gathered above the couch of your dying captain, filling his heart with grace, touching his lips with praise and glorifying his path to the grave; will she make this vision in which the last sight of an expiring soul breathed a benediction, a cheat and delusion?" This appeal, while perhaps appropriate at the end of the speech, is hardly subtle and requires little comment.
19. For an account of the event, see Benjamin Quarles, *Frederick Douglass* (Washington, DC: Associated Publishers, 1968), 276.
20. Henry Wilson, *History of the Rise and Fall of the Slave Power in America* (Boston: Houghton, Mifflin, 1872), 1:500; quoted in Waldo Martin, *The Mind of Frederick Douglass* (Chapel Hill: University of North Carolina Press, 1984), 272.
21. The life and career of Douglass is presented in three autobiographic books: *Narrative of the Life of Frederick Douglass, an American Slave* (1845), *My Bondage and My Freedom* (1855), and *Life and Times of Frederick Douglass, Written by Himself* (1881, with a revised edition in 1892). In addition to the biography by Benjamin Quarles, there is now William McFeely, *Frederick Douglass* (New York: Norton, 1991).
22. Martin, *Mind of Frederick Douglass*; Martin's assessment of Douglass's thought is briefly characterized in the preface to the book, ix–x.
23. Martin, *Mind of Frederick Douglass*, 260.
24. Quarles, *Frederick Douglass*, 277.
25. Jane Addams, *Twenty Years at Hull House* (New York: Signet, 1960), 38–39.

26. After delivering the speech in Chicago, Addams also presented it in Boston at the Twentieth Century Club and in other places. She submitted a version of the text for publication in several periodicals, but none would accept it. The speech was first published as an article, entitled "A Modern Lear," *Survey* 29 (November 2, 1912): 131–37. See Alvin Davis, *Jane Addams: An American Heroine* (New York: Oxford University Press, 1973), 113–14. To my knowledge, there is no detailed critique of the work, but Ray Ginger, *Altgeld's America: Chicago from 1892–1905* (New York: Marcus Weiner, 1986), 164–67, offers an interesting, brief commentary and assessment.
27. This characterization of Douglass's objectives comes from W. E. B. DuBois, who describes Douglass's program as "ultimate assimilation through self-assertion." *Souls of Black Folk* (New York: Bantam, 1989), 35.

PART FIVE

Rhetorical Pedagogy

Teaching rhetoric, like rhetorical criticism, was one of Leff's living arts. In the course of his varied career, he taught at Indiana University, the University of California at Davis, and the University of Wisconsin, and he chaired the Departments of Communication at both Northwestern University and the University of Memphis. He mentored countless undergraduate and graduate students at those institutions; he was also an active presence in the lives of students beyond his own university. Leff worked to build an infrastructure for rhetoric's future that could unite students and teachers of rhetoric across the country, even the world. Scarcely a month before his passing, he made a trip to China where he lectured and was developing a student exchange program. He was just beginning his term as president of the Rhetoric Society of America—the day before his death on February 5, 2010, he was at work on its May conference. He was immersed, too, in preparations for hosting the upcoming Southern States Communication Conference in Memphis in April, and teaching his protean seminar on Martin Luther King Jr.

Just as Leff regarded speech in its situated particularity as the "habitation" of rhetoric and the proper focus for rhetorical criticism, he as strongly—though in ways up to now less acknowledged—stressed the primacy of rhetoric's pedagogical orientation. This stress would sometimes assume a jeremiad-like quality, with Leff calling upon his peers to return their sights to the classroom. And yet, as the first essay in this part shows, this call for a return was, ironically, one for innovation and interdisciplinary awakening, too. "Teaching Public Speaking as Composition" starts self-reflexively: tasked with directing his department's basic public speaking course for the first time in twenty years, Leff rushes to "catch up" to how more recent textbooks and syllabi treat the subject. In doing so, he finds a conservatism in approach—the materials and objectives seemed to him to have changed little, if at all, since his time as a graduate student—that is at odds with wholesale transformations in what graduate curriculum in rhetoric had undergone in the meantime. This conservatism in approaches to teaching public speaking contrasts, too, with the "firm imprint" that changes in rhetorical theory had made on the teaching of composition in English departments. What explains the difference? At its core, and for historical reasons that Leff notes in the essay, the task of teaching the basic composition course had managed to maintain its integral connection to the scholarly identity of rhetoricians in English in a way it had not for rhetoricians in speech communication. In proposing that public speaking be taught "as composition," Leff's argument pushes rhetoricians to make what is still widely considered to be a service chore—the education of beginning college students in the art of public speaking—into a practice more intimately connected to the theoretical insights of its advanced scholarship and more esteemed by the field's senior faculty. In "Kenneth Burke in the Classroom," Leff exemplifies the very move he asks his peers to make. Turning to one of the twentieth centuries' most renowned critics, Leff does not simply "apply" Burke to pedagogy; he uses Burke's essay on "The Four Master Tropes" to reveal a close tie between irony and the constitutive paradoxes of rhetoric instruction. Taking Plato's *Phaedrus* as an illustration, Leff notes the tension between the technical, prescriptive rules for effective rhetorical performance and the fluid process that is the life of rhetoric as a socially situated activity and habit of mind. Leff avers that teachers err by opting for one pedagogic fundamentalism or the other—insisting on rigid adherence to rules that may blunt adaptive response, or (what is equally as bad) letting go of the rules and leaving students without guidance. Burkean irony is a middle path that teaches the situated art of teaching conventional rules while violating them to enlarge the perspectives of speakers and audiences.

Again returning to the classroom for orientation, "Theory and Practice in Undergraduate Education" illuminates the career of the theory/practice divide in Western thought from the standpoint of the basic public speaking course. Beginning with a detailed meditation on citations from Ronald Beiner, Michael Billig and Stanley Fish, Leff shows how the ancient opposition between theory and practice is now being challenged or dismantled. Leff notes how such epistemological rethinking always brings renewed interest in rhetoric. But herein lies an irony: "We find ourselves alienated from our own heritage just when it has become respectable." Leff notes how emphasis on abstract theory rather than giving attention to the situated particulars of practice and general principle "pulled [rhetorical precepts] out of their historical context and ordered them in accordance with epistemological constructs alien to their own purposes." In one of his most arresting statements Leff observes: "For the most part, then, what we have called the 'history of rhetorical theory' is actually a history of rhetorical pedagogy, or more accurately, a history of that part of the pedagogy which survives in written form."

Taking that history into the broad scene of debates over the purpose and identity of the liberal arts, "Cultivating the Useless: Rhetoric and Liberal Arts Education in an Age of Consumerism," a lecture Leff gave at the University of Washington in 2000, gives fresh meaning to many of Leff's central themes and is his fullest defense of rhetoric *as* a liberal art. Using Bruce Kimball's *Orators and Philosophers* as his point of departure, Leff reframes a historic debate between two modes of liberal education that have divided the West for 2,400 years. Leff contends that an educational program that would enable students to accommodate difference, appreciate novelty, and pursue common values and the common good—the foundation of traditional oratorical education—would not only benefit students but offer the university itself a coherent educational vision that it currently lacks.

The final piece, "What Is Rhetoric?," is a previously unpublished lecture that Leff delivered before the Canadian Rhetoric Society at the University of Windsor just months prior to his death. Arguing that the question he was assigned ("What is Rhetoric?") is the wrong question, Leff supports his claim by summarizing the historical streams of rhetoric to demonstrate how, in fact, rhetoric never had a single essence to begin with. And yet, amid this multiplicity, he places himself in the Isocratean, Ciceronian, and Quintilianic branch of the larger tradition, and then goes on to explain the difference his pedagogic/civic view makes for understanding rhetoric. He stresses why the views he rejects are not simply mistakes to be banished but resources that give them a valuable dialectical role in illuminating his own view and the views of other schools.

For all its familiarity, the essay strikes the reader with the surprise one experiences on entering a room in which familiar furniture has been artfully rearranged. Not just fixtures but the fixed relations they seemed to embody are cast in an unexpected light by an essay suggesting possibilities for further development as yet unforeseen.

FURTHER READING

"Isocrates, Tradition, and the Rhetorical Version of Civic Education." In *Isocrates and Civic Education*, ed. Takis Poulakos and David Depew (Austin: University of Texas Press, 2005), 11–30.

"Revisionist Historiography and Rhetorical Tradition(s)," with Richard Graff. In *The Viability of the Rhetorical Tradition*, ed. Graff, Arthur Walzer and Janet Atwill (Albany: State University of New York Press, 2005), 235–54.

Teaching Public Speaking as Composition

This article is intended as a call for reform, but I must begin by confessing some uncertainty about what it is that I am attempting to reform. The fact is that I do not have a secure understanding about the state of the art as it is now practiced in teaching public speech. I have not made a survey of the methods now used in classroom instruction, nor undertaken a systematic study of the textbooks, and I have not reviewed the current scholarly literature. What I have to say is based upon personal experience and depends on anecdotes, hunches, and analogies. Thus, I fear that my view of the current situation may be badly distorted, but if it is, this seems the right place to expose the error and stand ready for correction. I can only ask those more familiar with this territory to bear with my speculations long enough to consider the argument I want to develop.

From *Basic Course Annual* 4 (1992): 116–22.

Last year, after an absence of almost twenty years from the basic course, I became the director of the fundamentals public speaking course at Northwestern. My first step, obviously, was to find out what the instructors were doing and to catch up. To my surprise, however, it did not seem that I needed to catch up. The syllabi for the course looked very much as they did in 1970, and the instructors (all of them graduate students) adhered to the same objectives and methods that were in vogue two decades ago. The textbook was more attractive in format and better written than the ones I had used, but it included almost the same set of topics arranged in more or less the same order. A quick glance through a few other currently popular texts indicated that this book was no exception.

Now, everyone knows that teaching is a conservative business and that things change rather slowly at the base of the curriculum. Nevertheless, I was still greatly puzzled by the conservatism displayed in this area. During the past two decades, the academic study of rhetoric has passed through profound and revolutionary changes, and both theory and criticism now appear much different than they once were. In fact, what graduate students in rhetoric are now taught at the top of curriculum bears only a generic resemblance to what I was taught as a graduate student. Yet they still teach public speaking very much as I taught it. Why?

This question becomes all the more puzzling when we look next door and consider recent developments in English departments. In that precinct, the rhetorical revolution has made a firm imprint on the basic composition course. The venerable "product" model and its accompanying typology of assignments (e.g., exposition, narration, argument) have receded and seem on the way to extinction. Attention has shifted to the process of composition; students are no longer expected to make a finished product without some help in understanding the process of writing, and assignments have changed accordingly. New approaches to instruction have evolved: Small group conferences are frequently used so that students can critique their own work as an assignment proceeds; classes are taught in a "studio" or "workshop" environment, where the instructor plays a much less dominant role; and perhaps most dramatically, the writing across the curriculum movement has signaled a fundamental change in attitude about how students can best develop composition skills. At the same time, a variety of different rhetorical theories—expressionist, cognitive, social-epistemic, and others—compete for allegiance, and differing theoretical positions really do have an impact on teaching practices. And the ideological arguments that appear in the scholarly literature have assumed some importance in thinking about pedagogy. In short, the English composition course reflects what is happening in the scholarship, and it presents itself as a scene of intense activity, heated controversy, and constant experimentation. So far as I can tell, nothing of the sort has happened in our domain. How can we account for this difference?

In a recent issue of *College Composition and Communication*, I found an article that suggests at least a partial answer to this question. The article, "Identifying and Teaching Rhetorical Plans for Arrangement" by Joanne M. Podis and Leonard A. Podis,[1] obviously does not concern the issue I have just raised. Nevertheless, the stance of its authors reveals something that, if it is not typical, is at least frequent in the composition journals, and the contrast with our literature offers some interesting grounds for speculation.

Podis and Podis want to improve the teaching of arrangement by bringing into focus patterns and expectations that teachers invoke but often do not consciously recognize. For this purpose, they refer to cognitive theory, which offers a way to identify these patterns and raise them to conscious attention. Significantly, however, they use this theory as a general guide for their inquiry rather than as a source for specific principles. The patterns they discover arise from their direct experience in the classroom. That is, they reflect about the draft papers students have submitted, about their reactions to these drafts, and about the results of the rewriting process. As a result of this self-reflection, they identify eight "plans" for textual organization (e.g., the obvious should precede the remarkable). They make no claim that this taxonomy is absolute or exhaustive, and they are mindful that it proceeds from assumptions built into cognitive theory, which places stress on clarity and ease of understanding. Other theoretical interests, they acknowledge, lead to different attitudes about the value of clarity. Consequently, the essay concludes with a consideration of the limitations of their approach and a thoughtful argument about how their findings might prove useful for those who hold a different theoretical position.

From my perspective, the most striking feature of the article is the implicit but clear sense of the subject being studied. The article is *about* composition, specifically about the teaching of composition in a basic course. The rhetoric of the essay itself hinges on the assumption that the audience has a common fund of experience based in the teaching of composition, and the authors also assume that this experience is more fundamental, more basic to the constitution of the audience, than theories that can be applied to or abstracted from practice. Thus, as they blend theory into practice, the authors can pursue a line of theoretical inquiry without losing sight of the primary subject, and they can sustain an appropriate balance in assessing the practical advantages and limitations of their own perspective.

My impression is that rhetoricians who teach public speaking lack this kind generative connection between theory and practice. We do not seem able to invoke an implicit but vital understanding of our own practice as teachers of a practical art. For this reason, among others, our direct experience as in the classroom fades indistinctly into the background and the pedagogical interest tends to center on theories and methods per se. Typically we consider how abstract methods or theories might determine our course objectives or how we might exploit research findings developed elsewhere for some specific application, or how we might discover methods for assessing our effectiveness as teachers. In other words, our scholarship informs our teaching, insofar as it does, from the outside in, and the teaching experience itself seems theoretically uninteresting. The result is that the fit between theory and practice in teaching becomes rather awkward and artificial.

If this speculation has some merit, we might be able to explain *what* has made our pedagogy theoretically inert—namely a lack of commitment to the subject we teach and a corresponding failure to make an organic connection between this subject and our scholarship. Nevertheless, we still would not have answered my original question, which had to do with *why* our pedagogy seems so far removed from our rhetorical scholarship.

Pursuing the comparison and contrast with rhetoricians in English departments, I would argue that institutional politics are crucially important. For rhetoricians in communication departments the public speaking course rests securely at the base of the curriculum, and it is something that mature scholars escape as they climb the rungs of the career ladder. In our domain, teaching composition or performance, at least in the research institutions, is a task for graduate students and lecturers. Senior faculty teach cultural rhetoric, critical theory, nineteenth-century public address, or some other "content" subject. On the other hand, rhetoricians in English departments normally operate within a more restricted environment, since, insofar as they are actually rhetoricians and not literary scholars going through a probationary ritual, they must retain connection with the teaching of composition and cannot flee the subject. Consequently mature, theoretically sophisticated scholars continue to teach composition, or at any rate, teach advanced courses that are supposed to have a more or less direct bearing on the teaching of composition.

If we are inclined to make invidious comparisons (and academics always are), we might interpret this difference as an advantage to rhetoricians on our side of the fence. After all, the rhetorician in English seems confined, chained to the basics. Yet this same image might also suggest a less comforting assessment. Lacking connection through teaching the basics, we are not so well linked together in community, and given the amorphous nature of rhetoric as a subject, our scholarship runs the risk of scattering, specializing, and losing the texture of shared experience. That this hazard is actual and not just potential becomes clear when we move away from the public speaking course and consider areas that fall within the central focus of rhetorical scholarship.

In the case of rhetorical criticism, for example, the tenuous connection between theory and practice is as much apparent as it is in our pedagogy. Moreover, efforts to remedy this problem (my own included) have been frustrated because of the sprawl of rhetorical practice and the strong temptation to turn from the study of practice toward rather abstract theory. That is, in the absence of a reasonably well defined domain for practice, critics tend to speculate about practice in theoretical terms rather than to focus upon specific instances. Moreover, since the theories and ideologies that enter into such speculation are almost boundless, critics do not often share common ground even in respect to their experience as critics. Theory, thus, becomes detached from grounded arguments about the interpretation of practice. In a recent essay, Thomas Benson indicates a manifestation of this problem in terms of an odd asymmetry that exists in our literature. Rhetorical theorists, Benson observes, "typically do not draw heavily upon historical and critical studies. It is more common for theorists to cite other theorists. . . . Historians and critics are more likely to cite theory or attempt to contribute to theory than theorists are likely to draw on history and criticism."[2]

In other words, the study of practice generated in our own literature seems to have little influence on our theoretical work. This situation raises a substantial problem in respect to the fit between theory and practice, but perhaps more important, it also encourages a dispersion of effort. Since the study of practice does not build on itself, the range of the scholarship remains unlimited, and individual studies become additive rather than cumulative. Unfortunately, we seem to lack the common experience working on the same subjects that seems required for a disciplinary consciousness.

My point, then, is that by concentrating on public speaking as composition, we might serve two purposes at once. We might be able to generate better, more innovative, and more theoretically interesting approaches to teaching the basic course. At the same time, if we viewed the public speaking class as an important arena of rhetorical practice, and not just as a burden imposed upon us, we might discover a shared referent that could help focus and invigorate rhetorical scholarship as a communal enterprise. A serious interest in public speaking as rhetorical composition might provide precisely what we now lack—a practical ground for blending theory and practice—since it offers us a common locus for experiencing the interplay between theory and practice.

I realize that this is not a modest proposal and that it runs counter to a well-established tradition that segregates "skills courses" from what are normally conceived as our higher and more "scholarly" concerns. Thus, to accept it would require some fundamental changes in our thinking and our behavior. We would have to stop thinking of the public speaking course as nothing more than a "service" enterprise; we would have to conceive it as something integral to our mission as teachers and scholars; we would have to engage senior faculty in the course and challenge them to connect what they know about rhetoric to the fundamentals of practice; and we would have to be willing to open the course to new ideas and to experiments that might alter its familiar and comfortable structure. These changes will not be easy to effect, and perhaps the task is impossible. Yet one of the functions of the rhetorician is to turn the impossible into a possibility, and I hope that this essay is a step in just that direction.

NOTES

1. J. A. Podis and L. A. Podis, "Identifying and Teaching Rhetorical Plans for Arrangement," *College Composition and Communication* 41 (1990): 430–42.
2. T. W. Benson, "History, Criticism, and Theory in the Study of American Rhetoric," in *American Rhetoric: Context and Criticism*, ed. T. W. Benson (Carbondale: Southern Illinois University Press, 1989), 16.

REFERENCES

Benson, T. W. "History, Criticism, and Theory in the Study of American Rhetoric." In *American Rhetoric: Context and Criticism*, ed. T. W. Benson (Carbondale: Southern Illinois University Press, 1989).

Podis, J. A., and L. A. Podis. (1990.) "Identifying and Teaching Rhetorical Plans for Arrangement." *College Composition and Communication* 41 (1990): 430–42.

Kenneth Burke in the Classroom

Of all the lessons I have learned from Kenneth Burke, none is more valuable than what he shows and tells about irony. For Burke, irony is not simply a strategy that allows us to say one thing when we mean something else. Instead, irony becomes a point of coalescence between strategy and substance—a way of talking and thinking that simultaneously constructs, engages, and alters our encounters in the social world. Among other things, Burkean irony suggests a way for us to teach rhetoric rhetorically, and that is the issue I want to explore in this paper.

To begin, we need to appreciate how Burke attempts to instruct us as we read his work. He does not simply explicate a conception of irony, but he uses the concept as he explains it—that is, the treatment of irony is

Previously unpublished. Delivered in 1993 at the Western Speech Communication Association Convention, Albuquerque, New Mexico.

itself ironic. This interplay between "substantive" inquiry and rhetorical strategy emerges rather clearly in his essay "Four Master Tropes," where irony both directs and synthesizes the movement of his argument.

On one level, Burke invites us to read the essay as a conventional exercise in theoretical argument. He starts with a thesis: his concern is to demonstrate that the master tropes refer not just to purely figurative uses of language, but that they play a role "in the discovery and description of the 'the truth.'"[1] Each of the master tropes is then redefined in terms of its more "realistic" or "literal" application. Metaphor becomes "perspective," and as such provides the ground for understanding the reality of any "character," where character is used as a general term for understanding any distinct thing, pattern, situation, person, object, etc. Metonymy is equated with reduction, for it allows us to understand the character of something belonging to a higher or more complex level being in terms of a lower or less complex order of being—most notably by translating the intangible into language that applies to our experience with the tangible. Synecdoche functions as representation where a part can "stand for" the whole of a character, or the whole for a part, and where the part-whole representation is convertible. (That is, where the identity between part and whole works equally well in either direction.) Finally, irony involves an orchestration of all other terms and characters such that their interaction with one another produces "a *development* that uses all the terms."[2] In other words, irony manages and synthesizes the other terms used to describe reality.

Burke treats each of these redefined tropes separately and explains how each functions as a strategy for naming and understanding "literal" reality. At the same time, however, he consistently emphasizes that his terms overlap and interact with one another, suggesting that they operate in an ironic relationship. Moreover, the common character of all the terms seems to arise out of an ironic redescription. Where we normally think of the poetic strategies as wholly distinct from a literal understanding of reality, Burke renames things so that the literal reality of human understanding is itself a product of poetic strategies. Thus, the theoretical and analytic argument of the essay is subsumed within a pattern of dramatic/dialectic action, where terms become characters, and these characters interact in a cooperative competition for the naming of the real.

Reread in this dramatistic key, the essay has two central actors—scientific realism and poetic realism. Scientific realism, the villain of the piece, has a character formed by its proclivity to chart reality through metonymic reductions. The scientific approach to human relations assumes that we can locate their substance in terms of models drawn from a lower order of being (for example, animal behavior). This strategy, often adopted unwittingly, ignores the way that motives and interests inform the substance of the human condition and reduces all human action to naturalistic correlations. Thus, scientific realism traffics in mere correlations and mistakes statistical representations for a substantive representation of human reality. Poetic realism, the hero of piece, is not innocent of reductionism, for it too must simplify the human world if it is to represent it. But poetry does not end in reduction, for, although the poet, like the scientist, must reduce the spiritual to the physical in order to produce a work of art, the poet would not have the process end in a one-way reduction. Instead, poet makes the work so as to lead the reader from a tangible experience to an understanding of something that is less tangible and more spiritual. In other words, the character of poetic realism is synecdochic, since it entails the fluid movement between the representation of part and whole, between, for example, the concrete representation of an emotional experience and the nature of emotion itself. Poetic realism, moreover, locates its perspective in the distinctively human medium of language, and it produces models that embody the essential motives conveyed in human speech. Poetic strategies, then, incorporate the metonymic strategies of science, but expand and supplement them in the effort to achieve a more substantive encounter with human relations.

The entrance of irony into the essay effects a peripety in its dramatic form. Just as the strategies of poetic subsume the strategies of scientific realism, so does irony now subsume the poetic perspective. But this second shift is more significant than the first, since it elevates the issue to a new level. Metaphor, metonymy, and synecdoche deal with perspective, but irony—in classical terms a figure of thought rather than of speech—offers a perspective on perspectives, a master term for the coordination of perspectives, since irony produces a development which uses all the terms. This progression, of course, enacts Burke's concept of irony, for even as he defines it, the concept functions to illustrate his definition within the plot line of the essay. Moreover, this ironic perspective on perspectives leads us to conclude that no one perspective is precisely right or precisely wrong. Rather, through a process of dialectical mortification, all the competing perspectives are absorbed into the body of a larger development.

Finally, Burkean irony ironically perfects this view of perspectivism by inoculating us against perfection. The other tropes open new perspectives, and as irony gathers them together, it yields a maximum proliferation of perspectives within an ordered scheme. In rounding out this development, irony discounts any single angle of vision and keeps us in contact with the necessarily plural and relative character of the substance of human relations. Blind use of any single perspective encourages the perfection of that perspective until it reduces everything into its own abstract economy. Irony counteracts this reductive impulse by sustaining controversy and dramatic conflict. As it tests perspectives against other partially true perspectives, it recalls us to a broader context of motives and reminds us that substance cannot be reduced to form. Substance can only come into being through the enactment of form, and this point is itself demonstrated through Burke's progression from science to poetic to irony—a progression that is strategically motivated and open to ironic subversion. Irony, then, represents a mobile term of completion that allows us to take a stand by ordering the voices in controversy while it leaves the controversy open to on-going developments and to other voices.

Burke, then, offers a rhetorical justification of rhetoric as a substantive activity, and his essay instructs us as much by what it does as by what it says. This effort to hold form and content in solution and to connect what we say with how we say it has obvious implications for teachers of rhetoric. Let me hasten to say, however, that I am not advocating an effort to imitate Burke in our classrooms. Few of us could succeed in such an effort, and if we did, the likely result would be massive confusion among our students. What I want to suggest is a less radical, but still important and difficult alteration in our attitude toward the subjects we teach. We should, I think, become more sensitive to rhetoric as a medium that ironically seeks to resolve particular controversies for practical purposes while it sustains the on-going process of controversy. In the few minutes, I have remaining, I want to indicate how this attitude might affect the way we teach two traditional subject areas in our discipline: the history of rhetoric and public speaking.

The history of rhetoric has been and still largely remains a subject dominated by the study of canonical texts (i.e. Plato, Aristotle, Cicero, etc.). Traditionally, we have approached these texts in order to extract doctrine from them and to set them in an abstracted schematic of theoretical positions. The objective of this enterprise is to locate the possibilities of rhetorical theory according to fixed references in the tradition. In the process, we are liable to forget that these texts do not fix themselves in a tradition, but that they are placed and valued according to an interpretative process that evolves through a history of controversy.

Consider, for example, Plato's *Phaedrus*, a pivotal text in most accounts of the history of rhetoric and one that has undergone several generations of re-interpretation. A century ago, scholars generally agreed that this was a strangely divided text, split between a philosophical section concerning love and the soul and a rather mundane, technical section dealing with rhetoric. A later generation argued that the text was in fact unified in an effort to prescribe a genuine or philosophical rhetoric. More recent scholars have viewed the *Phaedrus* as work that achieves unity through its rhetorical form which ends in an ironic deconstruction of the rhetorical doctrine it enunciates. And even more recently, we find the work interpreted as an effort to maintain a productive tension between the technical and philosophical dimensions of rhetoric.

What, then, is the proper theoretical placement of the *Phaedrus*? The answer to that question is hardly fixed, and the various answers reflect both internal and external developments that influence those doing the interpretative work. Thus, in respect to internal developments, the stress on the unity of the *Phaedrus* is, in some large measure, the result of an earlier view of its disunity. And in respect to external influences, it is clear that all the various interpretations reflect changing views about philosophy, rhetoric, and their relationship to one another that characterize the history of the academic community. Consequently, I believe we should make clear to our students, and to ourselves, that the meaning of this work is the product of controversy, and that to understand the text we need to encounter not just its "doctrine," but the rhetorical form in which it is articulated and the successive voices that influence our judgment about what that form is and how we ought to determine its significance. Our reading of the text, in other words, is a parliamentary rather than an isolated, disinterested enterprise.

One of the reasons that interpretation of the *Phaedrus* has proven so controversial is that it locates a problem central to rhetoric as an academic subject. The end of rhetoric is adaptive and mobile, for the function of rhetorical performance is to encompass specific situations and circumstances. Yet, when we teach public speaking, we resort to technical precepts—general principles that establish standards for competent performance. There exists, then, a tension between the open-ended purposes of the activity and the static body of doctrine that informs the lore used to teach it. In the face of this problem, some teachers attempt to purify their effort to avoid the dilemma. The more conventional approach is to stress the technical rules and hold students to them. This makes it possible to control the academic exercise and insure that students really learn something. But it may leave them so dependent on a fixed, artificial routine that they lose all rhetorical sensitivity. The unconventional approach is to ignore precepts and let the students experiment. This strategy may help them realize the need for adaptability and creative response, but it may leave them without the skills necessary to encompass situations—and rhetorical situations are always social and thus always hedged by conventional expectations.

Burkean irony, I believe, offers a better solution—one that avoids the either/or dilemma presented by a rigid distinction between preceptive order and performative creativity. Even though the requirements of performance have priority over preceptive knowledge, we can still employ the precepts so long as we ironically discount them. We can teach them to students, so that they learn something about conventional expectations, and then we can teach them how to violate the precepts to alter or enlarge those expectations. The living purposes of the art can absorb the static rules because we can use the fixed referent as the ground for encountering the constantly shifting occasions and motives that enter into rhetorical discourse.

In short, public speaking is a necessarily ironic activity, for it thrusts the speaker into the plural space of the public world, and if we are to be our worthy of the subject, we need to find an ironic way to teach it.

NOTES

1. Kenneth Burke, *A Grammar of Motives* (Berkeley: University of California Press, 1945), 503.
2. Burke, *A Grammar of Motives*, 512.

Theory and Practice in Undergraduate Education

The question posed for this panel is both new and old. In the context of our own lives and careers, it is something new to question the nature and role of theory in our work. As Jo Sprague said, in her letter attempting to orient today's speakers, not so long ago we were quite confident that we knew what theory was and how to use it as teachers. Theory, on this view, was something that stood apart from and above practice. It consisted in a set of hierarchically ordered abstract propositions (i.e., laws or rules) that were capable of explaining practice. Theory was the stable and static goal which we aimed to achieve in our research, and the better our theory, the better our teaching. That is, we assumed we could improve the practice of communication only by transcending the rough ground where practice occurs.

Previously unpublished. Delivered in 1994 at the Speech Communication Association convention, New Orleans, Louisiana.

Of course, not everyone accepted this view, but the dissenters were relatively few and mainly disreputable—an odd assortment of lost souls who thought that teaching speech was actually a practical and honorable business and of antiquarians whose noses remained affixed to the texts of Webster or Cicero. For most of us, the priority of theory was an unquestioned premise, bolstered by the prevailing fashions in the academy, and ingrained so deeply that no other alternative seemed respectable.

Fashions, however, change, and during the past two decades, the once fixed relationship between theory and practice has been reconsidered. This trend is evident throughout the academy, in the humanities, the social sciences, and even in the physical sciences, but the main lines of development are fairly consistent across these disciplinary boundaries. The reversal of the older priorities almost always takes one of two basic forms—a weaker or a stronger claim about how practice resists theory. The more restrained version of this revision holds that theory has its limits, since general principles cannot encompass important aspects of human conduct.

Thus, in *Political Judgment*, the political theorist Ronald Beiner argues that questions of judgment

> can only be resolved in the concrete, when confronted by particulars. . . . Theory itself cannot displace judgment. If theory alone could answer the question, judgment would be rendered superfluous, and political man deprived of that quality of responsibility which we have argued is inalienable. The study of ethics . . . does not tell one what to do or furnish maxims for conduct; rather it forms the kind of person one is—making one, for instance, more reflective, more discriminating, more attentive—and it is only in this indirect way that it has an influence on practice.[1]

The stronger version debunks theory altogether, regarding it only as a form of practice disguised in arcane language. Thus, the literary theorist (or more properly antitheorist) Stanley Fish maintains in *Doing What Comes Naturally*:

> Theory has no consequences. . . . Theory . . . is a name for a set of principles or rules or procedures that is attached to . . . no particular field

> of activity, but is of sufficient generality to be thought of as a constraint on (and an explanation of) all fields of activity. Since there are no such principles—no constraints that are more than the content of a practice from which they are indistinguishable—there can be no such thing as theory, and something that does not exist cannot have consequences . . . it may be the case that in a particular discipline engaging in theory-talk and asserting its impossible claims are efficacious and even obligatory strategies, and in that discipline the presence of "theory" will certainly have consequences, but they will be no different from, or more predictable than, the consequences of any form of talk that has acquired cachet and presence. In short, when theory has consequences, they will be rhetorical, not theoretical.[2]

Beiner, though less directly and dramatically, also argues that the dethronement of theory encourages attention to rhetoric. Aristotelian rhetoric, Beiner notes, was designed to deal with deliberation about particulars in circumstances where no special theory or method can offer guidance. In this sense, rhetoric operates within the same conceptual space as political and ethical judgment; rhetoric engages contingent particulars, and since the contingencies are infinite, it is an activity that cannot be reduced to fixed theoretical principles. Another moderate revisionist, Michael Billig, a social psychologist, makes much the same point in *Arguing and Thinking* as he draws a lesson from Quintilian:

> The rules of rhetoric do not lack the certainty required by Plato because of the insufficiencies of the rhetorical theorists themselves. Quintilian was arguing that the rules must necessarily be provisional. It is the novelty of each moment which produces uncertainty, and thereby the need for hunches or judgment. . . . We can call these arguments against the possibility of definite rules Quintilian's Principle of Uncertainty. The principle asserts that we can never capture the infinite variety of human affairs in a finite system of psychological laws. At any moment the finite laws are likely to be embarrassed by unforeseen and unforeseeable events.[3]

I have quoted Beiner, Fish, and Billig at length partially because I want to indicate something of the texture of contemporary efforts to weaken or dismantle the theory/practice dichotomy. But obviously I have also selected these quotations in order to promote my own agenda (i.e., I have my own rhetorical purpose here), which is to suggest the close connection between traditional rhetoric and the current antiepistemological turn. This selection, of course, needs to be noted and emphasized, because revisionism does not always lead to the rediscovery of rhetoric. Nevertheless, the pattern found in Beiner, Fish, and Billig is not unusual, and in both its weaker and stronger forms, the tendency to stress practice over theory often encourages a revival of interest in rhetoric.

For those of us in speech communication this development is rather ironic. Insecurely located at the tail of the academic kite, we hang on as the latest breeze of fashion blows us back toward the place we have tried to escape—back to the domain of practice and perhaps back to the old rhetorics that we once relegated to antiquarians. Twenty years ago we thought we were finally moving with the prevailing wind—we were distancing ourselves smartly from the basic course and talking theory just like the rest of the tribes of the academy. But now as the wind has shifted, we find ourselves alienated from our own heritage just when it has become respectable.

In fact, the premodern rhetorical tradition, if examined with care, offers much that can help in grappling with the theory/practice issue. Unfortunately, however, our own disciplinary history involved a rewriting of that tradition in the idiom of modern epistemology and thus blinded us to its nuances. Originally, speech teachers appropriated the classical texts for pedagogical purposes—the precepts found in these works were applied to the contemporary classroom. Often this appropriation was rather sterile and mechanical, and it drew criticism for this reason. But the main objection was that such concentration on precepts distracted attention from theoretical issues. And beginning with Otis Walter's "On Views of Rhetoric, Whether Progressive or Conservative," scholars began to rewrite the history of rhetoric in terms of the philosophic "starting points" or "systems" that supposedly rested at the base of all rhetorics.[4] Given the existing intellectual climate, this effort led to an epistemological reduction of the tradition. Rhetorical treatises were to be read for their (usually latent) connection with a particular theory of knowledge. This maneuver gave these works a "theoretical" value and thus vindicated study of them from a modern perspective. But it was also a perspective that pulled them out of their historical context and ordered them in accordance with epistemological constructs alien to their own purposes.

In fact, epistemology is almost never an issue of much concern in the pre-Cartesian rhetorical tradition. Most works in this tradition are textbooks designed for students, and they typically consist of precepts ordered in relation to the divisions and subdivisions of the art. For the most part, then, what we have called the "history of rhetorical theory" is actually a history of rhetorical pedagogy, or more accurately, a history of that part of the pedagogy which survives in written form. In some instances, authors express concern about which precepts should be included, what they should be named, and where they should be placed. But this concern is hardly theoretical, and where the authors reflect on their task, they almost always indicate that the preceptive lore is an ancilla to practice; it is not something to be constructed for its own sake, but to provide what Nancy Struever calls an armamentarium for practical use. These rhetorical treatises, then, are more like tool kits than theoretical works. The classical system of rhetoric is not a "theory" of rhetoric—at least not in the modern sense of the term.

The tradition also includes other kinds of works—such as Aristotle's *Rhetoric*, Cicero's *De oratore* and *Orator*, and Quintilian's *Institutes*—that treat broader, more philosophical issues concerning rhetoric. But these sources generally are not much concerned about a "theory" of rhetoric per se. The one possible exception, of course, is Aristotle's *Rhetoric*, and it is just for that reason that modern (i.e., nineteenth- and early twentieth-century) scholars attached themselves to the *Rhetoric* and made it represent the whole of the tradition. In fact, however, the *Rhetoric* is an anomaly in the premodern history of the art, and it is far less prominent than the works of Cicero, Quintilian, or Hermogenes. Moreover, even in Aristotle, the "theoretical" status of rhetoric is unclear, since notions of practice and production also enter into his conception of the art. Late nineteenth- and early twentieth-century scholars glossed these difficulties and offered interpretations of Aristotle that forced his *Rhetoric* into the then dominant model of a proper theory. This reduction was followed by a second and even more dubious reduction, when, contrary to the historical evidence, this sanitized version of Aristotle's "theory" was used to represent the entire classical tradition.

If we remove the blinders imposed by this double reduction, a more complex view of the tradition emerges, and we can find much that speaks to us powerfully as teachers of communication, for it is a tradition grounded in the enduring practical problems of our profession. From this perspective, our "new" problem of engaging the theory/practice issue is really an old problem—one that Cicero and Quintilian, for example, address with energy and intelligence.

In its older variant, the issue is not the tension between theory and practice, since the modern theoretical psychosis had not yet developed. Rather the problem centers upon the related tension between "art," on the one side, and performance or practice on the other. Relatively early in the history of classical civilization, rhetoric had been codified as an art—that is, as a systematized body of principles that could be taught. Such principles proved useful for students and teachers, but, in themselves, they could not impart rhetorical competence, since the precepts are necessarily general, whereas the requirements of practice and performance are necessarily particular. That is, the end of the educational process is not to impart knowledge about art, but to development the flexible competence needed to respond to actual situations, and because these situations are infinitely various, no general principles (i.e., no theory) can teach us how to encompass them.

As a consequence, the relationship between general principles and practice cannot be fixed, and the principles cannot become autonomous. As Quintilian says at the end of his technical analysis of topical invention, whoever has no more than a knowledge of topical principles possesses a "dumb science" (*mutam scientiam*). Rhetoric as performative art always has priority over rhetoric as a preceptive, or "theoretical," art, since rhetoric is not a static object of study but a dynamic activity. In order to teach students to master the activity, general principles are useful, but only if the study of them does not become a fetish. Thus, the classical program of rhetorical education involves much more than simply learning a list of precepts; it entails exercises that require students to embody the principles in their own writing and speaking, and it entails the study of model discourses that allow students to recognize how the principles are embodied in the discourse of others. These and other measures are designed to encourage a fluid interaction between precept and practice in which the precepts take on life only as they come into contact with and are altered by practices. And when approached in this spirit, the teaching of rhetoric itself becomes an activity in which the dichotomy between art and performance, or between theory and practice, simply dissolves.

This fluid, situational conception of the relationship between principles and particulars is a special characteristic of the rhetorical tradition, and it reflects the pedagogical orientation of the discipline; to teach rhetoric is to teach a practice, and hence rhetoricians who take their work seriously must harness their preceptive lore so that it does not outrun the concrete demands of practice. Scholars outside the discipline, such as Billig and Beiner, have identified this feature of the tradition and used it as inspiration and support in their efforts to overcome the brittle modern distinction between theory and practice. Scholars in our discipline, ironically, have been slow to recognize this point and have had to be told by outsiders that their subject, precisely because of its intimate connection with practice and performance, offers a unique and important perspective on a crucial issue.

Our blindness is a direct result of the attempt to "modernize" communication and reform it in accordance with the once dominant epistemological model. As we attempted to escape from our inescapable connection with practice and performance, we lost serious interest in the "basic courses" where we taught "skills." We relegated these courses to graduate students or junior faculty; we regarded them as an embarrassment we had to endure or disguise and often restructured them as lecture courses where mute students could hear about our theories. And once the lure of theory caught hold, we could hardly understand our own disciplinary history, and so we changed our history, reducing it to its epistemological foundations. This was a history based on thumbnail sketches of how rhetorics fit within prefabricated philosophical niches; it was a history that tried to forget its subject, and it succeeded so well that only external forces could begin to deprogram our own thinking and open us to the more fluid and practical conception of theory that was always already there. Had we stuck to our business of teaching communication as a practical art, we might have understood the legacy we inherited from past teachers of art, and we might have led the way in correcting the theoretical psychosis of the modern academy. We still have much to contribute, I believe, for we actually teach rhetoric and communication, and that experience should give us special insight to the process others have noted. But to do so we need to heed a point that Jo Sprague has made repeatedly—by marginalizing our basic courses, we do not simply impoverish these courses, we also do a disservice to our research. In a practical discipline, research does not so much improve teaching (though surely it does), as experience in and reflection about teaching proves essential to research that matters.

NOTES

1. Ronald Beiner, *Political Judgment* (London: Methuen, 1983), 144.
2. Stanley Fish, *Doing What Comes Naturally: Change, Rhetoric and the Practice of Theory in Literary and Legal Studies* (Durham, NC: Duke University Press, 1989), 14.
3. Michael Billig, *Arguing and Thinking: A Rhetorical Approach to Social Psychology* (Cambridge: Cambridge University Press, 1987), 92.
4. Otis Walter, "On Views of Rhetoric, Whether Conservative or Progressive," *Quarterly Journal of Speech* 49 (December 1963): 367–82.

Cultivating the Useless: Rhetoric and Liberal Arts Education in an Age of Consumerism

Liberal arts education is education to virtue. It aims to be more than an instrument for enhancing the material prospects of students. It has less tangible ends, such as making students better citizens or better, more critical thinkers. And liberal education claims intrinsic merit; what it provides students is not meant to be simply useful but good in itself.

This broad definition leaves ample room for variation and diversity, but the two main possibilities are indicated by the word "liberal," and as that term shifts in meaning so also does the conception of the purpose and nature of the liberal education. The root of liberal is the Latin *liber* (free), and to be free may mean either free to do something or to be free from something. In the first or positive sense, the liberal arts prescribe the best

Previously unpublished. Invited lecture, delivered in 2000 at the University of Washington, Seattle.

education for those who have the freedom to cultivate their minds. Liberal education, in this sense, develops the potential of people who have leisure, who are enslaved neither by other people nor by economic circumstance and who seek to exercise leadership within a community. The virtues at stake here are connected with social arrangements. In the other or negative sense, the liberal arts prescribe the best education for those who seek freedom from bias, or prejudice, or other distortions that interfere with the ability to know things as they really are. Here the function of liberal education is to liberate the mind, to enable the pursuit of knowledge, and the virtues at stake are intellectual.

In his important book *Orators and Philosophers: A History of the Idea of Liberal Education*, Bruce Kimball calls the first of these options the orator's version of liberal education, and he calls the second the philosopher's version.[1] Both can be traced back to classical authority and then followed forward through the history of our culture. The oratorical track begins with Isocrates in the fourth century BC, moves forward to Cicero, who provides its most influential formulation, and then to Quintilian, and from there to the Renaissance humanists and their successors. The philosophical line also traces back to classical Athens, where Plato and Aristotle begin a tradition that reasserts itself in medieval scholasticism, in Enlightenment thought, and most recently in the modern research university. These two perspectives were born in competition with one another and have remained competitive through most of their twenty-four-hundred-year history. The competition, however, has not always been equal, and at various times one alternative has asserted itself so powerfully that the other has been virtually banished from the academy. Yet the displaced perspective has always ultimately taken its revenge—scholasticism's displacement of the older rhetorical tradition, for example, was itself displaced by the revived Ciceronianism of the Renaissance humanists, only to have the Cartesian revolution overturn the humanist program. So this is a complex history, and it is hazardous to reduce it to thumbnail descriptions. Nevertheless, from our current vantage, three points seem reasonably clear and undoubtedly relevant to our interests. (1) If we view the whole stretch of this history, it is the orator's version that has been most prominent. (2) But over the past century, coincident with the rise of scientific education and the research university, the orator's version has been driven so far into the background that this history has almost disappeared from sight. (3) During the past two decades, however, there has been a significant effort not just to recover memory of the orator's version but to invoke it as a viable alternative to the now dominant variant of the philosophical perspective. Kimball's book, published in 1986, is one sign of this development.

I want to offer my own contribution to this recovery of the rhetorical version of liberal arts education. Specifically, I want to concentrate on an issue Earl F. Cheit calls "one of oldest and most persistent problems in education," and that is the relationship between the useful and the liberal arts.[2] As my general definition of liberal education indicates, none of its incarnations can find justification in sheer utility, in the material benefits or consequences associated with the program. Thus, liberal and useful must always be distinguished in some sense, and the useful subordinated to or subsumed within the liberal. But this alignment can be effected in several ways, and the oratorical and philosophical versions of liberal arts education tend toward significantly different resolutions of this issue. As I hope to demonstrate, the social orientation of the orator's perspective generally tends toward a more fluid relationship between the useful and the liberal than does the intellectual orientation of the philosopher's perspective. Moreover, this characteristic difference has become heightened and exaggerated because of special characteristics that mark the contemporary variant of the philosophical perspective (the "liberal-free" variant, to use Kimball's term).

The philosophical ideal of education has always tended to isolate the individual thinker. It is, after all, an ideal connected with the contemplative life, and it is contrasted with the busy sociality of the orator's active life. Contemplation is a private affair, and the pursuit of knowledge of things as they really are invites skepticism about how things are ordinarily conceived. Thus, the liberation of the philosophic mind entails cultivation of attitudes and acquisition of mental disciplines that set the philosopher apart from, and sometimes even in Socratic tension with, the practical business of the community. Historically, however, powerful counterforces worked against the perfection of the isolated, free-thinking mind as an general cultural or educational ideal. Plato, for example, founded the Academy, a philosophical school that offered a place for the free exercise of the intellect, but it was only one of many options available in the world of Greek education.

Furthermore, the school persisted as an intellectual tradition rather than a bureaucratic institution, and hence its doctrine kept changing as successive generations of free-thinkers continued to do their free-thinking business. Aquinas, to cite another prominent champion of this position, lived at time lived when the European university provided the means of maintaining uniform curricula on an international scale and of preserving a considerable degree of consistency in philosophical doctrine over time. But the scholastic tendency toward pure rationality was hedged by the theological dogma and the institutional realities of the church.

In the late nineteenth century, when the research university was born in America, conditions permitted, in fact encouraged, a steeper ascent toward intellectual purity. The strong individualism inscribed in the dominant political ideology, the rationalism and skepticism characteristic of the scientific ethos, and the specialization sponsored by both science and the industrializing economy all contributed to a very strong form of the philosophical perspective on education. Thus, liberal studies came to be identified with the advancement of knowledge undertaken for its own sake. The liberal arts were, in the words of Harvard president Charles Eliot, those which were "pursued for truth's sake," and G. S. Hall added that research was the "highest vocation of man."[3] Its promotion required the student to become a tough-minded, skeptical individualist, liberated from the shackles of a priori prejudice and capable of contemplating the higher truths that eluded minds too much contaminated by practical interest.

I think it important to stress the affinity between these views about liberal education and the conception of liberal individualism that arose at about the same time. The research university brought with it a specialized and departmentalized conception of education that broke sharply with the older rhetorical/literary program. The older system offered a set curriculum for students that reflected traditional values; certain subjects and texts were selected and studied by all because they were thought to have substantive, ethical value; they represented the virtues stored within communal memory and which, when assimilated by the students, would make them better citizens. By contrast, the new program accepted all knowledge as the province of the university, and it allowed students to elect different subjects and to pursue different major concentrations. Eliot found this system not only conducive to scientific education but also morally uplifting: "The permanence of the elective system is assured by the demonstrated fact that it provides on a large scale an invaluable addition to human freedom, and provides this precious freedom for the most highly trained, and therefore the most productive and influential persons."[4]

Eliot's judgment rests upon the conviction that deliverance from "terror or oppression," or the advancement "of some sort of freedom," constitutes almost the only durable achievement of the human race. This point, of course, generalizes well beyond the elective system and establishes an ideological ground for defining and defending the liberal-free program of the research university. The university commits itself to expanding the domain of knowledge, which is a self-justifying activity, and the students, unconfounded by tradition or authority, are free to choose whatever useless subjects they elect to take and by studying them become critically rational and autonomous individuals. By the middle of the twentieth century, this position had become so well established that it spread from the research universities to the liberal arts colleges, and coupled with historical amnesia, it led to an almost complete identification between liberal education and the Enlightenment system of values. Hence, in 1960, the president of Sarah Lawrence (Harold Taylor) could say:

> Liberal education is the intellectual and cultural instrument through which the basic ideas of liberalism are transmitted and developed. . . . The central idea of liberal education is therefore the idea of individualism and individual freedom. . . . It has its origin in the Western world, in political and social changes which began in the seventeenth century and with the discovery of a new universe and a new world.[5]

This ideal of freedom, however, did not always fit comfortably within the institutional realities of the educational system. The departmentalization of knowledge threatened to fragment the educational experience, for if students were and ought to be free to elect courses, what common elements could hold the curriculum together? This problem was noted as early as 1896, when University of Chicago president William Rainey Harper promised that "the work of the student in the future will not be cut off into departments; on the contrary, it will be the study of problems which will lead him into and through many departments of study. The need for correlation does not receive from most of us the appreciation it deserves."[6] This language is somewhat remote from us, but the problem is painfully familiar, and its persistence vividly testifies to the difficulty of controlling the centrifugal tendency of the research university.

Nor is the root cause of the problem difficult to locate. If the end of the university is to pursue knowledge for its own sake, it is very unclear how to determine that some branches of knowledge are more basic than others. A search for truth is a search for truth, and one line of inquiry seems to provide opportunity for mental discipline just as well any other. Justifying core subjects on scientific and not arbitrary grounds seems virtually impossible. Thus, Abraham Flexner, writing about the general education curriculum just after the turn of the century, concludes that "every item is a separate scrap; the whole is a patchwork, suggesting in its method of composition, a political platform rather than a rational educational program."[7] Ironically, then, the advent of specialization, a hallmark of the new rationality, renders general education necessary, but the content of general education has to be determined by the far less than rational mechanisms of politics, not by any principle indigenous to the liberal-free program. Moreover, the inability to identify core subjects raises a disturbing question about the purposes of the whole enterprise. Aside from preparing students to do research in specialized fields, what is the use of higher education? As Charles Wegener argues, the only goal seems "to be offered by a 'specialty' or a 'profession.' Having in effect redefined and expanded the intellectual world in its institutional embodiment, the founders of 'the university' had, it would appear, deprived it of any purposeful structure."[8]

The circularity of this system also helped to rigidify the supposed difference between the liberal and the practical arts. Unlike the literary/rhetorical program that proceeded it, the strong version of the philosophical position did not and could not regard an art as liberal because of its cultural or ethical significance. There was only one internally consistent standard for including an art within the circle of liberal studies, and that was its absence of any practical application. So the liberal arts were defined negatively; they were the arts that had no marketplace value, or were not professional or vocational, or had no end beyond their self-contained academic limits. Kimball has documented the appearance of this rigid dichotomy as early as the 1890s, has charted its persistence through the twentieth century, and concludes that it is impossible to overcome it within the logic of the liberal-free worldview.

In short, the version of liberal arts education that we have inherited from the rise of the research university and to which we still largely adhere leaves us with only a tautology to defend the liberal arts. The goal of the university is the pursuit of knowledge for its own sake, and therefore the liberal arts are those that are studied for their own sake and have no practical value, and we can justify the intangible value of the arts thus conceived because our own definition of the goal justifies this judgment. Despite the question-begging flaw in this formulation, it proved sufficient so long as the university remained connected with scientific progress and science remained a god-term in our culture. But things have changed recently and changed dramatically.

Science no longer commands the unqualified respect that it once did. As Joseph Featherstone observes, "The ideal of science detached from any obligations to human community no longer has an entirely glorious sound to it."[9] The bottom line had begun to loom larger than the scientific ideal, and universities are being called to accountability. Richard Lanham asserts that the liberal arts have long operated on the "'General Motors rule' ('What's good for General Motors is good for the country')."[10] What's good for the arts must be good for the country. To doubt this only proves that you are Philistine." But fear of being called a Philistine no longer deters legislators and trustees who want explanations about what they are getting for the huge investment in higher education. And, worse yet, students have begun to discover that they are consumers. Instead of being content to shut up and pursue truth, they are demanding a return on the money they spend for their educations, and although most professors feel something ranging from anxiety to outrage when confronted with this demand, we don't really have an adequate counterargument. The old tautology won't work against the persistent student customer.

So when Jane Consumer comes to see Dean Liberal-Free, the dialogue quickly runs the dean into self-contradiction:

> JANE: Look here I am spending a lot of money, and I want practical results, not a lot of courses that teach useless subjects.

DEAN: Tut, tut. You don't understand that learning useless things is good for you because it makes you an independent thinker, frees you from dependence on authority and prejudice. Stick with the traditional curriculum, and you will be able to think for yourself someday.

JANE: Sorry, Dean, but I am already thinking for myself, and I want courses that deliver something I can use.

DEAN: Well, so you think, but you are still young. Believe me, experience shows that useless things make you a better person.

JANE: If I believe you about that, then I can't believe what you say about thinking independently.

So, as Jane's words leave our dean sinking into the liberal sunset, the time has come to look at our other alternative. Perhaps this oratorical version of liberal arts education can provide a better, more balanced perspective on the student as consumer. This perspective certainly contrasts with the one we have just examined, for the philosophical project tends toward rigor and independence of thought, while the oratorical project tends toward elegance and appropriateness of expression.

The key terms in the oratorical domain, elegance and appropriateness, contrast so sharply with the liberal-free version of the arts that we might wonder whether it belongs in liberal territory at all. Appropriateness (*to prepon*, decorum) indicates the oratorical hankering for accommodation, for meeting the requirements of a particular time, place, or occasion, and elegance (*eloquentia*) reveals an appetite for formal pleasures of language. Such conformist and aesthetic biases seem to make rhetoric entirely instrumental, a knack used to deceive or cajole others through nice-sounding but empty words. But, as I said at the beginning of this talk, a liberal art must have some intrinsic merit; how can a verbal art of accommodation claim to be liberal?

This problem is an ancient one, and it has been answered in various ways. The one common feature of these responses is that they idealize the orator's function. This may sound odd to a contemporary audience, accustomed to disdain oratory as verbal persiflage and rhetoric as mere pandering, but the argument has excellent references among premodern authorities, and it is now being revived by respectable academics. Let me try to explain this position first by describing some of the key features that distinguish the oratorical perspective and then by showing how that perspective might yield to an idealized interpretation.

The orator (I'll use this term as a synecdoche for anyone who acts as public advocate in whatever context or verbal medium) is someone who seeks to intervene in public situations so as to alter them through persuasive discourse. The end of this process is functional, practical, and local—something is supposed to happen in a particular situation. The situations the orator confronts are infinitely various and constantly changing, and thus it is impossible to devise a comprehensive, scientific set of rules to guide performance. Instead the orator must draw from common sense and general knowledge in order to size up the situation and must have a command of language sufficient to make an appropriate response to its demands.

I suppose everyone would agree that this task is complex and that the required skills are difficult to attain. The ethical status of the endeavor, however, is open to quite different interpretations. One response is cynical: Oratory can be dismissed as salesmanship or dirty politics. There is, as Plato says in his *Gorgias*, nothing noble about it; rhetoric is inherently evil, since it is a vulgar form of manipulation that corrupts language by substituting cosmetic devices for intelligent speech and subverts deliberation by substituting emotional appeal for genuine reflection.

A second response is neutral. Rhetorical skills, on this view, are instruments, tools, that can be used for good or ill. It makes no more sense to inquire into the ethics of rhetoric per se than it does to conduct an ethical inquiry about a hammer or a knife. Rhetoric is neither a virtue nor a vice but something that can be used to promote either depending on the purposes of the user.

Both these positions preclude consideration of rhetoric as a liberal art or of an oratorical version of liberal education.

The third response is found in Isocrates, Cicero, and Quintilian, among others, and makes rhetoric a virtue by idealizing the function of the orator. In this humanistic conception, not everyone who speaks is an orator; that title must be reserved for those who not only possess technical skill but who use it to good purpose. The orator, in Quintilian's famous phrase, is a good man speaking well. The virtue of the orator, moreover, cannot not be located outside the province of the oratorical art, for to do so would be to take the instrumental position. Instead, adherents of the liberal arts perspective maintain that the rhetorical process itself encapsulates and instills certain virtues.

The most crucial of these is the capacity to accommodate to different people and circumstances. Although unethical speakers may do this to promote their own selfish ends, the ideal orator has a genuine concern for the welfare of others, works toward the good of the whole, and strives to harmonize differing perspectives. In the conflicted scenes of public argument, the orator must consider not just reason, but the opposing reasons that always enter into controversies and must be able to argue on both sides of an issue in order to recognize and encompass the demands of the situation. Philosophical education cannot impart this socially sensitive faculty, since it deals with the acquisition of knowledge and tells us nothing about how knowledge connects with action in concrete situations. The orator, instead, must draw upon common sense and a general fund of knowledge to size up each situation in its full ethical and political complexity. The classical humanists associate this mental agility with the virtue of prudence, and prudence is a kind of wisdom that allows good judgment in cases where abstract rules cannot resolve differences; it is an ethical and intellectual discipline that offers, to paraphrase Martha Nussbaum, a keen and flexible insight into particulars and a way of discovering practical truth that avoids relying upon a set of simplified principles. In the idealized version of the art, the orator's prudence is intimately connected with the exercise of decorum in language—the ability to treat a subject in language appropriate to the situation. Decorum yields eloquence, and eloquence informed by prudence is not empty verbiage; it is the point at which knowledge becomes articulate, thought and word coalesce, and wisdom enters the service of the community.

The rhetorical art, then, operates in practice and application. Knowledge is sought for the sake of effective action rather than for its own sake. But effective action must be understood in a broad sense, since, in the humanistic tradition of the liberal arts, rhetoric does not offer a simple blueprint for effectiveness in this or that situation. (It is not equivalent to a manual that show how to install or repair something through predetermined stages.) Instead, the objective is to produce students who possess the faculty of adapting to different cases. This faculty represents a virtue in itself, since it encompasses principles basic to the life of humans as political and ethical animals, as creatures who constantly adapt to the social environments they create and sustain and who learn to accept and manage their differences with a dignity and respect. Or to put this point another way, useful or practical issues become, in the orator's art, occasions for embodying and bringing to life the "useless" knowledge of the theoretical disciplines. The orator cultivates the "useless" knowledge of philosophy because it offers a needed balance to the sheerly pragmatic tendency of oratorical practice and because it encourages a habit of mind that allows a broad, reflective perspective on human situations as they are encountered in their particularity.

I am proposing, in short, that the future of liberal arts education would be more secure if we made room for a revived conception of oratorical education. I have already suggested that this revival would have a number of benefits, and I will conclude on a more explicit note by listing and briefly discussing three main benefits that I envision: first, that the oratorical perspective offers a counterstatement and partial corrective to the now dominant view of liberal education; second, that this perspective, because of its tendency to balance and sustain opposing perspectives, helps to promote a lively and fluid conception of the liberal arts; and third, that in an age of consumerism, the oratorical perspective provides reasons to maintain an interest in subjects and inquiries that do seem immediately useful.

My first point is intended not as a critique of the philosophical perspective on the liberal arts but as a warning against the consequences of an unchallenged and hyperextended version of that perspective. Against the view that we ought to perfect the solitary intellect, we need the balance of a more socially and politically sensitive attitude toward education. As Kimball has observed, this point is the underlying lesson conveyed through the oratorical tradition, since that tradition teaches us that the "searching for truth without giving commensurate attention to the importance of public expression inevitably leads the individual to isolation and self-indulgence and the republic to amoralism and chaos" (238).

Second, a viable conception of the liberal arts must recognize the need for change and development as circumstances demand. The oratorical view, since it cannot rest in monologic isolation, offers a vehicle for making adjustments. The insistence on two-sided argument, the requirement to acknowledge and respect other positions, applies to the orator's art as an educational program just as much as it does to any other venue of its application. Thus, the philosophical "other" always remains present in this version of the liberal arts, and so too does skepticism about the value of liberal education. Rather than dismissing such opposing views, the oratorical program tries to engage and incorporate them. This argumentative tolerance is well illustrated in the masterwork of the oratorical tradition, Cicero's *De oratore*. In that dialogue, Cicero offers an eloquent defense for his broad, liberal view of oratorical education. But he also argues other positions, sometimes with such emphasis and force that the reader is tempted to think that Cicero regards philosophical culture as the better alternative or that the orator needs no philosophy, but only ingenuity and practice. Some modern readers of this text are scandalized by Cicero's apparent inconsistencies, by his unwillingness to fix on a single, clear position and to devote all his effort to supporting it. But such readings miss the crucial point conveyed both by the form and by the content of the work: oratorical culture must work in an impure social world where opinions differ and circumstances keep changing. This fluidity of thought and language, this capacity to "toggle" between different conceptual domains, recommends itself to us both as a way of teaching the liberal arts and as mechanism for changing our teaching when conditions change.

Finally, the oratorical approach to the liberal arts gives liberal arts educators some room to maneuver in a consumer culture. The goal of oratorical education is emphatically useful; it teaches students how to manage practical situations and how to apply what they learn. And for just that reason that this program demands that they engage apparently useless subjects, subjects that do not correspond to the interests of the moment. To concentrate only on such interests and to learn only practical methods of engaging them is to chart a course for obsolescence. The practical world presents us with changing and uncertain conditions. We can never be certain how we can apply our skills to a given case, and we are always faced with problems that extend beyond the repertoire of skills we already possess. The need to develop a faculty for practical action is more important than the need to learn any specific protocol for action.

Students, then, are well advised to unlimber their minds by dealing with subjects that expand the range of their intellect and require reflective concentration. The orator knows that useless subjects impart knowledge about the culture that sometimes have striking relevance for practical matters and that the flexibility of thought and speech needed for practical affairs is facilitated by intellectual exercises that stretch the mind beyond the immediate here and now.

Again I want to illustrate this point by reference to Cicero and to conclude by quoting a short passage from the second book of *De oratore*. One of the main characters in this dialogue is Antonius, who is represented as a man of practical action, a Roman lawyer and statesman and not some little Greekling (*graeculus*) who is filled with theoretical learning. Yet, as the dialogue proceeds, Antonius's comments reveal a surprisingly broad and deep familiarity with Greek literature. When another character remarks on this, Antonius replies:

> It is not because I am on the look-out for aids to oratory, but just for pleasure that I make a habit, when I have time, of reading the works of these authors and a few more. To what purpose then? Well, I own to some benefit; just as, when walking in the sunshine, though perhaps taking the stroll for a different reason, the natural result is that I get sunburnt, even so, after perusing these books rather closely . . . I find that under their influence my discourse takes on what I may call a new complexion.[11] (2.14.60)

NOTES

1. Bruce A. Kimball, *Orators and Philosophers: A History of the Idea of Liberal Education* (New York: Teachers College Press, 1986).
2. Earl F. Cheit, *The Useful Arts and the Liberal Tradition* (New York: McGraw-Hill, 1975), 3.
3. Charles Eliot cited in Kimball, *Orators and Philosophers*, 167; G. S. Hall, *Life and Confessions of a Psychologist* (New York: D. Appleton, 1923), 33.
4. C. W. Eliot, *University Administration* (Boston: Houghton Mifflin, 1908), 172.
5. Harold Taylor, "Individualism and the Liberal Tradition," in *The Goals of Higher Education*, ed. Willis D. Weatherford Jr. (Cambridge, MA: Harvard University

Press, 1960), 9–12.

6. From *The University Record* (Chicago: University of Chicago Press, 1896), 384.
7. Abraham Flexner, *The American College: A Criticism* (New York: Century Company, 1908), 77.
8. Charles Wegener, *Liberal Education and the Modern Research University* (Chicago: University of Chicago Press, 1978), 12.
9. From the foreword to Kimball, *Orators and Philosophers*, xiii.
10. Richard Lanham, *The Electronic Word: Democracy, Technology, and the Arts* (Chicago: University of Chicago Press, 1993), 104.
11. From the Loeb edition, trans. E. W. Sutton and H. Rackham (Cambridge, MA: Harvard University Press, 1942).

What Is Rhetoric?

I need to begin on two rather different notes—conventionally but sincerely with some words of gratitude and then somewhat unconventionally (and perhaps a bit less sincerely) with an apology. First, I want to express thanks to Tony Blair and his colleagues for their invitation to visit here and their kind hospitality over the past several days. It is real pleasure to meet and talk with members of the Centre for Research in Reasoning, Argumentation and Rhetoric and to make another pilgrimage to this mecca for the study of informal logic. The apology concerns the subject of the lecture and my reasons for deviating from it. I didn't choose the topic. In fact, originally Tony invited me to come and speak on an unspecified subject, and I consented with thoughts about retrieving one of the several papers I had incubating in my computer. Just a month ago,

Previously unpublished. Invited lecture, delivered in 2009 at the University of Windsor, Ontario, Canada.

however, those thoughts were dashed, and I was asked to answer the question: "What is Rhetoric?"

Of course, this is not the first time I have been asked this question. As an openly professing teacher of rhetoric, I have had to engage it in barbershops, barrooms, and faculty lounges across several continents and now for almost forty years. And it is not easily answered—as I have learned from an anecdotal reception history that features blank stares, suspicious glances, oblique comments, suppressed mutters, and the less inhibited response of the father of one of my students, who took his son aside and said, "But isn't that bullshit?"

Before this audience, I won't have to deal with these prejudices and misconceptions, but speaking to sophisticates still raises problems, and I am mindful and a bit weary of the personae involved in this question-and-answer exercise. Tony Blair is a philosopher and I a rhetorician, and there is a long and often contentious history to this business of a philosopher asking a rhetorician the "What is" question. And I cannot help but recall the first known instance—that scene in Athens where Socrates's apparently innocent question leaves the rhetorically eloquent Gorgias tied in dialectical knots; and this precedent hardly bodes well for someone in my position.

Nevertheless, I can take heart from the rhetorical principle that persons, times, and places alter the possibilities of discourse. Windsor is not Athens; I am not Gorgias, and Tony Blair—well—I know him and have worked with him, and I can say that—at least as far as his attitude toward rhetoric is concerned—he is no Socrates. Moreover, Gorgias's failure provides a lesson for rhetoricians that applies directly to this situation and tells us something about the nature of his art and its relationship to the question before us.

Gorgias falls into Socrates's trap precisely because he agrees to play the game according to the philosophical rules that Socrates stipulates. While this concession indicates one aspect of rhetoric—the desire to accommodate to the audience, it runs counter to another dimension of rhetoric—its power to reconsider and reconfigure the rules of the game. In this respect, an important difference between rhetoric and dialectic emerges, and I can best explain it by borrowing a metaphor that Max Black uses in a somewhat different context. Black asks us to imagine that in addition to the game of chess as we know it, we also conceive of a game of metachess. In chess, the players are allowed to move pieces only as the predetermined rules allow, but in metachess, players can make any move that they wish, provided that they can persuade their opponent that it is acceptable. Dialectic, from this perspective, is chess and rhetoric metachess, and so as a rhetorician I claim the right (in fact, in this instance, perhaps the obligation) to change the ground rules for this talk, and specifically to do so by amending the question that has been posed.

"What is rhetoric?" is the wrong question. And the reason is, to my knowledge, most clearly explained by Richard Whately, when, in the introduction to his *Elements of Rhetoric*, he warns that it is a "common error" to suppose "that a general term has some real object, properly corresponding to it, independent of our conceptions;—that, consequently, some one definition in every case is to be found which will comprehend everything that is rightly designated by that term . . . in fact, it will often happen, as in the present instance," that competent authority allows "a variation in the definitions employed; none of which perhaps may be fairly be charged with error, though none can be framed that will apply to every acceptation of the term."[1]

Consequently, the question should be reformulated to ask something of this kind: "How might we define rhetoric?" or "What is your preferred conception of rhetoric?" Since the first of these options implies a systematic inventory of differing positions that I do not have time to cover, I will attempt to answer the second and to explicate a conception of rhetoric that follows from my own affinity with the civic humanistic tradition. In order to explain this position, I will have to refer to several other definitions or conceptions of rhetoric, which I will pass over quickly or use as foil to my preferred view. But, in the spirit of Whately's advice, I want make it clear that I do not regard these other options as wrong or inferior but only as different and that attention to the differences is both unavoidable and desirable when working from within the pluralistic thicket of rhetorical scholarship.

Let me begin with Kenneth Burke's distinction between rhetoric as practiced (*rhetorica utens*) and rhetoric as an academic subject (*rhetorica docens*). For present purposes, I limit myself to the academic side (*rhetorica docens*) of this division, but the conception of academic rhetoric is decisively influenced by its perceived relationship to rhetorical practice, and at least two major approaches to this relationship have evolved through the history of rhetoric and still remain live options.

One of these options emerges when we turn to Aristotle and his definition of rhetoric as the "faculty of observing the available means of persuasion in any given case." In a very careful analysis of this passage, Jeffrey Walker demonstrates that the emphasis falls not on the discovery and use of particular rhetorical strategies but on the critical judgment needed to sort out such strategies and determine or understand their relevance to particular cases.[2] The key term in this passage is "observing," which is an English translation of the Greek *theoresai*—a word whose meanings include to view, judge, speculate, or gaze, and in this passage, as in the English cognate, indicates a theoretical interest—so that we may understand it to mean that rhetoric theorizes about the available means of persuasion. When the definition is interpreted in that sense, as a good many modern rhetorical scholars have interpreted it, rhetoric becomes a theoretical discipline whose business is to provide abstract principles or standards that explain how persuasive strategies do their work.

A very different attitude appears in the civic humanistic tradition that stretches from Isocrates through Cicero and Quintilian and from there to the Renaissance and beyond. This is, as Janet Atwill has put it, an "eloquence" tradition where the emphasis falls on developing the performative capacity of the rhetorical agent (i.e., the orator), rather than on the principles of the art.[3] Consider, for example, this passage from Quintilian:

> Some arts are based on examination, that is to say on the knowledge and proper appreciation of things, as for instance astronomy, which demands no action, but is content to understand the subject of its study; such arts are called theoretical. Others again are concerned with action, so that, the action once performed, nothing more remains to do; these arts we style practical, and dancing will provide us with an example. Thirdly there are others which consist in producing a certain result and achieve their purpose in the completion of a visible task; such we style productive, and painting may be quoted as an illustration. In view of these facts we must come to the conclusion that, in the main, rhetoric

> is concerned with action; for in action it accomplishes that which it is its duty to do. (2.18.1–2)

In *De inventione*, Cicero offers a definition of rhetoric that is consistent with Quintilian's remarks and typical of the humanistic tradition. He associates the art of rhetoric with eloquence and oratorical ability (*oratoriam facultatem*) and maintains that the function or duty (*officum*) of the art is to "speak in a manner suited to persuade an audience," while its end (*finis*) "is to persuade by speech." The distinction between the "duty" and the "end" of rhetoric is a matter of some importance, and I will return to it later, but for the moment, I want to focus on the rather clear difference between the Aristotelian interest in rhetoric as a theoretical art and the Ciceronian interest in rhetoric as a propaedeutic for achieving a performative capacity.

The tradition, then, allowed for two conceptions of *rhetorica docens* that differ in the immediacy of their connection with *rhetorica utens*. Through most of the twentieth century, the Aristotelian, or more theoretically oriented approach, dominated scholarship in the United States, which was practically the only site where disciplinary rhetoric still survived. More recently, however, as the so-called renaissance of rhetorical studies has stirred the academic waters, Aristotelian rhetoric and its distinctive theoretical proclivities have lost favor. But often it has been displaced by conceptions of rhetoric that sustain an even greater distance between the objects and purposes of study and the teaching of a performative art. Thus, Father Ong, a leading figure in the effort to rejuvenate rhetoric, observed that it had become "a more and more fascinating subject of study—not so much as a skill to be used by ourselves (Cicero's way of studying it) but rather as a historical phenomenon. Seen through history in its full sociological and noetic context, rhetoric throws a great deal of light on much in the past that is otherwise obscure and mystifying."[4] So rhetoric has become a hermeneutical lens, a medium for entering into and understanding cultural history. More recently, the influence of poststructuralism has stimulated interest in rhetoric not as a means of constructing discourse but as a method for uncovering and deconstructing cultural and political structures that function as forces of domination and repression. And perhaps at the end of this line of development, rhetoric has been represented as a philosophy of life and a mode of living in the postmodern world:

> Rhetoric today is neither a unified doctrine nor a coherent set of discursive practices. Rather it is a transdisciplinary field of practice and intellectual concern that draws on conceptual resources of a radically heterogeneous nature and does not assume the stable shape of a system or method of education. . . . Rhetoric is no longer the title of a doctrine and a practice, nor a form of cultural memory; it becomes instead something like the condition of our existence.[5]

Cultural hermeneutics, ideological critique, and postmodern rhetorical indeterminacy all are far removed from Aristotle's *Rhetoric*, and at least the last two of these concepts explicitly reject the premises upon which the *Rhetoric* is constructed. Thus, it may seem odd that I have placed them all in the same bin, but I have done so for a specific and limited purpose and that is to illustrate various conceptions of rhetoric that contrast with the civic humanistic conception of rhetoric as a teaching discipline.

The intimate connection with pedagogy delineates some of the characteristic features of civic humanistic rhetoric. To teach rhetoric within this perspective invites attention to the situated character of discourse and to the way that the context of particular situations limit and enable discursive performance. The context is a complex, interconnected network of circumstances that may be conceived in different ways generally and always assumes a different and unique configuration in each case, but normally includes recognition of the time, place, and occasion, the issues and subjects under consideration, the persona of the rhetor, the composition and character of the audience, and the presence of opposing rhetors and attitudes. Operating within this matrix of contingent circumstances, the rhetor seeks to adapt the discourse to its end, and the end is connected somehow with influencing the audience. The goal of the teacher of rhetoric is to help the student develop the capacity to speak or write effectively as the situation demands.

In the sketch I have just provided, you might have noticed how I have shifted and qualified terms that relate to effect—that is, adapting discourse to its end, "somehow" influencing the audience, and to speak or write "effectively." All these locutions refer to the purpose of rhetoric, which has to do with effect, and it might seem obvious that effect simply means the actual impact on audience—that is, success or failure in persuasion. But, as my verbal maneuvering suggests, "effect" proves to be more complicated than that, and while all versions of civic humanistic rhetoric accept it as a key element in rhetoric, it is conceived in a variety of different ways and never treated without some qualification and explanation. This complexity arises from two critically important concerns about teaching rhetoric—one of them artistic, the other ethical.

Rhetoric, like medicine, is an empirical art that deals with numerous and often recalcitrant circumstances that fall outside the control of the practitioner. Thus, in the case of the physician, failure to cure a patient does not necessarily indicate medical incompetence. Likewise, a rhetor's inability to persuade an audience does not prove artistic failure, since rhetorical situations involve chance factors and intractable obstacles that art cannot encompass. Consequently, although rhetorical art aims to produce a desired effect, it cannot guarantee success, nor can it be assessed only in terms of its actual results. It is for precisely that reason that Cicero distinguishes between the end of rhetoric (i.e., its empirical goal), which is to persuade, and the duty of rhetoric (its artistic goal), which is to speak in a manner suited to persuasion.

This separation between what the art does in words and what happens to the audience by words allows Cicero and his humanistic fellow-travelers to sidestep one problem, but it also raises another even more difficult issue. How are we to teach or assess an art of persuasion that cannot claim to achieve persuasion when it is applied to actual cases? Obviously, the art must have standards or norms that are related to effective performance but that cannot guarantee the desired outcome. And to respond to this problem, we might turn to Aristotle's *Rhetoric* and its theoretically motivated inventory of strategies related to probabilities—strategies that may work in particular cases but can do no more than indicate possible or likely effects. The humanists, however, are skeptical about theory and discount the importance of preceptive systems. All of them, even Cicero, refer to an extensive lore of precepts and give them a qualified recommendation as rules of thumb or rough guides for practical application. But they are incidental to the art they teach, for as Quintilian puts the point, whoever commands no more than a knowledge of abstract rhetorical strategies commands a dumb science (*mutam scientiam*). Theories, principles, and precepts are general; cases are particular, and the goal of rhetorical education is to nurture the capacity to encompass situated cases.

Civic humanism, therefore, does not seek to produce an art of rhetoric that consists in abstract principles but rather to cultivate an art that the speaker or writer enacts in rhetorical performance, just as the dancer's art manifests itself in the movements of the dance. It is an educational program that nurtures the student's capacity (*facultas*) to use discourse appropriately—to size up the situation accurately and to discover, use, and combine the argumentative and linguistic strategies best suited to meet the demands of the situation.

But the question remains: how do we teach or evaluate an art that is so closely tied to the moments of its enactment and so vaguely connected to any abstract norms? The answer resides in a kind of judgment that avoids the horizontal movement of inference from principles to or cases or from cases to principles and instead moves laterally across cases—an abductive or analogical type of reasoning that allows for understanding based upon comparison of fully realized examples. In the teaching of rhetoric, this requires that the students learn through practice and the study of models. The models become sources for imitation, not in the contemporary sense of imitation as mechanistic reproduction, but in a generative exercise where students study the model discourse carefully, identify its rhetorical strategies as they are embodied in the original text, and then learn how to reembody these strategies by applying and adapting them to a new composition of their own making. Over time, if all goes well, the cycle of analyzing and imitating model texts and of practice in composition inculcates linguistic skills and habits of mind that allow the student to invoke the art as effectively as possible within the limits of a situation, and it enables others who have gone through this process to recognize artistic excellence when they see it.

Among other things, this program inculcates the ability to accommodate to changing circumstances and develops the technical verbal skills to speak or write persuasively. These characteristics, of course, are associated with the long-standing negative view of rhetoric—rhetoric as an art of deception and trickery that enables unprincipled but glib charlatans to shift positions with every fashionable breeze and to promote their own selfish interest at the expense of the genuine public good. This is the basis of the case Plato makes so powerfully against rhetoric and that has continued to plague the discipline to this day. It is also a problem that engaged the civic humanists, and not just as a response to external criticism, but as a troublesome issue embedded in the logic of their own educational program. The claim to promote civic education entailed a commitment to teach virtue, but in the absence of explicit, intrinsic normative standards for rhetorical performance, how could the rhetoricians distinguish between sheer technical virtuosity and genuinely virtuous uses of their art? How could they claim to teach virtue when they were unable to specify or justify durable ethical standards that transcended and regulated the operation of the rhetorical medium?

Isocrates, the earliest known figure in the tradition I have identified, addresses these issues in detail and, in my judgment, his views still retain interest. While Isocrates rejected Plato's belief in absolute, abstract, and objective truth, he was equally opposed to the extreme relativism associated with Gorgias and other Sophists. He sought to establish a middle ground between these two extremes and to develop practical standards of knowledge that were responsive to ordinary experience and that would enable citizens to make generally appropriate and reliable judgments about particular cases. Good rhetoric was not simply discourse that pleased or persuaded an audience but rhetoric that helped to generate and sustain the knowledge and values necessary for this purpose. Virtue in this sense was decisively political, and while it could never be absolute and unalterable, it did need to rest upon relatively stable and durable ground, and that ground was the history of the political community. As the community developed and changed, it needed values that would sustain its identity but that would also allow for adaptation to new circumstances. Good rhetoric recognized existing values and reframed and rearticulated them in order to meet the evolving needs of the community. Or to put this in somewhat different terms, human values did not descend from an otherworldly source but were produced by and within communities and were sustained, improved, and changed through the medium of public deliberation as it manifested itself in political speech. Thus, politics was the source of values, and political speech was the medium that produced, sustained, and refurbished these values. Rhetoric was a self-regulating engine for generating virtue, but its internal operations were checked and bounded by the history of the community and its collective memory. History could be used selectively to promote different conceptions of virtue or to sanction the application of different virtues to a particular situation, but there was a limit to what could be promoted or adapted—the rhetoricians could change the rules of the game but only insofar as they could persuade a community to change itself.

I must confess that this is a very brief and broad summary of Isocrates's thought, and it is tinctured by implicit comparisons with more recent views of political ethics. I have pulled Isocrates in a communitarian direction and perhaps pushed him into a modified frame for deliberative democracy where political speech replaces conversation as the main instrument of deliberation. Nevertheless, I hope that this reconstruction is sufficiently plausible to indicate that a real affinity exists between the political and ethical underpinnings of civic humanism and some live options in the repertoire of political theory. If that is so, then the teaching tradition of rhetoric may have deeper and more extensive roots in the academic garden then is generally assumed, and the tendency of some contemporary rhetoricians to abandon or underplay the pedagogical heritage of the discipline may represent a misplaced effort to appear current by forgetting the past.

But I am lapsing into the kind of judgment that Whately warned us to avoid, and so let me summarize. To the question "What is rhetoric?" I can reply that it is the practice of adapting discourse to its purpose, or a theory of persuasion, or an aspect of cultural history, or a mode of ideological critique, or a condition of life, or good many other things. To the question "What is your preferred conception of rhetoric?" my answer is a teaching tradition designed to cultivate the ability to intervene in complex social and political situations through the use of discourse. It is an art whose function consists in a capacity for action rather than in theoretical principles or preceptive lore; it distinguishes between artistic excellence and empirical results, and it cultivates and assesses artistic merit mainly through analogical inference rather than through a deductive consideration of how cases conform to abstract criteria. And finally, it is a bounded but self-regulating engine for producing, applying, and altering the political values that inform its practice. Or, to modify Cicero's definition, rhetoric is a teaching discipline whose end is training speakers and writers to influence audiences and whose function is to cultivate the capacity to speak and write in manner suited to influence audiences; its instruction concerns the instrumental purposes of the rhetor and the social and political good of the community, since civic rhetoric is both a tool for action and a generative resource that helps to allow us to act together.

NOTES

1. Richard Whatley, *Elements of Rhetoric*, 5th ed. (London: B. Fellowes, 1836), 2.
2. Jeffrey Walker, "On Rhetorical Traditions: A Reply to Jerzy Axer," presented to the plenary session, Alliance of Rhetoric Societies, Northwestern University, Evanston, IL, September 12, 2003.
3. Janet Atwill, *Rhetoric Reclaimed: Aristotle and the Liberal Arts Tradition* (Ithaca, NY: Cornell University Press, 1998).
4. Walter J. Ong, *Rhetoric, Romance, and Technology: Studies in the Interaction of Expression and Culture* (Ithaca, NY: Cornell University Press, 1971), vii.
5. John Bender and David E. Wellbery, "Rhetoricality: On the Modernist Return of Rhetoric," in *The Ends of Rhetoric: History, Theory, Practice*, ed. John Bender and David E. Wellbery (Stanford, CA: Stanford University Press, 1990), 25.